AT HOME

THE AMERICAN FAMILY

1750—1870

AT HOME

The American Family 1750–1870

Elisabeth Donaghy Garrett

Harry N. Abrams, Inc., Publishers, New York

FOR R. M. PEARDON DONAGHY AND FRANCES MARY DONAGHY,
MY FATHER AND MOTHER

PROJECT DIRECTOR: LETA BOSTELMAN
EDITOR: ELLYN CHILDS ALLISON
DESIGNERS: CAROL ANN ROBSON
WITH GILDA HANNAH
PHOTO EDITOR: J. SUSAN SHERMAN

Library of Congress Cataloging-in-Publication Data

Garrett, Elisabeth Donaghy.
    At home : the American family, 1750–1870/Elisabeth Donaghy
Garrett.
      p.   cm.
    Bibliography: p. 288
    Includes index.
    ISBN 0-8109-1894-3
    1. Home economics—United States—18th century.   2. Home
economics—United States—History—19th century.   3. Dwellings—
United States—History—18th century.   4. Dwellings—United States—
History—19th century.   5. Family—United States—Folklife.
I. Title.
TX23.G37   1989
392′.3′0973—dc19   89–312
                                                          CIP

Published in 1990 by Harry N. Abrams, Incorporated, New York
All rights reserved. No part of the contents of this book may be
reproduced without the written permission of the publisher
A Times Mirror Company

Printed and bound in Japan

PAGE 1: *The Artist's Family*. Oil on canvas, by Benjamin West.
1772. Yale Center for British Art, New Haven; Paul Mellon Collection

PAGE 2: *Meditation*. Oil on canvas, by J. G. Brown. c. 1890.
The Metropolitan Museum of Art, New York City; George A. Hearn Fund, 1909

PAGE 8: *By Candlelight (Mrs. Jedediah Morse)*. Oil on canvas mounted on panel,
by Samuel F. B. Morse. 1820. Yale University Art Gallery, New Haven; gift of Mr. R. C. Morse

CONTENTS

ACKNOWLEDGMENTS

Writing, though a solitary exercise, ultimately becomes a collaborative effort. Many are the teachers, students, friends, associates, and kin who have contributed to the composition of this volume.

The inspirational teaching of the late Charles Montgomery was the catalyst. His ever-questioning mind and illimitable enthusiasm engendered in me a desire to examine his beloved American arts from yet another perspective. How much I would have enjoyed discussing these pages with him.

Friends such as Nancy Goyne Evans, John Quentin Feller, Florence Griffin, Joseph Ott, and Susan Swan have offered constructive suggestions for source material; while my associates at Sotheby's Susan Garbrecht and Vals Osborne kindly allowed me to take off those few extra weeks to complete the text. Library staffs have been obliging and accommodating, and I am particularly appreciative of the creative counsel and professional assistance of Susan Davis, Beatrice Taylor, and Neville Thompson.

Illustrative material has been generously donated by a number of private collectors, fine arts galleries, museums, and historical societies, and I am especially grateful to Sandra Brant of *The Magazine Antiques* for her invaluable help with pictorial material. Alberta Brandt, Jane Hankins, Richard Kugler, M. P. Naud, Cammie Naylor, and Kathleen Stocking weathered my persistent requests with grace and efficiency. Arthur Vitols of Helga Photo Studio has added visual enhancement with his many photographs. Susan Sherman of Harry N. Abrams helped ensure pictorial appeal. Carol Robson and Gilda Hannah are responsible for the attractive design and layout of the book.

Many friends have contributed to the physical presentation of this volume. A fortuitous asset came in the guise of Ellyn Childs Allison, my editor, whose deft touch, like that of a master couturier, strengthened style and conferred clarity of line. Two former students, Shari Hubner and Karen Parles, were generous with their encouragement, their copy checking, and their computer skills. Phyllis Stimler's gentle tutorial prompting almost succeeded in bringing me into the computer age, while Allison Ledes shared hours of her multifaceted talents.

I am indebted to Allison and George Ledes, Enid and Hugh Menzies, and Lin Smith-Vincent, who have affably obliged as surrogate parents when I sought a moment for research or seized a minute to write. My deepest appreciation goes to my children, Maria, Abigail, and Nathaniel, who have excelled in their own endeavors while assisting me in mine, and to my husband, Wendell, whose generous spirit, creative mind, and great good humor have made all pleasantly possible.

FOREWORD

BY PETER THORNTON

An article appeared with the title "The American Home" in *The Magazine Antiques* in January 1983. It was the first of six articles to come out over the following twenty-four months. They were by the author of the present book and were in a sense a trial run for this fascinating publication. Perspicacious readers noted, as these articles made their appearance, that here was something rather new. People had, of course, many times before written about life indoors in the past, about domestic practice or the use of household equipment. Indeed, *Antiques* and numerous other magazines had carried articles on this or that aspect of these subjects for many years, and a host of books exist which touch upon these matters. What was fresh about these new articles, and is an outstanding quality of this book, is the sheer weight of evidence that has been marshaled and the manner in which it has all been presented.

Earlier toilers in this field have extracted facts from inventories, culled pertinent information from newspaper reports, quoted advertisements, and cited from memoirs, diaries, and biographies, but no one has previously done so in quite such an extensive manner, and other writers have not usually had such a good understanding of the contemporary furnishings and interior architecture which help to put flesh on the bones of quotation. If one adds to this the parallel evidence provided by contemporary pictures, with which this book is so liberally sprinkled, a very rich pudding is the result but, unlike most rich puddings, this one has been stirred by a skillful cook who has managed to keep it light. This is important because almost everyone is interested in the subjects treated in this book and, however much the historian's methods have been brought to bear on the fundamental study, special attention has to be paid to putting across this kind of material in an easily accessible manner. The contemporary illustrations are an enormous help in achieving this because of their immediate appeal; the many quotations from memoirs and diaries also add lightness to the presentation of so much fact and remind the reader that it is the human lives of our forefathers that are thus being revealed to us.

The publication of this rich offering reflects an interest which has grown amazingly in the past decade or so. People are evidently fascinated by these matters and it is interesting to speculate how this has come about. Europeans of an antiquarian cast of mind were aware, already in the late Middle Ages, that their forebears had lived differently from themselves. They knew they had worn different clothes, for instance, and sensed that their habits had also been different. Interest in the past increased enormously during the sixteenth and seventeenth centuries, and it was then that antiquaries began collecting the odd relic of bygone ages. Such objects, divorced from their original context, were the first "antiques" but they were collected as curiosities or on account of their associations, not because they were valuable or regarded as symbols of status. Nor, for the most part, were they thought beautiful. Intricate workmanship was admired; aesthetic quality rarely came into the antiquary's calculations.

As antiquarian studies advanced, a better understanding of past customs evolved and this serious approach reached its apogee during the second half of the nineteenth century. Nothing so exhaustive has been published in this realm since Henry Havard's *Dictionnaire de l'Ameublement*, which came out in Paris in four thick volumes in 1888–90 and concentrated solely on French matters. This impressive work was by no means the only one to appear during this, the heroic phase of antiquarian effort in this field. Edmond Bonaffé's work of the 1870s marked its beginning, as did some of the first catalogues of the new South Kensington Museum in the 1860s, which were full of incidental information introduced along with the detailed descriptions. At the turn of the century, learned Italian scholars were much preoccupied with the meaning of terms in early inventories, and just before the First World War acute observations were made by such giants in the field as Wilhelm von Bode when writing about Italian Renaissance furniture. The last manifestations of this great wave of antiquarian research in this field are well represented by Troels Lund's *Dagligt liv i Norden i det 16de aarhundrede* (*Daily Life in Scandinavia in the Sixteenth Century*), which appeared in 1929. These works were all scholarly, and much in them has not since been bettered. Their chief failing lay in their illustrations, which were usually gray and depressing—and, in the case of Havard's dictionary, often downright misleading or irrelevant. Indeed, a great advantage that modern scholars enjoy over their predecessors lies in the way their work can be supplemented by excellent illustrations in color, which makes their contribution so vastly more attractive to the average reader (and, indeed, to other scholars, although they may not always so readily admit it).

Antiquarian studies in this particular field seem to have gone underground about the time of the First World War and did not really surface again until after the Second World War, and the revival did not really gain much momentum before the 1970s. The phase between the first wave and the postwar revival was the Great Age of Antiques. It was then that the object in isolation came to fascinate the public, including those who had previously been keen readers of antiquarian essays. What the object was for, how it had fitted into the context of life as lived when it was new, seemed no longer to be of quite so much interest, and this became especially the case as antiques became ever more expensive—and hence valuable in their own right. The age of an antique now mattered seriously; so did its quality (although not, for a long time, if the object dated from the nineteenth century, however exquisite its crafts-manship) and also "patina" which, for all its appeal, was essentially a product of age, wear and tear, and dirt. Museum curators and collectors and, of course, the whole vast trade that tried to supply their needs thus came to venerate "antiques" seen as objects set apart, in a showcase, on a stand, in a showroom, in a position of honor in surroundings where there was sometimes a tendency to be self-conscious about these matters. Journals sprang up to support this widespread interest; the very name of *The Magazine Antiques* reflects the passion of the time when it was first published. Indeed, one can follow the change in emphasis that has taken place in recent years simply by studying back numbers of this journal.

Nevertheless, while it is easy enough to see that change in emphasis has oc-curred, it is still far from easy to explain why this happened. Some suggest it sprang from the high cost of the better sort of antiques, once they had become a major form of investment and as a result of so many people wanting to possess them. As the cost rose, as these desirable objects got increasingly out of reach—or so the reasoning goes—

people were forced to turn to other realms, to whole classes of "collectibles" that were formerly regarded as lumber (unearthed at jumble sales and from junk stalls) or, on the other hand, and with a new awareness, to seeing what might perhaps be available in the realm of modern design. At any rate, as the contents of attics emptied into the drawing rooms of the modern collector, new interests were generated. What did one do with this curious object? Where did this thing fit in?

The huge prices being paid for high-class antiques also produced a backlash among quite a few people, mostly young and of radical inclination, who tended to disapprove of what to them seemed to be disproportionate financial involvement in the field; but many of these people were nevertheless interested in the past and eagerly sought information about past practices even while not wanting necessarily to acquire and possess the artifacts that went with such activities. So this faction also entered the scene as potential consumers of information.

Rampant nostalgia for a past which seems to many to have been a great deal pleasanter than our own times is also often given as a reason for the current growing interest in the customs and ambience of former days. This accounts particularly, no doubt, for the delight with which people today pounce upon contemporary watercolors and other illustrations of rooms as they were in times past. Of course most of these scenes tend to idealize the setting depicted (after all, one mostly recorded rooms one liked, in which one was happy) and this may partly explain why they almost invariably seem so charming to us. This widespread interest has in turn increased the demand for explanations of what can be seen in these pictures.

A further reason why studies in this field have increased is simply that professional historians are always seeking new fields to conquer as their own numbers grow. All those students seeking subjects on which to write their theses cast around, sometimes with desperation, for some as yet unworked field—and domestic studies offer a whole fresh row of options. Their tutors have likewise looked with interest at patches that have not already been tilled by others. However, thesis writers, and even their teachers, tend to concentrate on too particular an area; someone who can execute a wide sweep through new territory with real authority is not so easy to find.

The chief reason that the subject treated here has so unmistakably come into its own in recent years lies more in the fact that antiquarian studies in this field have surfaced again, after largely lying dormant between the wars. The difference between the first great wave that had spent itself by 1910–20 and the present revival is that there now exists a much larger public interest in such matters, and this has generated a considerable extra demand for information and, let us face it, for entertainment— because you do not have to be a learned scholar to find enjoyment in reading about these things.

It may well be that the revival of serious antiquarian research in the social history of domestic life was widespread. Perhaps it revived in Germany, in the United States, or in France during the 1940s and 1950s but this movement, if it existed, has not yet been studied (what an interesting subject for a thesis, incidentally). In one country, however, this revival is rather well charted, and that country is Denmark. Indeed, it is possible that the Danes were for a while isolated pioneers of this revival. If so, it may not solely have been due to a revival of interest among Danish scholars and museum curators; it could have arisen because during the Second World War, when this work first started, their energies had of necessity to be confined to studies within their own country.

Whatever the case, it was in the 1940s that a few people from the National Museum in Copenhagen began to spend the summer holidays surveying the contents of one or two Danish country houses. They took photographs of everything; not just grand items but commonplace objects like wastepaper baskets, towel rails, and lamps. They described and measured it all. They drew plans of each room to record how everything stood in 1942 or whenever it was they were carrying out a particular survey. They checked with old servants about their household duties, then and in former times, and they quizzed the dowager countess about her life as a young wife. As the years went by, an enormous mass of information accumulated and the museum staff became very expert in what might be called "furniture history," although it was of course much more than that.

Dr. Tove Clemmensen, the leader of the small team from the National Museum, went on to write several books on the subject and brought out a delightful book of old illustrations of Danish interiors, which has recently been amplified and republished. Unfortunately, very little of her work has been translated into English and thus remains largely inaccessible to a wider public, but her work influenced other Scandinavian scholars and, because the Keeper at the time happened to read Danish, stimulated the Department of Furniture and Woodwork in London's Victoria and Albert Museum to look at the subject from what was, in the 1960s, still a rather fresh point of view. Since then, this approach has gained adherents in many countries, not least in the United States but also in Germany and Italy.

There was a time, not all that long ago, when English scholars smiled condescendingly at Colonial Williamsburg or at Old Sturbridge Village (to name only two of the prime centers where life in early America has been studied with great seriousness and dedication), with their staffs all dressed up in coifs and clogs, hand-milking their cows, ironing their aprons with flatirons, spinning wool by candlelight, and brushing up their periwigs. But the English have long since learned to be deeply respectful of the knowledge that the staffs of such centers in the United States possess. The tradition established by the East Coast preservation societies is today much admired in Britain. Until quite recently, if, over in London, one wanted to know about the design of old rainwater hoppers, or window catches, or doorknobs, it was wise to get in touch with the Society for the Preservation of New England Antiquities, in Boston; and if one had a problem to do with historic paintwork, it was to American experts that one turned because the information was not readily available in Britain. Today, such matters are being studied with enthusiasm and fast-growing expertise in Britain, but many English people are aware that it was Americans who were pioneers in this field. Of course, both in the United States and in Britain, the availability of such information has since become vital as the preservation of historic houses has developed into such a major field of activity—a movement that gathered momentum worldwide during the 1970s in quite an astonishing manner.

The publication of the present book may therefore be seen not merely as a felicitous event. It also marks the bringing together of several strands to form a sturdy rope, the core of which derives from the scholarly concerns of the ancient antiquary. It represents a further contribution to the field of "preservation-society studies." It reflects a notable shift of interest among collectors of antiques. And it answers a need among a wide public who are fascinated by the past, who want to know more about the way their ancestors lived, and who often suspect that the lives of their forebears were rather more satisfying than in many ways are their own today.

This book is about the American home and the American family, but one should not be misled into thinking that what is described is in all cases peculiarly American. Parallel customs and practices can in many instances be found to have been current in other countries belonging to the Western cultural tradition. Certainly, readers in many parts of Europe will find this book of enormous interest and will discover in it facts that throw light on problems that are puzzling them in their own countries.

In the realm of domestic life, human requirements are much the same everywhere at any given time within the same cultural area. What studies in this large field teach us is to recognize the common tradition during each phase in our history, and subsequently to identify how this varied in practice in various localities, among various classes of people, or in answer to needs that arose from certain special circumstances. One might perhaps say that this book shows us both the Highest Common Factor of the great Western domestic tradition and the Lowest Common Denominator, which is represented by some very localized American customs. But if, dear Reader, you feel disinclined to see the subject expressed in such giddy terms, let me commend this book to you quite simply as a delightful read.

SIR JOHN SOANE'S MUSEUM
LONDON, SUMMER 1989

PREFACE

Historic houses and antique furnishings continue to elicit our interest in the everyday life of the past. The neatly dovetailed drawer of a chest, the vivaciously grained doors to a secretary desk seem to tell us of a meticulous people of British taste who found pleasure in forms that combined the beautiful with the useful. But such interpretations are not satisfying—the tedium of the general has smothered the animation of the specific. Time has obscured the fact that each of these pieces was made by an individual craftsman for a particular patron, for use in a specific room, in a unique home.

Several years ago I asked myself if there might be a way to personalize these objects once again, to understand and visualize them in their original setting. If the houses and the objects were mute, stubbornly secretive of their connection with the people and places of the past, then perhaps the people themselves would be more amenably revealing. I turned, therefore, to written materials, to the scribblings of the middle and upper classes, whose homes I hoped to understand better, concentrating on the region east of the Mississippi River.

The personal murmurings of diaries and letters place one immediately in the domestic setting. Often written at or about home, these documents are filled with the minutiae of the day-to-day and were my most generous source. Travel accounts, the literature of those who came specifically to observe and record, to compliment and condemn, were also instructive. But although many of these chroniclers were enlightening in their observations on men and mores, towns and townscapes, favors and foibles, few were intimately acquainted with the American domestic interior. Personal reminiscences provide a telescoped vision of life at home. The proliferation of this literary genre in the second half of the nineteenth century betrays a people perplexed by a tyrant progress, which was relentlessly snuffing out ways of life that had endured for generations. If the physical surroundings and the character of society seemed too rapidly changing, then the old should at least be preserved in writing. Many Victorians felt an obligation to pen their reminiscences for the sake of their children and grandchildren. Nostalgia for a vanishing past was the not very effective but emotionally soothing attempt to rein in the acceleration of life. To novels and poetry I have also turned, for their authors often give us the homely lispings of the many in a felicitous turn of phrase. In their effort to create a realistic setting, these writers indicate what was accepted and expected, drawing upon their own experiences. Household inventories, newspaper advertisements, and housekeeping manuals offered many a clue. And, finally, I examined contemporary paintings, prints, and drawings for domestic detail.

Taken individually, each of these mediums is fallible. Journals and letters are not always truthful; travel accounts are burdened with prejudices and plagiarisms, reminiscences rose-tinted, novels embroidered, household inventories incomplete, newspaper advertisements puffed up, and paintings subject to the artist's fancy. But when these disparate sources accord with each other again and again, there is a certain assurance of veracity.

This book is not about the peculiar or the exceptional. It is about the familiar patterns of living that emerge when these heterogeneous cards are shuffled together. The pack is rich in clues. One may learn that the neatly dovetailed drawer belonged to a mahogany chest of drawers that stood in the best bedchamber. It was crammed with snow-white linens, some made at home, others purchased afar. When closed, it was securely locked. When opened, by the key hung suspended at the housewife's waist, it exuded a pungent odor of cedar with which the drawer was lined, and an intimation of rose leaves and lavender—a pleasure to the nose and a deterrent to insects. Though well-constructed, this drawer sometimes closed hard, and Charlotte Tappan might need walk on crutches all winter for having slammed the drawer shut with her knee in exasperation. The secretary desk stood in the back parlor. Its dramatically grained doors came alive at eventide when candles were placed on the candle slides before them. But the black scar from a flame that burned too close is proof of the ever-present danger of fire.

One cannot impose strict temporal boundaries on ways of life, and I have quoted from sources outside the core dates of 1750 and 1870 to illustrate continuity. I am, however, primarily addressing a 120-year period during which the American home exhibited both change and continuum. The stark, linear aspect of many eighteenth-century interiors softened into the Victorian as the poetic picturesque replaced the rational, and as the symbolic became as significant as the real. Possessions accumulated, rooms multiplied, pieces grew grander, and privacy was enhanced as the furnace in the basement and gas lighting encouraged the family to spread out through more rooms a greater part of the year in comfort. But privacy had been desired in 1750, and there are many other areas of comfort and discomfort that would not change radically until electricity and modern medicine separated the world of today from what Peter Laslett has called "the world we have lost" and Robert Wells, "the world we have escaped."

The domestic world of the past was exigent. Uncertainty hovered over all. Yet from 1750 to 1870, home was the seat of whatever happiness one might chance to find on earth. It was an asylum from the yet more rigorous and rancorous outside world. Emily Dickinson's perception of professional duty as "black and brown" and home as "bright and shining" gave visual expression to the Victorian rift between the world of business and the sanctuary of home. It was by then a contrast of long standing. In 1801 Thomas Jefferson had pictured himself in Washington, worn down by pursuits in which he took no pleasure, surrounded by hostile people and pining for home and that society where all was peace and harmony, where one genuinely loved and was loved by all. Five years later William Wirt, also away from home on duty, would further testify that however much the noise of the children and the inconvenience of housekeeping might annoy him, yet "home is still the place for happiness."

There are many aspects of colonial and Victorian life that seem obscure to us today. But human emotions provide a timeless bond. We recognize the affection and the pique, the fear and the frustration, the grief and the joy that animate these early documents. Pitched on the rude edge of a western New York State forest, separated from the congenial, refined circle of her New Haven friends and family, Maria Silliman Church wrote her sister one November day in 1837, "Your letters and Mamas are the golden threads that connect me with a whole world of beloved objects from whom I should else be totally separated." Let us also follow a skein of golden threads back to a world of beloved objects, at home in early America.

A bright and bracing air and a glittering, plenteous sunshine were quintessential features in the portrait of early America as sketched by foreign observers. To those who came from smoke-enshrouded Old World cities like London, the glorious sun and coal-free atmosphere were invigorating. Far into the nineteenth century, European commentators praised the pure, unsullied air, which seemed to contribute to the cleanliness and chromatic intensity of the houses and garments. New York harbor's "singularly bright and lovely" aspect reminded one London correspondent in September 1829 "of the sea-bound cities of the Mediterranean but with more variety of color"; and William Tallack echoed both the sentiment and the enthusiasm when he wrote from Philadelphia in 1860 of the radiant red-brick and white-marble facades gleaming in a "Mediterranean clearness." Americans lent their pens to this cheerful delineation. It seemed to James Fenimore Cooper that the three components of that paradigmatic neatness and domestic comfort which overspread the native landscape were the brilliancy of the climate, the freshness of the paint, and the exterior ornaments of the houses.[1]

Like Cooper, Captain Thomas Hamilton attributed some of the sparkle of American towns to the ever-fresh paint. He believed that New Yorkers must have inherited their taste for colorful houses from their Dutch ancestors, and he admired the agreeable effect of gaiety and lightness. In many New World towns, fire regulations stipulated that bricks be used and these, too, were often annually coated in red, yellow, or light gray enamels, which not only acted as a sealant, preventing the clay from freezing and scaling, but lent a "cheerful, bright and daylight aspect" to the streets. John M. Duncan attributed the singular neatness of New York residences in 1818 to the bricks, which were made of a very fine clay, affording a close and smooth grain, and to the fact that they were always "showily painted either a bright red with white lines upon the seams, or a clean looking yellow." This precise outlining of each brick with white paint bespoke Enlightenment attention to clarity through distinctly demarcated spaces, a precision reiterated behind the front door in curtain trimmings, carpet, and wallpaper borders. James Stuart liked the pronounced contrast of red brick and white seam, which he thought gave a clean, fresh, and cheerful countenance to Manhattan buildings and to the city in general, but not everyone had such kind words for the practice. Lydia Maria Child found the white-bordered compartments of these facades "as numerous as Protestant sects, and as unlovely in their narrowness." It seemed to her, during the sultry, oppressive days of August, as if the sun were staring at you from these bright red walls "like the shining face of a heated cook."[2]

Paul Svinin, a Russian traveling in the States between 1811 and 1813, maintained that "the greater half of all the houses in the United States is built of brick painted with oil paint and outlined in white." He further complained, "Almost all the private residences in America are built on the same plan. They have the same facade

The Old State House and State Street.
Boston. Oil on wood panel, by James
Marston. c. 1801. Massachusetts Historical Society, Boston. The clarity of
the air, the glitter of the sunshine,
the vivid feminine costumes, and the
freshly painted facades with contrasting white trim impressed those who
came from coal-darkened cities of Europe where, as James Fenimore Cooper
remarked, "a diamond will hardly glitter." To one observer, Boston seemed
almost as free from smoke as a lady's
drawing room. If the air was clean, the
streets were not, and the ladies here
hoist their skirts to protect them from
the dirt and dust of street and walkway.
The imposing Old State House and the
modern bow-fronted shops with residences above them attest to the easy
commingling of public and private
space in early American towns

and are laid out in the same way. Having seen one house, you may confidently say that
you know them all. This is so completely true that of the millions of houses to be found
in the United States there are hardly a thousand that differ from the rest." Here was a
criticism voiced by many others as well. The desire to conform has long been
recognized as one of the most deep-seated impulses of the Victorian mind, but it was a
powerful factor in colonial and Federal home design as well, conspicuous in both
exterior and interior detail. In 1795 Thomas Twining denounced the repetitiousness
of Philadelphia streets, lined with houses of mathematical exactitude, as wearying to
the eye. Shortly thereafter, Félix de Beaujour opined that there was nothing so gloomy
as this uniformity unless it was the sadness of the Philadelphians themselves.[3]

The sameness of architecture, the brightness of the atmosphere, and the freshness of the paint continued out beyond the cities. To one British observer in 1829, the
banks of the Hudson River, dotted with white houses and free of smoke, seemed
"uncommonly gay and *riant.*" To another, the white frame houses of New England
possessed a peculiar neatness, cleanliness, and freshness. "There is nothing in
Britain that bears resemblance to a New England town," he wrote shortly after his
visit to the States in 1818 and 1819. "Such houses would soon look rusty and weather

beaten, were they in our climate, but they enjoy here a purer atmosphere, and the smoke of coal fires is unknown. The painting is renewed about once a year."4

To many foreign eyes the American house had a weightless, ornamental aspect more usually found in the decorative and fine arts than in architecture. Julian Niemcewicz thought that the thin brick walls, the abundant clear windows, the

carefully carved door pediments, and the aura of cleanliness gave urban homes "more the air of nice furniture than of buildings." John Shaw, whose *A Ramble through the United States* was published in 1856, found many of these red-brick and green-shuttered houses so gay that they resembled "paintings rather than dwellings"; and when Charles Dickens scrutinized the "whitest of white" New England domiciles with their "clean cardboard colonnades," he concluded that they had "no more perspective than a Chinese bridge on a teacup." Indeed, this enigmatic weightlessness, this repetitive precision, this spic-and-span freshness of American houses brought to mind "the little Toys with which Children build Streets & Cities." In Manhattan, the cheerily painted facades looked rather "like Baby houses" to Ann Maury in 1831; and when Sir David Wilkie looked with an artist's eye at Oswego, New York, in 1834, he, too, was struck by the houses, "as gew-gaw and gingerbread-looking as one could desire, stuck together like so many rows of bright-coloured pasteboard boxes in a toy shop."[5]

If the houses seemed unreal, the roads were demonstrably not. Emilie Cowell, who accompanied her husband, Sam, "the king of comic song," on his concert tour through the States in 1860–61, vowed that next to the revolting habit of spitting nothing was so shocking as the condition of Yankee roads. She was convinced that no city in the civilized world could compare with New York for filthy streets. Conflicting opinions abound, however. Though Mrs. Cowell roundly denounced the situation in New York, Boston, Providence, and Worcester, Anne Royall maintained that in hilly Providence at least, where everything was "on a descent," the rain kept the streets always clean, and in Philadelphia she allowed how the streets were swept and the pavements washed every day.[6]

It was generally conceded that Philadelphia was the tidiest American city, with Boston ahead of New York, Washington, and also Charleston, where Peter Neilson observed that all offal and garbage were laid in the street early each morning to be quickly conveyed away in carts. Residual matter was devoured by "the natural scavengers of Charleston"—turkey buzzards. Because of the role they played in clearing the streets, these birds of prey were respectfully tolerated, and the penalty for striking one was five dollars. The Chevalier de Bacourt thought Boston quite clean in 1840, in part because the residents were not allowed to put out any debris until trash

Runaway Pig at the Jersey Market Terminus. Front and Market streets, Philadelphia. Watercolor by an unknown American artist. c. 1850. The Library Company of Philadelphia. Cats, dogs, horses, and pigs contributed to the debris, the cacophony, and the dangers of the early American street. Note a typical paving pattern, with longer, flat stones forming the crosswalks

Bridewell and Charity School. New York City. Watercolor by Baroness Hyde de Neuville. 1808. I. N. Phelps Stokes Collection, The New York Public Library; Astor, Lenox and Tilden Foundations. Cattle were driven through cities in large droves and pigs had complete freedom of the streets. Here cows, pigs, and pedestrians amiably share the footpath before a somewhat ironically situated Office of the Board of Health. Flapping laundry seems further to impede the walkway. Both linens and line would have been taken in at sunset, for one can readily understand how perilous such an obstruction might be to the unsuspecting pedestrian groping his way in the obscurity of nightfall

collectors came by to pick it up each morning. In New York a law was passed as early as 1731 prohibiting the disposal of carrion or filth in the streets and further stipulating that the inhabitants "shall on every Friday, rake and sweep together all the dirt, filth and soil lying in the streets before their respective dwelling-houses, upon heaps, and on the same day, or on the Saturday following, shall cause the same to be carried away and thrown into the river, or some other convenient place." Some seventy years later Joshua Brookes confirmed that there were professional carters to take up refuse in Manhattan two or three times a week, with each householder responsible for sweeping his contribution into a hillock. Yet numerous witnesses swore that the slops or "uncleanly matter" of the houses was insouciantly thrown into the streets and there

Voices of the Night. Spruce Street Orchestra! Will Perform Every Night This Season!! Doors Open All Night. Admittance Free. Nashville, Tennessee. Pencil drawing by William Marshall Merrick. Sketchbook, 8 June 1864. Print Collection, The New York Public Library; Astor, Lenox and Tilden Foundations. Complaints of nocturnal noises abound in early journals and letters. The city dweller was robbed of sleep by lowing cows, grunting pigs, whining mosquitoes, rumbling carts, clopping horses, tolling bells, and stentorian watchmen. Country insomniacs bewailed the din of caterwauling cats, crowing cocks, and clamoring crickets. To all these might be added the seasonal ring of the ax and the scrape of the snow shovel

suffered to remain except in the steamy fever-haunted months of July and August.[7]

Volunteer carters in the four-legged form of hungry pigs scavenged among the pickings. It seemed to one observer, improbable though it might be, as if the hair-covered trunks in the bedchambers had actually sprouted legs and were trotting about the streets. John Sturtevant, whose reminiscences cover the years 1835 to 1905, wrote that during his boyhood these marauders had afforded much amusement to his New York clique on icy nights, when they would stretch a long rope across a street and trip the pigs—" 'As graceful as a hog on ice' was an expression that we then saw exemplification of." The Chevalier de Bacourt shared no such levitous recollections. He groused from Washington in 1840 that not only were there pillaging pigs but roving cows as well, and it was a nuisance to be sprinkled with milk each morning as one passed by women milking their cows on the sidewalk.[8]

In addition to the swill and the swine, there were phalanxes of carts, wagons, drays, trucks, and wheelbarrows, "continually obstructing the passage" and threatening to run the pedestrian down as they advanced at a gallop or fast trot. All was noise and bustle. By day, the clamor of iron wheels on stone was augmented by the cacophony of men, women, and children stridently crying things to sell with almost deafening noise. By night, according to one insomniac, the grunting pigs and lowing cows joined vociferous dogs and cats in creating an infernal racket.[9]

The horses that pulled all conveyances contributed with the pigs and garbage and the pools of stagnant water—due to inadequate drainage—to the miasma of American cities. Abigail Adams found the Philadelphia streets "so nausious," while Baron Ludwig von Closen attributed Baltimore's disagreeable odor to the filth of the main street and, interestingly enough, to the scent of brick dust from the multitude of recently built houses. Yet farther south, an editor for the *Picayune* described with chagrin the piles of garbage, clutter of carrion, and pools of reeking, stagnant water that befouled New Orleans roadways in 1860.[10]

If one survived so far there was yet the footing, or lack thereof, to contend with. Sand, mud, dust, snow, slush, and ice impeded vehicular and pedestrian traffic alike. Streets were irregularly paved, although improvements were more noticeable from the 1820s on. Stone, brick, macadam, and even plank were used on main thoroughfares; lesser streets received scant attention. Sidewalks offered little refuge from iron-rimmed cart wheels, and flying hooves kicked up dirt and splattered mud all about. In 1744 Peter Kalm remarked that in Philadelphia a gentleman always kept his lady to the side nearest the houses to shield her from the filth of the street. In 1851 Philadelphians were again reminded in the aptly subtitled *Facts for the People, or Things Worth Knowing* that the "right, being the post of honour, is given to superiors and ladies except in the street, when they take the wall, as farthest from danger from passing carriages." But danger came from all directions. Walkways were often treacherously uneven, and so different from city to city that a pedestrian's gait might reveal regional origins. A Philadelphian tackling New York streets, with their sharp, prominent stones, walked "with as much painful caution, as if his toes were covered with corns, or his feet lamed with the gout; while a New Yorker, as little approving the plain masonry of Philadelphia, shuffles along the pavement like a parrot on a mahogany table." Anne Royall was bemused by the singular gait of Savannah residents, who had become so accustomed to wading through sand that they walked "as one would walk through a bed of tough brick mortar," rising and falling with each step. And there were further inconveniences. In New Orleans, the brick sidewalks were loosely set in sand so that in wet weather every step triggered an unwelcome geyser of liquid mud.[11]

In muddy Philadelphia in March 1792, Elizabeth Drinker called on Sarah Logan Fisher, who had fallen in the street and hurt her foot; it was Elizabeth's first outing since the same accident befell her, two weeks earlier. Another young lady was able to call upon her risibility when she fell into a ditch while ambling about Washington in March 1809; in fact, she "laughed so much afterwards that she was quite ill and had to take medicine." The majority saw no humor in the situation. In Charleston, where the streets were "either mudpooles or ashpits," J. B. Dunlop spluttered wrathfully in 1810, "It is not unusual to see the cariages rolling along up to the axletree in mud and in less than one week afterward the wind whirling the Dust and sand in such opake clouds as not to be able to perceive a person on the opposite foot path." Sand was a particular problem in Virginia, South Carolina, and Georgia. To John Davis, traveling in the States between 1798 and 1802, windy Savannah seemed "a desert scene," and "every inhabitant wears goggles over his eyes, which gives the people an appearance of being in masquerade." Dust was inevitable wherever there were unpaved roads or macadamized streets not regularly watered. From Charleston, Anne Royall wrote that a man went through the streets daily with a cart and barrel of water, "so contrived as to wet the streets while he drives through them"; and Frederick Van Wyck, who was born in 1853, recalled the street-watering carts of his Manhattan childhood. "The water was paid for by such residents as wished the street in front of their houses dampened. Some blocks you would find watered only part of the way, or only at each end and not in the middle, since some of the residents would not pay for watering, preferring dust, rather than part with a little cash." From Memphis, where there was no paving, "or so little as not to be worth mentioning," and apparently not many watering carts either, Emilie Cowell complained in March 1860 of the clouds of dust that flew through the streets, filling rooms and throats and tainting even food with a taste of dust.[12]

Mud was universal. It seemed to Faith Wadsworth, writing on 3 January 1830 from Hartford, Connecticut, somber in its muddy guise, that never did she "expect to

Broadway. New York City. Watercolor attributed to Nicolino Calyo. 1840–44. Museum of the City of New York. Out on the street, the stifling heat of summer was intensified by a relentless sun reflecting off brick facades. Closed venetian shutters might offer cool refuge within. First advertised in American newspapers in the mid-1700s, slatted shutters had become universal by the mid-1800s, for they protected household furnishings from the effects of sunlight; they discouraged the free entry of flies and mosquitoes; they screened out the dust and sand that blew about the streets; they enhanced privacy; and they promoted summer comfort

The Beauties of Street Sprinkling. New York City. Watercolor by Thomas Worth. 1856. The New-York Historical Society, New York City. To pedestrians, street sprinkling might in itself be a hazard, while the driver of a watering cart had to have a sure sense of balance

witness so long a continuance of such deep Black Pudding as our streets are now filled with." It did not, however, seem to deter the staunchest females, who "venture out & often with the fluttering display of finery above, while their poor feet look like those of a Peacock—black & hedious." Mud was only one of a multitude of trials encountered by Mrs. Wadsworth's niece Maria Silliman Church when in 1831 she followed her husband, John Barker Church, to the western New York outpost of Angelica. Here she was greeted by "as much mud as when Noah first came out of the ark." Even the horses were coated with what her father, Benjamin Silliman, the celebrated Yale professor of chemistry and natural history, called the "Allegany coat of arms." Well might Mrs. Church complain that it was "so disagreeable to have it tracked into the house so much." Caroline Dustan, who kept a diary in New York City in the 1850s

and 1860s, often griped about the alternately muddy or dusty streets. On 5 January 1859, she noted the hibernal inconvenience of carts loaded with coarse salt passing through Broadway, the walking consequently all slush. Two days later she appended, "Many pieces in paper condemning the practice of salting the Streets as it injured dresses and boots." In January 1861, Salomon de Rothschild also recorded the liberal sprinkling of salt on New York's snowy streets and its consequence of black mud "so deep that you literally risk your life." One of his hapless friends slipped in crossing Broadway and disappeared! "The mud covered his head and if it had not been for several kind souls who devoted themselves to pulling him out from this annoying situation he would have smothered." Catharine Beecher recommended scattering ashes on slippery ice at the door—or better yet, removing it. Young Henry Shute of

Philadelphia. Engraving by Thomas Nast in Charles Dickens, *Pictures from Italy, Sketches by Boz, and American Notes* (New York, 1877). In Philadelphia the beautiful, templed Schuylkill Water Works supplied a bounty of fresh water which, according to Charles Dickens, was "showered and jerked about, and turned on, and poured off everywhere." Paul Svinin, a Russian traveling in the States in 1811 and 1813, thought no city in the world could compare with Philadelphia in the cleanliness of her houses and streets. On Saturday afternoons not only the windows, the outer walls, and the steps but the very sidewalks were scrubbed with soap and water. Anthony Trollope observed some fifty years later that once the frost arrived in winter, the marble steps were encased in protective wooden boxes

Saturday, N.Y. Pencil drawing in a sketchbook, by an unknown American artist. 1800–1850. The Winterthur Library: Joseph Downs Collection of Manuscripts and Printed Ephemera. The Saturday ablution of the front steps was a ritual observed in Boston, New York, and Philadelphia. Strollers in these cities had to choose their footing carefully and defensively or run the risk of having a bucket of dirty wash water thrown against their legs by conscientious housewives dousing the front steps

Exeter, New Hampshire, wished he had performed his duty of strewing ashes one January morning in the 1860s, for "everything was covered with ice and when father started for the depot he tumbled down the front steps from the top to the botom. . . . i herd him swaring aufuly about that dam boy, and i gess he wood have come up and licked time out of me, but he had to hurry to get the train." Yet when George Combe, slipping all over Philadelphia's icy streets, asked why sand or ashes were not strewn on them, he was told that "visiters would bring it into the houses on their feet and dirty the carpets."[13]

Tenacious mud, dripping slush, salt and ashes, sand and dust had tremendous implications for conscientious housekeepers. We can easily understand why they kept their shutters closed and their parlors shut up; why Ebenezer Parkman of Marlboro, Massachusetts, hurried off to the blacksmith in February 1740 to get "an Iron Hoop fitted for dirty Shoes at my west Door"; why Philadelphians washed their front steps regularly; and why many Americans placed large mats before their doors. Such conditions could be confining, particularly for women in rural situations during spells of wet and wintry weather. "I dont expect to go out of my own door," sighed Maria Silliman Church on 22 January 1842, "til the leaves and the birds come back."[14]

The inadequacy of street lighting was an additional hindrance to evening perambulations. Struggling to maneuver around Boston's narrow, crooked cobblestone streets in August 1793, John Drayton received little assistance from lamps, yet "if ever they were necessary in any place, they certainly are in this." Just as the town fathers frugally limited paving to the main streets, so, too, were they chary of lamp oil. Anne Royall observed that though there were lamps in all of Washington's streets and avenues in 1826, they were only lighted in winter. In New York, as John Sturtevant affirmed, the whale-oil lamps, which were placed about fifty yards apart

on opposite sides of the street, were lit only on dark nights — "when the almanac said the moon did not shine. If the moon rose, say at 12, Billy [the lamplighter] must go at that hour and put them out so as to save oil." Scant indeed was the light provided in any case. Caroline King, who lived in Salem, Massachusetts, from 1822 to 1866, recalled her juvenile pleasure in watching the lamplighter come running along at dusk, ladder over his shoulder, to light dim oil lamps "that only served to emphasize the darkness of the streets." In rural areas the lack of artificial light and the abominable roads often precluded evening visiting.[15]

Though winter brought isolation and other miseries to rural Americans, urban dwellers were delighted to exchange the noise, hurry, dirt, and confusion of city summers for a quiet, calm, and healthful country life. With a sigh of relief, in July 1793 John Drayton left Boston, where "a continual clatter is kept up throughout the day, by carriages rolling upon the paved streets," and arrived at Portsmouth, New Hampshire, where "a calm, and quiet reigns, inviting one to every mental gratifica-

A Street Scene in Winter: Evening. Oil on canvas, by an unknown American artist. c. 1855. Museum of Fine Arts, Boston; M. and M. Karolik Collection of American Paintings, 1815–1865. Hibernal travel was not facile. In the eighteenth century, women sometimes attached wood-and-iron pattens to their delicate slippers to protect them from the mud, slush, or ice of the street, but many are the accounts of turned ankles arising from this unsatisfactory solution. Evening perambulations were further complicated by the inadequacy of street lighting

tion." And it was with great reluctance that Sarah Logan Fisher prepared to leave her country home in Germantown at the end of the summer to return to center Philadelphia in September 1778, exchanging "the calm delights of Stenton for the noise & hurry of a tumultuous throng, to leave Green Feilds & Shady walks for Brick Walls & Dirty Streets to give up Solitude Retirement & peace for Noise hurry & Confusion." In theory at least, country living was more intimate and informal and offered temporary respite from the rigorous social sentence of town life. Sitting in her parlor in the capital one evening, a figure in Margaret Bayard Smith's 1824 novel, *A Winter in Washington*, wished to be transported to the relaxed and soothing intimacy of a country home. "I love *country tea* better than *city tea;* don't you?" she asked, and a male companion responded, "I perfectly agree . . . and think not only *country tea*, but *country evenings*, far happier than city evenings."[16]

Harvey Schuyler Ogden and His Sister. Oil on canvas, by George Harvey. 1842. Private collection. A center hall with doors at either end gave an airy, roomy feeling to the interior, and Nathaniel Hawthorne was one of many who believed that one could breathe the easier for it. Here the floor is flagged in cool marble and the stair treads are protected by a strip of carpeting held taut with brass stair rods. When doors were closed, the hallway received little natural light, particularly if there were no fanlight above or side lights flanking the doors. At night a hall might be illuminated by a lantern or globe lamp; later in the century, perhaps by a gas jet. Eliza Leslie, author of *The House Book*, suggested that for evening parties the front door be additionally furnished with a lamp placed on a shelf or bracket in the fanlight, which would illumine the step and shine down on the pavement where the ladies alighted from their carriages

Mrs. Joseph Wright. Oil on canvas, by Ralph Earl. 1792. National Museum of American Art, Smithsonian Institution, Washington, D.C.; gift of Joseph Alsop. By day, early Americans delighted in sitting at open windows for air, for light, for the pleasure of the prospect. Anne Royall, an outspoken nineteenth-century traveler in the United States, was convinced that one of the greatest luxuries in the world was to sit in a large, airy room, your chair drawn up close to the window, with a mountain, a river, a street, or some other novelty to engage the eye

Large and numerous windows, often fitted with window seats, offered vantage points from which to admire the pastoral setting. Many foreign observers remarked upon this typical abundance of windows, which gave American houses a light appearance (though some were puzzled by the chronic deficiency of window glass in southern homes). American portraitists frequently picture the sitter at a window and occasionally, with artistic license, include the prospect or, even more imaginatively, a frontal view of the sitter's house. Not only did the pose make an attractive composition, it was also highly creditable. For if one looked up upon arriving at home in early America there was sure to be someone at a window—for air, for light, or for entertainment. Sarah Logan Fisher was just one of many who frequently pictured herself there—"setting writing at the Blue Room window," "setting at the front Chamber window so anxious about my dear little Girl that I cannot Sleep," "setting writing at

Family in Garden, detail of *"Harlem," Estate of Dr. Edmondson.* Gouache by Nicolino Calyo. 1834. The Henry Francis du Pont Winterthur Museum, Winterthur, Delaware. In warm weather, families often spent their leisure hours in the cool of the garden. Lightweight yet sturdy Windsor or painted "fancy" chairs might easily be carried out from piazza, hall, or sitting room to provide temporary seating

my Dressing Room window," and "sitting writing now . . . very pleasantly by the back parlour window, the fine view of the Garden & the Birds sweet harmony make it very delightful." Often it was an elderly person, no longer able to get around easily, whose chair was pulled up to the window to help while away the hours. When Emily Barnes returned to the home of her uncle in Walpole, New Hampshire, after his death, she was pleased to see that his easy chair was yet at a window in the sitting room, "where, in dreamy meditation, or in contemplation of the lovely scenery, of which he could never tire, he sat many hours in the day." Long Island artist William Sidney Mount wrote that his grandmother's last wish before she died, in January 1840, was to be led one final time to her accustomed seats at the front-room window and the window in the kitchen.[17]

If one arrived at home late on a summer afternoon, there might well be family members strolling in the garden and on the lawns, perhaps taking tea under the shade trees, for early Americans enjoyed their scented gardens, the beguiling prospects, the cooling shade, and the refreshing breezes. Afternoon tea was often taken alfresco during the summer months. Even in town, tree-shaded lawns provided refreshing possibilities. When clergyman and botanist Manasseh Cutler called on Benjamin Franklin at home in Philadelphia in 1787, he found him in his garden, the tea table spread beneath a large mulberry tree; and Thomas Jefferson wrote from that same city in July 1793 that he never went into the house but at bedtime, preferring to breakfast, dine, write, read, and receive company under umbrageous plane-trees. Some families owned sturdy stationary chairs and settees specifically designed as garden furniture. More commonly, lightweight chairs and folding tables were carried from the house to the garden. Windsor furniture, strong yet portable and easily maintained, was considered particularly adaptable to outdoor use and could be found

in English gardens from the 1720s. In New York, Windsor chairs and settees "fit for Piazza or Gardens" were available by mid-century.[18]

Having arrived at home, perhaps we should climb the front steps, open the door, and walk into the entry hall. Very possibly this hall runs straight through the center of the house, bisecting a symmetrical floor plan. With large doors at either end, it is commodious, lofty, and airy, bespeaking a growing concern for the healthfulness of one's surroundings. Spacious rooms, soaring ceilings, and cross-ventilation all contributed to a lung-strengthening free circulation of air. In winter, drafts of frosty air from the entry doors could be confined to the hallway by closing doors to the adjoining rooms.

Throughout the eighteenth century and during the early nineteenth century, the hall (and all first-floor rooms) was often elevated above a story or half-story basement. In town, this meant that they were further removed from the noise, smell, and dust of the street. In the country, this elevation took advantage of picturesque prospects and salubrious breezes. With its front and back doors opened wide, the through hall is a metaphor for the Enlightenment's self-confident embrace of nature for human pleasure and benefit. Nature could be enjoyed outside on carefully planned grounds, or inside from strategically positioned doors and windows. Front-hall doors and drawing-room windows were calculatingly placed to take best advantage of the view.

By the mid-nineteenth century, first-floor rooms were often moved back down to ground level as Romantic thought preached a further rapprochement with nature. Homes were to nestle into their landscape settings. In houses of modern design, the hall was frequently reduced in height and breadth, demoted to a less central position in the floor plan and sentenced to become more of a service area than a living space.

Minard Lafever adamantly maintained in his *The Young Builder's General Instructor* of 1829 that a wide hall running through the house was room lost—an invitation to cold air in winter and of little merit in summer. Andrew Jackson Downing, whose *The Architecture of Country Houses* was published in 1850, believed that some kind of an entry passage was necessary, for it not only shielded family rooms from sudden drafts of air, "but it also protects the privacy and dignity of the inmates," who might otherwise be disturbed by visitors walking directly into their parlors. Yet he thought the through-hall plan too emblematic of town conditions and wanting of "local truth" for country situations where variety and convenience need not be precluded by spatial restrictions. Moderation and a sense of the appropriate seem to have guided Downing, for when he sought dignity and airiness in the design he referred back to this broad passageway. There were others arguing for the retention of the center-hall plan in the mid-nineteenth century, and in an age that treasured privacy and stressed the virtues of a plenitude of ever-circulating fresh air, these debates did not fall on deaf ears. Christopher Crowfield (a nom de plume of Harriet Beecher Stowe) spoke ably for this group, contending in 1865 "that the first object of a house-builder or contriver should be to make a healthy house; and the first requisite of a healthy house is pure, sweet,

Mrs. Daniel Truman and Child. Fair Street, New Haven. Oil on canvas, attributed to Reuben Moulthrop. c. 1798–1810. The New-York Historical Society, New York City. Early Americans delighted in handsome grounds, handsome houses, and a handsome prospect. Grounds were planned with key vistas in mind, one of which would have been the view from the center hall. On a warm day this hall provided a refreshingly cool and often delightfully scented seat as the fragrance of flowers from the garden and perhaps vines on the portico or potted plants on the doorstep wafted through. Bare floors seemed to enhance summer coolness

Two Children. Oil on panel, by an unknown American artist. c. 1810–20. Abby Aldrich Rockefeller Folk Art Center, Williamsburg, Virginia. The floor of the hall might typically be flagged in marble, left bare, or covered with a woven carpet, straw matting, or painted canvas floor cloth. The latter seems to have been the choice in this summertime view. Sturdy and easily wiped clean, floor cloths were well suited to the rough usage of the entryway. Women were advised in buying a floor cloth to purchase one that had been manufactured several years before as the paint would be more durable and less likely to flake off. Evidence points, nonetheless, to their having been repainted on a regular basis. In some homes these cloths were used only in the summer months, giving way to warm woolen carpets during the cold season, and housewives were cautioned to store them on carpet rollers, taking care not to crack the paint by incautiously bending the edges

elastic air. I am in favor, therefore, of those plans of house-building which have wide central spaces, whether halls or courts, into which all the rooms open, and which necessarily preserve a body of fresh air for the use of them all." Further, if furnished as a pleasant sitting room, this ample central room, on both the first and second story, would not be space lost, but rather the most agreeable lounging rooms in the house; "while the parlors below and the chambers above, opening upon it, form agreeable withdrawing-rooms for purposes of greater privacy."[19]

The floor of the hall in the most elegant homes might be flagged with marble, which promoted coolness in summer and cleanliness the year round. By the mid-nineteenth century, glazed tiles offered the same benefits at a fraction of the cost. Throughout the eighteenth century, hall floors might be left bare, particularly in summer, or a painted canvas floor cloth might protect the boards. These cloths were typically imported from England and were of bright color or dramatic pattern. One of the most favored designs featured alternating light and dark squares or diamonds in simulation of marble flagging. When Charles Carroll of Carrollton placed an order for an oilcloth with his London agent in 1771, he voiced the usual preference for a pattern of black and white. By the 1790s, however, these bold geometric designs were giving way to more delicate ones in the Federal style, and when Carroll sent for thirty yards of yard-wide canvas for floors in 1791, he wanted it painted "not in diamonds, but a waving Pattern." Floor cloths were admirably designed to withstand rigorous hallway traffic, for on them could be wiped the mud, sand, slush, or salt that were inevitably carried in on boots and slippers. The floor cloth prevented dirt from being tracked about the house, and its water-repellent coating offered a significant advan-

Paysage Indien. French wallpaper, gouache on paper, designed by Joseph Dufour. 1815. The Saint Louis Art Museum; Museum purchase. Scenic wallpapers of large scale, vivid color, and lively motif demonstratively transformed the aspect of many early-nineteenth-century interiors and were favored for expansive rooms such as the entrance hall. This particular example once enlivened the walls of the Putnam-Hanson house in Salem, Massachusetts. The graphic scenarios of these panoramic papers offered to innumerable young Americans a thrilling introduction to world history, geography, and anthropology. Many are the fond testimonials in diaries, reminiscences, and letters to the lasting effect of these lessons

tage over wooden floorboards or woolen carpets, which once wet required considerable time to dry out. Colonial opinion equated dampness with ill health, and one of the most crucial obligations of the housewife was to avoid or quickly eradicate any trace of dampness. Fastidious women made sure that these cloths were frequently wiped clean and, on occasion, coated them with milk and buffed them dry for augmented brilliance. Account books reveal that they were regularly repainted. In 1840 Eliza Leslie assured the readers of her *The House Book* that there was nothing so suitable for the hall or vestibule as a painted oilcloth, but by 1855 Mrs. M. L. Scott, author of *The Practical Housekeeper*, was of the opinion that "a carpet is preferable to an oil cloth for a hall, as oil cloth requires wiping off twice a day to make it look bright and clean."[20]

Wool carpets could be found in American halls with some frequency from the close of the eighteenth century. As early as 1788 Brissot de Warville commented upon the "ridiculous prodigality in carpets" in America and offered the anecdote of a Quaker from Carolina who, when he went to dine at the house of one of the wealthiest Quakers in Philadelphia, was so offended at seeing the front hallway ostentatiously covered with a carpet that he refused to enter the house. Often the carpet scaled the stairs as well and was held tautly in place by stair rods, which in the houses of the wealthy might be silver-plated and elsewhere of brass or iron. Carpeted stairs not only cushioned the feet parading endlessly up and down them but their sleek surfaces could oblige in more unusual ways. According to the reminiscences of Edward Hewitt, who was born in New York City in 1866: "One day, when we had been sledding on the street, the snow melted so that the sledding was not good. However, we wanted some more coasting. So Cooper, my elder brother, suggested that we try the sled on the front stairs of our house, which went straight down toward the front door. We thought that it would go slowly, on carpet, but instead it ran down with lightning speed, crossed the hall, and smashed against the large panel of the front door. Fortunately, the panel burst, and let us through without our hitting anything else." Canvas floor cloths were also used on the stairs, although they must have been dangerously slippery, propelling the unsuspecting down the stairs at a speed well nigh that of a sled. Straw matting was a favored covering for hall floors from 1750 to 1870, especially in summer. Denigrators found it a harbor to vermin and its impractical pale color susceptible to the disfiguring discoloration of hearth smoke and flyspecks, but *The Improved Housewife* (1854) and numerous other sources assured that straw carpets could be washed in salt and water or sand and water with a little hard soap.[21]

Black smoke and pin-dot flyspecks disfigured not only the matting but the engravings that often hung in considerable numbers in the hall and stairwell. As early as 1765 John Blott, a Charleston paperhanger, was promoting the use of wallpaper with the claim that "the expense of papering a room does not amount to more than a middling sett of Prints." By the 1780s Johann David Schoepf observed that the houses of Pennsylvania were seldom without "paper tapestries, the vestibule especially being so treated." Specifically designed for lofty spaces, hall papers were often bold in design. Papers of classical motif were much approved. Trompe l'oeil papers imitating marble or dressed stone superseded pillar and arch designs in stairways and entries during the early 1800s and remained popular for another fifty years, while scenic papers enlivened many nineteenth-century hallways with their colorful narratives. Some could be frightening. Eliza Chinn Ripley recalled the trepidation with which she mounted the stairs at a friend's plantation in Ascension Parish, Louisiana, in 1849:

> The hall was broad and long, adorned with real jungle scenes from India. A great tiger jumped out of dense thickets toward savages, who were fleeing in terror. Tall trees reached to the ceiling, with gaudily striped boa constrictors wound around their trunks; hissing snakes peered out of jungles; birds of gay plumage, paroquets, parrots, peacocks everywhere, some way up, almost out of sight in the greenery; monkeys swung from limb to limb; ourang-outangs, and lots of almost naked, dark-skinned natives wandered about. To cap the climax, right close to the steps one had to mount to the story above was a lair of ferocious lions!

By the 1850s such bold drama was decidedly outré. Not only had the entry been reduced in scale in many homes but its muted decoration was to be very definitely subservient to the éclat of the parlor. As Downing counseled, "The *hall*, and all entries, staircases, and passages should be of a cool and sober tone of color—gray, stone color, or drab," because "the effect of the richer and livelier hues of the other apartments will then be enhanced by the color of the hall."[22]

Hanging prominently in the entry hall might be a pair of fire buckets and bags. "As soon as that fearful cry of 'Fire, Fire' was heard," explained Caroline King, "my father would take down his leathern fire buckets which always hung in our back entry, shake out the strong canvas bags which were kept in the buckets ready for service, and rush away, to give all the help he could, as did every other able-bodied man in the town." James Smithwick, a Boston mariner, kept a pair of fire buckets, bags, and a "Bed Winch" in his entry in 1779. The buckets were for throwing water to quench the blaze, the canvas bags for salvaging small valuables, the bed key or bed wrench for dismantling a bedstead in a house afire or likely to take fire, for the best bed and its expensive hangings were a highly prized possession. A nagging fear of fire plagued all early Americans. Open hearths and blazing candles demanded close and constant supervision, but masters and mistresses were often distracted and servants irresponsible. Clothing and furnishing textiles often took fire, and journals frequently mention toddlers falling into the fire, children being scalded by burning fat or water,

Ira Merchant as a Fireman. Oil on canvas, by an unknown artist. c. 1850. Collections of the New Jersey Historical Society, Newark. Blazing candles, smoking lamps, open fires, and sooty chimneys meant that a nagging fear of fire was an unpleasant, daily aspect of life in early America. Often a pair of leather fire buckets, such as the one in the lower right corner of this painting, hung in the hall, ready to be taken down at the alarm of fire by an able-bodied man of the house and carried to the scene of the conflagration, where they might help quench the blaze. From Boston in the 1790s, William Priest reported that the women of the family would respond to the nocturnal tocsin by placing candles in the windows to light the path of the firemen

The Children of Nathan Comfort Starr. Middletown, Connecticut. Oil on canvas, by Ambrose Andrews. 1835. The Metropolitan Museum of Art, New York City; partial gift of Nina Howell Starr. The broad, airy expanse of the center hall augured well for a gymnasium, and here the children of Nathan Comfort Starr enjoy a game of shuttlecock. The elevated position of the Starr house should have provided a dry and therefore healthful setting, yet even under optimum conditions it was difficult to secure health at home in early America. Fifteen-year-old Emily Helen keeps a watchful eye over her sister and brothers. Twelve-year-old Grace Anna, named after a sibling who had died an infant, returns the cock to nine-year-old Henry, while six-year-old Frederick stands by ready to join in. Little Edward, with hoop and rolling stick, was born in July 1832 and died in October 1835, suggesting that this painting was commissioned by parents who wished to memorialize a dying or recently deceased child

maids stepping into kettles of boiling water, and similar accidents. Though many were conscientious—checking all fires and lights before retiring, teaching servants the proper way to carry a candle, and training children to fear the fire—yet one was always at the mercy of one's neighbors, for, once started, a fire often cut a broad swath. Faith Silliman Hubbard was relieved that she had no neighbors to set her house on fire in Hanover, New Hampshire, in November 1837 and reassured her mother that she was herself very careful; though fear of a fire remained her greatest anxiety, "all we can do is to be as careful as possible and trust a kind Providence for the rest." Incendiaries were not an uncommon problem in urban centers, heightening the terror—one might almost say paranoia—that seized residents at each alarm. The night tocsin and the cry of "Fire!" were sounds dreaded by all.[23]

Moreau de Saint-Méry, who was in America in the 1790s, tells us that when one went out for dinner one left cane, hat, and topcoat on a coatrack in the front hall. Some sixty years later, a book that promised to contain only what "Is of Practical Use to Every Body" reiterated, "You leave over-coat, cane, umbrella, &c., and if the call is of any length your hat in the entry." Indeed, by this date arborescent umbrella stands and hat stands branched out over many a vestibule, but pegs and pins might serve as well. Mary Palmer, who was born in Massachusetts in 1775 and married the first successful American playwright, Royall Tyler, recalled that as you entered her grandfather's house there hung on the left "a splendid pair of buck's horns, on the crags of which my grandfather and his guests hung their hats, and across which lay grandpa's gold headed cane whenever he was not walking with it." A thermometer might hang nearby, decreeing the comfort of the day, and often a venerable tall-case clock stood either in the hall or "half-way up the stairs," long before Henry Wadsworth Longfellow brought it literary fame.[24]

The remaining furnishings of the vestibule characteristically varied according to the season, for although the hall might be a comfortable breezeway in summer, outfitted with supplementary tables and chairs brought in from adjoining rooms, it was in winter but a chilly interval to be quickly passed through. The introduction of the airtight stove in the first half of the nineteenth century made it possible for some families to frequent the hallway year-round. Jane Haines pictured herself at home in Philadelphia in December 1821, "sitting in the Hall which is made comfortable by a coal fire in the stove"; and Phebe Ann Beach Lyman of Cherry Valley, New York, told her sister in February 1842 that some mutual friends had established their living quarters by their coal stove in the entry for the duration of the cold weather. It was far more typical, however, during the eighteenth century and early nineteenth century for the hall to be furnished as a living room in summer and stripped to its essentials in winter.[25]

From 1750 to 1850, Windsor and other painted chairs were common both in the entry hall and in the corresponding passage on the second floor. The early American entry hall was a large and convenient storage space, and folded or disassembled dining tables often lined the walls. On occasion, tea tables could be found in the entry hall, more often in the upstairs hall. This second-story passage might contain card tables and a settee or daybed as well, for the large windows at either end made this an open, airy, well-lighted, and solar-heated apartment for relaxing and informal entertaining. Here also stood the stately linen press or clothespress with its neatly folded bed linens and towels, as its height and breadth were easily accommodated in such a space and it was conveniently located near the bedchambers. By the close of the eighteenth century, there might be an upholstered sofa in the hallways of the well-to-do. At the time of his death, John Hancock, whose bold signature is a familiar icon, boasted a "spinnett" in the "Great Entry" of his Boston home, where "1 Copper plate Sopha" and "1 Leather Sopha" had also found houseroom; and when Philip Fithian, the Princeton-trained tutor at Robert Carter's Virginia plantation, arrived at Colonel John Tayloe's neighboring estate, Mount Airy, one August morning in 1774, he found the young ladies in the hall playing the harpsichord. On a rainy day the hall might reverberate with laughter and the lively ping of battledore and shuttlecock, for this spacious passage could oblige as a nursery and playroom as well. It was with many fond memories that Ellen Rollins retraced her girlhood steps, back through the green country lane to the old New Hampshire farmhouse. Let us accompany her as she pushes open "a door which leads into a hall, wherein I have sported away many a day in childhood. At the other end of this hall is another door, through which came . . . the odor of sweetbrier and honey-suckle."[26]

THE BEST PARLOR, OR DRAWING ROOM

Many American homes between 1750 and 1870 could boast two parlors. One was aloof and ceremonial, the other unpretentious and informal. The best parlor was a reception room, the apartment to which a guest would first be shown. It was strategically located on the main floor, frequently at the front of the house, just off the entry hall; as the view could play an important part in the overall éclat, however, the room might be shifted to take advantage of an expansive prospect or breathtaking garden at the back or side of the house. The intent was to impress through a display of fine possessions. The furniture should be rich and delicate and the wall and furnishing colors cheerful and light so that the "brilliancy of effect" would not be lost in evening twilight. The atmosphere was formal, the use occasional—for entertaining and such rites of passage as weddings, christenings, and funerals. And the appellation was various—parlor, front room, best room, drawing room, or a compass-point designation such as "southwest room," in reference to the position in the floor plan.

Best-parlor furniture was variably mahogany, walnut, rosewood, or cherry; invariably uncomfortable; and, in a long-standing tradition firmly established in seventeenth-century France, ranged about the walls. Drop-leaf Pembroke (breakfast) tables, fold-top card tables, and hinged-top tea tables and stands were specifically designed for such boundary positions along the walls and in corners. Catharine Beecher was yet directing with unbending authority in 1843 that one arrange the parlor furniture straight and square with the wall, never leaving the chairs standing awry "as if dancing a jig with each other." When Letitia Burwell looked back from the cluttered 1890s to this neat arrangement, so typical during her girlhood in mid-nineteenth-century Virginia, she mused that perhaps the old-fashioned furniture had simply "thought too much of itself to be set promiscuously over the floor, like modern fauteuils and divans." The resulting open space in the center of the room facilitated housekeeping; promoted the easy arrangement of the furniture for tea drinking, card playing, sewing, reading, or eating; and prevented family members from tripping over furniture left standing about in these often dimly lit interiors.[1]

Tables and chairs were brought out into the room for use and subsequently returned. Anne Royall cringed at the jarring sound of a table being dragged across a bare floor to be set up for a meal in the 1820s—a dilemma that the use of carpets might abet. This could be one reason why carpets in American parlors were typically stretched from wall to wall and nailed tightly to the floor: tautness prevented them from bunching as furniture was moved about. Casters of brass, wood, and leather facilitated this transport around the room and were advertised in colonial newspapers from the 1750s. But it is not surprising that one of the repairs most often mentioned in

Conversation Piece ("Hartford Family"). Oil on canvas, by an unknown American artist. 1840–45. The White House Collection, Washington, D.C. Opinion differs as to whether the family depicted is northern or southern, but the spirit of this elegant interior accords with A. J. Downing's dictum that the drawing room be elegant, light, and cheerful. Downing preferred soft hues and gilding for in-town drawing rooms so that the brilliancy of the effect not be lost at evening. Indeed, the delicate colors and the abundance of gilding in woodwork, wallpaper, and frames suggest that there would be considerable sparkle when the paired lamps were lit before the extravagant expanse of mirror glass. The piano, workstand in the background, and sewing box on the footstool reiterate the emphasis on social status and accomplishment. The mother holds some needlework in her lap. If, as Frances Byerley Parkes counseled in her *Domestic Duties* (1829), a lady was engaged in light needlework ("and none other is appropriate in the drawing-room") when guests arrived, she might continue, for such genteel occupation encouraged ease in conversation. Other parlor pursuits such as music, reading, or drawing, however, need be suspended

eighteenth-century and early-nineteenth-century cabinetmakers' account books is to broken table legs. Chairs were subjected to the same constant rearrangement, the same exacting wear and tear. Eliza Farrar advised American girls in 1837 that nothing which added to a mother's cares should be considered a trifle, so that "even setting up your chair is a duty, if it saves her the trouble of doing it." Late one evening seventeen years later, Ellen Birdseye Wheaton would wearily note in her diary that it was time to retire: "The children are asleep. The chairs are set back."[2]

The desirability of servant help under these conditions is obvious—not only did the furniture have to be regularly conveyed about the room, but this must be done with care, keeping a hand behind to prevent the corners and edges from damaging the walls. The spooned, curved, and angled backs of William and Mary, Queen Anne, and Chippendale chairs, though perhaps designed for human comfort and stylish appearance, offered the supplementary benefit of preventing all but the crest rail and, yet more, the tips of the splayed back legs from touching the stucco—areas that were often also protected by a dado or chair rail and the baseboard or washboard. Chairs, sofas, and tables continued to hug the perimeters of the parlor far into the nineteenth century. In 1840 Eliza Leslie recommended the use of carpeted slats, about a foot long, to serve as buffer between furniture and wall, and the following year Catharine Beecher approved the use of carpeted blocks behind tables and sofas in all rooms with nice walls or wallpaper.[3]

From the seventeenth century, parlor chairs had typically been commissioned in multiples of six, and in many eighteenth-century and nineteenth-century parlors a dozen side chairs remained the preferred number. In eighteenth-century Boston, sets of six or of twelve side chairs were often supplemented by one armchair, while Charleston residents favored a dozen side chairs and two elbow chairs—that is, chairs with open arms and, sometimes, padded armrests. Wool and leather were the favored seat coverings throughout much of the eighteenth century. When in 1783 Rebecca Rawle Shoemaker of Philadelphia made out a list of furniture, "which I think thee cannot do very well without," for her soon-to-be-married daughter, she included twelve mahogany chairs with woolen moreen bottoms for the parlor. By the end of the century, silk and haircloth (an early horsehair fabric) had eclipsed wool and leather in fashionable circles and would reign supreme for another hundred years. In cosmopolitan Charleston, where there was little delay in introducing the latest London taste, Andrew Johnston's establishment boasted "Twelve Mahogany Chairs with hair bottoms & 2 Armed Dº" by 1764; and to Edward Everett Hale a full century later, "twelve decorous heavy chairs, probably hair-seated, with their backs against the walls," were yet synonymous with Boston parlors.[4]

To sit in these uncompromising chairs, with their rigid backs and firmly stuffed seats, demanded physical and mental self-presence. George Channing had learned this exigent lesson in the parlor of his late-eighteenth-century Rhode Island home, where the chair seats were polished leather, and as these seats "sloped forward, it required no little skill to sit upright." It is not surprising that when Harriet Beecher Stowe sought to evoke the quintessential image of the early American parlor, she conjured up "exactly one dozen stuffed-seated cherry chairs, with upright backs and griffin feet, each foot terminating in a bony claw, which resolutely grasped a ball. These chairs were high and slippery, and preached decorum in the very attitudes which they necessitated, as no mortal could ever occupy them except in the exercise of a constant and collected habit of mind."[5]

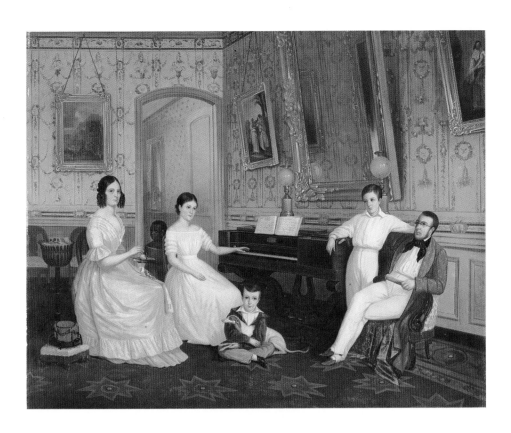

Child in Interior. Oil on wood panel, by an unknown American artist. c. 1850. Collection Mr. and Mrs. Norman Hirschl. Catharine Beecher, who prescribed harmony of color as the great, simple principle of beauty in home decoration, would have approved the carpet and upholstery treatment in this delightful interior, but both she and Eliza Leslie would have found fault with the wall color, which on no account was to resemble that of the furnishings but should instead offer a decided contrast, lest the room appear "indistinct" and "ungenteel"

Detail of a tin-glazed earthenware tray possibly from Bristol, England. 1743. By courtesy of the Board of Trustees of the Victoria and Albert Museum, London. This detail provides rare pictorial evidence of someone moving his chair out from the wall to join a group at a tea table set up in the center of the room. At the conclusion of this repast, and of countless others in England and America throughout our period, chairs and table would be returned to their outlining position. On 1 June 1744, William Black, who burned his lips more than once while simultaneously sipping tea and contemplating the fair beauties of one of the Logan daughters at Stenton, in Philadelphia, had the self-presence to record in his journal that after tea the tea table was removed

Checking the Barometer. Wood engraving by Alexander Anderson in [Arnaud Berquin], *The Looking-Glass for the Mind; or, Intellectual Mirror* (New York, 1804). Special Collections, Baker Library, Dartmouth College, Hanover, New Hampshire. A dozen side chairs typically lined the walls of eighteenth-century and early-nineteenth-century parlors. To Abram Dayton of New York, such stiff, thickly set mahogany chairs ranged at precise distances plumb against the wall looked like nothing so much as sentinels at a present. Observe how the height of the chairs accords with the chair rail and also how the sprigged wallpaper above helps to emphasize this divisional belt around the room. The chairs have been placed slightly out from the wall so that the wallpaper, paint, and chair backs themselves will not be damaged—advice reiterated in household manuals far into the second half of the nineteenth century. The raking rear legs and the slightly tilting backs of eighteenth-century chairs kept all but the tips of these legs and perhaps the back of the crest rail from coming in contact with the wall, thereby ensuring the safety of the splat and other delicately carved areas of the chair

Eighteenth-century and early-nineteenth-century parlor rituals necessarily mirrored the rigid formality of the seating furniture and its placement. "Made a *set, starched stiff Lazy Trifeling* Wedding Vissit," grumbled Esther Burr, after fulfilling that obligation on 18 July 1757. At company teas, the ladies would either sit along the wall or bring their chairs into a semicircle so geometrically precise as to suggest its

having been drawn by a compass. Tea and refreshments were then handed around. Ferdinand Bayard observed a group of Virginia ladies in 1791 typically "arranged in a semicircle on the right of the mistress of the house," and looking "as grave as judges on the bench." Margaret Hunter (Mrs. Basil) Hall, who had been raised in genteel British society at a moment when the English were adopting easy and informal patterns of living, was entirely fed up with the formality of American parlors by the end of her sojourn. She bemoaned the ubiquitous "most formidable circle," and after attending a parlor wedding in Holyoke, Massachusetts, in October 1827, she groused, "The company were seated according to the American fashion as if they were pinned to the wall."[6]

Parlor seating furniture of the 1750s and 1760s might include a couch or daybed rendered comfortable by a squab or a mattress and bolster in color harmony with the chair seats. In the succeeding decade an expensively upholstered sofa challenged the hegemony of the daybed in the best parlors, and by the 1830s the sofa had become the icon of this apartment and all other furnishings were to support it in character. Perhaps because of the softened comfort it provided or because women and textiles had long been affiliated, the sofa was also something of a metaphor for the female sphere of influence, and it was often seated upon this prized possession that the lady of the house chose to be portrayed. A gentleman in portraiture, on the other hand, rarely sits on a sofa unless accompanied by his wife.

As the sofa had come into vogue in the 1770s, when paired forms were particularly admired, a duo of sofas might provide colorful emphases in symmetrical room arrangements. These pairs were placed to complement architectural elements, enhancing the harmonious effect of the room. Thus, Mary Boardman Crowninshield hoped to purchase two little sofas or couches "which will just fit our recesses" for her Salem, Massachusetts, home in 1815, and Harriet Silliman intended "to have 2 small sofas one to be placed on each side of the new door" in her recently refurbished New Haven drawing room in 1836. Alternatively, they might flank the fireplace, as George Hepplewhite had recommended in the third edition of his *The Cabinet-Maker and*

Portrait of a Lady. Oil on canvas, by John Singleton Copley. 1771. Los Angeles County Museum of Art; Museum Acquisition Fund. The comfort of eighteenth-century sofas was often enhanced by an additional seat squab, with a row of pillows along the back or a pair of bolsters at either end. Both squab and pillows are present here. Note the loose tufting, the attention to outline expressed in the brass nails and pronounced welting cord, and the dramatic pattern of the crimson damask in what was then the most popular color choice for furnishings fabrics

Upholsterer's Guide (1794). Because sofas were moved about for comfort or to make conversational groupings, they were often fitted with casters. In summer a breezy location was important; in winter a sofa or a pair of sofas sometimes stood out from the fireplace, perpendicular to it. When Thomas Twining called upon George and Martha Washington at their Philadelphia residence in 1795, he was ushered into a medium-sized, well-furnished drawing room with a wood fire on the hearth, to the left of which was a sofa, which "sloped across the room"; and when Margaret Bayard Smith visited a friend in Washington in 1834, she was delighted with the elegantly furnished room "cheerfulized" by a bright fire, on one side of which, "drawn forward, was a handsome pianno, on the other side a comfortable sopha."[7]

The vote in favor of the comfort of American sofas was not unanimous, however, particularly after haircloth became well-nigh universal in the late 1820s. It seemed to one sufferer that the very bolsters themselves were "hard as logs of ebony"; and Margaret Hunter Hall avowed that a comfortable sofa at the end of "a fagging day's work" was one of the things she missed most in this rigid land of haircloth and mahogany. Even in the most luxurious homes she found the sofa "a miserable, nasty, narrow thing with wood on which to break your elbows at every corner." Abram Dayton of New York agreed that these horsehair affairs, "unimpressible as flint," were no couch of ease, but at least to a child the rounded, unyielding, and slippery seats "afforded capital *coasting* for youngsters, when the lynx-eyed guardian of the sacred domain was too busily employed in household duties to check the contraband sport."[8]

Anna Maria Smyth. Oil on canvas, by Sarah Miriam Peale. 1821. Pennsylvania Academy of the Fine Arts, Philadelphia. Not everyone found American sofas comfortable, and many were the complaints of uncompromising corners, unyielding edges, and insufferable seats

Except when covered in haircloth, the sofa upholstery was to accord with all other fabrics in the room—including curtains, chair seats, fabric-covered fire screens, and even the carpet—in color if not in material. In eighteenth-century Boston, where window seats were favored, these cushions were also to match. Stephen Greenleaf's "Best Room" must have been resplendent in 1795, with a red damask sofa to suit a baker's dozen of side chairs and armchair, all with red damask seats, and four red damask curtains with color-coordinated squabs.[9]

As with seating furniture, tables—and preferably pairs of tables—were arranged symmetrically about the parlor with architectural enhancement in mind. The window piers offered stunning possibilities. Marble-topped pier tables, or slabs, were particularly esteemed, and the best parlors might boast a pair on cast-iron or carved-wood bases with looking glasses suspended above. Looking glasses were essential features of the best parlors and in both scale and decoration they often made the most declamatory statement in a room. Indeed, their size and number were a sure index of the wealth and pretensions of a family. They were available in a wide variety of type and design from 1750 to 1870, with the most admired being consistently the largest. Typically, the frames were of polished mahogany or gilded or painted soft wood. John Parkinson, a Charleston carver and gilder, could oblige with frames in mahogany or white, or painted in colors to the client's own fancy in 1783; and the mid-eighteenth-century British taste for exuberantly carved frames painted white, on occasion tipped with gold, had been well established in the American colonies by 1770. It is pleasing to envision the theatrical effect of these airy white silhouettes against the rich, saturated colors of the parlor walls, painted, perhaps, in "Verditure blue, Prussian blue, pea-green, straw, stone, slate, cream, cloth, or pink colours." The window piers and the overmantel were customary locations for hanging glasses, whether they came in the guise of sprightly rococo C-scrolls; or delicate, restrained Federal-period rectangles and ovals; or the broad expanses of nineteenth-century plate glass, towering toward the cornice enframed in earnest allusions to some misunderstood past. Pairs were, of course, admired and a typical drawing-room ensemble was an overmantel and accompanying pair of pier glasses—perhaps fitted with candle arms and thus termed "sconce glasses." Calculatingly suspended beside or across from the windows or above the fire-enlivened mantel, looking glasses played an important supplemental role in lighting the drawing room. The best parlor was used most often either for the morning reception of visitors, when natural light would suffice, or in the late afternoon and evening, with tea, cards, music, or simply conversation as the social fare and, with the alliance of artificial light, looking glasses, gilded edges, and polished surfaces providing the drama.[10]

When Henry Hill of Philadelphia wrote Mary Hill Lamar, in London in the 1770s, sending a plan of his house on Fourth Street and asking that she procure looking glasses, his sister's response was quick. She had given the plan to an upholsterer who would in turn make her some drawings, "when I shall strive to fix on something that is handsome, and as cheap as possible. . . . I have some thoughts of sending only one large handsome glass for the best room . . . in the front; there being but two windows, one large glass will do with handsome girandoles or something more fashionable." From her enviable seat in the fashion capital she then went on to advise this brother in the American provinces, "A best room furnished in the present style and plainest taste is nothing more than two sofas, twelve or more chairs, a marble half circular table under the glass or glasses, glass lustres on the slabs to hold four

lights . . . or, in place of them, silver or plated branches for three candles; or, in place of the marble slabs, inlaid wood, which are very pretty and come cheaper." Her emphasis on the pier grouping underscores the importance of this element in the eighteenth-century parlor. Further, the restraint of this "present style and plainest taste" favored by many in London in the 1760s and 1770s was well suited to the pragmatic New World consumer, and an elegant simplicity and an emphatic sparseness were the salient features of many drawing rooms in eighteenth-century and early-nineteenth-century America. A pair of sofas, a dozen chairs, a twain of pier glasses, and tandem tables might well suffice for those who wished to furnish their homes "in the neatest and most genteel manner."[11]

Mary Hill Lamar went on to counsel her brother that "neither tea or card tables stand in the best room, but are brought in when wanted"—a fastidiousness that few

Yankees observed, regardless of how attuned they were to the latest London dictates. Tea tables and card tables (which frequently masqueraded as pier tables) abounded in American drawing rooms. Parlor tables were often covered with a cloth to protect their polished surfaces from dust and scratches and to provide protection from dripping wax, staining ink, and the tracings of a pen nib, for tables had to oblige in a number of different capacities. The cover might be "a Carpet Cover," like the "4 List Carpets for Tables" tallied in Benjamin Backhouse's Charleston inventory in 1767, but more typically it was of green baize—a coarse woolen fabric resembling felt. This could just overhang the tabletop or fall almost to the floor. Except for a cloth, however, most tables in eighteenth-century and early-nineteenth-century parlors were bare, ready to be moved into position for use. Exceptions were the kettle stand and its kettle companion, particularly admired by Charlestonians, and tea tables and rail-edged tables called china tables, which might display mahogany or japanned waiters and tea boards (trays), tea china, and silver. As the one exception to bare tabletops, these were all the more conspicuous.[12]

With the earliest appearance of tea china in the American seventeenth-century home, tea wares had sometimes been placed on a mantel—perhaps for display at this fire-lighted focal point, perhaps at this height to prevent accidental breakage, for closets were few and small. But as the eighteenth century progressed, growing concern for order, neatness, and convenience paralleled expanding consumer desires for luxury goods. Mantels in genteel homes were now decorated in an orderly way, often with small objects specifically designed as chimney garniture. Table china and glassware were taken off the mantel and displayed in a china cupboard or buffet (or variously referred to as the boffett, beaufat, or bowfat), which had become common to many homes by the 1730s and would remain in fashion into the next century. They were usually built into a corner of the room or to either side of the chimney and are not

York, Pennsylvania, Family. Oil on panel, by an unknown American artist. c. 1828. The Saint Louis Museum of Art; bequest of Edgar William and Bernice Chrysler Garbisch. Carpeting, wallpaper, and paint lend bright color and variegated pattern to this Pennsylvania interior, where simple painted furniture abides in harmony with hardwood pieces and looking glasses claim their wonted positions over the mantel and in the window pier. Note the absence of accessories and the attention to such niceties as having the window cornice box echo the wallpaper behind. A trusted servant is included in this family portrait as one is also in *Conversation Piece* and *The Children of Commodore and Mrs. John Daniel Danels* (see pages 41, 215).

always mentioned in household inventories as they might be considered architectural elements. Ebenezer Thayer's Roxbury, Massachusetts, parlor provides a transitional example, for he had in 1732–33 "China Plates in the Boffett other Earthen Ware in the Boffett & mantle Tree."[13]

Silver, tea china, the best table china, fine glass beverage wares, and other items used in the service of tea or other meals, such as a plate basket, breadbasket, and a shagreen case of knives and forks, were usually kept in the best-parlor buffets. The multiplication of consumer goods in the nineteenth century meant that even simple, rural interiors vaunted a china closet in the best room. These china cupboards are an important feature in the conception of the best parlor as a room for display. They often had glazed doors, and there is no question but that guests took full notice of their contents. To substantiate her characterization of Sam Lawson in *Oldtown Folks* as someone who "knew everything about everybody," Harriet Beecher Stowe cited his knowing "just all that was in Deacon Badger's best room, and how many silver table-spoons and teaspoons graced the beaufet in the corner."[14]

Not only was the display within lustrous and gleaming but often the cupboards themselves were japanned or painted in imitation of Oriental lacquer that they might, too, "shine and glister like looking-glasses." Japanned buffets were esteemed in eighteenth-century parlors in urban centers both North and South. The glittering effect of cupboards and contents would have been enhanced by candles and firelight. Lydia Howard Huntley Sigourney, who was born in Norwich, Connecticut, in 1791, could recall the parlor closet, "whose open door revealed its wealth of silver cans,

Gardiner and Samuel Howland. Silhouette by an unknown American artist, c. 1835, in Mrs. Eliza Newton Howland, *Family Records* (New Haven, 1900). U.S. History, Local History and Genealogy Division, The New York Public Library; Astor, Lenox and Tilden Foundations. This silhouette illustrates the use of a leather or fabric fringe nailed to a bookshelf edge to protect the books from dust and to add its own decorative touch

John Phillips. Oil on canvas, by Joseph Steward. 1793. Hood Museum of Art, Dartmouth College, Hanover, New Hampshire. John Phillips, founder of Phillips Exeter Academy in Exeter, New Hampshire, sits in a bright green Windsor chair beside a table that has been protected from ink and nibs by a cover of green baize. Baize-covered tables were so commonly used as a desk that they frequently appear in portraits as a surrogate for the desk and an attribute of male learning. The carpeting appears to be painted canvas floor cloths. Perhaps Phillips is seated in a hall, for in that part of the house drop-leaf tables, Windsor chairs, and canvas floor cloths were *de rigueur*. Observe the clarity of line in the contrasting curtain fringe and in the wallpaper border defining surbase, window surround, and cornice in the adjoining sitting room. The view from the window and the placement of the table beneath it suggest that this too offered a pleasant spot for work or relaxation

tankards, and flagons." As a little girl she had particularly "enjoyed brief glimpses of that parlor at night, lighted by two stately candlesticks, and an antique candelabra and [she thought] it was as the hall of Aladdin." Mrs. Sigourney also pictured the large brass andirons, "with their silvery brightness," but, she continued, "what particularly riveted my attention in that fair parlor was an ancient clock, whose tall, ebony case, was covered with gilded figures, of strikingly varied and fanciful character." There were handsome clocks, such as this undoubtedly japanned example, in many American parlors and perhaps a bookcase desk as well, although both of these forms might just as well be found in the back parlor.[15]

By the late 1760s there might be a large mahogany or japanned copper cooler for wines and a rum case, and by the close of that century one could find new, elegant forms in the urban parlor. One was the sideboard, sometimes marble-topped, arrayed

Home Sweet Home. Lithograph by Parsloe and Vance. 1875. Peters Collection, Smithsonian Institution, Washington, D.C. By the end of the eighteenth century, a parlor harpsichord or pianoforte made a clearly understood statement about the cultural pretensions of a family and the refined accomplishments of a promising daughter. A century later, as illustrated here, the piano had become a ubiquitous parlor furnishing, often embellished with its own cloth or scarf. That the number of qualified performers had not kept pace with the increase in instruments is evident in the horrified expression of the late-admirer at left, who precipitously seeks his escape from the jarring chromatics of a would-be siren. Observe how the paintings — perhaps further testimonials to this lady's dubitable talents — tilt forward to facilitate viewing

with welcoming decanters. Frances Trollope, who traveled in America between 1827 and 1831, had trouble concealing her disapproval of a sideboard in the prototypical Philadelphia drawing room, yet conceded, "it is very handsome, and has very handsome decanters and cut glass water-jugs upon it." Sarah Anna Emery recalled a particularly stylish and cosmopolitan best room in Newburyport, Massachusetts, where the seating furniture "was handsomely carved mahogany with coverings of a golden tinted damask, and curtains to match; with marble top tables, and marble mantels and hearths, which were imported from Italy. A marble topped side-board and a piano had been purchased in Paris; the carpets were from English looms, and the rest of the furniture was as splendid as American warehouses could furnish." On occasion, such a piano or harpsichord in an eighteenth-century parlor or music room bespoke genteel pretensions. The proliferation of the form in the early nineteenth century was an indication of the diffusion and diversity of consumer demand and of the growing emphasis on the polite accomplishments deemed necessary to a polished young lady. When a daughter sat down to perform for a parlorful of guests, such tunes pronounced the genteel education her parents had procured her, and not without considerable expense. Even if not used, "the diminutive, thin-legged, wheezy piano, purchased during some paroxysm of thoughtless extravagance," stood triumphant as a symbol of the family's recognition of polite refinements. By 1850, when A. J. Downing pronounced the pianoforte "the universal accompaniment of the drawing-room" and condoned the unequal ratio of many pianos and few pianists — as long as the desire for musical attainments was there — the piano had swelled in size as well as in number, assuming the bulbous contour of a "kettle in disguise."[16]

In rural homes from 1750 to 1870, there was on occasion yet another ostentatious presence flaunting itself in the best parlor — a bed. Huckleberry Finn applauded the conspicuous absence of the customary bed as he surveyed the niceties of the Grangerford's parlor vis-à-vis their Mississippi neighbors': "There warn't no bed in the parlor, not a sign of a bed; but heaps of parlors in towns has beds in them." An expensively draped bed and a small underbed or trundle bed, which could be wheeled out from underneath the larger bed for the safe stowage of children, had been a common furnishing in seventeenth-century parlors. Here amid the finest possessions guests had been entertained, and here benighted friends had slept. A bed, and its trundle companion, remained a regular feature in Hartford, Connecticut, parlors through the 1770s, and here in 1813 Samuel Bolles yet displayed a chintz-draped bed and an underbed in his "Front Room" — the most expensive bed in the house, although there were four bedchambers. Abbott Lowell Cummings has provided documentation for the use of the parlor bed by the master and mistress of the household in the seventeenth century; but by the third decade of the nineteenth century, and probably long before, the handsome bed in the rural best room had taken on the character of a seldom-used exhibit item in a room of display. Ellen Rollins, who was born in 1831, could call to mind her grandparents' best room, or "fore room," in Wakefield, New Hampshire, where the china and glass in its cupboard were marvelously fine, but "most noticeable of its furnishing was the bed, — more for show than use. . . . not to be leaned against or carelessly indented." And it stood in a room seldom used: "a store-room for household treasures. . . . a sort of show-room."[17]

Drawing-room floors in the homes of well-to-do colonists might be carpeted with the products of British looms. Wilton and Turkey carpets were favored in the eighteenth century, but they were not common. When Charles Carroll of Carrollton

ordered "1 Best Turkey Carpet 19 foot Long & 17 foot broad" in February 1784, he asked his London agent to "examine well this Carpet to see that it is clear of puckers which Turkey Carpets often have and which besides being ugly occasions them to wear out sooner in such Places"—understandable enough with the traffic of people and furniture back and forth. The carpet, as we have seen, was generally laid wall to wall and fitted to the contours of the room by the housewife or upholsterer. Carpets, curtains, and upholstered furniture, which had been the prerogative of the wealthy before 1800, had found their way into the parlors of the middle class by the third decade of the nineteenth century. "On entering the house of a respectable mechanic, in any of the large cities of the United States," marveled Francis Grund in 1837, "one

The Hobby Horse. Oil on canvas, by an unknown American artist. c. 1840. National Gallery of Art, Washington, D.C.; gift of Edgar William and Bernice Chrysler Garbisch. Red and green were favored colors in mid-nineteenth-century parlors, and green remained a common choice for table covers far into the nineteenth century, although the selection was by then extensive. In this parlor, the astral lamp sits in a nest of crocheted yarn, which not only was decorative but preserved the table cover from oil spills. Wallpaper and carpet each attest to the taste for large-scale motifs and to the vogue for color-shading effects

cannot but be astonished at the apparent neatness and comfort of the apartments, the large airy parlours, the nice carpets and mahogany furniture." Those who could not afford to purchase a carpet might make one, but everyone aspired to a carpet by this date—for the parlor at least. A Brussels, Axminster, Wilton, or common ingrain carpet might be a most conspicuous feature of the parlor throughout the first half of the nineteenth century, its bright colors—crimson and green were favored—and lively design contrasting with the dark furniture and simple walls. Large, soft carpets liberally strewn with gargantuan roses retained their decorative supremacy in many middle-class homes throughout the nineteenth century, but in the homes of the well-to-do they increasingly became just one more luxurious presence in a sea of opulence.[18]

The extension of trade routes worldwide contributed to the profusion of objects in American nineteenth-century drawing rooms. "Indeed, the whole world contributes to their luxury," exulted James Fenimore Cooper in 1828: "French clocks, English and Brussels carpets, curtains from Lyons, and the Indies, alabaster from France and Italy, marble of their own, and from Italy, and, in short, every ornament below the rarest that is known in every other country in christendom, and frequently out of it, is put within the reach of the American of moderate means, by the facilities of their trade." By 1849 Sir Charles Lyell, the celebrated geologist, would maintain that

Family Group. Oil on canvas, by Frederick R. Spencer. 1840. The Brooklyn Museum; Dick S. Ramsay Fund. Romantic thought preached a rapprochement with nature, which is clearly evident in the neat, compact bouquet of fresh flowers on the center table, in the clambering rose at the wide-open window, and in the picturesque view so easily accessible from the beckoning door. Wall colors in this period must also bespeak nature—stone gray, moss green, or fawn brown

he "had heard it said in France that no orders sent to Lyons for the furnishing of private mansions, are on so grand a scale as some of those received from New York; and I can well believe it, for we saw many houses gorgeously fitted up with satin and velvet draperies, rich Axminster carpets, marble and inlaid tables, and large looking glasses."[19]

The chaste reserve of the Enlightenment parlor had given way to the Victorian propensity for accumulation and love of ornament. Chairs "deep and luxurious," chairs "of the light fanciful Kind," side chairs, armchairs, sofas, lounges, ottomans, hassocks and footstools "in profusion" swallowed the staid lineup of a dozen side chairs and pendant pair of elbow chairs. A multiplicity of small stands and a great variety of light and fanciful tables were touted by A. J. Downing and others because they "are not only useful in the drawing-room for books, ladies' work, flower-baskets, etc., but they give an air of feminine taste and occupation to an apartment, without which it is apt to look stiff and solemn." The drawing room had long been regarded as feminine in character because of the elegance and delicacy of its furnishings and colors, but the

Victorian cult of domesticity gave an intensified fervor to this emphasis: the "arrangement of the multitudinous furniture and ornaments must be left to the taste of the lady of the house; none but a lady can do it," asserted J. C. Loudon.[20]

Tabletops might yet be covered with a cloth. This was often of traditional green color, but there was a much broader assortment of materials and colors to choose from. In fact, Downing felt that the parlor center table and sofa tables "depend for their good effect mainly on the drapery or *cover* of handsome cloth or stuff usually spread upon their tops, and concealing all but the lower part of the legs." These covers were now in turn covered with a variety of knickknacks, trinkets, books, and lamps—"Most of the tables must also have something upon them to make them appear of use," directed Loudon. Multishelved forms, such as the étagère or whatnot, the easel, corner shelves, hanging cabinet, and tall cabinet for curios, were introduced for the display of "whatever trifles of useful or ornamental character may accumulate." Indeed, no trifle was too trifling in an age that extolled individualism, for Victorian theorists

Mr. and Mrs. Alfred Dwight Foster and Their Children Dwight, Mary, and Rebecca. Worcester, Massachusetts. Oil on ivory, by Eliza Goodridge. 1838. American Antiquarian Society, Worcester. Beginning about 1820 one starts to see books, small bouquets, lamps, and other objects decorating the tops of tables, which would have been left bare earlier. The high polish of this table and the diminutive size of the bouquet are typical

Children in an Interior. Oil on canvas, by an unknown American artist. c. 1840. Collection Kathryn and Robert Steinberg. In many homes, the parlor was reserved for formal occasions and was as little used by the family on a daily basis as the dome-protected vase of artificial flowers that often stood on the center table. Writing tables and other necessaries for employment would not be found here, for what use would they be in the typically blind-darkened, curtain-shrouded, closed-up parlor, where even the carpet might lie folded toward the middle, dumpling fashion, to safeguard its glorious colors

postulated that each and every possession was imbued with the ability to elucidate the unique character of its owner.[21]

Eighteenth-century home owners treasured clarity, stability, balance, and order—an order that was evident in the arrangement of the furniture in symmetry with the architectural elements; the careful attention to color and proportional harmony; the neatness of uncluttered, highly polished surfaces. When Charles Carroll of Carrollton ordered one fashionable sofa and a dozen chairs from London in October 1771, he wanted them upholstered not only in chromatic harmony with the crimson silk damask curtains at the windows but also in proportional accord with the room, which was twenty feet square. A "skilful upholsterer will suit the size of the Sopha & Chairs to the Size of the Room—& be careful not to send them too large," cautioned Carroll, revealing himself to be a true disciple of Enlightenment thought. Spatial definitions were made clear in precise linear borders and contrasts of color and/or material. Woodwork might stand out against paper, fabric, plastered walls, or woodwork of another hue. Often there was a chair rail, which provided a visual division of wall space; wallpaper borders or gilded fillets of carved wood or papier-mâché might emphasize these clarifying lines. Similarly, the edges of tabletops were beaded, gadrooned, carved, and inlaid, while chair seats were fringed or lined with brass tacks for emphatic outline. Window curtains were edged with contrasting tape or fringe; carpets had borders. Between 1820 and 1870 these divisional elements were stripped away amid new concerns for homogeneity. Chair rails were removed and walls painted or papered in uniform fashion from floor to ceiling. When Harriet Silliman asked her daughters for advice in redecorating their New Haven home in 1836, the girls suggested "having the chair rail removed" in both parlors and, further, that the wallpaper "have no border . . . or a very narrow one." Vibrant eighteenth-century colors became increasingly muted that they might blend easily together.[22]

Further, each room in the eighteenth-century home was perceived as a separate entity; used for many purposes, perhaps, but insularly decorated in regard to its own four walls and floor. The paint color, wallpaper, and carpet bore no relationship to that of an adjoining apartment. In the nineteenth century, however, not only were the decorative elements of the parlor to meld but they were to flow into those of the connecting room as well: curtains, carpets, and wallpaper must be reciprocal. Offering her mother advice on improving their parlors, Faith Silliman stipulated, "by all means have both rooms papered *alike*." Two decades earlier, in December 1817, Elizabeth Wirt asked her husband to have the curtains for the two lower rooms of their future home in the capital made of the same color if not the same material, and to order common carpeting of the same pattern for each—"also chairs alike for both rooms might be advisable—as such things would look better when both rooms are thrown open, upon an occasion." That fashionable reception rooms, divided by folding doors, might be integrated for special functions was observed by John M. Duncan in New York in 1818: "In the modern houses the principal apartments are on the first floor, and communicate by large folding doors, which on gala days throw wide their ample portals, converting the two apartments into one." (The phrases "to throw wide" and "to throw open" capture some of the bold drama of the occasion, for it was often done for effect—an open solicitation for compliments on the congruity of decoration.) The smaller apartment remained a parlor, often used for the morning reception of female visitors. The other was in some houses the dining room. Although Frances Trollope had to concede that "when thrown open together they certainly make a very noble apartment," yet she did not approve the arrangement, for "no doors can be barrier sufficient between dining and drawing-rooms." This English traveler would perhaps have been better pleased with what Isabella Bird Bishop found to be the typical floor plan in affluent middle-class Manhattan homes in 1856, by which time there were generally three reception rooms: "a dining-room, small, and not striking in appearance in any way, as dinner-parties are seldom given in New York; a small, elegantly-furnished drawing-room, used as the family sitting-room, and for the reception of morning visitors; and a magnificent reception-room, furnished in the height of taste and elegance, for dancing, music, and evening parties."[23]

The axial rethinking of the parlor was in part allied with new concerns for airiness and proper ventilation and in part an outgrowth of new precepts of informality and ease that had begun to circulate among the fashionable folk about 1800. Harriet Manigault was relieved that her tea party for forty or fifty friends in December 1813 was not at all stiff and that "every body was standing up & walking from one room to the other"; and when Lady Emmeline Stuart Wortley visited Daniel Webster at his home in Marshfield, Massachusetts, she admired "a number of remarkably pretty drawing rooms opening into one another, which always is a judicious arrangement I think; it makes a party agreeable and unformal."[24]

Parlor furnishings might readily express this new informality in an easy arrangement of chairs and tables scattered about to encourage impromptu conversational groupings, but such carefree informality was rarely the case in the drawing rooms of America. Having traveled in the States in the mid-1850s, Thomas Grattan felt qualified to censure the prototypical Yankee room, where "scarcely any object seems meant for use, all are so prim and formal, in pattern and position." The center table was another product of the new concern with informality. Introduced via France and England, it was intended to stand in the middle of the room, covered with interesting books, papers, and prints—a magnet for easy social groupings. In the first

Parlor design by George Platt. New York City. Drawing in ink and wash. c. 1850. Collection Russell Lynes. By the mid-nineteenth century, a double—even triple—enfilade of parlors had become the norm in the better sort of urban home, and looking glasses might be calculatingly placed to further extend the effect. Here, Rococo Revival chairs and stands hug the walls with as much stubborn tenacity as they had a century before

parlors of America this casualness was retained. Thus, when on 23 November 1828 Margaret Bayard Smith called on Elizabeth Wirt, now established in Washington, she was ushered into a very large and elegant drawing room, "in the middle [of which] was a round table cover'd with books, engravings, workboxes &c &c lit by a splendid lamp. Round the table was seated the young ladies and 2 young gentlemen." In the generality of American drawing rooms, however, the center table was erroneously plunked down on an imaginary island with as much frozen formality as every other object in the room. And there it remained, sometimes supporting a seldom-used sinumbra lamp or an inutile alabaster vase of artificial flowers, parlor-protected by a chilly glass dome. This center table is the clue to the interpretation of the nineteenth-century parlor. If it was around the drawing-room center table that the family assembled in the evening, then the whole room assumed an easier, lived-in informality. But such was not usually the case. More commonly, it was around a table in the unceremonious back parlor that the household ended its day.[25]

By 1870 the whole idea of a formal room for the reception of guests, and to the exclusion of the family, was coming under increasing fire. A new word was being bantered about—instead of a parlor for proper parlance, a family might prefer a *living* room for all the lively activities of its bustling, close-knit membership. But, for generations of Americans from 1750 to 1870, the best parlor–drawing room was an accepted, if chilly, aspect of life at home. "We never sat in the parlor but usually visited it," as Andrew L. Winton summed it up. The front parlor was removed from the pulse of the family. It was, in the words of social historian Russell Lynes, "an island of formality in a turbulent sea of family comings and goings." Perhaps, then, we should trespass no longer, but shut the door and tiptoe to the back parlor, where we'll hope to find the family.[26]

THE BACK PARLOR, OR SITTING ROOM

The second parlor in an American house was variously termed parlor, sitting room, keeping room, living room, dining parlor, or back parlor—the last in reference to its location behind the best parlor. The role of this apartment was family room, the intent was convenience, the atmosphere was informal, and the use was frequent. The furniture was more diverse in type, quality, and material than that in the codified best parlor. If the front parlor was decked out in mahogany, the back parlor was often arrayed in walnut or even more typically in a patchwork of walnut, mahogany, and

61

maple. There were fewer paired forms, and although furniture lined the walls, the arrangement bespoke convenience more than symmetrical nicety and traditional formalism. Many families had only one parlor, in which case the room usually combined the salient features of both—a panoply of display furnishings and a good deal of useful furniture.

Often there were several tables in the sitting room—generally from two to four—of varying shapes, sizes, and materials. Several of these were designed for eating and drinking, and the varying sizes and shapes offered flexibility in table arrangements, dependent upon the number of diners and the meal served—breakfast, dinner, tea, or supper. For from 1750 to 1870, the sitting room was often used as a dining room and the dining room, in turn, frequently doubled as a sitting room. Thus, as Elizabeth Drinker noted in her journal on 4 April 1792, her family and invited guests had "dined in ye back parlor"; while on 28 December 1844 James Colles reported from New York that "our Dining Room, being very pleasantly situated, we will use it for the double purpose of Dining and Sitting Room."[27]

Convenience dictated that the kitchen be nearby, and proximity to the center hall was also important, for here a dining table or parts of a dining table were often stored when not in use. On occasion, in the summer months, these hall tables might be set up *in situ* to take advantage of cross-ventilation, but at other times they could be brought into the dining parlor either to be set up for the meal and returned, or to supplement an existing table when the number of diners was larger than usual. That dining tables were brought into the dining parlor from the hall we hear from Elizabeth Wirt, who wrote her husband in December 1812 suggesting that two or three tables in their Richmond, Virginia, home be moved to the front entry, which would leave space in the dining room for a couch. She assured him with acerbity, "It would only be a little

A Domestic Scene. Probably Newburyport, Massachusetts. Drawing in pen and wash after an English print source, by an unknown American artist. 1823. Society for the Preservation of New England Antiquities, Boston; gift of Nina Fletcher Little. A Pembroke table with hinged leaves and a drawer might oblige as a desk, workstand, tea table, or dining table—and all in the course of a day. Casters facilitated its transport around the sitting room, where it was a standard furnishing in the Federal period. Observe the mother's workbasket, momentarily set aside, and the way in which she secures the cricket, or footstool, with her feet so that her daughter may safely stand upon it to recite the alphabet. It was an English practice to leave the floor bare between the carpet and the baseboard, thus clearing the way for furniture that would typically be ranged along the walls. In America, carpets were more often laid wall-to-wall; yet Abraham Brower of New York maintained that when carpets were first introduced into Yankee parlors in the late eighteenth century, they "only covered the floor outside of the chairs around the room"

more trouble for the servants to go a few steps further for the Tables at meal times, which I hope they would be able to live through." John Rattray had "Two Large Square Mahogany Tables" in his Charleston dining room in 1761 as well as two square tables in the passage outside it. His brace of square dining-room tables offered admirable adaptability, something that Rebecca Rawle Shoemaker probably had in mind when she added "2 small dining tables of a size" to that list of requisite furniture for her daughter in June 1783. Thomas Elfe had supplied a customer with "2 Large Mahogany Tables 4 feet 3 Inches Long & 5 feet 5 Inches wide," in January 1772, and nine months later Charles Carroll placed a nearly identical order for "Two Substantial square mahogany Tables each 4 feet 4 In. broad & 5 feet 6 Inches long— exactly of a Height—and so Contrived as upon occasion to be fixed together & make one Table—with substantial legs." This last directive was most certainly necessary as the pieces were regularly shifted about to meet the needs of the moment, and it doesn't

Rhode Island Interior. Oil on canvas, by an unknown American artist. 1800–1810. Collection Fenton Brown. Wall space is clearly divided by chromatic contrast in a room where green lends color harmony. The carpet's decorative role brings to mind an Italian's observation, contemporary with this painting, that a majority of Americans displayed few pictures, statues, or ornamented furniture, preferring instead mahogany furniture and fine carpets. The simple starkness of this apartment remained a characteristic of American interiors into modern times. Note the green baize writing surface on the portable desk, the hearth rug, and the neatly stashed fireplace equipment. The drop-leaf table appears to have just been brought out into the room to be set up for use before the fire. A pair of silver-plated candlesticks appear with some frequency in early-nineteenth-century inventories, and here a pair flank a clock on the mantel shelf. They would not be fitted with candles until the moment of need

take too much imagination to conjure up the scenario that led to Thomas Elfe's supplying a fellow Charlestonian with four new dining-table legs in September 1773. Hooks and eyes and other connective devices were used to join these pairs. When Benjamin French, clerk for the House of Representatives, sketched a picture of his East Capitol Street home in November 1838, he delineated the typical arrangement of double parlors divided by folding doors, which were at that moment open: "and the center table with an astral lamp upon it stands in the doorway, our venetian blinds are half drawn up, there is a fire in our new stove . . . our mahogany chairs with hair cloth seats are in the front parlor, our cane seat cherry wood chairs, are in the back parlor, our large side board stands on one side of the back parlor, our small side board between the windows of the same room, one of our pair of tables is in the front passage, the other in the back parlor." Simple sideboard tables might be found in both dining rooms and dining parlors from 1750 on, and by the 1780s there might be a true sideboard with deep bottle drawers. As a purveyor of hospitality, attired with decanters, tumblers, and wineglasses, it was a rightful occupant of the sitting room where intimates might be received.[28]

Further documentation of the use of the second parlor as an eating room are the closets or cupboards filled with china: not the fine china and silver of the front parlor buffets, but good, serviceable table china—plates, dishes, tureens—and sometimes a coffee mill for those who abjured tea at breakfast. Marianne Silsbee pictured her grandmother's house on Front Street in Salem, Massachusetts, where in the second parlor, "on the upper shelves of a closet by the chimney were the remnants of the handsome India china imported by grandfather: plates and bowls of brilliant colors, and about half of a delicate tea service with a border of faint hues, relieved by dull gilding and his initials, I. D., in the same style." Here, too, was the dining table, with its two drawers—"not to hide dinner in if unexpected company arrived," assured Mrs. Silsbee, "but to keep the damask cloths handy for daily use." This was probably one of the so-called Pembroke tables, alias breakfast tables, which, with their two hinged flaps and a drawer, were admirably suited for informal repasts. When not spread with a damask cloth for a meal, the breakfast and other sitting-room tables were often protected by that same bright green baize cloth we have already become acquainted with in the best parlor.[29]

A desk was often placed in the back parlor, and its writing surface was similarly protected with baize or shalloon, another woolen fabric. Some homes could boast a separate library, occasionally located on the second floor (perhaps for greater privacy and quiet), but in most houses books, bookcases, and a desk or desk-and-bookcase were found in the parlors, often the back parlor. Such pieces connoted male learning and business acumen, and when the master of the house sat for his portrait, it was frequently at his desk. Among the furnishings in one room at Thomas Burling's New

"Mr. Wing." Painting in watercolor and gouache, by an unknown American artist. c. 1830–45. Museum of Fine Arts, Boston; M. and M. Karolik Collection of American Water Colors and Drawings, 1800–1875. The so-called Mr. Wing chose to be portrayed with his books and other attributes of learning. The glazed doors of the bookcase have been lined with pleated silk—a frequent practice—which not only protected the leather volumes from the rays of the sun but gave a pretty, unified look to the piece

York home in 1833 were a desk-and-bookcase, a sideboard, a dining table with ends, two card tables, and a good deal of china—testimony to the easy blending of occupations in these early rooms. J. C. Loudon reminded his readership that the secretary desk or desk-and-bookcase should never be positioned across from a window, "for nothing can be more awkward than the idea of a person sitting down to write with his back to the light, or, should the room be small, to an open fireplace."[30]

When the desk had a bookcase top with glazed doors, the glass was often lined with silk, which was usually green and sometimes pleated. This gave a pretty, unified look to the piece by day and a vivacious color by candlelight. Throughout the second half of the eighteenth century, green silk had been used in French and English libraries to protect delicate leather bookbindings from light and dust and was recommended for this purpose by Thomas Sheraton, George Smith, and other British cabinetmakers and designers, so it seems natural to hear Faith Silliman overriding her father's objection to the installation of floor-to-ceiling bookcases in their Connecticut home ("all our books are not handsome") with the recommendation that they "line the book cases with green," which would make them "a very great ornament to the room." By concealing ordinary books or a collection of baubles, this curtain promoted a neat and tidy appearance. Caroline King remembered following her aunt into the dining parlor of her New England home and watching with delight as she "went to the secretary, and from behind the latticed doors lined with green silk . . . took out many queer things for my entertainment." Green was the usual choice as it was considered soothing and "friendly to the Eyes."[31]

A clock was a customary adjunct to the desk. Bostonian Thomas Tilestone had a desk-and-bookcase and an eight-day clock in his northeast parlor in October 1794, together with a square table, a round table, and a tea table; while Elizabeth Buffum Chace recalled that the tall eight-day clock stood in the corner of many Rhode Island

Brooklyn. Watercolor by H. G. Cantzler. 1851. Print Collection, The New York Public Library; Astor, Lenox and Tilden Foundations. Simple, spare furnishings, a hanging bookshelf, and musical instruments suggest a student's room in a boardinghouse. Both piano and music stand are fitted with candle arms for evening practicing and performing

Alexandria, Virginia, Interior. Watercolor by Sterling Turner. 1845–50. Collection Peter and Leslie Warwick. Flowering plants, striped wallpaper, and a figured table cover lend charm and pattern to this cool and airy room, which seems to have been arrayed for summer. Hanging bookshelves were practical and decorative and were often found in sitting rooms and bedchambers. Birds abounded at home in early America; this little warbler's cage hangs from a bracket placed as close to the open window as possible. Canvas or linen window shades were universal

sitting rooms and beside it, in the best homes, hung a barometer and thermometer in one frame.[32]

Considering the vehemence with which foreign travelers excoriated the American male for his tobacco habits, it is not surprising that tobacco tongs are found with regularity in that room with the desk. On occasion, there might be a spittoon or spitbox as well. Dr. John Nacy's "5 Spitting Basons" at home in Charleston in October 1776 shared hospitable company with a writing desk and box of short pipes, a backgammon table, and three rum cases. David Hatch of Boston owned "a Spontoon" in 1794, while "1 Copper spit Box" glittered in James Townsend Leonard's New York front room in 1833. That these were used we can infer from the antics of little Roger

Beach, who, though not yet walking on his own, could adroitly imitate his expectorating elders: "He 'halks' and *spits* in the spitbox, and does a good many other funny things which furnish *not a little* amusement," wrote his doting mother in 1851.[33]

There was one further picturesque scrap of evidence of the male presence in the sitting room—a spyglass. Andrew Sigourney kept his "Spye Glass" in the front room of his Boston home in 1762, along with his clock and glazed door "bookcase," and Ebenezer Simmons probably kept his on the mantel of his Charleston "Back room," for it is listed with the fireplace equipment in December 1763 in a room that also housed the prototypical brace of mahogany tables and an eight-day clock. Of course, the spyglass might also be found, although less frequently, in a bedchamber or kitchen. And it was used not only by men to sight their ships but by men and women to look out for an expected visitor or to identify an unexpected one. Anne Eliza Clark pictured herself at home in Providence, disappointed that her mother had not yet returned—although "we had been looking out for you all day with the spy glass."[34]

Simple hanging shelves might supplement bookcases and are often seen in views of nineteenth-century sitting rooms. A. J. Downing maintained that a few pieces of board and some strong cord would suffice for a cottage, although he rhetorically imbued them with a symbolic import belying their common appearance: "The walls of an humble cottage sitting-room, decorated in this way, have a higher meaning there than those of the most superb picture-gallery in a villa—since we know that it signifies intellectual taste in the former case, while it *may*, perhaps, be only a love of display in the other." Hanging bookshelves played a part in Harriet Beecher Stowe's recollection of her Aunt Esther Foote's room in Litchfield, Connecticut, where "the floor was covered with a neat red and green carpet; the fireplace equipment resplendent with the brightest of brass andirons; small hanging book-shelves over an old-fashioned mahogany bureau; a cushioned rocking-chair; a neat cherry tea-table; and an old-fashioned looking-glass, with a few chairs, completed the inventory. I must not forget to say that a bed was turned up against the wall, and concealed in the day time by a decorous fall of chintz drapery." A bed that could be folded up, called a press bed, was on occasion found in the back parlor, and a looking glass was seldom absent. Miss Foote had one further piece that was found with some regularity in late-eighteenth-century and nineteenth-century middle-class sitting rooms—a bureau.[35]

John Peirce, a Boston distiller whose small estate was settled in 1794, had furnished his combination dining-sitting room with the typical medley of bureau, dining table, mahogany card table, pine table, mahogany tea table, dozen green chairs, looking glass, and tablewares. By 1850, when *Godey's Magazine and Lady's Book* gave a description of a suite of new and elegant furniture for the benefit of "those at a distance from cities," they knew full well that this might "cause divers groans from 'honest country folk,' where chairs, a bureau, a looking-glass, and a table, are still considered the essentials of parlor furniture." Rutherford B. Hayes recalled that his family's resources were so limited in the 1820s that his boyhood home in Delaware, Ohio, had been scantily furnished, yet his mother had a new bureau and stand and a gilt-edged looking glass in the parlor. Sometimes the mirror was attached to the bureau—a form that in upper-class urban homes would have been strictly confined to the bedchambers. Nonetheless, Polly Bennett of Bridport, Vermont, was undoubtedly proud of the "1 Mahogany Dressing Beauro with L. Glass attached," which graced her rural sitting room in 1849, and her little daughter, Lucy, may have been equally gratified, for standing nearby was her own small "beauro and glass."[36]

Some form of lounging furniture—a couch, daybed, settee, or sofa—was an important amenity in American sitting rooms from 1750 to 1870. Captain John Indicott furnished his Boston keeping room with a desk-and-bookcase, an eight-day clock, a couch with a red woolen squab, and seven chairs with red leather seats. The latter attest to the popularity of leather in eighteenth-century sitting rooms and suggest an attention to color harmony in the back room as well as in the front room. Such a settee or sofa had to be sturdy, for it obliged the demands of boisterous children as well as sedate adults. Frances Sellers Garrett could easily recall "the settee which accommodated so many of us" in the sitting room of her childhood home in Delaware in the 1830s and 1840s, and where her "Mother took her nap after dinner, while we played about, and made no end of noise." There was an old-fashioned daybed with a cane seat and slanting headboard in the Danvers, Massachusetts, parlor belonging to Louisa Crowninshield Bacon's grandmother in the 1840s. Here, too, was a set of white Windsor chairs with stuffed and fringed leather seats. In one of these seats there was a small hole, which made an audible squeak if anyone seated himself incautiously— "How many times I have watched," reminisced Mrs. Bacon, "hoping, some large, fat person would take that particular chair, so that we could hear the squeak and at the same time enjoy their dismay."[37]

Windsor chairs and cane-bottom or flag-bottom seating furniture were common to the sitting room. We have heard mentioned the cane-seated cherry chairs in

Benjamin French's Washington back parlor, and Mary Hill Lamar advised her brother in the 1770s that she considered cane-seated chairs and sofas with fabric-covered hair cushions to be the best for American drawing rooms as well as common sitting rooms. Windsor chairs were available from the very beginning of the period we are considering, and painted "fancy" furniture, in vogue by the end of the eighteenth century, was followed by enameled cottage furniture and lacquered pieces, so that between 1750 and 1870 some form of painted seating furniture provided brilliant spots of color around the perimeters of many upper-class and middle-class sitting rooms. They offered a maximum effect at a minimum expense and were unabashedly intermixed with more demure mahogany or walnut pieces. Among the furnishings in one Newburyport parlor, for example, were a mahogany desk-and-bookcase, a pair of mahogany card tables, and a half-dozen dark green wooden chairs with a pair of rockers to match.[38]

Rocking chairs abounded. By the end of her stint in America, Anne Royall was convinced of one thing at least—"I abhor rocking chairs." One was sure to stumble over their bold crescent projections, and Mrs. Royall departed the country with "hardly a sound toe left." Austin Foster, on the other hand, remembered with malicious self-satisfaction for years thereafter the pleasure a rocking chair had afforded him in the early 1830s, when he had retaliated against his sister and her beau for making him light the parlor fire by filling the cushion of the suitor's accustomed seat—the rocking chair—with pins. By 1853 Eliza Leslie felt it necessary to inveigh against the "dizzy and ungraceful practice of rocking in a rocking-chair," adding that in genteel parlors these had been supplanted by handsome stuffed easy chairs that were moved on casters. Easy chairs, of the old-fashioned, deep-winged variety, though more common in the bedchamber, could be found in sitting rooms and parlors.[39]

Although most sitting-room chairs were ranged along the walls, a pair of comfortable seats was frequently pulled from the lineup and placed at either side of the fireplace or stove. This was a comfortable, common-sense arrangement given literary sanction by Harriet Beecher Stowe when she decorated Simeon Brown's keeping room in *The Minister's Wooing:* "On one side of the room stood a heavy mahogany sideboard, covered with decanters, labelled Gin, Brandy, Rum, etc.,—for Simeon was held to be a provider of none but the best, in his house-keeping. Heavy mahogany chairs, with crewel coverings, stood sentry about the room; and the fireplace was flanked by two broad arm-chairs, covered with stamped leather." Eliza Susan Quincy pictured Ebenezer Storer's dining parlor as having "capacious arm-chairs, cushioned and covered with green damask, for the master and mistress of the family," on either side of the fireplace; and the 1807 inventory of that room lists "2 Lolling Chairs" and "2 Arm Chairs." A lolling chair, what we today sometimes call a Martha Washington chair, was an open-armed easy chair, which was sometimes sold with a cushion and often with casters. In the Federal-period sitting room, a pair of them was considered a most fashionable amenity. John Hancock had a pair in his sitting room, and Marianne Silsbee recalled one in her grandmother's second parlor, together with a huge sofa, two wooden rockers "cushioned to render them endurable," and half a dozen chairs "hard enough to make the children seated on them sufficiently uncomfortable." In his Boston middle room in 1806, Joseph Cutler also had arranged a lolling chair, a half-dozen chairs, a rocking chair, two children's chairs, and a cradle.[40]

Home from School. Oil on canvas, by William E. Winner. 1865. The Historical Society of Pennsylvania, Philadelphia. The joy of freedom is gymnastically expressed by this ebullient young man before a window of bloom and song. Plants were much admired, particularly after improved heating methods ensured their survival through frosty nights and days. Here a set of shelves has been erected on which ivy, calla lilies, and geraniums appear to thrive. The gray shutters attest to the fact that by this date green was no longer the universal favorite color for blinds. Decorating manuals now counseled that as blinds were intended for convenience, not conspicuous ornament, the color ought to match as closely as possible that of the wall. Besides, green soon faded, spotted when wet, and showed the dust too clearly

In this room in which the family ate, studied, read, sewed, played, and relaxed, children's furniture was often practical. Mary Walkley Beach could yet envision the pleasant south front room—the living room—in her Southington, Connecticut, home in the 1820s and 1830s, with its child's chair and crickets—that is, little stools. And, in a family which eventually grew to nine children, "there was always a little wooden cradle there painted red, one of father's own make and a baby." The crickets were commonly used as children's seats and were often found in a sitting room, for this was one of the apartments where mothers regularly gathered their little ones for morning

Mother and Child. Detail of a water-color sketch by Baroness Hyde de Neu-ville. 1808. The New-York Historical Society, New York City. Footstools were considered essential in homes where there were women and children. This little child stands upon her stool, or cricket, to recite a lesson to her mother—a common sight in the sitting room–schoolrooms of America

lessons. Here, children not more than two or three years of age were introduced to the perplexities of the alphabet, numbers, and needle and thread. James Fenimore Cooper's daughter Susan Augusta, who was born in 1813, has portrayed just such a scene of parlor lessons at home in Cooperstown, New York. "My little sister Cally was my playfellow in those days, though she was still a baby, not yet two years old. Our education began, however, in the little parlor at Fenimore; we used to sit on two little stools near our Mother; I learned to read in a primer, and to sew; Cally, I fancy, was considered too young for the primer, and her sewing was done with a thread tied to a pin. . . . When we had finished our hour of school we followed our Mother into the pantry, and each holding up our little apron . . . we were rewarded with a few raisins, or ginger bread, or perhaps a bit of maple sugar." J. C. Loudon pronounced the footstool to be "an article of essential utility to every cottage where there is a mother; and it also forms a seat for a child." He suggested that it could be either plain or covered with carpeting. The hard wooden cricket was indeed often softened by a cover of leather or ingrain carpeting, something Joshua Brookes observed while traveling in the States about 1800: "It is very common to have a little stool covered with carpet or black leather and a fringe to put the feet on." Little Lucy, a fictional character of the nineteenth century well known to young American readers, reminded them that they had to put their chairs and crickets away after play, a caution that suggests the walls and corners of sitting rooms perhaps displayed the uneven profile of adult and children's furniture admixed.[41]

By the early years of the nineteenth century, there was often a stove in the sitting room, placed purposefully in that apartment which was often occupied, by young and old alike, and for much of the year. It might be a Franklin fireplace which, in time, would be replaced by an airtight stove. Mary Walkley Beach could remember the open Franklin stove that stood in that south front room, "thereby making two nice corners for us children to place our one little chair and crickets" in. Susan Lesley described the old parlor of her Northampton, Massachusetts, home of the 1820s, which was of moderate size—the better to retain the heat of a large Franklin stove with its brass finishings, fender, and andirons. Around this the family "lived for eight months of the year," undoubtedly pulling the sofa, rocking chairs, and cane-bottom chairs with chintz-covered hair cushions as close as possible.[42]

A major drawback of the airtight stove was its dehumidifying heat and smell of hot iron, and household manuals were soon advocating the use of plants and other greenery as a means of replacing moisture and purifying the air. Houseplants, which had been used in a limited way in the eighteenth-century parlor, now became more general. Specially designed plant stands were introduced in the early nineteenth century, with stepped shelves offering one typical arrangement. Nineteen-year-old Faith Silliman was delighted when her father gave her "a flower stand, not the common steps, but . . . just like three oval shaped tables one above the other." A note from her mother in February five years later alludes to one reason why houseplants had not been a regular decorative feature in the colonial home: "It has frozen hard in our cellar & in all the closets in the dining room, but the plants have not been injured." Sarah Logan Fisher was not so fortunate, noting in her Philadelphia diary in December 1786, "Very Cold last Night, our Flowers froze in the front Parlour, tho' we had kept a good Fire yesterday." These late, lamented flowers were probably the hyacinths that she had purchased as bulbs in October and placed in her hyacinth glasses to bloom.[43]

Cut flowers were also used. Unfortunately, although many eighteenth-century diarists tell us that they gathered bouquets, they rarely tell us where they put them; but cut flowers were usually arranged in small, compact bouquets on the mantel. Joshua Brookes admired the "marble jars and blue china ones in which were placed some blue and red bachelors buttons" on the drawing-room mantel at Mount Vernon in February 1799. Charlestonians seem to have been very fond of flowers. In 1761 John Rattray owned several flowerpots and five flower horns—cornucopia-shaped flower pockets with flat backs that hung against the wall—and three years later one might have selected a flower container from Mrs. Ann Air, whose shop goods included five flower horns and "43 pr. painted Glass flower potts." In summer a large pot might sit imposingly on the hearth, and in winter small pots and vases would be arranged along the mantel; flower horns were hung, like overflowing horns of plenty, at the chimney breast—a fire-warmed location, which made good sense. Dried flowers and ever-greens might also decorate a winter mantel. Sarah Anna Emery, who was born in 1787, recalled the delight with which she had assisted her Grandmother Little each fall "to arrange in pretty vases of home construction the dried amaranths, which mingled with white-everlasting, milk-weed, bitter-sweet and evergreen, made pretty winter bouquets, to decorate the mantles of the parlor and living room." They had also roped garlands of evergreen around the mirror and clock—all of which elicited the censure of their pragmatic Newburyport neighbors, who sniffed, " 'Sich things did very well for some folks. If Miss Little had to delve and drudge like most women, she wouldn't want dried posies and greens alittering her house, but she always had contrived to live ladyfied.'" By the early years of the nineteenth century, commercial greenhouses supplemented the home garden, and by the second half of that century plants had become an integral part of interior decoration. Many a sitting room was transformed into a garden—if not a jungle—as trailing ivy and other vines twined themselves about the apartment.[44]

Also taking advantage of the warmth of the sitting-room stove might be a variety of feathered companions. Birds were popular pets at home in America, and many a sunny sitting room was enlivened with their song. When in 1833 Deborah Norris Logan of Philadelphia penned a picture of her winter parlor—the "old dining room"—it included a coal stove, a table under the south window embellished with a few cherished plants, a dining table under another window, sometimes similarly accoutred, a little maple desk, and a contented grouping of two cats, a cardinal in a nice new cage above the desk, and a beloved mockingbird. Of far more pugnacious mien was the salty old parrot who, despite his genteel living arrangements with a pair of maiden ladies in early-nineteenth-century Salem, yet "had always about him an air of having been out all night." This "ragged and battered" parrot, whose "colors, like his morals, were low in tone," had not only a wicked eye but, according to one victimized observer, "an unpleasant habit of roosting upon the chair-rails and unex-pectedly pecking at the legs of us children." He generally liked to sulk and glower on the back of a small sofa in the sitting-room corner. But on occasion the room became quite alive with his raucous cries, for when one of these eccentric old maids would pluck off her wig and toss it to the sitting-room floor—as she was wont to do if annoyed by the heat or excited by the conversation—"he would burst into peals of rasping, metallic laughter, swaying insanely on his perch, drawing long breaths, and appar-ently becoming quite exhausted with his mirth."[45]

Painted canvas floor cloths were recommended for rooms like the second parlor,

Ann Proctor. Oil on canvas, by Charles Willson Peale. 1789. Hammond-Harwood House Association, An-napolis, Maryland. Six-year-old Ann Proctor is here portrayed with what were undoubtedly her two favorite pos-sessions: an elegant doll and a colorful parrot. Prattling parrots were popular pets in the eighteenth century and nineteenth century, although their dis-course and demeanor were not always commendable

The Sargent Family. Charlestown, Massachusetts. Oil on canvas, by an unknown American artist. 1800. National Gallery of Art, Washington, D.C.; gift of Edgar William and Bernice Chrysler Garbisch. Haircloth-covered side chairs and an upholstered lolling chair were at the height of the mode for the parlor in the opening years of the nineteenth century. The two-toned straw carpet would not have been admired by all, however. Catharine Beecher believed that checked matting of two colors wouldn't wear well, while Eliza Leslie pronounced it common and "ungenteel"

where flowers and sun abounded. These might be quite simple or rather elaborate affairs, deceptively painted in close imitation of Wilton and Brussels carpets. Alternatively, the sitting-room floor itself might be painted. Elizabeth Buffum Chace, who saw no carpets during her girlhood in Rhode Island, remembered parlor and sitting-room floors being "painted in the mode called 'marbled.'" When there was a woven carpet, it was likely to be a poor but colorful cousin to the best-parlor carpet. Once store-bought oilcloths, commercial carpeting, wallpaper, and textiles came into their domain, rural housewives seem to have exulted in strong color and forceful pattern. Country sitting rooms were often a riot of pattern and color—with striped list carpeting, sprigged wallpaper, grained woodwork, painted chairs, and chintz cushions. When a Connecticut girl wrote her sister in 1855 to say that she had "papered my sitting room & put down my new carpet" and was "having the room grained," she fully expressed this busy country aesthetic.[46]

Of course, Brussels and ingrain carpets might also bring color into a nineteenth-century sitting room, and in summer the floor might don a straw carpet—what James Fenimore Cooper called "beautiful, fragrant, and cool India mats," in an allusion to their pleasing visual, olfactory, and tactile qualities. By the time Isabella Trotter reached Ohio during her tour of the States in 1858, she felt qualified to observe that "it seems the fashion all over America, as it is abroad, to leave the space open in the middle of the room, and the chairs and sofas arranged round the walls, but there is always a good carpet of lively colors or a matting in summer, and not the bare floor so constantly seen in France and Germany."[47]

Not quite bare floors but sanded ones were also common in rural sitting rooms, kitchens, bedchambers, and anterooms. Lyman Beecher recalled that during his early married life in East Hampton, Long Island, in the opening years of the nineteenth century, "we had no carpets; there was not a carpet from end to end of the town. All had sanded floors"; and William McKoy, the first teller of the Bank of Philadelphia, maintained in *Lang Syne*, a series of articles published in 1828 and 1829, that "parlour floors of very respectable people in business used to be 'swept and garnished' every morning with sand sifted through a 'sand sieve,' and sometimes smoothed with a hair broom, into quaint circles and fancy wreaths, agreeably to the 'genius for drawing' possessed by the chambermaid." The celebrated artist John Trumbull, who was born in 1756, also recalled that he had discovered some of his genius for drawing on the sanded floors of his Connecticut home.

> My two sisters, Faith and Mary, had completed their education at an excellent school in Boston, where they both had been taught embroidery; and the eldest, Faith, had acquired some knowledge of drawing, and had even painted in oil, two heads and a landscape. These wonders were hung in my mother's parlor, and were among the first objects that caught my infant eye. I endeavored to imitate them, and for several years the nicely sanded floors (for carpets were then unknown in Lebanon,) were constantly scrawled with my rude attempts at drawing.[48]

Such schoolgirl pictures, in silks and paints, were proudly displayed in many early parlors. A girl "was considered very poorly educated who could not exhibit a sampler," Sarah Anna Emery maintained; "some of these were large and elaborate specimens of handiwork; framed and glazed, they often formed the chief ornament of

OPPOSITE BELOW:
Popping Corn. Watercolor by Benjamin Russell. c. 1865. Old Dartmouth Historical Society, New Bedford, Massachusetts. Many are the heartfelt reminiscences of the simple joys of popping corn before the immense kitchen fireplace or at the cozy sitting-room hearth, and the beaming expressions of these young folk certainly convey such pleasure. Observe the housecleaning nicety of a dusting feather pendant from the mantel shelf and the immodest face peeking in the window—no privacy here! A trio of paintings, conveniently labeled for us, is suspended by cord above the symmetrically arrayed mantel. Both paintings and looking glasses were often thus suspended. Elizabeth Bleecker McDonald was dismayed to return to her Manhattan home on 19 March 1804 and find her parlor looking glass in several pieces on the floor, the cord having rotted through

Victorian Parlor. Engraving. c. 1850. Courtesy, Ridge Press. Typical furnishings in this middle-class parlor are the argand lamp on the mantel, the venetian blinds, the so-called dressing bureau, the étagère, center table, footstool, and sofa, and what is undoubtedly a rocking chair in the foreground. Observe how the mirror is propped up on the mantel shelf rather than hung suspended from the wall—an apparently common practice (see *York, Pennsylvania, Family* and *The Reverend John Atwood and His Family*, pages 49, 151).

the sitting room or the best chamber." John Jay Janney vouched that in every Quaker home in early-nineteenth-century northern Virginia "you might find a 'sampler' framed and hung in a conspicuous place in the parlor," and in a Troy, New York, sitting room Margaret Hunter Hall finally found something she could admire in this country—a needlework picture of Hector and Andromache, "worked, I suppose, by one of the young ladies of the house." All were not so liberal with their praise of these amateur efforts. Mark Twain, in evoking the quintessential Victorian parlor, would bracket over the whatnot—"place of special sacredness—an outrage in water-color, done by the young niece that came on a visit long ago, and died. Pity, too; for she might have repented of this in time." Nor did Huckleberry Finn (and many, many others) "somehow seem to take to" the lugubrious mourning embroideries and watercolors that darkened many a sitting-room wall—"because if ever I was down a little, they always give me the fan-tods."[49]

In a room much frequented by the mistress of the household, one might well expect to find a lady's worktable or sewing stand in the sitting room. For few wives and mothers, from 1750 to 1870, were ever free from sewing tasks—if only repairs and alterations. Introduced in the late eighteenth century, along with a number of other pieces specifically designed for a lady's convenience, these worktables were often fitted with casters. The tops provided a surface for thimble, thread, scissors, and candle or lamp, while a drawer, often divided into small compartments, provided for the efficient stowage of sewing implements. The deep lower drawer or fabric bag held unfinished work. Marianne Silsbee sketched the pleasant picture of a prototypical Salem housewife who, having completed her morning duties, was ready to take her seat in the parlor "with a basket of mending or sewing on the pretty work table, a book, perhaps the last Scott's novel, perhaps an 'Edinburgh Review,' lying in close neighborhood." Commonly the scene was not so hushed, for sewing duty was often coupled with that of child care. Mary Palmer Tyler remembered that day in January 1783 when her father had come dancing into the parlor, in most unwonted fashion, joyously announcing to his amazed wife, who was at her worktable "as usual," and to the children playing on the floor that the war was over—" 'Peace is declared!' "[50]

A sentence of this sort—"It is Eve^g and you can see us seated at our Table with Books & work &c."—runs as a leitmotiv through nineteenth-century letters and journals. In some sitting rooms, the table around which the family clustered was the workstand. Jane Margaret Craig, mistress of the Philadelphia estate Andalusia, wrote in 1809 that "in the evening all sit around a work table, and while five of us work the sixth reads." More typically, it might be a round center table, the form that A. J. Downing by 1850 pronounced to be "the emblem of the family circle." This it was to Maria Silliman Church, who rued her absence from it and who, one October evening at half past eight, indulged her homesick heart with the comforting vision of that distant family "all sitting round the parlour table." And when her mother wrote her on the evening of 4 March 1835, she was indeed "quietly seated at the centre table in our parlor" with a daughter on either side engaged in their lessons.[51]

The family sitting room seemed to offer emotional as well as physical comfort. Frances Sellers Garrett remembered the solace of the living room where her family gathered in the evenings of her Delaware childhood; on dark nights, when one of the children left the cheerful room to go into a far parlor for some work or book, "and heard the branches brush against the window, we felt eerie and uncomfortable, and hurried back into the warm room where were Mother and the lighted lamp, and

Father reading, and the boys and girls gathered around the center-table." But reading must come to an end as the family bedtime arrived. "When the old clock, that had stood like a tall sentinel in the corner of that sitting-room since long before I was born, struck the hour of nine," wrote Emily Barnes, "it was an invariable custom . . . for each member of the household to be in readiness for the night's rest. Grandmother, adhering to her usual custom, rose, bidding them good-night; and, following her example, we went to our rooms." Just maybe, however, if we peeked into this sitting room after the old folks had gone to bed we might find a gaggle of girls "at ½ past nine seated round the parlour fire, eating, drinking, & curling up our hair."[52]

Meals at home in early America were served in the dining room, sitting room, drawing room, bedchamber, kitchen, hall, piazza, and any other convenient location. Flexibility was essential when servants, weather, health, and family composition were ever-changing. When family members were ill, and they often were, they ate in bedchambers. Before central heating became available, in the second half of the nineteenth century, the family ate in a hearth-warmed room in winter. In summer they would gather where it was coolest. Anne Grant was grateful for the additional heat in the winter "eating parlour," located directly over the kitchen in the back section of an Albany home; and when in August 1806 Robert Sutcliff visited Wakefield House in Germantown, Pennsylvania, he was refreshed to dine "in a room on a level with the cellar," feeling that a "dining-room so situated, is a great privilege at this season of the year, in a climate like this." But such a room would have been intolerably cold and damp four months later.[1]

Dining rooms are mentioned in eighteenth-century and even late-seventeenth-century inventories, but their diverse contents betray their many functions; they were essentially the typical sitting room–dining parlor discussed in Chapter Two. In the course of the eighteenth century, fashionable English families followed French precedent and aspired to have a room set apart for the sole purpose of dining. The commonality of culture on both sides of the Atlantic ensured that the same practice prevailed here, but far into the nineteenth century Americans remained flexible in their dining arrangements. A specialized dining room was a symbol of economic success, and a spate of nineteenth-century architectural design books, published both here and abroad, jealously guarded this indicant of middle-class status for those who had both sufficient money and admirable taste. Many families never saw the need for a pretentious dining room and continued to enjoy their meals in the cozy kitchen or hospitable sitting room. Others had a formal dining room but continued to eat informal meals, such as breakfast and supper, in that back parlor. And just as few rooms in the American home were used for one purpose alone, even formal dining rooms had to accommodate a variety of activities. Writing at the center table in her drawing room in 1831, Margaret Bayard Smith penned a picture of the dining room as an apartment much frequented by the family throughout the day. First, "the girls sit of a morning in the dining room, which opens from this, where they read and sew together, seldom coming in to receive company." Next the entire family arrived for dinner. Finally, "after dinner and through the evening, all the girls come into the parlour, and Mr. Smith and Bayard [their son] sit and read and write in the dining room."[2]

The dining room was usually located on the ground floor, but in urban homes it might be in the basement, "so that we descend to dinner," explained one English visitor. A basement dining room was conveniently located near the kitchen and often

had the casual atmosphere of a sitting room, but the miserly, bleak view from its scanty windows was nothing more than "a monotonous procession of legs, passing and re-passing on the sidewalk." It was felt that the position of the dining room should be northward and somewhat secluded for subdued light and reposeful tranquillity; its atmosphere more "sober" and "substantial" than that of the drawing room; its appearance "that of masculine importance"; its furniture plain, neat, and mahogany. Predictable furnishings were a dining table and chairs, a sideboard and often a cellarette, a side or serving table, a china closet, one or more looking glasses, portraits, lamps, polished fireplace equipment, and sometimes a clock.[3]

In a dining room or dining parlor where the table was not *in situ*, the first step in preparing the room for a meal was to lay the table rug, or crumb cloth, on top of the carpet. Its purpose was set forth by Eliza Leslie in 1840: "In an eating-room, the carpet should be protected from crumbs and grease-droppings by a large woollen cloth kept for the purpose, and spread under the table and the chairs that surround it; this cloth is to be taken up after every meal, and shaken out of doors; or else swept off carefully as it lies." Thomas Jefferson's goal in purchasing a crumb cloth "to lay down on the floor of a dining room," was to protect the handsome *uncarpeted* President's House floors from grease "and the scouring which that necessitates." The use of a crumb cloth was universal; the materials and colors were various. Painted canvas had been used for this purpose since the early years of the eighteenth century and remained popular well into the nineteenth century. Eliza Leslie recommended drugget (a coarse wool fabric) finished round the edge with carpet binding; thick green baize; or very strong, stout brown linen. But green baize seems to have been the favored choice, although it did not wear well with heavy use. Martha Ogle Forman of Cecil County, Maryland, laid down her dining-room carpet for the winter on 11 December 1820, and two days later her husband went to town to buy her "four yards of Green baise to cover the Carpet"; subsequent diary entries, such as "I had the Bais made for the dining room," or "made a Green cloth for the dining-room," document its replacement every fall. Crumb cloth colors might be green, blue and white, brown, or black and white—Catharine Beecher advised that a "pepper-and-salt color" would show the dirt least.[4]

In those dining rooms where the table was regularly set up for each meal, the table was placed on top of the crumb cloth and square with the room, with leaves and legs properly fixed "so that all stand firm." At the conclusion of the meal, it was removed. Edward Kendall, at a Connecticut inn during his American tour of 1807 and 1808, observed that the servants, in conformity with "the manners of the country, carried away the table when they carried away the cloth, and drove away loiterers with an army of brooms." The men, he further noted, had previously carried their chairs to the wall, the women to a window. A great advantage of the formal dining room, however, was that the dining table might stand out in the center of the room and not have to be folded up and placed aside to make way for other activities. Long extension tables became popular in the Federal period, allowing for large numbers of guests in that convivial age. Faith Silliman, in Hartford on a buying spree three months before her marriage, in May 1837, wrote her mother that she could "get very nice cherry tables and they have a way of making them, with one table almost the size of our common table and an end that fits on and makes a table large enough to accommodate conveniently ten and can a dozen persons." The table end or ends, when not in use, could be placed symmetrically around the room as supplementary serving tables.[5]

In the eighteenth-century and early-nineteenth-century homes of the wealthy and upper-middle class, company dinners were usually served about two o'clock. These were leisurely, prolonged affairs. Sarah Anna Emery portrayed her easy girlhood in post-Revolutionary Newburyport, where "luxurious indolence, rich dinners, with long sittings over the wine and dessert, card parties of an evening, with a hot meat supper at nine or ten o'clock, was the usual routine in many of our first families." Robert Adam, the British designer and architect, had indeed remarked that whereas the French did not devote great attention to the decoration of the dining room because they left it promptly after meals, in England dining rooms "are considered as the apartments of conversation, in which we are to pass a great part of our time." Americans adopted the English example, as the duc de La Rochefoucauld-Liancourt observed: "The distribution of the apartments in their houses is like that of England, the furniture is English. . . . The cookery is English, and, as in England, after dinner . . . the ladies withdraw, and give place to drinking of wine in full bumpers, the most prominent pleasure of the day, and which is, consequently, very natural to prolong as late as possible." At the conclusion of an early-nineteenth-century dinner party in Philadelphia, Robert Waln, Jr. was horrified to witness the male glances, "short, quick, stolen, and expressive," which continually passed to that end of the table where the lady of the house presided. She, however, was undoubtedly relieved to quit the table "the moment the men announce they prefer Bacchus to Venus," for, as Eliza Farrar pointed out, "A dinner, well performed by all the actors in it, is very fatiguing and, as it generally occupies three hours or more, most persons are glad to go away when it is fairly done."[6]

Throughout the eighteenth century, tables were set for the English style of serving, in which all dishes for each course were placed out at once, and these bounteously laid tables ensured that foreign observers would think of Americans as a people of plenty. European-born Rosalie Calvert, living in Maryland in 1806, did not approve of this Yankee mode of serving all the meats and vegetables at once because "one has not time to eat sufficiently before half the dishes are cold." Caroline King

The Dinner Party. 10 Franklin Place, Boston. Oil on canvas, by Henry Sargent. c. 1821. Museum of Fine Arts, Boston; gift of Mrs. Horatio A. Lamb in memory of Mr. and Mrs. Winthrop Sargent. This fashionable Boston interior illustrates Thomas Sheraton's dictum that a large sideboard, handsome and extensive dining table, substantial chairs, a large looking glass, family portraits, marble fireplaces, and a Wilton carpet were the furnishings appropriate to the dining room. The carpet has here been protected by a baize floor cloth. Shutters and blinds have been regulated to block out distracting glare, and a candle is lit on the table, where the gentlemen enjoy a final course of fruit. The adjustable ceiling lamp has been suspended to reflect in the pier glass and there are stylish patent lamps on gilded tripods at either end of the mantel, for, as a knowing Englishman who had spent time in America observed in 1819, American mantelpieces were invariably very shallow and would not admit of large lights, so that small patent lamps set upon tripods offered the best mode of lighting. The serpentine front of the sideboard allowed one to reach across with ease and therefore to serve with agility; the large and undoubtedly ice-filled pitcher atop had become an expected amenity in American dining rooms by this date

remarked that one solution to the problem of cold viands was the silver-plated chafing dish that stood before each guest at her home, that he might cook his meat slices according to personal preference. These "were round, about the size of a large dinner plate, with pretty open work rims and with lion's head handles"; and indeed, in a New York newspaper advertisement in June 1800, we read of "new invented chaffing dishes, to use at the dinner table." Cold dinners were a frequent nuisance in the depths of winter, as meals had to be transported from cellar kitchens, back kitchens, or out kitchens, and genteel families appreciated a pair of silver chafing dishes to reheat chilled food, pewter dish covers and hot-water plates for keeping the dish and contents warm, and brass or japanned plate warmers for heating plates before the fire. Families of lesser refinement in search of a hot meal might adopt more innovative methods. A Maryland physician, Alexander Hamilton, was puzzled in 1744 when a Long Island matron, while at table, called for the bed-warming pan. "I could not guess what she intended to do with it unless it was to warm her bed to go to sleep after dinner," admitted Hamilton, "but I found that it was used by way of a chaffing dish to warm our dish of clams." We can be sure that Hamilton did not endear himself to this family, for in reaching out for a mug of beer, he brushed against the warming pan handle and "unfortunately overset the clams."[7]

The emphasis on these amply spread tables was on proportion and symmetry. "You should observe to have your side dishes in a straight line, and at a regular distance from each other, and also match in size and colour," cautioned Christopher Gore's butler, Robert Roberts, in 1827. Eliza Leslie reiterated the counsel in 1840, and Catharine Sedgwick wrote that when correctly set, the table might look as if the placement of every napkin, glass, spoon, knife, and dish had been determined by plummet and line. In the late 1830s the French or Russian style of service, in which the dishes were handed around, became popular. Philip Hone had trouble adjusting to this new mode and complained from New York after suffering through a dinner *"à la française"* in January 1838: "The dishes were all handed round; in my opinion a most unsatisfactory mode of proceeding in relation to this important part of the business of a man's life. One does not know how to choose, because you are ignorant of what is coming next, or whether anything more is coming. Your conversation is interrupted every minute by greasy dishes thrust between your head and that of your next neighbor, and it is more expensive than the old mode of shewing a handsome dinner to your guests and leaving them free to choose. It will not do. This French influence must be resisted."[8]

The table was to be covered with a cloth that should "always be *white.*" At both dinner and supper it was taken off the table after dessert but before the final nuts, fruit, and wine were served. The marquis de Chastellux commented on the order of the service in 1780: "The dinner was served in the American, or if you will, in the English fashion; consisting of two courses, one including the entrées, roast, and warm side dishes; the other, the sweet pastries and preserves. When the second course is removed, the cloth is taken off, and apples, walnuts, and chestnuts are served; it is then that healths are drunk; the coffee which comes afterwards serves as a signal to rise from table." By 1861 Isabella Beeton could yet caution the butler in families "where the old-fashioned practice of having the dessert on the polished table, without any cloth, is still adhered to," to "rub off any marks made by the hot dishes before arranging the dessert."[9]

Tablecloths, shiny and glossy, were to "hang down all round." "There is nothing of the sort superior to the best double French damask," advised Eliza Leslie, "it being not only fine and thick, but soft and glossy, like satin; and it looks as well after washing as before." Mrs. Leslie advocated the use of a mangle instead of ironing. A mangle was a set of two rollers for pressing linen and cotton, giving it luster. Charles Bagot, the British minister in Washington, then a provincial town, wrote in 1819 to the man who was to succeed him: "I used to regret on account of the appearance of my table linen that I had no mangle—they know of no such instrument & it might be worth your while to take out one of those small portable mangles which are sold in a shop in Oxford Street." This Bagot's successor did and found it "very useful." There were, however, "4 Mangle Cloaths" and a mangle in the laundry at the Governor's Palace in Williamsburg in 1770; several women advertised their services in clear starching and mangling in southern American cities in the 1790s; and in cosmopolitan New York, mangles were offered for sale by 1802, at least. If, as claimed, "a woman may do as

much in one hour with this Machine as in a day by ironing," then we can be sure that Martha Ogle Forman would have rejoiced to have one on 24 August 1818, inundated as she was with her "large Ironing, 12 Tablecloths, and every thing else in proportion." And, like the tablecloth, the mahogany table itself was to shine—a picture of which Caroline King sketched most effectively.

Once or twice a year my father gave a dinner party to his gentlemen friends, and then all the resources of our house (and sometimes of the houses of our friends) were called into action. The old mahogany dinner-table was rubbed with a brush and beeswax until one could see one's face in it. The large tablecloth of finest damask, representing a landscape with trees and flowers and impossible lambs frisking among them, was ironed until its polished surface was almost as bright as that of the table. And it was never allowed to be folded. No crease must dim its brilliant smoothness, so it was hung over chairs in the spare-room until the day of the dinner party arrived. . . . Imagine the Lamb Tablecloth bravely set out with sparkling glass and shining silver, and gay with my mother's best set of red and white India china.[10]

Sometimes two white cloths were used. Dining with the Hill Carters at Shirley in Virginia in 1833, Henry Barnard, a visiting Yale student, described the removal of an upper cloth before dessert, and of the lower cloth before the fruits and nuts were brought out—a practice yet *de rigueur* for Charlottesville dinner parties in the 1840s. Sarah Josepha Hale recommended the use of a scarlet cloth under a fine, thin damask in 1857, as it would give the damask "an imperceptible glow," but such could only be used, she cautioned, if the cloth was not taken off, "as nothing can look well in removing but linen." By 1870, it was standard practice to leave the cloth on throughout the meal.[11]

Breakfast tables, or Pembroke tables, as they came to be known in the Federal period, were covered with a tablecloth as well, although Henry Barnard noted that on the Carters' mahogany breakfast table each plate stood separate on its own little cloth." This was a regional practice also observed by Margaret Bayard Smith at Monticello, where "instead of a cloth, a folded napkin lay under each plate," and further corroborated by a Virginian, Letitia Burwell: "All was strange to us [in New York]—even the tablecloths on the tea and breakfast tables, instead of napkins under the plates, such as we had at home, and which always looked so pretty on the mahogany." *The Domestic's Companion* (1834) advocated the use of a press to ensure neat breakfast, lunch, and dinner cloths, but Catharine Beecher assured that this could be less expensively achieved by simply folding the cloths along the ironed creases and laying some heavy object on top.[12]

Napkins were used in the early American home but not as universally as the tablecloth. Many European visitors commented upon the conspicuous absence thereof. One Frenchman in the 1780s complained that a "table in the American style would seem extraordinary in France. The table is covered with a cloth, which also serves for napkins; it is ordinarily large enough to overflow on all sides, and each one wipes in front of himself (unhappily, they do not change it very often)." A contemporary compatriot who had traveled through the colonies was relieved to at last arrive in cosmopolitan Boston, where "they have capital wines and also napkins." The use of napkins seems to have been quite general in urban centers from the 1750s, yet an 1851 Philadelphia publication, *Facts for the People*, implies that napkins were not always present, for it counseled, "When napkins are provided, they are at once carefully unfolded, and laid on the knee." In rural areas, napkins were even less commonly used. Maria Foster Brown, who was born in 1827, reminisced that in her pioneering days in Ohio and Iowa there were tablecloths of cotton diaper, but handkerchiefs had to suffice as napkins; and Franklin Butler Van Valkenburgh, born in New York State in 1835, recalled that at least on Thanksgiving "the tables were always covered with snowy napery, on which I never saw a napkin." Yet at her Maryland plantation on 11 September 1818, Martha Ogle Forman had in her wash "48 Napkins, and table cloths without number"—many perhaps from the "one thousand four and a half yards of homespun" she had made that year, but all testimony to the extra burden of hospitality on the housewife in that social age.[13]

Guests in the American nation likewise criticized the segregation of the sexes at

the dining table. "It certainly does not, in my opinion, add to the well ordering a dinner table," remonstrated Frances Trollope in 1832, "to set the gentlemen at one end of it, and the ladies at the other; but it is very rarely that you find it otherwise." Bernhard Karl, duke of Saxe-Weimar Eisenach, observed this same arrangement while visiting in South Carolina in 1825, but he cavalierly remarked, "I broke the old custom," gliding in between the ladies, "and no one's appetite was injured thereby."[14]

In the eighteenth century, chairs for the dining room were generally mahogany, with the Chippendale "Gothick" taste much favored. Thus, in 1781 David Evans, a Philadelphia cabinetmaker, billed a customer for ten side chairs with Gothic splats, two dining tables, and a sideboard. Leather and horsehair, the recommended seat coverings, were often protected from spills by slipcovers. Windsor and other painted chairs were also suitable and were much in use by the end of the eighteenth century. When Boston merchant Joseph Barrell ordered eighteen of the handsomest Windsor chairs fit for dining and for his hall in 1795, he specified that they have arms and be rather less in seat width than common, so that more might be accommodated at table; and he wanted them painted a light blue-gray color, "the same as my summer dining room." Louisa Crowninshield Bacon remembered her grandparents' dining room,

"Law Sakes Alive! What Are You Doing Baby?" New York City. Oil on canvas, by Charles Markham. c. 1870. The New-York Historical Society, New York City. The bustling prosperity and well-stocked abundance of American markets, particularly in urban centers, and the implied bounty on American tables are the subject of this realistic and humorous depiction

Dining Room at Mrs. A. W. Smith's. Broad and Spruce streets, Philadelphia. Watercolor by Joseph Shoemaker Russell. 1853. Private collection. The decoration of this Philadelphia boardinghouse dining room relies on the boldly patterned wallpaper. The fireplace has been closed up for the summer and the mantel is unadorned, save for two small oil lamps. Venetian shutter and linen shade shut out excess light yet provide ventilation. The cloth has been carefully laid so that it hangs down evenly all around and the table is set with exacting symmetry. There do not appear to be any napkins

Sarah and Friends Going into Turkey. Watercolor by Benjamin S. Russell. c. 1865. Old Dartmouth Historical Society, New Bedford, Massachusetts. Sarah and friends look intent on the expected delights of roast turkey while the family cat girds itself for the unwanted attentions of the seemingly amiable dog loping through the doorway. The side table holds the viands and utensils for the dessert course—a practical arrangement in homes where there was scant servant help and where the housewife herself had to serve

"pretty well filled with the large dining-table, set round with old wooden chairs painted white, with little blue lines for decoration." They were not very steady, she recalled, and every now and then one would tip over, to the delight of the children. Certainly these lightweight chairs facilitated moving about, for written evidence suggests that dining chairs, too, were often placed back against the walls when not in use. In 1827 Robert Roberts advised servants to go immediately into the dining room after the gentlemen had at last quitted the table "and first put away all the chairs in their places." Robert Kerr thought in 1864 that an important aspect of the dining room was "the unbroken line of chairs at the wall," both because of the convenience of the arrangement and for its association with the purpose of the room.[15]

To facilitate serving in the best eighteenth-century and early-nineteenth-century dining rooms, there might be side tables, some with marble tops. When stationary, these marble-topped side tables were referred to as "slabs." If mobile, they might be called sideboards, sideboard tables, or serving tables. Many of these tables were rectangular in shape, and some were fitted with a drawer. Semicircular kinds were, in fact, the ends of the extension dining table. In February 1773 Charleston cabinetmaker Thomas Elfe, for example, billed one customer for "1 large Square Table & 2 Side Boards rounds to fitt the other"; and another for "two sideboard tables to fit to a large table" six months later. Extra plates, the cold meats and salad for supper, and in some cases silver spoons, forks, and knives were placed on these serving tables during meals. J. C. Loudon suggested a pair on opposite sides of the room, one for hot foods, the other for cold. These sideboard tables were often covered with a cloth. John Ball of Charleston had ten "side board" cloths of diaper, osnaburg, and damask for his simple "Square Cypress side board table" in 1765; and Robert Roberts was yet advising in 1827, "You must have a clean cloth spread upon" the side table.[16]

At the end of the eighteenth century, a new form was introduced. Called a sideboard, it was essentially a sideboard table with the important difference that it had deep cupboards or bottle drawers. Household inventories and other documents reveal a wide variance in the values placed on sideboards. When Boston cabinetmaker Benjamin Bass died, in 1819, he had in his warehouse "1 Grand Side Board" appraised at one hundred dollars and additional ones at forty-five dollars, thirty-eight dollars, fifteen dollars, and similar sums. Undoubtedly the cheaper "sideboards" were, in fact, serving or sideboard tables, the more expensive examples of true sideboard form with bottle drawers. By 1794 George Hepplewhite had effusively endorsed the form: "the great utility of this piece of furniture has procured it a very general reception; and the convenience it affords render a dining room incomplete without a sideboard."[17]

From its introduction and throughout the nineteenth century, the sideboard was considered the most important single piece of furniture in the dining room. In England its preeminence was sometimes acknowledged by placing the sideboard in a recessed area behind a columned screen. In America there were few columned screens, but a recessed area or niche was often designed for the sideboard. Paired sideboards set in niches were particularly favored for the balanced aspect they gave a room. When artist John Singleton Copley dined with friends in New York in August 1771, he admired the recessed arches to either side of the fireplace, each displaying a sideboard. Such an arrangement also meant that the sideboards would be conveniently out of the way of those serving the table. Again, in 1840, Eliza Leslie directed, "Two small side-boards, one in each recess, occupy less space than a large one standing out, and are therefore preferable, unless the dining-room is very spacious and expensively furnished, so that an elegant side-board may be classed among its ornaments." If the sideboard was large, a serpentine front was desirable, as it would allow the butler to reach across with agility and serve with ease. "Besides," pointed

After the Feast. Oil on canvas, by Eastman Johnson. 1872. Whereabouts unknown. The essential theme here is Victorian nostalgia for the tranquil hospitality of an irretrievable past. Decanters and wineglasses had stood atop the sideboard since its introduction almost a century before this painting was done, but the flower-filled bowl adds a decidedly nineteenth-century touch

out Thomas Sheraton, "if the sideboard be near the entering door of the dining-room, the hollow front will sometimes secure the butler from the jostles of the other servants." Robert Kerr suggested that the sideboard be positioned at one end of the dining room, behind the master's chair, that communication with the servants might be facilitated.[18]

The sideboard was convenient for the service of liquor and the storage of bottles. In addition, there was frequently a liquor case or wine cooler beneath the sideboard. George Channing recalled that in Newport in the opening years of the nineteenth century, "various stimulating beverages were exhibited in Dutch liquor-cases in an open space below" the sideboard "or in triangular liquor-stands above"; and Laura Richards remembered the dining room of her girlhood with its big sideboard and companionate wine cooler, "a piece of furniture dear to Brother Harry and me in a peculiar way. It was an oblong chest of solid mahogany, the hexagonal cover sloping upward toward a trophy of grapes. When I look at it to-day, it is hard to imagine that Brother Harry and I used to sit in it, facing each other. Our little boots were probably not at all good for the zinc lining." The sideboard also provided for the stowage of flatware, either in a drawer or in knife boxes, specifically designed cases on top. Charles Haswell, who was born in New York City in 1816, said that in all dining rooms there was a sideboard which was "the repository of liquors of various kinds," and "in which were held the knives, forks, spoons, etc., of the table." Steel-bladed knives were particularly difficult to maintain and required a thorough scouring with brick dust after use if they were not to rust. They should be inspected daily and, if stored for any length of time, particular care had to be taken to oil and wrap them in flannel. In Philadelphia in 1797, Julian Niemcewicz commented upon a number of fine sideboards, all "with a case on top filled with knives, forks, spoons, etc."; while a Marylander recalled visiting two fastidious maiden aunts during her childhood and watching their elderly butler polish "the knives after each meal, standing them upright in the mahogany knife boxes at each end of the sideboard." It was with amusement that she also recollected a peculiarity of this finicky butler who, before each meal, would come into the dining room armed with a roll of stair carpet. "This he unrolled gradually, laying it carefully over the floor carpet from pantry to cupboard to sideboard and around the table and walked on it while setting the table and bringing dishes from the kitchen."[19]

Sometimes the sideboard offered yet another convenience. Thomas Sheraton explained his design for a sideboard with a discreetly concealed chamber-pot cupboard, "made to hide itself in the end rail as much as possible, both for look and secrecy." If this nicety were not available, there might be "a closet to hold utensils sometimes required by gentlemen after dinner"; or possibly a night table or a "necessary" chair. In the 1790s Moreau de Saint-Méry pictured the Philadelphia gentlemen smoking, toasting, drinking, and running "to the corners of the room hunting night tables and vases which will enable them to hold a greater amount of liquor."[20]

The primary function of the sideboard, however, was display. It was the heir apparent of the medieval court cupboard which, resplendent with cupboard cloth and polished silver, had proclaimed the wealth of seventeenth-century Americans amid the panoply of the parlor—the room then used for formal dining. Like the court cupboard, the sideboard was a focal point and for a century it would remain the most conspicuous object in the dining room. Highly polished wood or glossy marble tops

L'Après-Dînée des Anglais. Engraving. c. 1814. Reproduced by courtesy of the Trustees of the British Museum, London. This French caricature jests at the British custom of segregating the sexes after dinner and graphically portrays a secondary service of the sideboard, wherein was often concealed a chamber pot for just such an emergency

offered admirable surfaces on which to display glassware and silver—Baron Axel Klinkowström, traveling in the States between 1818 and 1820, observed that in the American dining room "there is always a very elegant mahogany sideboard decorated with the silver and metal vessels of the household as well as with beautiful cut glass and crystal"; and Moreau de Saint-Méry, with characteristic hyperbole, remarked that "before dinner and all during dinner, as is the English custom, all the silver one owns is displayed on the sideboard in the dining room." Servants were cautioned to "study neatness, convenience, and taste" in setting out their masters' sideboards, "as you must think that ladies and gentlemen that have splendid and costly articles, wish to have them seen and set out to the best advantage." Many apparently took great pains to do so. When Josiah Quincy dined with Miles Brewton in Charleston in 1773, he couldn't help but admire the sideboard, magnificently laid out with plate, and commented effusively on "a very large exquisitely wrought Goblet" which he thought of "most excellent workmanship and singularly beautiful."[21]

A successful sideboard display was carefully calculated. Color was important. The sideboard itself should be of a rich hue, as this "sets off the service of plate to the best advantage"; *The Domestic's Companion* advocated that those who owned any blue wineglasses should "for ornament, intermix a few of them with the others, which will add greatly to its splendour." Fastidious placement was also imperative. Robert Roberts advised that the glasses be arranged in a crescent or half circle, "as this looks most sublime"; while *The Domestic's Companion* preferred a triangular formation: "or, to give a clear idea of what I mean, first place four, next to them three, then two, and lastly one." Dramatic lighting collaborated to give the desired theatrical effect. It was clear that the sideboard should never be surmounted by, or even flanked by, windows because "when a gentleman does honour to his guests by displaying his plate, its effect may be destroyed by the glare of the light." Rather, J. C. Loudon suggested hanging a lamp directly over the piece as a kind of spotlight. Robert Roberts recognized the drama of back lighting: "If you should have a light on your sideboard, you must leave a vacant place behind your glasses for it." Thomas Sheraton

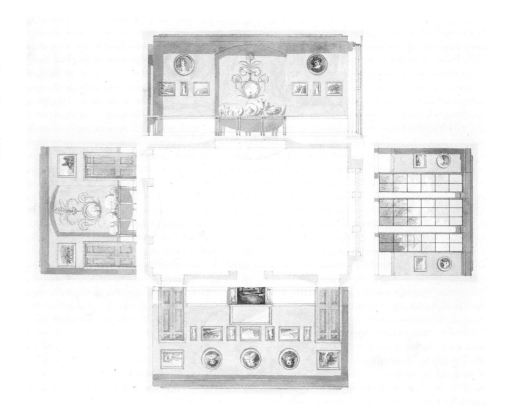

illustrated several designs for sideboards with a brass stay rail for silver hollowware and candle branches or lamp branches in the middle; these, "when lighted, give a very brilliant effect to the silver ware." The most effective way to dramatize the sideboard display, however, was through the conjunction of candlelight or lamplight and plate glass. It was with forethought aplenty, we can be sure, that Anne Eliza Clark Kane hung an elegant looking glass with candle arms above her sideboard with its "plate Vases &c." Round girandole mirrors with reflective convex glass were admirably suited to this demonstrative position over the sideboard, or sometimes the looking glass might be fitted into the back of the sideboard. Extant examples by Anthony Quervelle and other American cabinetmakers suggest the once sparkling, spectacular display of conjoined mahogany, marble, looking glass, silver, crystal, and candlelight.[22]

China was kept in a cupboard either in or near the dining room, but not on the sideboard, and bold was the display when it was brought out for use. David Erskine complained of the stiff formality of American dinner parties at the end of the eighteenth century, and was somewhat irked by the vast display of dishes and finery and the great fuss made about putting them on and taking them off the table. During the next two decades that vast display would become yet more vast, and hostesses might take great pride in their tea, dinner, dessert, and supper services, to say nothing of their matched sets of cut and engraved glass. The prince de Broglie, though somewhat affronted by the rusticity of American manners in general, enjoyed himself in Boston, where "everybody drinks out of his own glass, and the plates are changed as often as can be desired." Such a sufficiency meant that dinner tables might not only look nice but be served with pleasurable ease, devoid of the bustle and confusion attendant upon rinsing or washing tablewares during the course of a meal. Alice Izard

applauded the regularity of her daughter's South Carolina household in 1814, for it "abounds in excellent necessaries, such as plenty of glass & Wedgewood's ware," but she censured her sons, whose homes "have scarsely enough to serve the table once, & then be taken out to be washed &c." In general, tables in the South were more remarkable for their abundance of silver than their supply of china. Conspicuous, unbreakable, easily maintained, readily secured under lock and key, and convertible to currency if necessary, silver was admirably suited to plantation patterns of life.[23]

Display and arrangement were as important on the dining table as on the sideboard. And that housewives succeeded in this we hear from those guests who admired the "superb tablecloth," the "elegant cut glass," or the "brilliant service of cut glass." But perhaps the *ne plus ultra* of dining-room theatrics was achieved on those occasions when, in the words of the duke of Saxe-Weimar Eisenach, who attended a splendid dinner in New Orleans in 1826, "after the second course, large folding doors opened and we beheld another dining room, in which stood a table with the dessert. We withdrew from the first table, and seated ourselves at the second, in the same order in which we had partaken of the first." Eliza Leslie suggested that at summer dinner parties the dessert be served in another and cooler apartment, as the "beauties of the dessert appear to greater advantage, when seen all at one view on a fresh table." Florence Hartley would reiterate the virtues of such a summer setting in 1873, recommending that the party retire after the pastries to a cool, fresh room where the ices and fruits might be tastefully arranged amid a colorful scattering of flowers, "thus delighting every sense."[24]

In those towns steeped in the pervasive odor of tar and tropical fruit, Sumatran pepper and Arabian coffee, Spice Islands cinnamon, cloves, and nutmegs; in those towns enlivened with the animated banter of sailors, the saucy chatterings of green parrots, the lyrical airs of Java sparrows and other southern songbirds; in these towns the presence of the East suffused the dining room. It was here in the fruits—the oranges, shaddocks, pineapples, Malaga grapes, juicy figs, and "great purple raisins with the bloom of the plum still on them"—placed on the shining mahogany table when the cloth was removed. It was here in the exotic rich wines and the priceless Juno Madeira, aged and improved by its travels around the world. It was here in the coffee that ended the feast, made from the pure mocha bean, "enriched by cream so thick

Detail of *The Dinner Party* by Henry Sargent (see page 81). Following the English tradition, the tablecloth has been removed for the fruit course. Sweet wines and native and exotic fruits are reflected in the mirror-bright polish of the mahogany tabletop

that it had to be taken from the cream pitcher with a ladle," and served hot and fragrant in colorful India china mugs. And there were many animate tokens of the far-ranging adventures of American ships as well: Josiah Quincy was delighted with the very fine bird that "kept familiarly playing" about Miles Brewton's dining room, "under our chairs and the table, picking up crumbs, etc., and perching on the window, side board and chairs: vastly pretty!" Samuel Breck was much less amused by the undisciplined menagerie of cockatoos, poll-parrots, and monkeys at a friend's Boston home, pets "which, like spoilt children, were brought into the parlour at the fruit-dessert to gather nuts and gorge with raisins and apples." It was the custom in this household to place a well-filled punch bowl, always brought in with a little parade, in the center of the table as soon as the last cloth was removed. Here, surrounded by the choicest wines, stood the huge vessel, and Breck never forgot one occasion, when the ample bowl occupied its accustomed place and a mischievous monkey that was skipping about the table seized the wig of an Amsterdam merchant and, running to the bowl, soused it in.[25]

China-trade paintings might enliven the walls in port-town dining rooms, for paintings and prints were considered highly appropriate in this apartment. Robert Adam had decreed that dining rooms should always be finished with stucco and adorned with statues and paintings rather than fabric wall hangings, which would "retain the smell of the victuals." By the third decade of the nineteenth century, Frances Byerley (Mrs. William) Parkes would caution that persons of good taste would prefer a few pictures of high merit to walls "covered with inferior performances." And, she continued, "as no strong reflected lights should be permitted to fall upon a picture, the walls, the carpet, and the curtains, should be of a hue which is more likely

Natchez Porch. Pencil sketch by Charles A. LeSueur. c. 1830. American Antiquarian Society, Worcester, Massachusetts. A Yankee visiting Natchez, Mississippi, in the early 1830s observed that no planter's house was complete without a gallery or porch to enhance the lightness and beauty of the edifice and to provide a fine promenade and a refreshing dining room

to absorb than to reflect light." Mrs. Parkes believed a deep olive-green or a dull crimson to be the best colors for the dining room.[26]

Curtains were to be "of substance" in keeping with the character of the room. George Smith wrote in his *A Collection of Designs for Household Furniture and Interior Decoration* (1808) that the color could be selected "as fancy or taste may direct; yet scarlet or crimson will ever hold the preference." When Charles Carroll, the Barrister of Mount Clare, sent to England in 1764 for "58 yards of Substantial Silk and worsted Crimson Damask for window Curtains for a Dining Room," and when Julia Ward Howe said that at her New York home in the 1830s "the red room was that in which we took our meals," they stated the conventional preference for this color in the dining room.[27]

Robert Kerr felt adamantly that the chief characteristic of the dining room ought to be freedom from the heat and dazzle of sunshine at those hours when it was in use. He would have sympathized with Sidney George Fisher of Philadelphia, who complained about an uncomfortable dinner in 1848, with "the glare of sunlight blazing in at the windows." The nineteenth-century use of inner and outer curtains, painted shades, and venetian blinds reflected the contention that "during dinner the view should be shut out to prevent distraction." Venetian blinds and louvered shutters were particularly favored, as they provided a screen while allowing for circulation of air. "If it is summer, see that the sashes are raised, and the venetian blinds drawn down," counseled Eliza Leslie, "turning the slats, so as to make the room sufficiently light." Further, if the dinner was to commence in daylight but there was a possibility of its being protracted till after sunset, then the blinds should be closed from the beginning of the meal and the candles lit, for "it is extremely uncomfortable to have the company overtaken by the gloom of twilight, and obliged to wait almost in darkness while the lights are preparing."[28]

In *The Art of Dining* (1837), Thomas Walker expressed his belief that "justness of proportion, harmony of colouring, and disposition of light, are the most desirable qualities in any room, but especially in a dining-room, without any individual ornaments or objects to distract the attention." Lighting was a problem, however. "I rather think the best mode of lighting a table has not yet been discovered," acknowledged Walker, repeating Robert Roberts's contention that "Dinner Tables are seldom sufficiently lighted." Roberts endorsed the symmetrical placement of candlesticks and branches on the table "with half as many candles as there are guests," and with their flame "about eighteen inches above the table." Walker disagreed: "I think it desirable not to have the lights upon the dining table, nor indeed anything which can interrupt the freest communication with the guests." He recommended lights on the mantelpiece, which is probably what William Bingham had in mind when in 1791 he ordered "some of Argaud's [Argand's] Lamps of the most approved Form for Lighting Dining Rooms." Alexis Soyer agreed in 1849 that the lights were the first thing to be looked to on the dining table, and that they should be placed so as not to intercept the view of any person at table, "but at the same time they ought to be enough to show everything off to advantage." He preferred removing some of the lights from the table to the sideboard when the cloth was removed, "as the light after dinner ought to be more subdued." Wall sconces, with and without mirrors, often supplemented the illumination of the dining room, where candles continued to be a favored source of artificial light long after the introduction of gas lighting.[29]

The care of diners was an art in the early American home, and all five senses were indulged. Servants were to go about their work with as little noise as possible, treading lightly on carpeted floors. A clean and well-aired dining room pleased the sense of smell as did careful attention to such details as bringing in the cheese only at the moment of need. The sense of touch was catered to by comfortable chairs and close attention to the temperature of the room. Lord Botetourt, at home at the Governor's Palace in Williamsburg, kept his wintertime guests and their viands warm with a good fire, a mahogany fire screen, and a plate warmer in the dining room, where, in summer, cooling air passed through venetian blinds, and choice wines, chilled in mahogany coolers, promised to revive wilting diners. Sight was soothed by the absence of superfluous furnishings and ornaments, the symmetrical arrangement and harmonious proportions of the furniture, adequate yet subtle lighting, subdued colors, and a beautifully set-out sideboard and dining table. The cook made every effort to please palate and eye alike. Let us, then, step into the dining room behind Robert Roberts with his supper dishes "garnished with green parsley or flowers," thus giving the "supper table a most sublime appearance, and particularly in summer time, when every thing is green and in bloom."[30]

Every early American house had a kitchen, but its emplacement, use, size, and character could differ dramatically according to geographic location and economic and social distinctions: North or South, urban or rural, villa or farmhouse, with servants or without.

In the South, the kitchen was generally a detached outbuilding some twenty to one hundred yards away from the "Big House," thus removing at a distance the incessant commotion of the servants and the bothersome heat, troublesome smoke, and treacherous sparks of the open fire. In congested towns, such as Baltimore, Philadelphia, New York, and Boston, the kitchen might hunker down in the basement or sit at the back of the house; and there was often a supplementary out kitchen as well, for many northern families, because of the wide seasonal temperature variables, found maximum comfort in having two kitchens. Some used the basement kitchen in winter, the out kitchen in summer; for others the basement kitchen was a cool summer kitchen and the principal, main-floor kitchen performed winter service. In the rural North this generally large apartment might sprawl across the back of the house, embracing expansive views of flowers and fields, and gathering to itself the sweetened breath of meadow, garden, and orchard. Or the kitchen could nestle into a succession of annexed outbuildings, which might unfold as kitchen, buttery, sinkroom, laundry, wood house, carriage house, and privy: an arrangement that made New England houses seem "to be constructed on the model of a telescope; compartment after compartment, lessening in size, and all under one cover."[1]

Regardless of where it was located, there were certain universal qualifications for an efficient kitchen. It should be sufficiently large that duties could be performed smoothly, and it must be well aired and ventilated; receive plenty of light; offer easy access to the dining room or dining parlor; be remote enough that the family not be incommoded by the smell of cooking food and the noise of rattling pots; have readily available supplies of fuel and water; and share proximity with such supportive appendages as sinkroom, pantry, buttery, and storeroom.[2]

Family use of this apartment depended in large part on the housewife's involvement in kitchen operations. If she was blessed with able and sufficient servants and her role was merely supervisory, she only visited the kitchen, and the room entered little into family life, being more an efficient workroom than a lively living space. If, however, she performed many of the kitchen duties herself, then the room was more likely to become a multifunctional space frequented by the entire family; and a New England housewife's faculty to regulate this space as culinary workroom, dining room, and sitting room was proverbial—to her went the laurels for producing "the greatest possible results there with the slightest possible discomposure." A supplementary kitchen might aid her in this, for families that used the kitchen as a dining and/or sitting room might confine the hottest, heaviest, and hardest work to a secondary kitchen. In urban Boston in the 1820s, the Rice family kitchen served as a dining room year-round, but in summer the cooking was done in a small basement room arranged and furnished for that purpose. Often, a small nearby kitchen obliged in the same way. A. J. Downing extolled the combination kitchen-living-eating room for its ease of operation, but in order that this space might be kept neatly and provide a pleasant family dining space, he designed a small back kitchen adjacent, with a separate flue for a small range or cookstove.[3]

Seasons could determine the use of the kitchen as a dining room. Faith Silliman Hubbard had two kitchens at home in Hanover, New Hampshire, in 1837, and she intended to use the one next to the parlor as an eating room in summer; while Peter Neilson, a Scotsman traveling in the United States in the 1820s, observed that "in many of the houses, the kitchen, in winter, is most usually converted into the dining-room, being warm and comfortable." Suggestive of the use of the kitchen as a dining room are such furnishings as tables, chairs, eating utensils, and perhaps a tin horn or conch shell hanging near the back door and "usually winded by some kitchen Triton," to call the field workers in to their noontime dinner. Painted chairs, often with flag bottoms and sometimes with the amenity of cushions as well, and Windsors were common in the North; the sparsity of seating furniture in southern kitchens under-scores the use of that room as a laboratory rather than a living space.[4]

Despotic winter might command the use of the kitchen as a sitting room as well as a dining room, particularly in those homes where the kitchen fire was the only fire. "When the equinoctial gale came unseasonably," recalled George Channing, "the keeping-room, as it was called, was deserted, and the kitchen fireplace became the resort of both old and young. A piece of furniture called a settle, with its high back and of semicircular shape, was a highly esteemed seat at such times; and, when the coals were glowing of an autumnal evening, the old sepulchral chimney, with its cosey corners, was hailed as a godsend." At least for the old folks, the settle, with its tall, draft-shielding back, might well be the hibernal throne. Edmund Soper Hunt, who was born in Weymouth, Massachusetts, in 1827, could also recall that "in winter the house was cold. We had no stoves, but large, open fire-places for burning wood," and before the great fire "was a high-back settle where the old people sat to keep warm. This was the kitchen, or living-room of the house; all the other rooms were un-heated." Caroline Gilman, in her *Recollections of a Housekeeper* (1834), paid tribute to the settle as "that glory of New-England kitchens." Often fitted with casters so that it could be pulled closer to the fire or pushed out of the way, the settle might not only offer a place to rest but provide storage space beneath its lidded seat, and, if it had a hinged back, it might even metamorphose into what Catharine Beecher thought a very convenient article, for kitchen use, "a *settee*, or *settle*, made to serve also as an ironing-table." She suggested that it be made of pine stained a cherry color and that it have a seat with two lidded compartments, one for the sheets to be used as ironing-board cover, the other for diverse ironing apparatus. Gervase Wheeler likewise advocated the use of a space-saving "folding settee ironing-table" in 1851. The term "settee" is interesting here because it seems to have been used interchangeably with "settle"; Harriet Beecher Stowe opened the scenario in *The Minister's Wooing* in a great, old-fashioned kitchen where, by the side of the fire, stood "a commodious wooden 'settee,' or settle."[5]

Other furnishings suggestive of a sitting room might include looking glass, rocking chairs, desk, workstand, books, clock, and carpets. The well-fingered Bible

and weather-wise almanac were sure to find shelf space in the kitchen—or the latter might at least dangle from a peg. The fourteen chairs in Jonathan Davis's Dorchester kitchen in 1762 must have meant that there was sufficient seating furniture for a good part of his family to gather around at the commencement and conclusion of each day to hear him read from his large Bible and, on occasion perhaps, from the other bound books and pamphlets he kept there. A clock in or near the kitchen was considered important to secure regularity in family arrangements. Alternatively, there might be an "old worn hourglass, standing in two leather loops on a shelf above the fireplace," which would invariably be turned "exactly at eight o'clock in the evening, that we might be sure to go to bed duly at nine." When Abigail Adams wrote from Richmond Hill in New York City on 9 June 1790, it was to request that her sister send "my kitchen clock & Press which stands in the kitchen" in Braintree, perhaps in a vain attempt to regulate her "vixen of a House maid" and the other worthless servants who agitated her Manhattan household. Polly Bennett had comfortably furnished her

Vermont kitchen in 1849 with a calico-dressed settee and pillows, a rocking chair, six splint-bottom chairs, a pine table, cherry light-stand, and "1 clock with L. Glass" — a space-efficient and perhaps penny-wise combination. She also had two white window curtains and a rag carpet.[6]

Peter Neilson mentioned that American kitchen floors were in winter covered with rag carpets, and John Sturtevant concurred: "The dining room and kitchen were one — generally covered with a rag carpet except around the stove or open fire place where might be a piece of oil cloth, more commonly a piece of canvas." Sarah Trecothick had a floor cloth on her Boston kitchen floor in 1749, and ninety-two years later Catharine Beecher might still believe that an oilcloth was even better than a painted floor "because it can be removed, to be repainted," something which seems to have been done regularly. Eliza Leslie agreed, suggesting a coarse, stout, plain oilcloth, unfigured and of one color: dark red, blue, brown, olive, or ocher-yellow. She also thought it satisfactory to paint the floor itself with several coats of common paint, "yellow ochre being the cheapest, but slate-colour the best." New Englanders seem to have embraced the idea of saffron-hued floors, for when William Thackara walked through the town of Tisbury, Massachusetts, in August 1820, he noted that "all the floors are painted with a thick coating of yellow ochre"; and when Harriet Beecher Stowe filled in the outlines of a "large, roomy, neatly-painted" kitchen, it had green wooden chairs, a small flag-bottomed rocking chair with patchwork cushion, rows of shining tin, a neat well-blacked cookstove, and a "yellow floor, glossy and smooth, and without a particle of dust." Beach sand might also be rippled decoratively across the kitchen floor, and Sarah Anna Emery could picture her rollicking Aunt Hannah, a girl of eight or nine, seizing the broom and drawing "the freshly-strewn sand on the kitchen floor into a remarkable combination of zig-zags." Many a New England kitchen was scoured white and sparkled with beach sand in summer, though carpeted with homemade rugs in winter.[7]

Walls were often whitewashed "to promote a neat look and pure air," for thus treated they tended to make the room lighter and removed disagreeable smells. Martha Ogle Forman spent 21 May 1842 "Yellow washing the Kitchen." Three years later, in her *Domestic Cookery*, Elizabeth Ellicott Lea offered a recipe for a yellow-ocher wash, suitable for a kitchen. Composed of glue, water, yellow ocher, and whiting, it seems a little more appealing than the lampblack and molasses mixed with whitewash that she also thought "a good color for a kitchen." Wainscoting, when present, was often red or brown, and walls and ceilings might seem to converge in picturesque testimony to the bounty of the land, particularly in harvest-rich autumn. An astonished sojourner passing through New England in the 1830s vouched that he had not supposed there were as many dried pumpkins and sausages in the world as he had seen hanging from the kitchen walls of these rural folk. The picture of a be-raftered farm ceiling that Susan Augusta Fenimore Cooper conjured up in her *Rural Hours* (1850) was perhaps an omnium-gatherum of all she had ever seen pendant from this "sort of store-place," with "all kinds of things . . . on hooks or nails driven into the beams; bundles of dried herbs, strings of red peppers and of dried apples hanging in festoons, tools of various kinds, bags of different sorts and sizes, golden ears of seed-corn ripening, vials of physic and nostrums for man and beast, bits of cord and twine, skeins of yarn and brown thread just spun, and lastly, a file of newspapers." And there might be additional oddities swinging from or near the ceiling. A frilly garland of very white paper might dangle in the hopes of ensnaring a few of the less wily flies; and the horns of a stag could be nailed near the ceiling "for all the men, who could reach so high," to hang their Sunday hats upon.[8]

Of course, the focal point, the great scene of action, in the early kitchen was the braggart fireplace, which dominated the room, obliging as cookstove, lighting device, and furnace. As the eighteenth century advanced and fuel supplies dwindled in quantity while rising in cost, the voracious fireplace was scaled down, and by the 1820s it might even have surrendered to the iron cookstove. But many were the reminiscences of those who had sat by the fireplace and seen the stars or stood at one end and looked out of the top of the chimney and felt the rain falling gently on the face. Gervase Wheeler suggested that the fireplace be positioned at one end of the room rather than on a side wall, as it would thus be easier to avoid the heat and because there would be more room to move about, as well as additional wall space for shelving. To keep the kitchen cool was something of a challenge, but spaciousness and cross-ventilation helped, and there would not be one great heat-producing fire for cooking but rather a number of smaller fires scattered about the hearth, gauged to the various foods that were baking, simmering, stewing, or boiling.[9]

Typically, the fireplace was outfitted with a crane, from which hung a kettle, a pot, and perhaps an additional large water kettle with a spigot so that hot water might always be at hand for cooking and cleaning. All of these could be raised or lowered to suit the heat. Universal utensils of iron, brass, copper, or tin included chafing dishes, dripping pan, frying pan, kettles, saucepans, patty pans, skillets, skimmers, stewpan, and toaster. Wealthy families owned a good many more nonessential amenities, such as cake pans, ice-cream molds, fish kettles, and wafer irons, and a greater proportion of all their kitchenwares were crafted of copper. Whether iron or copper, all these pots and pans were heavy and cumbersome, and the requisite stooping, bending, lifting, and carrying were not only muscle-building but hazardous. Dismal indeed was the life of a cook in early America. Not only was she subjected to the danger of the flames, "the deleterious vapours and pestilential exhalations of the charcoal," the glare of the scorching fire, "and the smoke so baneful to the eyes and complexion," but she must live in the midst of these dangers "as a soldier on the field of battle, surrounded by bullets, and bombs, and Congreve's rockets," with the only difference being that for the cook "every day is a fighting day, that her warfare is almost always without glory, and most praiseworthy achievements pass not only without reward, but frequently without even thanks." In addition to being brave and stoic, the cook must be acute of sight, smell, taste, and hearing—the latter that she might "discriminate (when several saucepans are in operation at the same time) the simmering of one, the ebullition of another, and the full-toned warbling of a third." No wonder women who were financially able to hire and fortunate enough to find sufficient help looked first for a cook. Few housewives—in upper-middle-class urban homes, at least—troubled themselves with roasting meat or baking bread, although they might on occasion display their finer skills at making preserves or baking such delicacies as cakes, pies, and cookies. And if the cook became ill or marched off unexpectedly, chances were that the cooking chores would devolve on the chambermaid or nurserymaid, for cleaning house and caring for children seem to have been tasks less odious to the housewife than cooking the meals.[10]

Pokers, tongs, and bellows were requisite armor for the aggressive chef and stood close by, ready for action. Sometimes there was a jack, which through variant contrivances turned the spit automatically as it lay across a pair of weighty andirons.

Engraving on the cover of *The Kitchen Companion and House-keeper's Own Book* (Philadelphia, 1844). Science & Technology Research Center, The New York Public Library; Astor, Lenox and Tilden Foundations. This kitchen with its plate-lined walls and game-hung rafters seems providentially well supplied. Note the wall clock, the coffee mill on the mantel, and the tin kitchen on the hearth. Popping corks, stirring spoons, and burbling pots add resonance to the scene

Experienced cooks knew that it took rather more than fifteen minutes a pound to roast meats, although the age of the meat or the temperature of the day might complicate the timetable, for in frosty weather all kinds of meat took longer to roast. "In summer, twenty minutes may be reckoned equal to half an hour in winter," calculated one guidebook in 1831. A tall screen, often found in early kitchen inventories, would be beneficial in warding off time-consuming drafts of chilly air, but would also encumber the way. By the close of the eighteenth century, many families had a tin kitchen or reflector oven, which stood on the hearth to roast turkeys or chickens, cuts of beef, or legs of mutton as the obliging fire sent out its heat. A crank at the side enabled the cook to ensure even browning, and a small door at the back could be opened for basting with the flavorsome contents of the dripping pan below. Secreted within the bricks to one side of the fireplace might be a portentous brick oven, heated up every Saturday. The temperature was gauged by holding your arm in for the count of twenty for brown bread, meats, beans, Indian puddings, and pumpkin pie; and if it was not uncomfortable to keep that arm in to the count of forty, then all augured well for delicate fruit pies, cakes, and white bread. Busy indeed was this contrivance every Thanksgiving, when seventy-five to one hundred pies might emerge steaming from its portal, moistened with boiled cider and laced with good brandy "for its 'keeping' quality"— to be eaten at once or stored frozen, and lasting generally "till March."[11]

In the early 1800s, to either side of the fireplace or out in the yard-kitchen,

forward-looking families installed Rumford ovens complete with an impressive array of boilers activated by the fireboxes beneath them. It was only begrudgingly that some turned to this new-fangled device. Elizabeth Watters wrote to her aunt, Lydia Bowen Clark, in Providence in February 1803, apparently in response to an earlier letter, acknowledging that she was "pleased with my Uncles plan of Rumfordising the mode of Cookery for the summer but agree with the Cook that the sight of the Fire is far to be prefered in Winter." This prejudice in favor of the open wood fire lingered long. Though the cookstove began to meet with acceptance in the 1820s, cookbooks addressed both open-hearth and iron-stove cooking into the 1860s, and many families were yet savoring the tasty products of the open fire after 1870. According to Susan Augusta Fenimore Cooper's fictionalized account, one family used "a stove for cooking, and in the very coldest weather, they keep two fires burning, one in the chimney, another in the stove"; this is probably a pretty true picture of the transitional period in which many were not quite ready to give up the amiable aspects of the open fire. Fired with wood or coal, iron cookstoves were cleaner, a little easier to use, and certainly more economical. Faith Silliman Hubbard reported from Hanover, New Hampshire, in August 1837 that "we do all our cooking by a stove and thus far I am much pleased with it, and think it saves a great deal of work." But when Caroline Dustan's kitchen range ovens were out of order on 9 January 1861, the pudding was baked on the trustworthy parlor hearth.[12]

Kitchen Sketch. Pencil drawing by Frank Blackwell Mayer. c. 1830–50. The Maryland Historical Society, Baltimore. Some preferred the geniality of the open hearth to the economy of the stove, and in many kitchens the two abided side by side in an unspoken compromise

Warmers for heating plates before the fire and hot-water dishes for successfully conveying warm foods to a distant dining room were regular kitchen accoutrements. Genteel families might even have a pantry or service room between the kitchen and dining room, where the servants could collect plates and where there might be a steam table to keep dishes hot. At the opposite temperature extreme, there must be a supply of ice somewhere near the kitchen. Into the third decade of the nineteenth century, the icehouse out in the backyard would have to suffice, though always with a varying and often temper-raising degree of success. Catherine Chew had "1 Ice Chest" in her Philadelphia kitchen by 1840, yet Catharine Beecher felt it necessary to describe the term "refrigerator" shortly thereafter, presuming that everyone was not acquainted with the device. By 1870 iceboxes or refrigerators were pretty much universal, and George Makepeace Towle was only one of many to commend the "great boon of unlimited *ice*" in this bounteous country, and enjoyed his early morning strolls along American streets in summer where one might "observe at every basement door one of those huge, refreshing, tempting lumps, left there by the ice-man, awaiting the maid."[13]

There were, of course, numerous other devices to facilitate the preparation of food, such as scales, pewter measures, whisks, rolling pins, chopping knife and board, cleaver, coffeepot, knives and forks, salt box, pepper box, sugar nippers, sugar box, and a mortar and pestle of marble, brass, bell metal or lignum vitae. Many a kitchen rang with the sonorous thump of arm-wearying butter creaming, raisin stoning, herb chopping, and sugar pounding. "There was no cut nor granulated nor pulverized sugar, to be turned from the grocer's bag onto the scales," explained Eliza Chinn Ripley, who was born in 1832 and spent her childhood in New Orleans. "All sugar except the crude brown, direct from plantations, was in cone-shaped loaves as hard as a stone and weighing several pounds each. These well-wrapped loaves were kept hung (like hams in a smokehouse) from the closet ceiling. They had to be cut into chips by aid of carving knife and hammer, then pounded and rolled until reduced to powder." Eliza Leslie thought a pair of sugar nippers for "breaking small the loaf-sugar, after it has been cracked with a stout knife and a mallet or hammer," indispensable in the correctly furnished kitchen. The nipped, chipped, and pounded sugar was stored in a closely covered tin or wooden box.[14]

Additionally, there might be a tight-lidded box for the safe stowage of candles in the kitchen, for this was the apartment in which the household candlesticks were cleaned and kept ready for use. Thomas Tilestone's Boston kitchen displayed a conventional lineup of four brass and seven iron candlesticks with an accompanying four pairs of snuffers in 1794. Here also might be the candle molds to facilitate that unpleasant cold-weather task. John Guerard had four dozen candle molds at his plantation near Charleston in 1764. The considerably greater number of these molds in Charleston inventories than in Boston inventories perhaps attests to the easy availability of store-bought candles in that northern city and perhaps also to the larger number requisite to the smooth operation of a multifaceted plantation. A tin lantern for dawn and twilight chores often hung here, and here, too, was the tinderbox to oblige those careless enough to let the fire go out.[15]

There might also be a cache of cleaned and ready-for-action chamber pots stowed away in some kitchen corner. The four brass chamber pots listed with Philip Free-man's kitchenwares in Boston in November 1782 were perhaps placed here not only for cleaning and polishing but for warming before the fire—imagine their stinging

Engraving on the cover of W. A. Henderson, *Modern Domestic Cookery* (New York, 1828). Science & Technology Research Center, The New York Public Library; Astor, Lenox and Tilden Foundations. A large plate rack with fabric-lined shelves has been wheeled before the fire to warm the plates for a meal—a sedulous attention much appreciated by gourmands in frosty dining rooms

nip in bedchambers where the temperature hovered below freezing. Here, too, might be the little tin and wooden foot stove and the tall brass bed warmer, ready to be filled with a shovelful of warm coals in an attempt to moderate the discomforts of those chilly chambers.[16]

Mousetraps and rattraps were necessary to protect provender at times when the resident cat was lazy, overtaxed, or otherwise engaged. Joseph Edward Flower undoubtedly needed the wire rattrap and the mousetrap he owned in Charleston in 1757 to help keep the rodent population down, for with his "Dozen Bird Cages of different Sorts," a cat would have been a most unwelcome tenant. Cleaning supplies of all kinds—iron and tin dustpans, brooms and brushes galore, pails, and mops—would be stored here as well. And then there was the multitudinous laundry apparatus necessary to ensure the success of the Monday wash and Tuesday ironing: copper or brass kettle, tubs, baskets and clothespins, horsehair clothesline, folding board or ironing table, clotheshorse, flatirons, box irons, iron holders, iron wipers, and little pieces of beeswax or spermaceti to smooth the path of the iron over the fresh-scented, line-dried linens. When Theodore Dwight entered a Massachusetts kitchen one cold December morning in 1819, "It was tuesday—they were ironing," and two or three flatirons were "toasting" in front of the fire, where he was happy to place his frosted toes as well, while "a holder or two were pendant near the crane." A folding board and clotheshorse were neatly stowed in Ebenezer Pierpoint's Roxbury kitchen in 1768, and there were eight baskets and a clothesline in the Manhattan kitchen of Cornelius Bennett sixteen years later. Catharine Beecher gave explicit instructions for the tidy stowage of all this gear in 1841. But it wasn't only sheets and pillowcases, towels and tablecloths that were scrubbed white in this kitchen; the misted mirror and beady rivulets running down the windowpanes on a Saturday night intimated that there would be spanking-clean skins as well. "Saturday was bath night," sighed one who spent her girlhood in late-nineteenth-century Massachusetts, "and after supper began the dreary business of lugging round, wooden washtubs in from the shed and heating numberless kettles of water to fill them. In winter, the tubs were rimmed with frost; in summer, they harbored large, black spiders. It took at least one heavy iron kettle of boiling water to wash one small boy or girl. Woe betide that one who put in a dipper too much of cold; he or she sat shivering while another kettle heated and the next candidate hammered at the portals for his turn." Shaving apparatus—razor, hone, and strop—might be found in this hearth-warmed apartment as well: a much more hospitable setting than the chamber with its ice-rimmed washbowl.[17]

In or near the kitchen would be the sink, perhaps "with a pewter ewer and bowl where I washed my hands when coming in from play," as there had been in William Davis's kitchen in Plymouth, Massachusetts. Of course, any kind of piped-in water could be a problem throughout the winter: Deacon Enoch Little of New Hampshire cleared his sink of ice on 7 April 1817, it having "not thawed out this winter yet." Catharine Beecher advocated the use of two block-tin washbasins and an accompanying roller towel—to be changed twice a week—and a "nicer" towel for less rugged use. Tinwares were plentiful in the nineteenth-century kitchen; Robert Roberts rather preferred block-tin utensils for small families, as they were lighter and cheaper if properly cared for. Kitchen supplies of all kinds—wooden, iron, pewter, tin, etc.— could be purchased from a dry-goods merchant, at auction, or from a traveling tinker. Quantities of pewter might be found in the kitchen. In fact, household inventories sometimes laconically lump these wares by weight. Joseph Gooch of Milton, Massa-

Kitchen Scenes. Watercolor by John Lewis Krimmel. Sketchbook, 7 July 1819. The Winterthur Library: Joseph Downs Collection of Manuscripts and Printed Ephemera. Among these kitchen furnishings of wood, tin, iron, and brass are a roller-towel rack, candle box, washtub, colander, rolling pin, flatirons, and andirons. The diligent figure at the upper left is scouring steel-bladed knives with brick dust—a daily chore if they were not to rust

chusetts, for example, owned "90 ^{lb} pewter" in 1770. All this pewter might be stowed in a plate rack suspended on the wall; but often there was a more elaborate affair called a dresser—with cupboards or an open shelf for pots, beneath upper shelves with rails on which to rest the edges of pewter plates and dishes—"in order that they may lean forward, so as to protect their faces from the dust." J. C. Loudon, always alert for

symbolic significance, thought the kitchen best characterized by the grate or kitchen range and by the imposing dresser. Usually this piece occupied the wall opposite the fireplace. The dresser was either painted the color of the woodwork or scrubbed white with frequent scouring of fine white sand, and the pewterwares themselves were to be frequently polished. How numerous are the memories of the ostentatious glitter on those dresser shelves—the pewter plates bright as polished silver, capturing the flicker of the opposite firelight:

> . . . and the pewter plates on the dresser
> Caught and reflected the flame, as shields of armies the sunshine.[18]

When in 1788 Nathaniel Saltonstall gave instructions for the construction of his future house in Haverhill, Massachusetts, he desired the kitchen "to be ceal'd, Dressers with Draws under the same and a Cupboard—panelled Doores to the

Dressers and a Closet in some Part of the kitchen if desired and one over the Fire Place." Closets were essential in the kitchen, where safety and efficiency dictated a clean hearth, "as neat as a table," and clear of all unnecessary encumbrances. Mary Rice Livermore remembered that there was a deep cupboard over the kitchen fireplace at her girlhood home "for japanned lamps which burned whale oil, flatirons, skillets, spiders, and other kitchen utensils of iron."[19]

Closets played an important role in the cleanliness of American kitchens, and if we listen to Robert Roberts we shall hear that "cleanliness is the chief cardinal virtue of the kitchen." The chimney was to be swept often so that ashes would not trickle down upon the food, and it was suggested that the cook every morning brush down all loose soot within reach with a long-handled broom. The cook herself must dress in a washable frock with a clean apron, and all utensils must be regularly washed with soap and water or scrubbed with white sand. Wiping cloths should be washed daily. Brissot de Warville said that American "kitchens are kept clean, and do not give out the disgusting smell to be found in the best kitchens of France." Anne Royall thought New England kitchens and all their appurtenances "as neat as any gentleman's parlor," in 1828, though in the South they were invariably "filthy and the cooks abominable"; and she was much offended by one house near Richmond, Virginia, where the meat "stunk," the servants "stunk," and the house "stunk."[20]

Happily, kitchen odors were generally more pleasant. The condensed sweetness of the harvest wafted through in the aroma of apples ripening in the cellar and herbs drying above the hearth. A soupçon of smoke mingled with the scented vines that clambered at the window. And best of all was that spacious store closet, found somewhere between the dining room and the kitchen, whence floated flavorsome smells every time the door was opened. "The moment Grandmother turned the key in the door," recalled Ruth Huntington Sessions, "one perceived a fragrance, exotic and rare; a mixture of spices, fruits, syrups, nuts—words cannot describe the richness of that mixture, the product of age-old sweetness to which Europe and Asia had contributed and which seemed to cling to the very walls and shelves, immaculate though they were." Here stood rows of preserves, miniature casks of tamarinds, flat boxes of guava jelly, round-shouldered blue jars enclosed in a network of split bamboo and filled with fiery ginger, chests of green and black tea "with queer little Chinamen with long queues hanging down behind," bags of Java and mocha coffee, boxes of Malaga raisins, drums of figs, casks of grapes, jugs of molasses, and cones of purple-cloaked sugar, "their bright-colored labels fastened with little bows of red ribbon."[21]

And there was further testimony to the trade with foreign shores in the brilliant plumage of the birds who shared in the warm hospitality of the kitchen, joining their song with the warbling of the pots. Bird cages abounded in early American kitchens. James Smithwick, a Boston mariner, had hung his old sea buddy in his parrot cage in the warm lean-to off his kitchen in December 1779, and the kitchen is where Helen Davis kept and pampered her precious parrot a few decades later. This indurative spinster requested that her colorful companion be buried with her, and to her nephew fell the unpleasant assignment of wringing its neck, though "it was a tough old bird and made unfavorable comments" concerning this behest.[22]

For some families, particularly those in upper-class urban establishments or in servant-supplied southern homes, the kitchen was merely a place to visit and in which to supervise, to direct, and often to scold. But to the middle class and the rural folk, the kitchen was "the heart of the house," the symbol of all that was warm and generous

"You Want to See My Pa, I 'Spose?"
"Wa'al, No; I Come Designin'..."
Wood engraving by Augustus Hoppin
in *Harper's Weekly*, 23 October 1858.
Courtesy Vassar College Library.
Kitchens offered colorful testimony to
the quality and quantity of the harvest
and were typically festooned with
strings of dried apples and peppers and
bunches of seed corn, while crookneck
squash hung suspended from the mantel or lay in racks about the fireplace.
The glow of the wood fire and the glint
of the pewter provide illumination
enough for this coy courting scene

The Pedlar's Cart. Drawing in pen,
brown ink, and pencil, by William T.
Carlton. c. 1840. Museum of Fine
Arts, Boston; M. and M. Karolik Collection of American Water Colors and
Drawings, 1800–1875. Pedlar carts
laden with hats, brooms, inexpensive
lamps, tinware, earthenware, cloth,
and trinkets might come around two or
three times a season, and the inveigling
pedlar was often successful in talking
a housewife into some item for her
kitchen. Or, at least, he might find employment in remolding broken pewter
spoons and mending the household tin-
ware. Here both pedlar and itinerant
knife grinder ply their trades

and protective. What Mary Rice Livermore loved most in the "always clean and
orderly kitchen" of her girlhood was the daytime "freedom I found there. We could
play, shout, run, jump, stand on the substantial chairs to look out the windows, play
housekeeping, and set out the kitchen table with our little pewter dishes and tiny
porringers, bring in our individual chairs, stools, and crickets, and build up establishments in every corner of the room." To others, such as Ellen Rollins, it was by night
that the kitchen was "the best part of the house." All seemed "fire-changed, and were

mellowed into the bright scene," as the jocund and brilliant back log generously spread its radiant cheerfulness over the simple furnishings, and the pewter dishes upon the brown dresser "shone in dancing firelight like silver." This defiant back log—"eloquent with fiery tongues"—was at last no more, the benighted kitchen dark and silenced; yet "the stories it told to a child, with crackling voice, went not out with its smoke." Nor did the fond memories of that old-time kitchen.[23]

Jostling the best parlor for first-place position in the hierarchical room arrangement of early interiors was the best bedchamber. These were the two rooms first to display curtains at the windows and carpets on the floor; here were the choicest furniture, the richest sconces, the most expensive looking glasses. It might be difficult to ascertain which room won out in this contest but it is easy to discern how much more elegantly arrayed they were than all subordinate apartments.

The best bedchamber stood at the summit of a gradational chain of sleeping rooms, at the other end of which were the cold garret bedroom and the crowded back chamber or kitchen chamber—in both of which the bed (and usually beds) had to vie for floor space with textile-processing equipment and grain reserves. Even with the snow falling on his face, John Jay Janney believed he never slept better than in an early-nineteenth-century Virginia kitchen loft, which was large enough for a commodious " 'colonial chest' and three beds, and still [had] room for the flour barrel, the corn meal, the buckwheat meal, and the salt barrel, besides the 'big wheel' [the wool wheel], the 'little wheel' [the flax wheel], the reel, and the rats." British army officer Thomas Hughes, suffering a stay in America during the Revolution, was not so amenable to rural insufficiencies. Trying to sleep in a New England three-bedded garret amid nuts and apples, he opined, "If this is the kind of life the poets say so much of, and call Rural Happiness, I wish to my soul that they were here, and I in London."[1]

The best bedchamber, which might also be the guest chamber, remained aloof from all this. Here, the atmosphere was hushed, unhurried, reverential—"You tiptoed in," wrote a contributor to *Atlantic Monthly*. Blessed above all furnishings in this sanctum was the state bed—"the family Zeraphim, secretly worshipped." "Of course," wrote Caroline King, "the bedstead with its heaped-up feather beds and down pillows, its fine linen, fragrant with lavender, and its gorgeous or delicate bed-trappings, was the chief feature."[2]

Between the four posts of the typical best-room bed, from 1750 to 1850, were a rope or sacking bottom or wooden slats, upon which rested a straw-filled tick, then a feather bed, perhaps a mattress, a bolster, next the bottom sheet, two pillows propped up against the bolster, a top sheet, blankets (two were often recommended), and a crowning counterpane. There might well be the additional nicety of a little watch pocket for the nocturnal stowage of that accessory, made of white muslin, dimity, tick, or the same material as the bed curtains. And enveloping the posts were yards upon yards of this curtain material, suspended from rods concealed by the tester. When closed, these curtains would completely encircle the bedstead, making the bed seem to one contemporary, "a room in itself, with four carved posts, flowered curtains for walls, a chintz tester for ceiling, and steps conducting one into an acre of billowy bolstered bliss!"[3]

The straw-filled tick that lay at the bottom of this veritable cumulus cloud was to be emptied of broken and crushed straw, washed, and refilled with a fresh supply each spring. In the country, this straw did not have to be carried far, but Maria Foster Brown, who was born in Ohio in 1827, remembered that it had to be toted carefully, for her "father wouldn't let the straw be carried through the grounds because some of it would be dropped on the grass and give the place an untidy look." In the city, recalled John Sturtevant of Manhattan, it was supplied by local farmers, who "would drive in with their large, long hay rigging loaded with straw, driving through the streets crying, 'Oh straw, Oh straw!'" And in picturesque testimony to the littered aspect of New York streets, Sturtevant continued, "The crushed and broken straw from the beds was emptied in the streets where the boys set fire to it and did 'stunts' by jumping over it by which many of us were more or less burned."[4]

Next came the feather bed, which might be filled with some forty pounds of goose feathers and down. Americans in urban centers could purchase feathers or feather-filled beds from upholsterers or even at auction. But feathers were not always easy to procure. Joshua Brookes slept on feather beds in Geneva, New York, in the 1790s, yet noted that the residents had to send to Albany for them. Maria Silliman Church hoped to be able to locate forty pounds of feathers to fill a bed in her western New York home in November 1831, but by the following June had only been able to secure feathers enough for bolsters and pillows: "I can wait until Autumn for the beds," she decided, during which interval she used mattresses of wool, straw, and hair.[5]

As the bed, bolster, and pillows often weighed in at sixty to ninety pounds of feathers per bed, and as there were several such beds in well-to-do households, the threat to the poultry yard was real. Samuel Goodrich, who was born in Ridgefield, Connecticut, in 1793, recalled that the beds "were of ample size, and well filled with geese feathers, these being deemed essential for comfortable people. . . . every decent family had its flock of geese, of course, which was picked thrice a year, despite the noisy remonstrances of both goose and gander." Eliza Leslie recommended that the geese be plucked in August and not in cool or damp weather, lest the geese catch cold from the loss of their feathers—which brings to mind a delightful anecdote from Bennington, Vermont:

> My grandparents' geese were in the cellar where the wine was kept. The faucet on one of the wine kegs was open and the geese drank the wine. They got drunk, keeled over, and passed out! When my grandparents found the geese in the cellar, passed out, they thought they had died of something. They couldn't eat them because they might have died of something awful, so they plucked them all to use the feathers for feather beds. And then the geese woke up! They woke up and made a whole lot of noise. My grandparents had to keep them tied on a string to the house for the rest of the summer until their feathers grew back, so they wouldn't wander too far and get cold.

By the 1820s and 1830s, urban housewives might avail themselves of an ample supply of feathers at furniture outlets, such as the Eagle Furniture Warehouse in Boston, which could supply, in 1830, all manner of bedchamber furnishings, including bedsteads, dressing tables, looking glasses, counterpanes, ready-made bed linens, and a wide variety of feathers, "all of which are dryed on their own kiln and warranted free from smell or moths." Feathers did indeed have to be properly cured and free of oil or they would begin to smell. This could be remedied, according to

Details of an eighteenth-century English copperplate-printed cotton fabric, currently incorporated into a quilt in The Henry Francis du Pont Winterthur Museum, Winterthur, Delaware. The exotic imagery of the printed cottons that hung at the window and enswathed the bedstead fired the imaginations of many American children. Together with scenic wallpapers, these panoramic fabrics were the picture books of the period. Harriet Beecher Stowe, who went as a child to live with her Aunt Harriet Foote in Guilford, Connecticut, recalled with pleasure their magical effect. In her new home, the beds were enveloped in a printed, so-called India cotton, which had been brought home by a seafaring uncle: "And I recollect now the almost awe-struck delight with which I gazed on the strange mammoth plants, with great roots and convolutions of branches, in whose hollows appeared Chinese summer-houses, adorned with countless bells, and perched jauntily aloft[;] with sleepy-looking mandarins smoking, and a Chinaman attendant just in the act of ringing some of the bells with a hammer. Also here and there were birds bigger than the mandarins, with wide-open beaks just about to seize strange-looking insects; and a constant wonder to my mind was why the man never struck the bells, nor the bird ever caught the insect." (Quoted in Lyman Beecher, *Autobiography, Correspondence* [New York, 1865], vol. 1, pp. 310–12)

Eliza Leslie, by opening the bed or pillow seams and inserting lumps of camphor. Elizabeth Ellicott Lea recommended pounded cloves. Both methods certainly would have contributed their own pungency. Tick and feathers were to be washed, either together or separately, three or four times a year, according to some authorities, but it is doubtful that this frustrating exercise was ever performed with such exacting regularity. Reserve feathers were to be stored in paper bags or boxes and kept in a dry place, such as the garret.[6]

To propel oneself to the summit of the rotund feather bed required a near-gymnastic stunt, so bed steps were a frequent amenity in early chambers. Even then, there might be further obstacles to sleep. A Massachusetts girl could remember a time when "night and morning were made fearful to me by the prospect of having to climb up and down these 'bed steps,' as they were called. The fear was emphasized by the fact that the bed was piled up very high in the middle, so that unless I landed exactly in the centre of the mountainous island, on my first entrance, I passed my night in rolling down hill, or in vain efforts to scramble up to the top, to avoid falling out on the floor." These voluminous feather beds could be very uncomfortable on steamy, hot nights. Margaret Hunter Hall complained of being obliged to sleep on a feather bed

Mrs. Nicholas Salisbury. Worcester, Massachusetts. Oil on canvas, by Christian Gullager. 1789. Worcester Art Museum; gift of Stephen Salisbury III. Eighty-five-year-old Martha Salisbury, the mother of eleven children, is well deserving of this capacious seat of ease. Note how well the armrest is designed for exactly that purpose. The dramatically patterned damask upholstery, the highly polished round stand, and the glossy dress fabric would all have been enhanced by candlelight and firelight

in upstate New York one broiling June night in 1827, and thought it "strange that in a country where there is so hot a summer they should not universally use mattresses, but they have not learnt yet to adapt comforts suitable to the different seasons." Eighteenth-century Charleston inventories, however, very definitely show that mattresses were used in the warm-weather months. Catharine Beecher suggested that one place either a strip of straw matting or a thin mattress of hair, cotton and moss, or straw over a feather bed in summer; and Florence Hartley felt strongly in 1873 that one should have both a feather bed and a mattress at least in the guest room, so that the guests might place whichever they preferred uppermost.[7]

Sheets and pillowcases required hours of care, for even if sheeting was purchased it had to be fitted, hemmed, and maintained—washed, bleached, and ironed. Housewives were usually diligent in their care of the linens. Elizabeth Drinker retaliated against one who wasn't in August 1771 by tying up the sheets "Nutmeg fashion" and

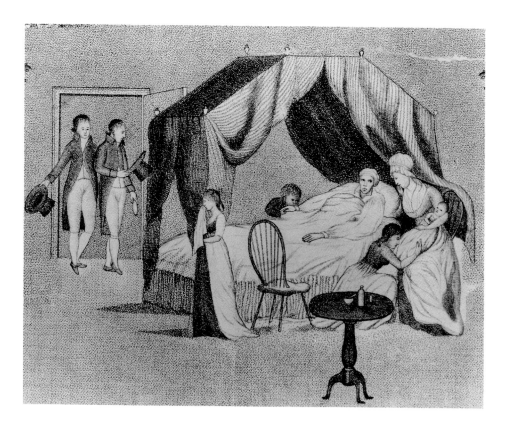

leaving them "covered up in ye Beds, for the old woman to tug and scold at." But Samuel Goodrich was one of many to report that the "sheets of the bed, though of home-made linen, were as white as the driven snow." In addition to the visual pleasure their snowy whiteness afforded, these linens often lent a delicate olfactory pleasance to the chamber, for they sometimes were stored with aromatic leaves, herbs, and spices. Recipes for sachets or perfume bags to secrete away in chests of linen or drawers of clothes were numerous; *The American Housewife* (1841), for example, proposed a potpourri of "rose and sweet-scented clover leaves, dried in the shade, then mixed with powdered cloves, cinnamon, mace, and pressed in small bags." Ellen Rollins could easily remember that the bureau in the foreroom at her grandmother's New Hampshire farmhouse "was always crammed with fine-twined linens, white as snow, and scented with lavender and roseleaves"; and Mary Jane Boggs, traveling in Virginia in 1851, was tempted to resign herself "to the *arms of Morpheus*," not only because she was tired but also because "the sheets are perfumed with roseleaves." Eliza Leslie, however, thought that the air of a bedchamber should be perfectly free from all scents—even a pleasantly perfumed one; and Nicholas Ridgely couldn't have agreed with her more. He was vexed indeed to be given a bed with scented sheets in Smyrna, Delaware, as he wrote his wife with indignation in 1818:

> I had arrived at Smyrna, about 6 oClock on Tuesday afternoon very well. When I went to bed, about 10, I perceived a very powerful Perfume in the Room, like a large Collection of highly scented Washballs. I hunted but could not perceive from whence the Scent came. I heard Ann Wakeman below & called her up. She came, and informed Me that the Clothes had

been laid in a Drawer among Rose Leaves. I told her I could not bear it. She said if the Windows were hoisted for a few Minutes the Scent would be soon gone. She went down and I had not Sense enough to have the Sheets etc. taken off & others put on; but I hoisted the Window and went to work fanning the Clothes, and at last shut the Windows down, & went to bed. I lay there, and tossed and tumbled till past 12 oClock, then I took the Sheets and Pillow Case off the Bed, and lay on the Bed without Sheets or Pillow Case, with an additional Counterpane which I got from another Bed.

Ridgely was convinced that the fever he suffered the next day was directly attributable to these scented linens. More typically held culpable, however, would have been the dampness of the sheets.[8]

In fact, to most early Americans damp sheets were an irrefutable prognosis for ill health, and the very thought of them brought consternation. Some advised the use of an inverted tumbler between the sheets after they had been heated with the bed warmer: if the tumbler showed telltale drops of water, the verdict was guilty. Benjamin Franklin checked a woman in the process of putting damp sheets on his bed, requesting that she air them first—which she did that frost-nipped January evening in 1756 out on the hedge, causing Franklin to sleep sandwiched between sheets "cold as death, and partly frozen," muffled up to his ears in his overcoat and woolen trousers. Sheets were to be well aired—though not at nightfall with the temperature below zero—and then stored neatly in a dry location.[9]

The use of bed curtains was general in homes of the better sort far into the nineteenth century. One purpose of these amplitudinous hangings was to keep out drafts of cold air and to help maintain body warmth in chambers that never knew a fire. Bed curtains and nightcaps—for child and adult alike—were prophylaxes to taking cold, which in that pre-antibiotic age was a source of considerable anxiety.

> For the curtains warm are spread
> Round about her cradle bed;
> And her little night-cap hides
> Every breath of air besides,

read a popular nursery rhyme. Margaret Izard Manigault was convinced that her daughter's cold in October 1814 had been "brought on by sleeping in a bed without curtains," and Catharine Beecher, writing in 1841, still thought high-posted bedsteads best, as it was often important to hang curtains "to protect from cold currents of air." But they were not needed in warm-weather months and were taken down, as they harbored dust and one "should not take cold by not having them."[10]

Additionally, bed curtains offered a modicum of privacy in rooms where there were several beds. Anne Royall was relieved to find two good beds with curtains at Wells Tavern, near Fayetteville, Alabama, one December night in 1817: "I was quite delighted with a place of concealment, should travellers arrive; and, drawing the curtains of a princely bed close, I lay still and snug out of sight." Mrs. Royall was unusually fortunate to have not only the luxury of bed curtains but also the privilege of sleeping alone in an American inn. Sleeping several to a bed was commonplace in early America, both at home and on the road; and drawn bed curtains were no guarantee of privacy, as Thomas Twining reluctantly discovered while staying with a

Quaker merchant in Philadelphia in 1795, where he was awakened by someone who "drew back the curtains, and placed himself at my side."[11]

But in multibedded chambers that held master and mistress, children, and often a servant, the curtains at least provided some seclusion. Testimony to the disparate sleeping arrangements possible was the demoniac scene in Alexander Anderson's New York bedchamber on 10 April 1798, five days after the birth of a son. Waking in a nightmare, this well-known wood engraver flew out of bed "with the most horrible bellowing," broke loose from his wife's grip, disentangled himself from the bed curtains, knocked over the toilet table and two or three chairs, sent the tongs and shovel clattering to the hearth, and careened into the bed where his mother-in-law, the nurse, and apparently the infant were sleeping! Some years later, when he argued against the use of bed curtains in his *The Domestic Encyclopedia*, Anthony Willich equivocated, "We do not, however, mean to insinuate, that curtains ought to be universally abandoned, as there may occur a variety of instances, in which the laws of propriety and *decorum* might render them useful and necessary."[12]

The richness and expense of some of these bed hangings are startling to us today. Plunket Fleeson, that improbably named Philadelphia upholsterer, billed the wealthy John Cadwalader a large sum in 1770 for a resplendent bed. The price included making "a phestoon bed full trim'd, with plumes, laces, & head board, fringed," sewing two "Venetian" window curtains that would draw up into poufs, supplying fifty-six yards of fine red-and-white copperplate cotton, sixteen yards of linen for lining the valances, one hundred and eighteen yards of fringe for the bed and window curtains, fifty-seven tassels, twenty-five yards of silk lace, and thirty-two yards of white-twilled lace.[13]

The earliest hangings were sewn from a variety of woolen materials. Sarah Anna Emery pictured her grandmother's bed hung with green moreen curtains, edged by a heavy gimp trim. The luxuriant trimmings along the edges of bed curtains and valances were important to the visual effect and were often of boldly contrasting color or material; while green, which was considered "very refreshing to the eye," was often recommended for the prevailing color of bed hangings. Mrs. William Parkes was yet advocating the use of moreen curtains in 1829, long after the introduction of cottons, as they did not require lining as did the then-popular chintz hangings. On occasion there were crewel-embroidered bed curtains, such as those that delighted Dorothy Dudley in an upper chamber of Joseph Lee's eighteenth-century home in Cambridge, Massachusetts, "all worked in gorgeous colored worsteds by the aristocratic fingers of Mrs. Lee," and lively with "gay figures of birds perched upon trees scarcely larger than themselves, the tempting strawberries corresponding in size to the plants by their side, the dogs and deer, and animals I could find no names for."[14]

As the eighteenth century advanced, such brightly colored, fanciful tableaux became generally available through the introduction of copperplate-printed cottons and block-printed chintzes. The aspect of the bedchamber was, in fact, transformed by these startlingly large-patterned cottons, some fifty yards of which might flutter about the bed and windows. In a sense, these fabrics were the picture books of the period, offering a fantastical, panoramic world of vibrant color and exotic motif to children whose books were scantily illustrated with small, staid, black-and-white wood engravings. "How well I remember lying in bed looking at the peacocks and other figures on the chintz curtain of my four post bedstead," wrote William Davis of Plymouth, Massachusetts; and Caroline King lovingly recalled the bedstead in their

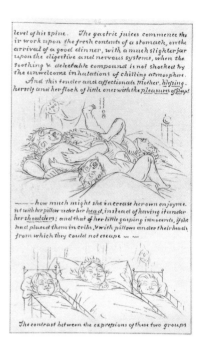

The Breath of Life; or, Mal-Respiration and Its Effects upon the Enjoyment of and Life of Man. Drawing by George Catlin for a book illustration. 1862. Museum of Fine Arts, Boston; M. and M. Karolik Collection of American Water Colors and Drawings, 1800–1875. Catlin's drawing humorously illustrates both the mid-nineteenth-century belief that pure, unimpeded air was the first premise of health and the truism that children often slept with their parents. When used, cribs were drawn up to the bed to facilitate infant care

East Chamber of the Peter Cushing House. Hingham, Massachusetts. Oil on canvas, by Ella Emory. c. 1878. Private collection. The copperplate-printed bed trappings in this late-nineteenth-century view confirm the supposition that furnishings were not always up-to-date, particularly on the upper floors. A prototypical chintz-covered easy chair and an old-fashioned Queen Anne side chair flank the bedstead. A small bedside rug and a straw carpet were common to chambers. In winter the strip of highly flammable straw carpet before the fire should be covered with baize to protect it from flying sparks

Salem spare room, hung with a canopy and curtains of soft, cream-color India cotton, scattered with small bunches of bright flowers. With obvious emotion the then elderly woman avowed, "A shadow of the childish awe with which I used to tiptoe into that sacred apartment, and gaze at the Eastern splendor of fruit and flowers, comes over me now as I write. I remember putting out a timid little finger to touch those forbidden fruits, and then quickly drawing it back as if I had committed a sacrilege." The bed had become a storied enclosure. Indeed, copperplates possessed great narrative power, and red, blue, purple, pink, or "chocolate" inks colorfully set forth all kinds of scenes and powerfully evoked all manner of circumstances. William Dunlap surrounded a narrow bed in an 1836 novel with scenes of "Lord Anson, his ship, his sailors, and the groves and fountains of the isles of those delightful climes"; while "William Penn's Treaty with the Indians" was the action-packed copperplate scene that encircled a bed in John Penn's Philadelphia home, Lansdowne, in 1788.[15]

Linen of checked pattern was much used in eighteenth-century chambers, with either red or blue with white being the universal favorite, although green-check furniture also had a following and a Philadelphia merchant carried "Crimson & Yellow Furniture Check" in 1774. Woven plaids were conventional. Sarah Frazier could never forget that dreadful day in 1777 when a band of British soldiers had ransacked her Chadds Ford home, rushing upstairs and taking the plaid curtains that belonged to a field bedstead, throwing them at her servant with the saucy suggestion that she put them on as a petticoat—which she, poor thing, tried to do but "in her efforts got her head through a slit and became completely entangled."[16]

Of course, the wealthy might boast of silk hangings. By 1840 notable choices for bed curtains included bright chintz, wool damask, rich silk, or broad-striped dimity. White dimity had become popular in the late eighteenth century, at a time when the fashionably dressed miss should be draped in Grecian white—the better to resemble a Diana or Aphrodite—and white bedchambers had come into vogue. White hangings would maintain their supremacy throughout the nineteenth century, as they could be easily washed and might "thus be always contrived to have a clean appearance," but there was mounting debate as to the hygiene and safety of bed curtains at all. Anthony Willich had argued in 1802 that children's beds, at least, should be stripped of curtains because, among other things, they were a fire hazard.[17]

New England Woman; or, A Lady from Connecticut. Oil on canvas, by Cecilia Beaux. 1895. Pennsylvania Academy of the Fine Arts, Philadelphia. Chambers furnished entirely in white had become fashionable in the late eighteenth century, and this portrait of Julia Leavitt Richards illustrates the old style lingering on. Innumerable are the early accounts of bed linens "white as snow" and a pleasure to behold

Bedchamber Fire. Wilmington, Delaware. Watercolor by Sophie du Pont. December 1832. Courtesy The Nemours Foundation, Wilmington. The proximity of candle flame to bed hangings, window curtains, and mosquito netting was always dangerous and sometimes fatal. A distracted servant putting a child to bed, a nursing mother tending her infant, a midnight reader: all are documented scenarios for a bedchamber conflagration. This particular fire, caused by the incautious snuffing of a candle, was successfully quenched by a motley and sleepy fire brigade armed with pitchers, pails, and chamber pots

This accusation was repeatedly proven valid. It is perhaps easier to understand the frequency with which bed textiles caught fire if we glimpse into Mary Guion's Westchester bedchamber at half past ten on the evening of 21 April 1803, for there she is writing "in the bead the candle sits on it my paper on the coverlids." "Never read in bed," commanded Catharine Beecher in 1841, "lest you fall asleep, and the bed be set on fire." But many a letter was written and many a book was read in bed regardless of the danger: "Being naturally an excellent mimic," chuckled a mischievous Massachusetts girl, "I often crept out of bed; went to the foot of the stairs leading to the sleeping apartments of my aunts, who were very prone to reading late o'nights, and, imitating the tone of my grandmother, said: 'Blow out your lights, this minute!' then stole laughingly back again, as I instantly heard the obedient puff!"[18]

By the fourth decade of the nineteenth century, concern was intensifying over the salubrity of bed curtains, which were charged with harboring dust and vermin, impeding a free flow of fresh air about the bed, or trapping stale air within. The ideal bedchamber of the 1850s, 1860s, and 1870s must be clean, spacious, lofty, unencumbered with unnecessary furniture and, most important, well aired. Mrs. William Parkes had submitted the equation of airy rooms to health and cheerfulness in 1829, and though everyone might not have the privilege and advantages of large, airy rooms, she conceded, yet "all may endeavour to keep their apartments clean, free from disagreeable odours, and may, also, contrive to have their windows open at proper seasons, that a change of air may be obtained." Catharine Beecher thought that it would be impossible to overstress the importance of well-ventilated sleeping rooms, and Mrs. M. L. Scott and others concurred that one could not have too much fresh air on the bed throughout the day. Once these concerns for hygiene were conjoined with those for safety, the use of bed curtains diminished. A. J. Downing might remark in his *The Architecture of Country Houses* (1850) that the "high four-post bedstead, with curtains, still common in England, is almost entirely laid aside in the United States for the French bedstead, low, and without curtains"; and Amelia Murray was very pleased to find a four-post bed in a New Orleans chamber in 1855 because "I never saw anything but French bedsteads in the North." Many French bedsteads were, in fact, at least partially draped; but the general trend throughout the second half of the nineteenth century, as power tools supplied Victorian chambers with conspicuous headboards and footboards—veritable cliffs of gleaming veneer and fancy carving—was either to throw back the curtains and discard them entirely or to retain a half-canopy with draperies at the head only.[19]

As long as there were bed curtains, these must accord, both in material and in

The Old, Old Story. Lithograph by Haskell and Allen. Boston. c. 1872. Peters Collection, Smithsonian Institution, Washington, D.C. Throughout the nineteenth century there was mounting debate over the healthfulness of bed curtains, and by the date of this print the majority vote was against them. No longer concealed in drapery folds, the headboard, such as this example in the Renaissance Revival style, might rise up in a towering triumph of carved walnut. The bed with its pillow shams, carpet with hearthrug, lamp with lamp mat, rocking chair with antimacassar, workstand, and bedside night table were standard chamber furnishings in the Victorian period and lend veracity to a scene which to some must have seemed only too familiar

"Why, Miss Anne," said Lucy, "isn't it any darker than this?" Engraving in [Jacob Abbott], *Cousin Lucy's Conversations* (Boston, 1842). Little Lucy's trundle bed has been pulled out from under the big bed for use in this nocturnal scene. A looking glass in the window pier hangs suspended so as to allow the glass to tilt forward, facilitating its use at the dressing table

form, with the window curtains. Before the American Revolution, and in some areas long afterward, there were few window curtains in comparison with bed hangings. But when window curtains are listed in early-eighteenth-century inventories, they are most often in the room with the best bed, underscoring the supremacy of this room at that time. Eliza Leslie reminded her readership in 1840 that the bed curtains and window curtains must be of the same material and corresponding form — counsel that Catharine Beecher reiterated a year later, adding the bed quilt to the ensemble. By 1870 a matching portiere might hang in the doorway. If there were window seats and squabs in the best room downstairs, the arrangement was echoed in the best chambers upstairs, where the squabs must also contribute to the unity. In fact, all upholstered furniture, and even the wallpaper, must be a part of the color harmony. When George Washington ordered a dozen chairs with seats of three different colors they were "to suit the paper of three of the bed Chambers." Two years later, in 1759, he sent an order to Robert Cary & Co. in London, specifying a tester bed with blue or blue-and-white curtains, matching bed coverlet, window curtains, cornices, and four chair seats to suit the wallpaper, "in order to make the whole furniture of this room uniformly handsome and genteel." Benjamin Franklin envisioned a similarly refined chamber for his Philadelphia home when he sent his wife from London in 1758 "56 Yards of Cotton printed curiously from Copper Plates, a new Invention, to make Bed and Window Curtains." But he, poor well-intentioned husband, erred in bedchamber decor etiquette, for he also sent her "7 Yards Chair Bottoms printed in the same Way, very neat; these were my Fancy; but Mrs. Stevenson tells me I did wrong not to buy both of the same Colour."[20]

Early household inventories suggest that there was usually only one bed in the best bedchamber (although secondary chambers might well be crowded with more). But the image of privacy and seclusion that this evokes can be erroneous, particularly if there were young children in the family. Chambers that by day looked relatively unencumbered might by night be littered with supplemental pallets, mattresses,

trundle beds, cradles, and cribs. When Anne Eliza Clark Kane pictured her Providence chamber in July 1812, she had two of her children in a trundle bed at the foot of her bed and two on a mattress that was every night spread on the floor; and when Elizabeth Wirt catalogued the sleeping arrangements at home in Washington in April 1820, her teenage daughter was beside her in the high bed, her toddler son and a younger daughter on a pallet at the foot of the bed. Each time a new baby was added to a household (often every two years), there might well have to be a reshuffling of these sleeping patterns. "Grandmother, when her first baby came, took it into her own bed," explained one author. "When another baby came to crowd it out, there was the trundle-bed that stood under the big bed all day, and rolled out at night with a sleepy rumble. And when more babies still came to crowd the trundle-bed, the first baby, a big boy, six years old now, had a bed made for him at the head of the back stairs, or up garret, under the sloping eaves."[21]

Little children frequently slept in their parents' room, particularly if they were infants, if there was no other responsible person for them to sleep with, or if they were ill. By the time Mrs. William Parkes cautioned that infants should never be left to sleep alone, in 1829, generations of American mothers had already followed such advice. Ann Maury thought, in 1832, that the devotion of Virginia mothers to their children "surpasses any thing I have ever seen elsewhere. I have not known the most delicate female shrink from the care of her Infant at night, & generally they have more than one in their chamber at night." Nursing infants often slept in their mothers' beds. Minerva Rodgers, who lived at Sion Hill in Havre de Grace, Maryland, told her distant husband in October 1807 that their infant son John "is so fond of his mothers bosom that he never sleeps quietly unless his head is resting on it." Three years later, she penned a picture of yet another lively bedfellow, year-old Robert, who "rides every thing—all his playthings are turned into ponies, and his eyes are no sooner open than he climbs up and bestrides the bolster, taking a braid of my hair for his bridle and whips and chirrups like a second Phaeton, till his nurse takes him away." Even if the baby slept in a cradle by day, it would often join its mother by night, and this arrangement, which precluded the necessity of her getting out of bed and perhaps taking cold, may partially explain the relatively sparse mention of cribs and cradles in early documents. Anne Eliza Clark Kane apologized to her mother on New Year's Day 1813 for a letter so badly written, "but I am rocking [the] Cradle with one foot all the time (I have been so extravagant as to buy me one)," and closed with the intelligence, "I am going to turn in by the side of my little boy whom I take from his Cradle every night and lay on my pillow."[22]

If there was a crib or cradle in the parents' chamber, it was placed conveniently next to the bed. J. C. Loudon suggested that the height of this crib correspond to that of the large bed, that it be made with one side to lift out, and that it be fastened by hooks and eyes to the side of the mother's bed, "so that she may have access to the child during the night, by merely stretching out her arms, and taking it to her." Alone in Norfolk, Virginia, in May 1805, William Wirt wrote with loneliness to his wife, picturing his chamber where "by the bedside stood our Robert's crib, just as he had slept in it . . . and on the other side, up in the corner, our Laura's cradle"; while Benjamin Franklin Perry, visiting in Columbia, South Carolina, reached out automatically in his sleep to make sure his son's crib covers were up, awakening to find that he wasn't at home after all.[23]

Additionally, when children were ill they were regularly promoted to the master chamber, where it would be easier to nurse and keep a close watch on them, and where there might be a light by which to administer medicines and a fire to keep them warm. An anxious Fanny Appleton Longfellow pictured herself one June night in 1848 moving the crib of a sick child into her chamber, where she "held his little hand all night." Sarah Logan Fisher brought her little Billy, who was suffering from "inflammatory fev[e]r," into her Philadelphia chamber in December 1787, noting in her diary seven weeks later that Billy had gone back to the nursery for the first time since he was ill. Caroline King recalled that it was a custom in her family that if she or a sister were sick they would be brought into their parents' bedroom and tucked into

Conversation in the Sick Chamber. Engraving in Mrs. [Sarah Stickney] Ellis, *The Family Monitor and Domestic Guide* (New York, 1844). The Winterthur Library: Printed Book and Periodical Collection. The conversation here seems to be a silent one of understanding. No loud noises were to disturb the requisite peace of the sick chamber. The patient has found comfortable sanctuary in the recesses of the easy chair while his bed is being refreshed. In cases of illness, bed linens were to be frequently changed and the chamber kept sweet and clean. When necessary, the air might be improved by sprinkling the bed and floor with vinegar, lemon juice, or some other strong vegetable acid. It was thought advisable to take the bed hangings down in cases of severe illness

the trundle bed. Here she awakened one evening, sick with a cold, and, peeping out from underneath her many coverings, saw a bright little scene of fireside comfort, which she fortunately shared with us: "A wood-fire was burning in the Franklin stove—'The light stand' (as we always called a pretty old-fashioned three legged round table) with two brass lamps upon it, was drawn up cosily in front of the fire, while on one side sat my mother with her workbasket, and on the other my father, wrapped in a long Russian dressing gown, a real coat of many colors, reading *A Midsummer Night's Dream* aloud to her [in] true Darby and Joan fashion."[24]

The pair of chairs in which Caroline's parents sat before their fire were undoubtedly two of a larger number in the room. Six were often found in chambers, and that was the quantity Rebecca Rawle Shoemaker suggested for her daughter's bedroom when she made that list of the basics required for housekeeping in 1783. Boston leather-dresser William Hall had six black walnut chairs with crimson harrateen (lightweight wool) bottoms in his red front chamber and six blue-bottomed ones in his blue-green back chamber in 1771, while there were sets of a half-dozen chairs in at least three chambers at William Banford's Charleston home in 1767. As in the parlor, these chairs were to be set back against the wall so "as not to be stumbled over in the dark, should you have occasion to rise in the night." Particularly in secondary chambers they might be old-fashioned, having been demoted from the parlors and banished upstairs. Low chairs, what we today call slipper chairs, are found with some frequency in bedchambers, where they would have facilitated cradle rocking as well as aspects of the toilette. Benjamin Godin had three "Low Chaires" in one Charleston chamber in 1749; and 124 years later, Florence Hartley could yet recommend the use of a low chair in the bedroom "to use while changing the shoes or washing the feet." Simple straw-bottom or rush-bottom chairs were common to chambers, and by the opening years of the nineteenth century painted "fancy" chairs had become popular.

On occasion there were rocking chairs as well; Eliza Leslie, who had banned them from the parlors, advocated their use in the chambers. Thomas Tilestone had two in his Boston southwest chamber as early as 1794, along with a dozen chairs and a large easy chair.[25]

Since the first half of the eighteenth century, an easy chair, or what is sometimes now called a wing chair, had been a regular feature in bedchambers, where it was often placed beside the bed or near the fire. Anne Eliza Clark Kane insouciantly laid her month-old son in the "easy chair by my bed and without conceiving it possible such a child could roll out"—but roll out he did, frightening his mother more than harming himself. The easy chair offered a comfortable place to rest. Elizabeth Wirt pictured herself "crouched . . . up in my easy chair determined to take a nap"; and Sarah Anna Emery "unintentionally fell asleep" in Susy Dole's capacious easy chair. Because of its frequent use and expensive upholstery, the easy chair was usually protected by a washable slipcover; in fact, there were usually two or three cases to each easy chair so that it might always have a clean cover. A potty might be concealed beneath the seat—a very common practice. Ribton Hutchison had an "Easy Chair with a Pan" at home in Charleston in 1753; and when J. C. Loudon illustrated what he considered a very comfortable easy chair in his *Encyclopaedia* in 1833, it too had a movable cushion as a seat, beneath which was discreetly concealed a "night convenience."[26]

With wings to deflect drafts, ample proportions, warm, down-filled seat, and potty convenience, the easy chair was admirably suited to the use of the elderly and infirm. When Anne Grant first came into the presence of the imposing Catherine Van Rensselaer Schuyler of The Flats near Albany in the 1760s, "she was sitting; and filled a great chair, from which she seldom moved"; and when Mrs. Samuel Cary called on a venerable friend, aged about eighty-six, in October 1814, she too "was seated in an old-fashioned easy-chair with a crimson damask covering." Susan Lesley claimed that her mother, following the birth of each of her eleven children, was able—the very next day—to sit up in her large easy chair, with her mending basket and book beside her. The easy chair offered a comfortable seat not only to the convalescent patient but to those kindly neighbors or family members who sat hours watching by the bedside of the sick. Someone was often sick at home in early America, and frequently for long periods of time. Abigail Adams, suffering from "inflammatory rhumatism" in Philadelphia in March 1792, complained, "Tis now the sixth week since I have been out of the door of this Chamber, or moved in a larger circle than from my Bed to the chair." Bedchambers had to be made comfortable for nurse and patient alike. "It has to be remembered," Robert Kerr counseled in 1865, "that every Bedroom must be considered not merely as a sleeping-room but as occasionally a sickroom."[27]

The sick room must be quiet. There should be no superfluous conversations. Creaking hinges and grating locks should be immediately oiled, and attendants were to abjure rustling silks for washable cottons and tread lightly in shoes that did not squeak. Noisy children must be hushed:

> When Philip's good mama was ill
> The servant begg'd he would be still
> Because the doctor and the nurse
> Had said that noise would make her worse.

Mrs. John Powell. Boston. Oil on canvas, by John Singleton Copley. 1764. The Cleveland Museum of Art; gift of Ellery Sedgwick, Jr., in memory of Mabel Cabot Sedgwick. Well-stuffed, broad-winged easy chairs offered a warm, draft-free comfort. Here an eighty-year-old widow, Anna Susan Dummer Powell, is familiarly portrayed in her wonted seat—the easy chair. The earliest ambition of one New England miss had been to grow up and wear a cap and sit in an easy chair knitting and looking comfortable, just as her mother did

During a period when President Washington lay ill in New York, Eliza Susan Morton Quincy recalled "seeing straw laid down in the adjacent streets, and chains drawn across those nearest the house, to prevent his being disturbed by carts and carriages"; and Samuel Canby Rumford remembered an example of similar solicitude during an epidemic of typhoid fever in Wilmington, Delaware, when several streets were closed to traffic, or a thick layer of straw was laid before the house of very ill patients "to prevent them being disturbed by the noises made by the feet of a horse or the wheels of the wagon." The sick chamber, as all apartments, was to be well aired but not drafty. Charles White suggested in 1793 that the door and windows be opened every day in warm weather, and that the fireplace opening not be stopped up with a fireboard or similar contrivance, but rather left open so that it might act as a ventilator. Furthermore, the sick chamber was to be kept "as sweet, as clean, and as free from any disagreeable smell, as any other part of the house" by frequent changes of linen and the immediate removal of all offensive matter.[28]

If there were aspects of the hospital ward in the sick chamber, there also had to be some of the comforts of the sitting room, for a patient and his attendants might spend weeks, even months, in this room. Comfortable chairs, good fires, and adequate lighting were essential, as were tables for eating, writing, and sewing. Chamber closets often contained a number of eating and drinking vessels, along with such accoutrements as sugar canisters and rum cases, attesting to the multifunctionalism of these rooms. Maria Silliman Church whiled away the final weeks before the birth of her second child, on 15 February 1834, in her bedchamber, sewing and reading aloud with a cousin who had come to assist. Four weeks later she wrote, "Little baby is now a month old and I am emancipated from my bed room." This was the standard interval between delivery and resuming household duties, but complications could keep the new mother chamber-bound for much longer. As many women of childbearing age might expect to spend a month in this way about every two or three years, a goodly proportion of their married life was thus spent confined to a bedchamber. At the time of the birth, this room became something of a reception room, as neighboring women came to help at the delivery, and there followed days of formal "sitting up" visits, during which female friends came to congratulate or condole, depending upon the health of mother and child. Sarah Logan Fisher noted in her diary in December 1776 that at the Quaker Monthly Meeting "Susy Lightfoot appeared in Testimony, entreating young Mothers not to make such great preparations for their Lying in as they generally do, & to avoid those formal Visitings upon the occasion which are too much made use of amongst us." But the custom persisted into the nineteenth century, and expectant mothers often went to considerable trouble to ensure that their chamber present a handsome appearance at this "public" time. Those who delivered in the summer months, when the bedstead was often devoid of curtains, had the curtains hung especially for the occasion and taken down about a month later at the conclusion of the visits. Sarah Logan Fisher was busy "Washing & getting my Bed put up" on 17 August 1779, a job which she finished on September 3, feeling that "I am now quite ready in that way"; a son was born shortly thereafter. Two years later, one of her maids was again "putting up my Bed in the Front Room," while another was "scrub[b]ing & getting ready" for the birth of another little boy. Preparations in August 1783 included "ironing my Beds," "cleaning the Paint," "whitewashing," "putting up my Bed," and "scrubbing the chambers that I am now nearly ready" for the birth of yet another son. And three years later, a month after the birth of a stillborn daughter, she sighed, "Betty took down my Blue Bed—will it ever go up again or not," implying that these blue bed hangings were reserved for the ritual of childbirth. Elizabeth Bleecker McDonald of New York had upholsterer Harry Lyons "put up my Valence to my Bed and Windows" on 20 July 1801; a son was born on 5 August, and on 8 September, she "took down the Valents of my Bed." The same ritual preceded the birth of a daughter in July 1804. Elizabeth Wirt, big with child six weeks before the birth of her son Henry, in June 1818, and "slipping about, one side at a time, *crab fashion*," wished that she had an upholsterer "here for a few days, to put up my curtains for me—for I hardly can master the courage to set about such a complicated affair." The hanging of the bed curtains specifically for birthings had something to do with concerns for health and, perhaps, privacy, but it had much more to do with pride. Women naturally wished to have their chambers appear to advantage at these social times and compare favorably with those of their friends. A handsomely draped bed in color harmony with other chamber furnishings would have played a strategic role in this.[29]

A supplementary harmony and elegance was achieved by ordering the bedchamber furniture carved en suite. Such a companionate grouping in the eighteenth-century chamber might include high chest, dressing table, and chairs; and in the nineteenth it might comprise bedstead, bureau, washstand, and wardrobe. The soaring high chest on S-curved cabriole legs and its matching dressing table were a prominent feature in many early northern chambers—the South did not favor this form. Nathaniel Hawthorne endorsed such "ante-Revolutionary Furniture" in 1842, feeling that "after all, the moderns have invented nothing better, as chamber furniture, than these chests of drawers, which stand on four long, slender legs, and rear an absolute tower of mahogany to the cieling the whole terminating in a fantastically carved summit." The high chest, with its broad expanse of figured wood grain and tiers of bright brasses, might be particularly attractive by candlelight and firelight. Mary Cadwalader Jones, who was born in Philadelphia in 1850, could remember lying close to the floor in her trundle bed, "watching the reflection of the wood fire in the polished brasses and mahogany of a towering chest of drawers." In colonial chambers of the urban well-to-do, a japanned high chest, and perhaps a coordinating dressing table and looking glass, might well contribute to the pageantry of this nocturnal apartment. Standing out in relief from the lustrous black-striated vermilion grounds—suggestive of glowing tortoiseshell—came an array of exotic figures in gilded gesso. Festive Chinamen and flying cranes, arched bridges and apocryphal beasts, preposterous pagodas and protective parasols might all be set in motion by the capricious flicker of burning taper and flaming logs. Just such a handsome grouping enlivened John Billings's Boston home in 1763: a japanned chest of drawers—decked out with beakers and glasses—a japanned dressing table, and a long japanned looking glass. The primary function of the high chest was the storage of clothes and other textiles, but in the early years of the eighteenth century flat-top high chests, similar to Billings's, did supplementary service as a display surface for china and glassware.[30]

Chests of drawers, double chests, bureaus, presses, and wardrobes provided for additional textile storage in drawers and on shelves. Inventories that catalogue the contents of these pieces suggest that the larger chests and presses were capable of holding enormous quantities. Table linens and bed linens were often stored in the room with the best bed—in the seventeenth century this might be the parlor and in the next century it would be the best bedchamber. Security and convenience may have prompted this. But whatever the reasons, it must have been soul-satisfying to the mistress of the household to know that the chests and clothes presses in her room were replete with clothing, bed linens and table linens, quilts, coverlets, towels, and even clouts, alias diapers.

Trunks appear with frequency in early chambers and in 1841 Catharine Beecher yet alludes to "the trunks in a chamber" as if they were still a universal feature. John Coles's "Trunk of Cloathes" in Charleston and David Ochterlong's "Trunk [of] Family Linnen consisting of Table Cloths sheeting Towells &c" offer examples of prototypical contents. Gilded leather chests or trunks appear with some regularity in inventories of the wealthy, both North and South, and would certainly have contributed to an animated, glittering evening scene.[31]

Portrait of Mrs. Catherine Cuyler. Albany, New York. Oil on canvas, by an unknown American artist. c. 1790. Collection Albany Institute of History and Art. The taste for white encompassed both costume and chamber furnishings, and this sitter was clearly a fashionable lady, for her portrait was painted when toilet tables skirted in white were just becoming popular. On the table sits a large pincushion filled with pins of various sizes with which to hold one's costume together. Sometimes the dressing table itself might serve as a pincushion, for covers of white Marseilles quilting with raised designs would soon come into vogue

There might well be a desk and a shelf of books in the bedchamber. Those particularly fortunate might even have a private closet adjoining the chamber, furnished as a study—an arrangement that had been standard in Old World homes from the sixteenth century. William Young of Boston had both a large red cedar desk and a cherry desk in his chamber in 1750, as well as part of a "Twilight," or toilet table, and a dressing box. There often was a dressing box on the table or the case piece used for dressing. Ephraim Chambers in his *Cyclopedia; or, An Universal Dictionary* (1783) listed the representative contents of a lady's dressing box as being paints, pomatums, essences, patches, pincushion, powder box, and brushes; and Sarah Frazier reported that during the fracas in Chadds Ford one of those British soldiers went into a downstairs bedroom and took from a dressing table a dressing box, "throwing pin cushions, combs, etc. on the floor." By 1840 Eliza Leslie was suggest-

ing, "On the toilet table keep always your dressing-case, your bottles of cologne, Florida water, etc., and a large pincushion, filled with pins of different sizes." A goodly supply of pins enabled a lady to hold her costume together in that age before zippers, snaps, or Velcro.[32]

For the dressing table, covers of snowy white Marseilles quilting with thickly padded designs served as a supplemental pincushion. This type of cover was made from the same quilting used for bed counterpanes or coverlets and ladies' petticoats. James Smyth had "2 dressing Tables Cover Lids" at home in Charleston in 1764; and when Faith Silliman returned from shopping in Hartford, Connecticut, in February 1837, she told her mother she had found "the most beautiful white counterpane I ever saw, they call it Marseilles, but tis just like in quality to the bureau covers that you said you made out of an old skirt of Grandmama's." Dressing tables and bureaus might alternatively display "carpets," or scarves, of damask, diaper, calico, or dimity, trimmed with fringe or frills, for unless marble-topped they were always to be covered. *The Workwoman's Guide* (1838) noted that some preferred a piece of oilcloth bound with ribbon upon their dressing tables, which they approved as being not only neat but durable. "Handsome oyl cloths for Tables" were advertised in the *Boston Gazette* in 1761, and Andrew Oliver of that city owned "1 Chamber Table & Oile Cloth" in March 1774.[33]

Dressing tables of plain, unpainted wood with white covers and full, deep, floor-length skirts of muslin came into fashion in the late 1770s and continued to find advocates throughout the nineteenth century. Sarah Anna Emery admired just such a table, "tastily covered with white muslin and ornamented by blue bows," which she had seen in a Newburyport best chamber; and Mary Palmer Tyler was proud that, although there were no carpets in any room but the parlor at her far humbler Vermont home, she did have curtains to the bed and windows and two white-dressed toilet tables. Anne Royall shared no such esteem for these flouncy trifles, complaining from the South, where she found them in universal use in 1838:

Beau Nasty. Charleston, South Carolina. Watercolor by Charles Fraser. c. 1800. Courtesy The Charleston Museum, Charleston, South Carolina. This actor puts the final touches on his costume with the aid of a small standing dressing glass, or "swinger," which could be rotated back and forth for greater viewing efficiency

Then comes high semi-circular tables in the chambers, they are called dressing tables, and from their uniform appearance, one would think they are indispensable; do the people ever travel? if they have never, they ought; they will see that no such abominable things are at all necessary. I could not imagine what the things meant, they are always in the way, placed exactly in the place where they ought not, that is, in front of some window, or where you wish to place your writing or reading table; if you offer to remove them out of the way, you are sure to get your hands stuck to pieces with the pins which confine an immense long apron in which this table is enveloped.[34]

Case pieces such as bureau tables and chests of drawers were also used as dressing tables. Small dressing glasses that could be swung back and forth for greater viewing efficiency often stood upon this dressing table, bureau table, or chest of drawers. By 1840, however, Eliza Leslie would pronounce these "swingers" out of favor, "as they scarcely show more than your head, and are easily upset." Rather, she continued, "it is now customary to fix a large glass upon the wall at the back of the table or bureau; suspending it by a double ribbon to a strong hook, and making the string long enough to allow the glass to incline considerably forward, so as to give the persons that look into it a better view of their figures."[35]

A bureau with a looking glass attached was a compromise acceptable to many in the early nineteenth century. Mrs. Leslie thought the most elegant dressing tables to be those of mahogany "with marble tops, having at the back a large mirror, with candle-branches or lamp-brackets on each side." Candle arms attached to the dressing glass would certainly have facilitated dressing in a tenebrous room by freeing the hands, unless one had, like the Chinn girls in New Orleans in the late 1830s, "two dusky maids to follow . . . all about, and hold [the candles] at proper points so the process of the toilet could be satisfactorily accomplished." Sconce glasses—looking glasses with candle arms attached—were favored for well-appointed chambers in the eighteenth century and, as in the parlor, pairs were particularly admired. The grouping of "a dressing Table & Glass & a pr Glass Shades" in James Postell's Charleston "Blue Room" in August 1773 suggests yet another attempt at efficiently lighting the dressing process by protecting the candles from drafts.[36]

The growing emphasis on personal cleanliness that began to manifest itself in the second half of the eighteenth century brought with it a novel diversity of furniture forms to assist in the care and cleansing of the body. Dressing tables, washstands, commodes, and beau brummels all frequently secreted looking glasses within their often-elaborate mechanisms. Washhand stands began to appear with frequency in the 1750s and remained in the bedchamber, or perhaps the dressing room, with a towel horse on which to dry towels nearby, long after the chamber bathing tub had sauntered down the hall and to the back of the house, where there was a more explicit "bathroom." The earliest washstands were of rounded section above a tripod base and were designed to hold a washbasin and a flaskett, or bottle. This bottle would burgeon in the nineteenth century into a gargantuan pitcher holding at least a gallon of water. The stand, too, changed, undergoing something of a geometric evolution—from rounded in section to triangular or squared and on to rectangular. With each successive metamorphosis it grew larger, in response to the growing importance of washing.

Cleanliness of person had been stressed in eighteenth-century guides to polite

Woman Bathing. Drypoint and soft-ground etching in color, by Mary Cassatt. c. 1891. National Gallery of Art, Washington, D.C.; Rosenwald Collection. The sponge bath in the chamber remained the norm in many homes throughout the nineteenth century, decades after running water had brought ease and comfort to the fashionably fitted bathrooms of the urban elite

behavior, but the nineteenth century placed even greater emphasis on the frequency and thoroughness of the ablutions as cleanliness and health were equated. The second American edition of the *Domestic Encyclopedia* stipulated in 1821 that every family ought to be supplied with the proper conveniences for warm and cold bathing, advocating a tepid bath three times a week "at least" in summer, "as the practice is not only very cleanly but highly healthful." By 1837 Eliza Farrar would insist that the whole body be washed in soap and water at least once every twenty-four hours. A heightened regard for privacy grew apace with these more exacting dictates of cleanliness. Eliza Farrar acknowledged, "Where two or three occupy the same room, without any dressing-room, or closet, large enough to wash in, it is impossible for the toilet to be properly made. A person must be alone and safe from intrusion for a quarter of an hour, every morning, in order to wash thoroughly; and the heads of families ought to afford every member of them the opportunity of being thus alone." She then suggested to young ladies that if they could not find this privacy in the morning they should try to command it at night, washing themselves "when the eyes of younger sisters are closed in sleep, or by retiring a quarter of an hour earlier than an elder sister." Some proposed the use of screens to promote privacy, and chamber screens might include the large, several-leaved folding screens useful for putting near doors to block drafts, and smaller screens of two folds, which were considered "very convenient to place by every washing stand, when two persons occupy the room." Catharine Beecher thought paper or chintz a tasteful covering for these lighter screens.[37]

Private dressing rooms began to appear with greater frequency in the 1770s. These apartments might be furnished with a dressing table, washstand, wardrobe, or chest of drawers, and there should be a fireplace to warm both body and clothes. Some thought it appropriate for this dressing room to contain sitting-room furniture as well — for example, a sofa that might be made into a bed, or a large easy chair, a sofa table, and a bookcase. Peter Delancey's Charleston dressing room in 1771 was handsomely appointed with a chest of drawers, a cupboard and a desk, a bookcase, a shaving stand and glass, a fire screen, and a stool.[38]

Bathing tubs and, more infrequently, bidets might be found in either a dressing room or a separate bathroom. Samuel Kempton, tinplate worker, coppersmith, and ironsmith, addressed Manhattanites in August 1785 with a bit of hard sell for "those truly useful Machines, called Bidets, so much used in England and France"; citing their acknowledged benefit in the "renovating of constitutions injured by luxurious excesses," as well as in removing barrenness — and even "imbecility" (perhaps because of the shock treatment one received from the "coldest" water with which it was to be filled). By 1831, Catherine Chew had a bathroom in Philadelphia fitted out with a shower bath, a bathtub, a small [water] closet, a painted table, and Windsor chairs. Alternatively, there might be a bathhouse outside in the backyard with a pool for bathing or a yard shower like the one schoolgirl Anne Eliza Clark forced herself to use in August 1791, though she "did not like it very well." Stationary bathtubs were uncommon in American residences until the second half of the nineteenth century because of the expense of running water upstairs. By the 1850s and 1860s, however, in the bathrooms of the urban well-to-do, at least, there might be "tub, douche, shower, and indeed various and universal squirt, — up, down, and promiscuous." Isabella Bird Bishop admired the large, lofty, and airy bedchambers she saw in New York in the 1850s and commended the bathrooms with hot and cold running water, which she found generally on three floors.[39]

Sidney George Fisher would gloat over the plumbing improvements at his new Philadelphia home in 1852, where he was wont to rise at seven, go to his dressing room in the back section of the house, and avail himself of "a bath with hot & cold water & a water closet adjoining, also a sink to carry off waste water & slops." He found the bath "a great luxury, exhilarating & refreshing," and "far preferable to my old fashion of a sponging bath which I used because I had no other in the old house." Yet for many the sponge bath in the chamber (or the kitchen) had to suffice for years to come, and *The Practical Housekeeper* (1855) would catalogue "a small bathing tub"

as a necessary furnishing for each chamber. Indeed, the canons of the chamber sponge bath were inexorable enough that one easily comprehends Fisher's willingness to give it up. The "formidable operation" began with spreading a piece of waterproof floor cloth, two yards square, on the carpet before and under the washstand. Next one would have to carry or, if one were fortunate, have carried six to twelve quarts of the purest and coolest water, which would be splashed into a leviathan washbowl. Then the face was dipped in and the neck, back part of the head, arms, and hands sprinkled in preparation for quickly and—it was to be hoped—deftly throwing water "all over your person." The subsequent application of a coarse towel soaked up the deluge while the scourging flesh brush ignited a "healthy glow." In conclusion, one need only take up the floor cloth and empty it into the slop pail. Or, if one preferred a shower, one might stand in a bathing vat or other vessel while a trusted assistant stood on a high chair pouring water from a tin shower head or common watering pot, "which answers the purpose perfectly." That adept tinsmith Mr. Kempton could provide New Yorkers with "a small convenient apparatus" of his own manufacture for

Bathing; Invasion of the Ganders. Wilmington, Delaware. Watercolor by Sophie du Pont. August 1831. Courtesy The Nemours Foundation, Wilmington. Outside in the yard there might be a shower house to which one toted one's own (unheated) water or a bathhouse with a pool. Here the tranquil scene at the du Pont bathhouse on the banks of Brandywine Creek has been clamorously transformed by the impertinent entry of a flock of geese

the purpose of a shower bath, which, because of its size, might be used in dressing room or bedchamber without detriment to the floor and furniture. This all seemed desirable enough, but the remainder of his argument would have discouraged all but the most intrepid from experimenting with this device, for it was recommended "by the most eminent physicians, particularly where violent shock is required to quicken the circulation of the blood." Mrs. Farrar assured that with practice "you will become so expert as not to make any slop on the carpet, and thus avoid bringing your ablutions into disrepute with the higher powers." Eliza Leslie suggested, perhaps more realistically, that a breadth of "oil-cloth" be nailed down upon the carpet before the washstand, and when Polly Bennett took stock of her household furnishings in Bridport, Vermont, in 1849, she listed "1 Washstand—bowl and Pitcher/ 2 Bits Oil Cloth," in the large chamber.[40]

The bowl and pitcher were supposed to be emptied into a chamber bucket by the housemaid each morning, the vessels cleaned, and the bucket carried away for disposal of its contents. Those with fewer scruples or of more slothful inclination, however, might save themselves some steps. Eleven-year-old John Davis Long pictured himself early the morning of 21 June 1849, going "to turn the water out of the washbowl. I was turning it out of the window when It slipped out of my hands and went smash onto the ground." Four years later, Frederick Law Olmsted was awakened in Fayetteville, North Carolina, by a servant "throwing up the window, to empty out the contents of the wash bowl, etc."[41]

Olmsted's "etc." may have included the chamber pot, although Louis Philippe, the king of France between 1830 and 1848, had complained of the absence of this amenity while traveling in the South in 1797:

Nowhere are there chamber pots; we asked for one at Mr. J. Campbell's and were told that *there were broken panes in the windows.* The reply was perfect for a game of cross questions and crooked answers. There were indeed many broken panes, and it is a rare thing here to sleep in a hermetically sealed room. The other day, being in a loft, we were looking for the window or opening that should do service for a chamber pot. We found it 10 feet up, and so we insisted on some sort of receptacle; they brought us a kitchen kettle!

Nonetheless, chamber pots were often at hand, and household inventories suggest that they were stored with equal frequency in bedchamber and kitchen. In the chamber, this pot might humbly reside under the bed or it might be more genteelly housed in the lower cupboard section of the washstand or in a more particularized piece designed specifically for this purpose and called a nightstand or night table. Often the chamber pot was concealed in a chair. Sometimes this was the easy chair, as we have seen. Charles Carroll of Carrollton, who regularly ordered one, two, or three dozen whitestone chamber pots from England—suggestive of their high mortality rate as family tripped over them and servants tripped with them—needed in November 1796 "4 pewter easy chair pans." Sometimes, the chair was a so-called closestool, such as the "1 Plain neat clostool chair with 2 pans" that Carroll ordered in 1784. Or it might be craftily disguised as to function, like the "very neat Night Chair" that this same gentleman commissioned in January 1775, fastidiously specifying that it be "formed with such a Deception as to appear anything *but* what it really is *tho not* troublesome to use." Eleven years later, Thomas Sheraton would illustrate designs for pot cup-

Pernicious Effects of Reeding Tails. Wilmington, Delaware. Watercolor by Sophie du Pont. c. 1830. Courtesy The Nemours Foundation, Wilmington. This sketch—whose title is a play on words, referring to the long pleated, or reeded, skirt worn by the pretty culprit—graphically documents one inconvenience of an earlier time and suggests why some householders were annually obliged to replenish the supply of chamber pots

135

boards which "are used in genteel bed-rooms, and are sometimes finished in satin-wood, and in a style a little elevated above their use." It is interesting that there is often no mention of a night cabinet or closestool in the best chamber in early New England inventories, although secondary bedrooms might well contain one. It does not stand to reason that there was no such convenience in this most convenient of chambers; more probably it was listed in its genteel disguise.[42]

In an allied move, in Charleston chambers of the 1760s, the corner or roundabout chair became increasingly popular as a night chair—perhaps in part because it would have been easier to clean than the upholstered easy chair, and perhaps also because its secondary function could be more easily disguised. Used in parlor, sitting room, and chamber alike, and often at a desk, many roundabout chairs were not fitted with potties at all, and thus function might be concealed by enigma; moreover, scholarship on New England examples suggests that many did not have the pan-concealing, deep seat-rails that so clearly bespoke function, so that when the pan was removed the chair might look like so many other roundabout chairs in the house. Perhaps, too, the fact that this corner chair—like the triangular washstand—could be pushed into a corner speaks of a concern for privacy. Privacy, whether for oneself and the natural functions of the body or for personal possessions, was important. Thomas Sheraton advocated the use of a pot cupboard, its upper section fitted with shelves "to keep medicines to be taken in the night, or to hold other little articles which servants are not permitted to overlook."[43]

Privacy and prudery paired up as the nineteenth century advanced. Della Lutes recalled that the china chamber pot of the Victorian era and its accompanying jar had each a crocheted hood, "not so much for the purpose of decoration as a contribution to the accepted rules of modesty. For . . . a visiting girl to have made a clatter, however mild, with either device would have brought the blush of shame to her cheek."[44]

Handsome china toilet sets, often numbering some six to eight pieces and comprised of variant combinations of pitchers, washbasin, slop bowl, chamber pot, soap dish, brush dish, sponge dish, tumbler, tooth glasses, and water bottle, provided colorful accents to nineteenth-century chambers. Bellamy Partridge would never forget the "wonderful" eight-piece set of bedroom china that he and his seven sisters had purchased and divvied up to give their mother one Christmas in those "pre-plumbing days."

> It was pink with a gold band around it—washbowl, pitcher, slop jar, and other articles too numerous to mention. Indeed there were so many pieces that we could not put them under the tree and had to hide them behind the parlor door. When the right time arrived all eight of us slipped into the parlor, and then came marching back in single file, each bearing a piece of the china set. The piece that fell to my lot was the slop jar, and just to make some fun I slipped it over my head. The caper made a great hit—but after the fun was over I found I could not get my headpiece off.
>
> We all struggled valiantly for a time and then sent for the doctor. He made a careful diagnosis and shook his head. "Get me a hammer," he said. It was Father who finally struck the blow. He held a flatiron against one side of my headgear and gave the other side a smart rap with the hammer. The crockery broke into a dozen pieces, leaving me a bit groggy from the blow—but free.

City Bedroom. Probably Brooklyn, New York. Watercolor by A. Mayor. c. 1850–67. Museum of Fine Arts, Boston; M. and M. Karolik Collection of American Water Colors and Drawings, 1800–1875. Observe the French bed with duvet, the bureau with scarf, the gas lamp with broken shade, the silhouette with cracked glass, and the washstand with accessories. By this date, one was admonished to wash the whole body with soap and water at least once every twenty-four hours. The artist may have intended us to see a sponge-bearing figure disappearing through the door at left. A judicious bather would have placed a strip of oilcloth before the stand to guard the carpet from liberal splashings. Both the washstand and the dressing bureau with mirror are painted and decorated in the style of "cottage" furniture then much in favor for bedchambers

Caroline King could picture many a Salem chamber brightened by rich old Canton china toilet sets of blue and white, or light green India china strewn with colorful flowers—the "stately long-necked ewers, and basins so large that a baby might be drowned in their gorgeous depths."[45]

And there might be further evocations of the exotic East in these old-time chambers. Mrs. King remembered well the magical power of the scenic wallpaper in one of the chambers of her girlhood home:

> It represented Turkish pictures. A river flowed all round the walls of the room, its banks covered with mosques and minarets and "stately pleasure domes." Just opposite the bed was a beautiful turreted Turkish house with steps leading down to the water, at the foot of which a pleasure boat with purple awning and cushions was moored. Once on a time when I was ill with a fever in that bed, just in the dead vast and middle of the night, I saw that door open, and a lovely Turkish lady (I must confess looking very like the Eastern figure on my nursery mantlepiece) issued lightly forth, escorted by a cavalier, who after arranging the cushions for her, tenderly helped her in, and "loosed the chain and down she lay, and the broad stream bore them far away," out of my sight.

The use of wallpaper in bedrooms, however, was controversial. J. C. Loudon thought the walls of a chamber looked best papered, and A. J. Downing observed that its use was general in this apartment, which both agreed should be light and cheerful. Advocates noted that it was cheap and easily applied, detractors that it could not be washed, was a harbor to vermin, and should therefore never be used in sleeping rooms. "Are not health, and cleanliness, and comfort, a thousand times more important than mere looks?" intoned one manual in 1856. Elizabeth Wirt would have answered yes, for there she was in Washington on 22 September 1818, battling with bugs and feeling that "this *papering of chambers* is a dreadful business." By the next day she had torn off a good part of the nursery paper, rubbed the wall cracks with spirits of turpentine, sent the bedsteads to be painted green, and pronounced emphatically, "If after this I do not get the mastery of *mine enemy* I shall give up."[46]

Carpets were considered healthful in eighteenth-century chambers, as they rendered washing the floor unnecessary and thus avoided dampness, but the hygiene of chamber carpets came under scrutiny in the following century. In rural homes this was no problem, as "the chambers were all without carpets" anyway. Ellen Rollins could remember yet another rural solution, for the chamber floors at her grandparents' New Hampshire farmhouse were kept strewn with sand—"a cheap, changeful covering which at night I used to scrawl over with skeleton pictures, to be scattered in the morning." Bedroom floors in more fashionable homes, however, might well be covered with carpeting. Smaller carpets around the bed might protect a large carpet from wear, or they might buffer bare feet from cold boards just as they had in Europe, beginning in the 1600s. Although the use of wall-to-wall carpeting in chambers was being discouraged by the second decade of the nineteenth century, the bedside carpet was retained. Straw matting was also much used, and if it was, woolen baize should be set down round the hearth in winter to diminish the fire hazard, as Maria Silliman Church did in November 1833; but it was actually much safer to replace or entirely cover the matting with a carpet, as she subsequently did, in October 1835, putting her drawing-room carpet in her bedroom and the matting below in its place—"as I did not feel safe to have a fire in my room with the matting."[47]

Elegance, comfort, utility, and health were important considerations in the decoration of eighteenth-century and early-nineteenth-century bedchambers. Furniture for sleeping, resting, washing, nursing, writing, and eating proclaimed the multifunctional aspect of these rooms, although their primary function was made clear in the towering presence of the curtained bedstead. Sets of side chairs suggest something of the semipublic aspect of the chamber in that period when the success of a birth, the recovery from an illness, the ease of a death were dependent upon the practical skills and emotional comfort of neighbors. When the family had the means, textiles abounded, providing brilliantly colored and dramatically patterned protection from drafts and dampness and offering bold evidence of social and economic advantage. By 1870 the bedchamber had become a more private apartment, for though birth, sickness, and death still took place in this room, they were more likely attended by trained professionals and the immediate family than by concerned neighbors. Elegance was no longer deemed necessary but the emphases on comfort, utility, and health survived. It was the concern for health that brought about the greatest changes, as healthful increasingly meant sanitary. Furniture that could be easily cleaned, preferably of light color to expose dirt and with a minimum of dust-entrapping ornamentation, was best suited to a germ-free environment. To secure an abundance of pure, unimpeded air, free from dust, all unnecessary furnishings were eliminated; bed and window curtains were scaled back or taken down; carpets were reduced to a narrow strip around the bed and perhaps a few small ones scattered about.

Of course, in many families nothing changed at all, and bedchambers displayed generations-old draped beds, upholstered easy chairs, and flouncy dressing tables. But all these chambers, whether upper class or middle class, colonial or Victorian, "showed that sleep was a luxury, well understood and duly cherished by all classes." Let us then extinguish the chamber light, lie back, and vicariously experience the sights and scents of an early nineteenth-century Massachusetts chamber as pictured by Ruth Huntington Sessions:

> When we spent the night at Grandmother's we were tucked into great softly pillowed beds, in rooms which, like the Christmas closet, were redolent of refreshing odors. Whether it was from the fragrant sheets—perhaps a suggestion of lavender—or the pungent, stimulating camphor in which the blankets had been laid away, or the fine Castile soap, or the delicate faintly perceptible aroma of old polished mahogany, or possibly a little vase on the bureau with a sprig of rose geranium or lemon verbena offsetting a few flowers, I would not venture to say. Probably all those perfumes had mingled and stayed in the air for years, renewed from season to season. Sea air blew in at the windows, and an old chair with high back and flowered Chintz hangings seemed to guard over the dreamers.[48]

Well-trimmed candles and lamps were icons of the punctilious housewife and indices of domestic comfort. If lights were clean and burning brightly, all augured well for comfort at home in early America. So important were well-groomed lights that nineteenth-century books on household management even equated good lighting with a good marriage, and Eliza Leslie forewarned the bride in 1840, "A neat and well-conducted house, with fires and lights always as they should be . . . are comforts that are not lightly prized by any married man."[1]

Brightly burning lights promised asylum. John Bill was as relieved to escape an "Egyptian darkness," which had spread over the Philadelphia outskirts early one December evening in 1827, and to enter that city, where "the lights in the Windows & the long Vistas of Lamps in the Streets, formed a striking contrast with the previous gloom," as Janet Schaw had been to emerge from the umbrageous depths of the North Carolina woods in March 1775 and find herself "in front of a large house from the windows of which beamed many cheerful tapers." Flickering candles and glowing lamps also evoked an inner warmth, conveying a feeling of solace and security. Levi Hutchins had intended to return home from his brother's New Hampshire farmhouse one cold winter evening in 1810, "but the social circle of my brother's household, cheered by the mingled light of the bright woodfire and his domestic tallow-candles, caused so much happiness, that I was induced to postpone our return till morning." And Ulysses Hedrick could recall the emotional comfort of lantern light on a northern Michigan farm in the 1870s: "When I was coming home late on a dark night, especially in a gale in winter, the tiny wick all aglow warmed me all the way through. There was nothing comparable to lamps and lanterns in our isolated home to raise the morale of its inhabitants, whether they were outside or inside the house."[2]

Candles were the primary source of artificial light until the second half of the nineteenth century. Catharine Beecher and Harriet Beecher Stowe yet felt it important to offer instructions on making candles in their domestic guide of 1869, *The American Woman's Home*, and Anne Gertrude Sneller, who was born near Cicero, New York, in 1883, recalled that her grandmother made all the family's tallow candles. Candles were also made of beeswax, spermaceti, bayberry, myrtleberry, and, ultimately, stearine. Candle making was a time-consuming, back-breaking, ill-smelling process to be performed in the cold-weather months so that the candles might harden more quickly. Louisa Jane Trumbull alluded to the noisome aspect of the task when she noted in her diary on 1 November 1836 that her mother was "trying suet tallow or some such thing which is wonderfully disagreeable to my nasal organs"; and Stephen Walkley conveyed the discomfort of the chore when he pictured his mother, bundled in a variegated abundance of shawls, trying out tallow, and laboriously dipping two hundred or three hundred candles at a time. Whether manufactured by dipping or by pouring into a tin or pewter candle mold, the quantities

Who's There? Oil on canvas, by Thomas Waterman Wood. Late nineteenth century. Courtesy Christie's, New York City. With nightfall, light was indeed scant at home in early America. It was often impossible to see across a room, and well might one need to ask, who's there? A Frenchman traveling in New England claimed that the penurious Americans lived by the light of the fire and that if they lit a candle for a visitor they extinguished it when he left

necessary for household use connote fatigue. Mary Guion made 260 candles on 26 January 1801; Maria Silliman Church made 360 on 10 January 1834; and Elizabeth Porter Phelps made nearly 600 in October 1790. Mutton tallow was prized above beef tallow for its whiteness, and Maria Silliman Church went to the extra trouble of bleaching her tallow candles "as white as spermaceti by spreading them in the sun." She found them "very nice" and was delighted that they "don't run, or smoke, at all." Most tallow candles did run and smoke, were of an unattractive yellow color, were easily softened by heat, had to be snuffed repeatedly, and were malodorous when extinguished. Frequent snuffing was necessary to remove the snuff, or charred end of the wick, before it could fall into the molten tallow and cause guttering. Maria Foster

The Trying Hour. Watercolor by William Sidney Mount. 1834. The Addison Gallery of American Art, Phillips Academy, Andover, Massachusetts. The pun here is on *trying*—trying out, or refining, animal fat for candles; a trying, or exacting, task, which was evil-smelling and backstraining. When this housewife had rendered the lard to her satisfaction, she would either dip wicks into the tallow or pour the hot tallow into pewter candle molds

By Candlelight (Mrs. Jedediah Morse). Oil on canvas mounted on panel, by Samuel F. B. Morse. c. 1820. Yale University Art Gallery, New Haven; gift of Mr. R. C. Morse. Many were the complaints of weak eyes, for eyestrain was endemic in an era when precision work had to be performed in nominal light. Candles were usually kept in the kitchen, where they would be lighted at the moment of need, and the phrase "candles have just been brought in" is a frequent time reference in early documents

Brown said that those candles at her Iowa home were "as thick as your little finger," so the importance of snuffing is obvious. Anthony Willich tabulated in his *The Domestic Encyclopedia* that a common candle needed to be snuffed forty times in an hour, and the operation required close attention and dexterity or the flame would be extinguished. The obligation to look up from one's book or work every two to fifteen minutes to check the candle, pick up the snuffers, and carefully remove the charred wick ends was counterproductive to concentration on a difficult text or a fine seam. But it was not until the discovery of stearine, about 1825, that a self-consuming plaited wick was developed. Candles of bayberry (genus *Myrica*) and the similar myrtleberry (genus *Myrtus*) offered several advantages. As elaborated by Robert Beverley in his *The History and Present State of Virginia* (1705), they were "never greasie to the Touch, nor melt with lying in the hottest Weather: Neither does the Snuff of these ever offend the Smell, like that of a Tallow-Candle; but, instead, of being disagreeable, if any Accident puts a Candle out, it yields a pleasant Fragrancy to all that are in the Room; insomuch, that nice People often put them out, on purpose to have the Incense of the expiring Snuff." Bayberry and myrtleberry candles, though more costly than tallow candles, were less expensive and less highly esteemed than those of beeswax and spermaceti. Janet Schaw, who thought these pale green candles gave "a very pleasant light, and when placed in a silver candlestick, look extremely pretty," wondered why in North Carolina, where myrtleberries abounded, "the people of fashion use only spermaceti, and if any green wax, it is only for kitchen use."[3]

Some housewives preferred to mold their candles, commonly using a mixture of tallow and beeswax. Though these exacted precision in the making, they were ultimately rewarding to the eye in their stately uniformity. John Jay Janney's mother was particularly proud of her mold at home in early-nineteenth-century Virginia, for it was "the only one in the neighborhood, and was frequently loaned on special occasions, weddings, and other such gatherings." In Plymouth, Massachusetts, Wil-

Snuffing the Candle for Grandpa. Detail of the cover illustration for *Harper's Weekly*, 17 March 1866. Colored engraving. It was estimated that a common candle required snuffing forty times in an hour—a deft operation that removed the snuff, or charred end of the wick, before it fell into the molten wax, causing the candle to gutter and the light to diminish. Wicks of loosely twisted cotton twine could be manufactured at home or purchased at a local store in balls "as large as your two fists." Many were the attempts to improve candlelight, but early-nineteenth-century experiments with waxed wicks proved that, although they might burn brighter, they would not burn better or longer

liam Davis's mother placed her pewter candle molds on the kitchen-dresser shelves in company with all the household pewter. But they were also stowed elsewhere, commonly in the garret or another storage area, when not in use. Housewives often supplemented the stock of homemade candles with store-bought beeswax, spermaceti, or bayberry candles for special occasions. From the Boston chandler Edward Langdon, for example, one could have purchased green-wax candles or molded candles, plain or fluted, in 1753; and by 1761 the choice had expanded to include large or small, plain or flowered, molded or dipped, tallow, bayberry, or spermaceti candles. Maria Silliman Church was amply supplied in December 1841, for she had made an abundance of tallow candles and had found spermaceti ones in the village. James Clemens had vaunted the advantages of these costly but superior whale-oil candles before a Boston audience in 1748: they exceeded all others for beauty and sweetness of scent when extinguished, lasted twice as long as a tallow candle of equal size, and gave a soft, easy, ample light. A soft, easy light was highly desirable, for in this era the typical text was printed in small type and sewing stitches need be tiny in

Boy with Sinumbra Lamp. Oil on canvas, by John Bradley. 1837–43. Courtesy Berry-Hill Galleries, New York City. Prototypical furnishings of the parlor in the 1830s and 1840s included the center table, often marble-topped, and a lofty oil lamp surmounted by a handsome glass shade. Like the astral lamp, the sinumbra ("shadowless") lamp was designed to cast an uninterrupted light. Oil lamps required hours of laborious cleaning and maintenance if they were not to smoke and smell and were therefore not used unnecessarily. Lighting devices incur the majority of pejorative comments on odor at home in early America

scale, though staggering in sum. Further, spermaceti candles did not become soft in the hand and required less snuffing.[4]

Although most candles did need frequent attention, all families did not own metal snuffers, as Anne Royall intimated. Writing from Alabama in 1818, she pictured herself seated before a bright fire with a stand, a lighted candle, and a pair of snuffers: "I have a snuffer-tray too, but one who was raised in the woods, you know, can easily dispense with a snuffer-tray; but I confess, I abominate that practice of snuffing the candle with your fingers." In 1853 Elisabeth Koren corroborated this suggestion that the use of snuffers was far from universal in the States: "The Yankees find they can use their fingers just as well—so why then procure snuffers?"[5]

Tubs of tallow and boxes of candles were to be stored in a cool place and secured against the ravages of gnawing rats and predatory cats. The cellar was one frequent repository, being cool enough that the candles would not melt. Martha Ogle Forman put 149 pounds of candles in four boxes in her cellar in April 1826, although in November 1828 she was obliged to remove her tallow from the cellar, as "the Cats eat it so much," and secure it in a safe place. There were 40 pounds of candles in Humphrey Devereaux's garret in Marblehead, Massachusetts, in 1774 and five boxes in a third-story storage area at the late William Bingham's Philadelphia home in 1805. Mrs. Jaques of Newburyport, Massachusetts, kept her candles in a bushel measure under the bed in a locked and, we can well expect, cold bedchamber. Those for immediate use could be found in a box hanging in some cool spot in the kitchen.[6]

Candles, therefore, were grueling to manufacture and tiresome to store, required frequent snuffing, were eye-straining, emitted heat, consumed oxygen, dripped tallow, and were often malodorous. Fortunate indeed were those women who returned from a gala occasion with their dresses unsullied by wax spilled from the overhanging chandeliers. There were, however, important advantages as well, and long after the introduction of oil lamps and gas lighting, many still thought that "candles, from their portability and other qualities, supply, upon the whole, the most convenient and most general mode of obtaining artificial light for domestic purposes." J. C. Loudon advocated that the nineteenth-century parlor be lighted entirely by wax candles, to the exclusion of oil lamps, which, he thought, always produce both smoke and an unpleasant smell.[7]

A piece of lighted pitch-pine made an acceptable, though dangerous, substitute for a candle in many rural homes. While researching his *The Slave States of America* (1842), James Silk Buckingham was intrigued to watch the choreography of a Georgia servant as he took a lightwood knot, ignited it at the kitchen fire and, carrying it in one hand as a candle, did all his work, whatever it might be, with the other; and if some operation required the use of both hands, he deftly fixed it in some part of the room where it would stand upright. Rushes dipped in tallow remained another inexpensive source of light throughout the nineteenth century. Elizabeth Oswald Chew's Philadelphia cashbook for 1814 to 1819 shows her buying rushlights as well as spermaceti and "dipt" candles; while Catharine Gansevoort of Albany purchased twenty rushlights and seventy-four candles in December 1817, providently reducing the expense by exchanging for them eleven pounds of tallow.[8]

Simple lamps fueled with animal fat smoked away in country cabins throughout the period, and more genteel oil lamps were used sparingly in better homes from the 1750s. George Cummings, who was born in North Groton, Massachusetts, in 1838, said that his mother made twenty dozen to twenty-five dozen tallow candles every fall

The Ring Family. New York City. Painting in sepia wash with black paper cutouts, by Augustin Edouart. 1842. The New-York Historical Society, New York City. Standard lighting apparatus for a drawing room at this date was a pair of argand lamps on the mantel and an astral lamp on the round table. Unless there was company, however, the mantel lamps would typically not be lit. The argand lamp, invented about 1782, had a tubular wick that allowed a current of air to pass both inner and outer surfaces of the flame, thus securing a brighter light. A glass chimney placed above the lamp increased the draft and intensified the light yet further. An astral lamp resembled an argand lamp, but the oil was contained in a ring flattened in such a way that the light thrown downward was uninterrupted. Observe the coal fire, the hearth rug, and the sliding door separating double reception rooms. Barely visible is the lofty pier glass and the pier table with a vase of dome-protected artificial flowers on its bottom shelf so that they "could save the whale oil, then much used in lamps for night service," and by that date many families were provided with this standard combination of oil lamps and tallow candles. Often a stately astral lamp stood in the center of the parlor table, while a pair of argand lamps or candlesticks might decorate the ends of the mantel. By 1859 Thomas Grattan would find the cheapness of lamp oil one of the most gratifying examples of domestic economy in the United States, and he observed that "tallow candles (the curse of middle life and moderate incomes in Europe) are never seen. Astral, solar, moderator, and other fanciful kinds of lamps, lustres lighted with glass, and wax or spermaceti lights, are to be found everywhere." But lamps could smoke and smell, and they broke easily; their fuels might congeal in cold weather and have to be placed before the fire to liquefy; and then there was the big problem of spilling oil. Laundresses had to know the secrets of extracting oils and wax from fine silks and glossy satins. Maria Silliman Church was irritated with her five-year-old son in 1849, for he "managed while I was out of the room, to upset the Astral lamp onto the matting, and his Father's new coat and pantaloons and I had ample employment in contending with whale-oil until bed-time. If we had had the gas arrangements one day sooner the disaster would have been avoided."9

Gas was an additional option in urban areas by this date. Thomas Webster and Frances Byerley (Mrs. William) Parkes addressed the advantages of gas in their encyclopedia in 1856, acknowledging that it could be conveyed easily by pipes to locations where it would be difficult to affix any other light; they found the light agreeable; and the smoke "which always proceeds from candles" was avoided. Further, there were no sparks, and gas was much brighter than any other artificial light yet in use. Samuel Breck's diary entry for 4 September 1839 conveys his euphoria with this then-novel light at home in Philadelphia (and at the same time betrays his shortcomings as a mathematician): "This day I lit for the first time the Gas, and a very splendid light it makes. I have in each parlour 8 burners, with tubes to add six or eight more, and there are in the vestibule and hall three; so that upon a gala occasion I can put in play about 35 burners. And as each burner is at least equal to three Astral lamps, and each lamp equal to 8 candles, we may state the gas power thus: $35 \times 3 = 105 \times 8 = 920$ candles!" Edgar Allan Poe, however, viewed gaslight as an example of the "perversion of taste" and maintained that its harsh and unsteady light was offensive, making it "totally inadmissible" for domestic use—"No one having both brains and eyes will use it." But there was no dripping of grease or spilling of oil, and a Russian traveling through Cincinnati in 1857 noted yet another advantage of this illuminant: "Gas is so cheap and popular that in the stores it is left on all night long until morning, for a thief will not steal into a lighted room where the watchman will immediately see him from the street." There were, of course, many disadvantages to gas lighting as well. It was not portable, and the gas jets added perceptibly to the heat of the room. Further, as Samuel Eliot Morison attested, "Many of the gas pipes and burners leaked slightly, so that there was always a faint odor of illuminating gas in the house." It was also fickle, threatening to go out at any time, and in cold or moist weather it either burned scantily or not at all. Caroline Dustan's New York diaries for the late 1850s and 1860s are replete with references to these periodic failures both inside her home and outside on the street. Such blackouts either precluded the use of a room or necessitated the recourse to candles. George Dallas wrote of a miserable evening at the White House in March 1849, when there had been "a terrible odour of gas in the East-Room. The experiment of lighting in that way began last evening, but

Charles and Emily Eaton. Medford, Massachusetts. Oil on canvas, by an unknown American artist. c. 1844. Fruitlands Museums, Harvard, Massachusetts. The globes of the pair of argand lamps over the fireplace face toward the center of the mantel. Paintings and prints frequently show them turned out toward the ends of the mantelpiece (see, for example, *The Ring Family*, page 144), but in all cases the globes are symmetrically disposed. The wreath of flowers around the base of the astral lamp protected the elaborate tabletop from oil spills and offered a softening touch to the room

owing to the badness of the construction, it failed and resort was had to dingy candles. The collection of escaped gas remained intolerable almost the whole time." In 1836 Philip Hone had been witness to a similar evening function in New York City where, suddenly, " 'Darkness overspread the land,'" and he concluded that although gaslight was handsome, its very fickleness made it "illy calculated for the ordinary uses of a family."[10]

One further advantage of gas lighting, however, was the vast saving of time and labor necessary to clean and trim oil lamps or to clean candlesticks and prepare candles. Faith Breckenridge of Meriden, Connecticut, had no trouble recalling that abhorred Saturday task of cleansing and polishing the steel candlesticks and snuffers—an onerous chore usually forced upon the younger girls in the family. Not only must the candlesticks be scraped of wax and polished bright but the candles

Sitting Room at Samuel Mount's Cabin. Watercolor sketch by John and Anna B. Collins, in their manuscript journal "Our Mission in East Tennessee." 1870–79. Courtesy of the Friends Historical Collection, Guilford College, Greensboro, North Carolina. In rural cabins, the open fire was not only the sole source of heat but the surest source of light. Heart pine and other resinous woods were gathered as "candlewood" or "lightwood"—names that chronicle their bright-burning contribution to the evening scene. Observe the petticoat suspended on the wall (no wardrobes here) and the men tipping back in their chairs—an American idiosyncrasy consistently condemned by foreign visitors

themselves must be kept clean and, if dirty, brightened with a flannel rag dipped in spirits of wine. Oil lamps also required hours of maintenance if they were not to smoke and go out and smell disagreeable. Robert Roberts warned servants in 1827 that it was a very important part of their work to keep drawing-room, dining-room, and entry lamps in perfect order so as to show a good light, for he had been "in some houses where the rooms were almost filled with smoke and the stench of the oil, and the glasses of the lamps clouded with dust and smoke." Indeed, when Harriet Manigault went to a ball at Mrs. Nathaniel Biddle's home in January 1814, there was "one great drawback which was that the room smoked so excessively that we could hardly breathe. I don't mean the smoke of a fire, but of lamps. They had some new fashioned coloured glass lamps, which had a pretty effect altho so disagreeable a one. Our noses were all black, & our clothes were prefectly grey. Charlotte & I were dressed in white crape over white satin, and they were quite ruined." Margaret Hunter Hall similarly suffered through an evening in Washington in 1827, during which "two of the lamps went out almost immediately and smelt the whole night in the most abominable manner." Franklin Butler Van Valkenburgh, who lived as a small child in New York State in the 1830s, said that whale-oil lamps were "dirty and stuffy, and apt to smoke, and to smell awfully unless the mother herself gave them attention." Catharine Beecher, therefore, found it imperative to forewarn housewives that "there is no work intrusted to domestics, which it is so difficult to have properly attended to, as the care of lamps." She applauded those ladies who, though they might keep a full supply of domestics, chose to clean their lamps themselves, thus ensuring a bright, a clean, and a sweet flame. A "sweet" flame was, indeed, difficult to ensure, and the prime culprit in references to bad smells at home in America from 1750 to 1870 is artificial lighting, whether in the smoky guise of candle, lamp, or gas burner.[11]

Kerosene was widely used by 1870, but, for all its advantages, it did not put an end to the daily cleansing of lamps. "Asked to name her most arduous work," Ulysses

Hedrick surmised, as he surveyed the kerosene lamps in use, ". . . my sister would have said 'cleaning lamp chimneys and lanterns,' a daily task as long as she was in her father's house." Anne Gertrude Sneller remembered that when her grandfather had brought home the first kerosene lamp, the family had felt that illumination could go no further, but "as lamps finally replaced all candles, the womenfolks learned to their surprise that filling, washing, and trimming lamps every day and polishing the lamp chimneys took more time than lighting a candle and blowing it out—or even cleaning the dripped tallow off the candlesticks. But lamps had come to stay."[12]

Candlesticks and lamps were to be readied for use each morning and until the moment of need were kept in the kitchen, where inventories suggest they were lined up along the mantel or the dresser shelves. Candlesticks were occasionally left out in the parlor but would not have been fitted with candles until they were to be lighted. This rule applies to the standing candlesticks that were so popular in Boston front rooms before the 1780s; to the pairs of brass or glass candlesticks, each protected by a glass hurricane shade, favored in eighteenth-century Charleston; to chandeliers, which were found primarily in the reception rooms of the wealthy; to the candle branches, or sconces that brightened the walls of parlor, dining room, and bedchamber; and to the pair of candlesticks that might adorn the parlor mantel.

Considering the difficulties involved, artificial light was not used at all whenever possible. Having spent so many hours making candles, we can be quite sure that Mary Cooper was grateful to be able to come back to her Long Island farmhouse on Sunday evening, 26 July 1772, and go to bed "with out liteing a candel." Sometimes one could take advantage of natural light. Peggy Rawle of Philadelphia spent an evening in May 1781 "in the parlour without a candle; as the moon shone bright it was pleasant"; and when Elizabeth Drinker called on friends in that same city one July evening in 1805, "They had no light in ye parlor, as is much the custom for some years past in ye summer." The blazing fire was a most important supplemental source of illumination until the general acceptance of the airtight stove and the coal-fueled furnace extinguished the genial glow of the open hearth in the second half of the nineteenth century. The enlivening flame and crackling snap of an amiable wood fire was the stuff that late-nineteenth-century nostalgia was made of, but in an earlier era it had sometimes had to suffice as the only light. Laura Wirt pictured herself at home in Washington in November 1818, "writing by a dim firelight. I can scarcely see." Frederick Law Olmsted's request for a candle so that he might write in a firelit North Carolina room in 1853 was countered in the colloquialisms of a local servant: "Not if you hab a fire. Can't you see by da light of da fire? When a gentlemen hab a fire in his room, dey don't count he wants no more light 'n dat." On the frontier and in the deep country, heart pine or other resinous wood was gathered for candlewood; among the regular duties of Daniel Drake while a boy in Kentucky was picking up "chips in the corn basket for kindlings in the morning, and for light, through the long winter evenings when 'taller' was too scarce to afford sufficient candles, and 'fat' so necessary for cooking, that the boat-lamp, stuck into one of the logs of the cabin over the hearth, could not always be supplied."[13]

Though it was often difficult to read or write by the dim light of the fire, its glow was sufficient for story telling and games, and winter sitting rooms were often enlivened by such entertainment at eventide. Emily Barnes recalled with pleasure those childhood evenings when her grandmother had "proposed stories, and she had a marvellous treasury of that kind to draw from, how eagerly we sought our places in

Going to Bed. Woodcut from *The Rose Bush; or, Stories in Verse* (New York, n.d.). Old Sturbridge Village, Sturbridge, Massachusetts. As a fire precaution, children were often sent to bed without benefit of lamp or candle, but here adults help light their way through the tenebrous depths of a stairwell. It was important for all family members to know the correct way to carry a candle if floors were to be free of wax and fires were to be avoided

the sitting room around the low-cushioned chair, which was placed in the warmest corner, the room all aglow with the bright, blazing fire. 'There is no need to light the candles,' she would say; and we were very glad to avoid the interruption occasioned by snuffing them, especially when so unfortunate as to snuff them out." Virginia Randolph Trist similarly reminisced of winter evenings she had spent with her grandfather Thomas Jefferson at Monticello. "When it grew too dark to read, in the half hour which passed before candles came in, as we all sat round the fire, he taught us several childish games, and would play them with us. I remember that 'Cross-questions,' and 'I love my Love with an A,' were two I learned from him; and we would teach some of ours to him."[14]

When artificial light was used, it was used sparingly. "As may be supposed," confirms Faith Breckenridge, "the candles were used with severe economy." Characteristically, a room would be lit by one candle, or one or two small lamps, or one larger lamp. When Sarah Ridg accidentally snuffed out the candle at her sister's Burlington, New Jersey, home in August 1809, these two young women were left in darkness, for it was "the only one burning in the house. The family, all but ourselves, were asleep, the fire in the kitchen had gone out, and we were compelled to go to bed in the dark as well as we could." The use of a single lamp is implied in Eliza Leslie's instructions for cleaning an astral lamp: "A lamp that is nightly in use should be trimmed and replenished regularly every morning, otherwise there will be no certainty in its burning, and it will go out unexpectedly at any time in the evening, leaving the room in darkness." And it is explicit in Caroline Cowles Richards's description of the typical evening scene at home in Canandaigua, New York, in 1857, as she and her sister shared "the funniest little sperm oil lamp with a shade on to read by evenings and the fire on the hearth gives Grandfather and Grandmother all the light they want, for she knits in her corner and we read aloud to them if they want us to." Artificial light was thus a cement which held the family together—imposing a temporal regularity on its members, who were forced to gather closely together to benefit from the single light source, and to retire when it was extinguished.[15]

George Channing recalled that during his Rhode Island boyhood, "candles were a great luxury (little children were obliged to find their way to bed in the dark)." Indeed, with nightfall, most of the house would be cast in gloom. Stygian hallways, blackened stairwells, groping about for a light, falling over furniture—are all referred to. This paucity of light was certainly one good reason for placing the furniture back against the wall after use—it would be all too easy to trip over pieces left out. Nathalie Boyer said that at their Pennsylvania home in the second half of the nineteenth century, guests were given tin tubs in their bedchambers, put there while they were at dinner, but "as the rooms were unlighted, it was an easy matter and one that often happened for the unsuspecting guest to tumble into the bathtub." Elizabeth Drinker bumped into her Hessian stable boy as she entered her tenebrous kitchen one evening, thus acquiring a smarting eye and swelled cheek. And as he mulled over the injustices of life, young Henry Shute of Exeter, New Hampshire, recalled the time his father was walking toward the door in the dark, "with his arms out to feel for the door, one arm went on one side of the door and the other arm on the other side and he hit his nose a fearful bump rite on the edge of the door, and i wish you cood have heard him swear, well if i swear he licks me, and he smokes and if i do he says he will lick me and he dont go to church and if i dont go he says he will lick me. O dear i gess i wont smoke enny more."[16]

The scarcity of light had tremendous implications for the early family. Candlelight, firelight, and lamplight created only pockets of illumination, leaving much of a room in darkness. The difficulty of seeing in such dim surrounds meant that the privacy the extended family lost because it was so numerous was in part compensated for by the secrecy of darkness. Court records and early American fiction are filled with references to the unperceived "telltale" witness in the corner. These same conditions, so favorable to concealment, were undoubtedly an encouragement to that urban problem of burglary.

In the typically half-darkened room, the wavering flame of fire or light sent exaggerated pulsating shadows over walls and ceiling, bringing to mind John Greenleaf Whittier's couplet

> The cat's dark silhouette on the wall
> A couchant tiger's seemed to fall.

Firelight breathed life into the inanimate devices of the carver. The bold outlines of a Queen Anne chair-splat might be projected on the wall as a pair of nodding parrots,

The Reverend John Atwood and His Family. Concord, New Hampshire. Oil on canvas, by Henry F. Darby. 1845. Museum of Fine Arts, Boston; gift of Maxim Karolik to the M. and M. Karolik Collection of American Paintings, 1815–1865. Reverend Atwood, chaplain of the state prison in Concord, and his wife and children encircle the center table, which had by this date become synonymous with domesticity and the valued lessons learned at home. Scarcity of light was a bond that held the American family together, for members had to gather in a group to benefit from the single light source at eventide. Note the crocheted lamp mat on the table, the mourning picture on the wall, and the wallpapered fireboard, which secured the fireplace opening in the summer months

Making Believe. Oil on canvas, by Seymour Joseph Guy. 1870. Collection Jo Ann and Julian Ganz, Jr. The vigorous crest rail and stiles of a Chippendale side chair cast an exaggerated shadow on the wall, suggesting the drama of the benighted interior, with huge, capering shadows dancing about in the ruddy glow of candle, lamp, or firelight

the openwork splat of a Philadelphia Chippendale chair as a grotesque, winking mask. William Fletcher King, who had lived in a log house near Zanesville, Ohio, had no sentimental nostalgia for the shadow-enlivened interior, however—writing in 1915: "In this day of bright illumination the thought of a candlelit room seems gloomy. Besides giving a feeble light, the tallow dip had to be frequently trimmed with snuffers. While the candle in a small room and for a few people might have looked cozy and done fairly well, it did poor service in a larger space. I have seen at spelling schools and at religious meetings weird effects on faces and walls, where the room was dimly lit by a few candles in tin reflectors on the walls."[17]

These tin reflectors were one of many contrivances by which eighteenth- and nineteenth-century homemakers maximized what little light they had. Lighting devices were specifically designed to magnify and reflect light with cut glass—

Detail of *The Tea Party* by Henry Sargent (see page 47). References to reflection run as a leitmotiv through accounts of early interiors, and looking glasses play a prominent role in these narratives. The dramatic alliance of artificial light and plate glass was clearly stated in the conspicuous use of sconce glasses in parlor, dining room, and bedchamber and was reiterated in the strategic placement of candles, lamps, and chandeliers before all manner of looking glasses

polished or mirrored surfaces often being an integral part of the design. Glass, and particularly cut glass, was much favored for its glittering presentation of light, and pendant prisms might further refract light. Candlesticks, lamps, and chandeliers were calculatingly positioned so as to reflect in looking glasses. Mirrors with candle arms attached glittered about the walls and over the mantel, and there might be a desk-and-bookcase with doors of mirrored glass, to be enlivened by candles placed before them on the candle slides. By the early nineteenth century, the circular, convex girandole mirror was considered a most fashionable accessory, and one further alliance of light and looking glass was the parlor pier arrangement. The typical pier grouping as it evolved in elegant European interiors in the 1670s was composed of an elaborately carved and often gilded table, with a looking glass suspended above, and a pair of candle stands to either side. By day these pieces were illuminated by incoming

Cornices, Curtains and Draperies for Drawing Room Windows. Illustration in Thomas Sheraton, *The Cabinet-Maker and Upholsterer's Drawing-Book* (London, 1794). The Winterthur Library: Printed Book and Periodical Collection. Large expanses of plate glass were common to the reception rooms of the wealthy, despite their expense. The more elegant the interior the larger and more numerous the glasses. The pier arrangement offered stunning possibilities for such a declamatory statement. Observe how this pier tabletop, in both profile and decoration, has been designed with its doubled image in mind. Frequently, a lamp stood on the table to lend further glitter to the composition, and in eighteenth-century Charleston a pair of candlesticks with draft-excluding hurricane shades often claimed this place of honor

Family in Silhouette. New York City. Painting in sepia wash with black paper cutouts, by Augustin Edouart. 1842. The Henry Francis du Pont Winterthur Museum, Winterthur, Delaware. The pier glass extends to the floor, and it was with considerable forethought that the curtain tassel, lamp, and shell collection on the bottom shelf were placed to reflect in it. Sanction of such shell arrangements was provided by a New Englander who reminisced about the eagle-supported tables in the piers of a Massachusetts parlor, with marble tops above and the great sea shells below, "in which we used to hear the sound of the sea." The elaborate window treatment with alternating dark (usually red) and white curtains could be seen in better homes all along the Eastern seaboard. In his thumbnail sketch of Washington, D.C., in 1842, Charles Dickens mentioned the ubiquitous private house "with a red curtain and a white one in every window"

Girl Coming through Doorway. Oil on canvas, by George Washington Mark. c. 1845. Collections of Greenfield Village and the Henry Ford Museum, Dearborn, Michigan. Doors were often painted to simulate mahogany or some other dramatically grained wood, and the flicker of candlelight would set the whorls and spirals into gyrating motion. A high-gloss finish would enhance the lively effect as would the polished doorknob, particularly if it were silvered or of cut glass

light filtering through the flanking windows. By night the light from the candle stands would reflect in the great glass and play about the carved and gilded elements of this so-called triad. By the eighteenth century, the candle stands had disappeared, but often there were candle arms attached to the glass or a light on the table illuminating its marble, inlaid, veneered, or painted top. Pier tables were often designed, both in form and in surface decoration, to be seen doubled in the glass which, by the close of the eighteenth century, might appear to extend down to the floor behind. Inlaid and painted semicircles along the back edge of the tabletop seemed to come full circle through reflection—shells opened up, flower buds unfurled. Nineteenth-century housewives often took advantage of these reflective possibilities and displayed their shell collections before the glass on the bottom shelf of the pier table.

Despite their expense, looking glasses were common to the reception rooms of the middle and upper classes, and the more elegant the interior, the larger and more profuse the glasses. The typical arrangement, designed both to give the illusion of greater spaciousness and to maximize reflection, was to place pairs of chimney glasses and pier glasses or a chimney glass and a pier glass across from each other. Often there were candle brackets or lamp brackets or even gas jets framing the glasses and a chandelier or ceiling lamp suspended between them.

Perhaps the most surprising testimony to this quest for luster was the silver, mirrored globes that hung from New England ceilings, serving no function other than to reflect light. Lucy Clark Allen, who was born in Hingham, Massachusetts, in 1791, recalled childhood visits to a neighbor's home, where she was intrigued by a "glass globe which hung on the great beam in the middle of the room, and reflected the whole room in its mirrored surface in miniature, very wonderful to my childish eyes." Eliza Susan Quincy remembered that from the center of the large summer beam that traversed Ebenezer Storer's drawing room and dining room there "depended a glass globe, which reflected, as in a convex mirror, all surrounding objects"; and the 1807 inventory of Storer's estate tellingly tallies "1 Glass Globe" in the front parlor and "A Globe" in the dining parlor. If one turns to fiction and Royall Tyler's attempt to portray the quintessential parlor in a stately Boston mansion, one finds that "from the middle of the ceiling, in the center of a circular department of stucco work, was depended a glass globe, the inside coated with quicksilver." Most significant, therefore, is the 1771 inventory of Royall Tyler's father's Boston estate, which lists "1 large Glass globe," apparently hanging in the parlor. Further research may determine whether or not the many glass globes listed in both northern and southern inventories were of this mirrored variety.[18]

Furniture, woodwork, wallpaper, and textiles were all given polished, glossy finishes, which not only made them easier to keep clean but enhanced their appearance by candlelight and lamplight. Robert Roberts recommended that furniture should be rubbed and polished to "a good gloss" and "a most brilliant polish." Ten years later, Frances McDougall also published directions for polishing tables in a way that would "produce a gloss like a mirror." "Sattin Painting" vied for favor with shiny satin paper. When in 1796 John Mifflin and his wife ordered wallpaper for their Philadelphia home, they wished the paper "glossed or varnished over"; and more than fifty years later, Orson Squire Fowler would favorably mention coating wallpaper with varnish, thereby giving "a shining or glistening appearance to the room." Shiny lustrings and glossy satins were fabrics favored for both upholstery and dresses by ladies who admired these polished apartments. Other fabrics might be rendered dramatic by candlelight via their bold patterns in strongly contrasting light and dark shades of the same color, or by the lively movement of their watered, waved, and glazed surfaces, which were tightly stretched over the frames of sofas and chairs or draped in ample yardage at the windows. Rainbow wallpapers, which appeared to change with every flicker of light, teased the eye and animated candlelit drawing rooms as changeable silks enlivened costumes. Louisa Crowninshield Bacon recalled what fun it had been to watch these silks "and count the different combinations of colors that made the silks changeable." Movement was clearly as important as gloss. The panels of mahogany doors, the drawer fronts of chests, the tops of tables, and the serpentine facades of sideboards were all highly polished to emphasize the dynamic grain of the wood, for carpenters and cabinetmakers selected their cuts carefully,

exploiting the drama of bold, vivacious graining by day and its yet more powerful effect by candlelight. It is not surprising that the favored cabinet woods during much of the eighteenth and nineteenth centuries were mahogany and rosewood—each of which was inspirited with a lively, showy grain.[19]

Because lighting was the hallmark of hospitality, much additional lighting was

provided for entertainment. Maria Silliman Church commented in September 1840 upon a party at her in-laws' house, where "the rooms were brilliantly lighted, with upwards of 30 candles in one, besides lamps." And after a party at her home in Mobile, Alabama, in 1848, Mrs. George Fry proudly observed, "Our house was as light as day, having thirty solar lamps and sixty candles throughout the house." These festive nocturnal interiors must have been spectacular, with the lively grain of waxed mahogany spiraling up the front of a towering case piece or swirling across the shiny top of a pier table. Carved and polished flame or corkscrew finials and carved pinwheels and sunbursts would be set to revolving by the wavering light as petal-based candlesticks and spiral-turned andirons swayed into the motion. Gold and silver glittered all about. Gilded chairs, tables, picture frames, looking glasses, cornices, hardware, brass curtain pulls, ormolu mounts, and polished fireplace equipment sent out glints of light. If there were golden accents in the design of the carpet or

Mrs. Isaac Smith. Boston. Oil on canvas, by John Singleton Copley. 1769. Yale University Art Gallery, New Haven; gift of Maitland Fuller Griggs. A wealthy patron's high esteem for sparkling, polished surroundings is evident in the pearls in Mrs. Smith's hair, around her neck, and at her elbows; in the blue-green changeable silk lining of her plum-color robe; and in the sheen of the glazed gold fabric that has been tightly stretched on the polished mahogany armchair and emphatically outlined in gold nails

in the upholstery fabrics and decorative fringes, these too would be highlighted. Brass and light-colored wooden inlays or ormolu mounts defined edges, giving gold-toned outlines to brightly polished tables, just as a sequence of brass nails traced the contours of upholstered furniture. Even the wall divisions might be dramatically demarcated by papier-mâché bordering in burnished gold, which trailed along the chair rail and up and over the window and door frames. Wallpaper could be one of those on "the most fashionable Silver Grounds" or perhaps one of the "Gold, Silver and Cloth Papers on embossed and enamelled Grounds." Isinglass, or mica, was used to spangle papers: one could have purchased "frosted, spangled and velvet papers with frosted and spangled borders" in Boston in 1790. Silver- and gold-spangled needle-work and mica-flecked sconces might further enliven the walls, while the very floor cloth itself might be "tinsel'd." Fire screens of glass, gilded leather, flame-stitched crewels, or frosted papers and silk were all designed for maximum effect before a flickering flame. After Sidney George Fisher returned from a call upon Mrs. Israel Pemberton Hutchinson at her home in Philadelphia one Friday evening in February 1841, he wrote effusively of the handsome rosewood surrounds and heavy gilt furniture, the immense mirrors and splendid chandeliers, the abundant candelabra, lamps, and ormolu ornaments—but what intrigued him the most was the pretty scene around her fireplace, with its "firescreen composed of a single, large plate of glass, very thick & set in a rich and massy gilt frame, so that you see the fire & are protected from its heat. This frame corresponds with that of the mantel mirror, so that the whole, the blazing fire thus framed in, the gold ornaments on the mantel & the large mirror above glittering with lights from candelabra and chandeliers, produce a very beautiful effect."[20]

Glittering "frost" was as important to the ladies in their dress as it was in their surroundings. Fully cognizant that "colours seen by candle light will not look the same by day," ladies dressed for these candlelit festivities carefully, often selecting glossy white fabrics spangled with gold or trimmed in silver, pearls, and diamonds. Eliza Bowen Ward was delighted with the supper party she attended in Charleston in 1791, for "it was so well lighted we could see every body," and she particularly admired the dress of one lady—a tiffany gown with festoons of painted flowers accented with foil spangles "so that it was extremely brilliant." When Charlotte Chambers walked into President Washington's birth-night ball in February 1795, she found the ladies "glittering from the floor to the summit of their headdress," their jewels and sparkling fillets of diamonds "reflecting the light from a hundred directions"; and when yet another Washington visitor dined at the President's House in November 1810, she was dazzled by a lady dressed in a white muslin thickly spangled with gold, with a lace handkerchief bordered and spangled like her dress and spangled white satin shoes. She also noticed that the dining and drawing rooms were lighted by splendid chandeliers and antique lamps placed on brackets around the walls.[21]

Frances Byerley Parkes would have approved of this arrangement. In 1831 she suggested that the best way to light a ballroom was "by a chandelier or lamp suspended from the centre of the ceiling, which diffuses an equal light, while it adds to the elegant appearance of the room. Lustres placed on the mantel-piece, and branches on tripods in the corners of the room, are also extremely ornamental." It was essential that the lighting devices be arranged so that they might not be easily overturned by a crowd of guests. Chandeliers and sconces were favored, and there might be supplemental candles and lamps high up on the mantel shelf or wall brackets, or on sturdy corner tables and center tables. Margaret Hunter Hall, who had to admit that the one thing Americans did do well was the lighting of their rooms, admired a festive setting in Philadelphia in 1827, where the rooms were "lighted entirely with candles and very well done. They were not in lustres, but in the middle of each room there was a circular frame in which were placed three or four dozen candles and at the sides of the rooms were semi-circular frames fitted with candles in the same way. Each of the frames was entirely concealed by a wreath of artificial flowers."[22]

The felicitous union of lighting with flowers and leaves, both fresh and artificial, was fashionable by the late eighteenth century and in vogue throughout the nineteenth century. Elijah Hunt Mills attended "a very brilliant ball" in Washington in March 1819 and noted that "the room was hung with festoons and semicircles of

Proposed Ballroom for a Theater in Richmond. Drawing in watercolor and pen, by Benjamin Henry Latrobe. 1797–98. Library of Congress, Washington, D.C. Chandeliers and a carpet might add the final touches to this design for a ballroom. Large-scale looking glasses enhanced the luster of a candlelit reception room, and ladies dressed with a sophisticated understanding of the sovereignty of brilliance and the allure of reflection, often selecting glossy white garments spangled with gold or trimmed in silver, pearls, and diamonds

Connecticut Interior. Watercolor with crystalline decoration, by an unknown American artist. c. 1810. New York State Historical Association, Cooperstown. The American taste for glitter extended even to walls and floors, where the wallpaper or floor cloth might be spangled with isinglass or mica. The silver baskets on these walls have been so treated. The theme of Charity offering a bun to a beggar child was derived from an English print and appears frequently in American schoolgirl embroideries. The idea of placing the figure in an interior, however, is innovative

flowers and variegated lights." Letitia Burwell recalled those parties at home in Virginia during the first half of the nineteenth century, when "the house was illuminated by wax lights issuing from bouquets of magnolia leaves placed around the walls near the ceiling, and looking prettier than any glass chandelier." Chandeliers were decked out in flowers. One of Julia Ward Howe's earliest memories was of being led into the family parlors one night in the early 1820s and beholding a circle of wax lights and artificial flowers glittering from each ceiling. James Nicholson commented upon yet another effective and typical arrangement at Mrs. Benjamin Cohen's Baltimore home in 1837, where the rooms were "all most brilliantly lighted by Lamps which blazed from amidst bunches of flowers"; and Eliza Leslie penned a pretty, though fictional, picture of a ballroom "illuminated with astral lamps, whose silver rays shone out from clusters of blue and purple flowers, and with crystal chandeliers, whose pendant drops sparkled amid festoons of roses." The very candles might be dressed out in paper flowers. Robert Roberts suggested that "if you have branches around your drawing room, and they are to be lit up when there is a party, you must trim your wax candles most sublimely, with some white paper cut in the form of a rose, to go round the end of the candles, and fit neatly round the socket of the branch," as "this looks very well at night."[23]

Eliza Susan Quincy detailed her preparations for a party at home in Boston on 21 April 1819, and they included sending to the Botanical Garden for flowers, "with which we decorated our drawing rooms,—placing them in vases on the mantelpieces, and in glass vases over the folding doors which were surmounted by a fan light." By half past seven, lights shone brilliantly from the center and around the walls of the rooms and all was in readiness for the arrival of the guests. Draped in gold and silver muslins, lace and jewels of all descriptions, the ladies fit easily into a scene to which they were only too happy to contribute their glitter. As the adjective "brilliant" was the compliment most coveted for an evening party at home in early America, with what evident and well-deserved pride could Eliza Susan Quincy proclaim, "Our rooms were universally admired & it was pronounced the most brilliant and successful party of the winter."[24]

I have been at work, providing the "food that perisheth," scaring the timorous dust, and being obedient and kind. I am yet the Queen of the Court, if regalia be dust and dirt, have three loyal subjects, whom I'd rather relieve from service. Mother is still an invalid, though a partially restored one; father and Austin still clamor for food; and I, like a martyr, am feeding them. Wouldn't you love to see me in these bonds of great despair, looking around my kitchen, and praying for kind deliverance, and declaring by "Omar's beard" I never was in such a plight? *My* kitchen, I think I called it — God forbid that it was, or shall be, my own — God keep me from what they call *households*, except that bright one of "faith"!

With this jeremiad Emily Dickinson announced her lamentable, though temporary, promotion to housekeeper at home in Amherst, Massachusetts, in May 1850. Hers was the voice of the many, for the uncertainty of servants and the certainty of other family vicissitudes meant that most women would, at least on occasion, don the regalia of the Queen of the Court of dust and dirt, of soapsuds, and of rolling pins. Many brides commenced housekeeping physically forearmed with such incidentals as dusters, cleaning rags, and dishcloths. Maria Silliman Church said that her mother-in-law was impressed with the quality and quantity of her dowry goods — "even to *holders* and *dish cloths*"; while Caroline Gilman recalled in 1834 the calico bag she had been given years before, "containing iron holders, kettle holders, wipes and dishcloths, presented me by an old aunt, who had quilted them" as a wedding present. Emotionally, many found themselves not so invincibly armored against this "prickly art" of housekeeping, which not only tired the body but tried the spirit. The comfort of traditional verbal counsel was often no longer possible as families scattered across the troublesome vastness of nineteenth-century America. Written counsel, in personal letters and published manuals, became all-important. From the late eighteenth century an ever-increasing number of household manuals and domestically directed periodicals sought to offer both practical advice and moral sustenance to the house-wife. That they were consulted we hear from Maria Silliman Church, who found herself in 1833 removed from her family, sentenced, as she would have said, to the solitary uncouthness of western New York State, and troubled at having misplaced her copy of Lydia Maria Child's *The American Frugal Housewife.* "I quite miss it," she allowed.[1]

In the eighteenth century and early nineteenth century, a housewife's duties might encompass the production, preservation, preparation, and presentation of food, and the fabrication of cloth and clothes, candles, and soap. Although these commodi-ties became increasingly available for purchase in the first half of the nineteenth

Mrs. Patty Porter. Perhaps Washington, Connecticut. Oil on canvas, by Ralph E. W. Earl. 1804. The Brooklyn Museum; gift of Colonel and Mrs. Edgar W. Garbisch. Lucy "Patty" Pierce Merwin Porter is portrayed with her laceworking tools. The woman of faculty never spent an idle moment but knew how to make the most of every second of the day. Paintings indicate that the practice of nailing baize or oilcloth covers to a table was rather widespread

century, store-bought goods usually supplemented rather than supplanted home-made products.

Cooking seems to have been the chore turned over to the help with the greatest alacrity, as we've seen, and the kitchen role of some housewives was purely supervisory; the hearth duties of those blessed with adequate help amounted to nothing more than making sweetmeats, regularly boiling them over to discourage mold, and baking additional delicacies for the tea table. All women, however, were expected to be versed in kitchen skills, for they might at any moment become a principal in its operations. Emily Dickinson, called upon during the momentary absence of her kitchen maid in 1864, "winced at her loss, because I was in the habit of her, and even a new rolling-pin has an embarrassing element."[2]

Maria Silliman Church spent Wednesday, 27 September 1837, "looking over the clothes from the wash—doing little jobs of mending—looking into my sweetmeats (which seem in good order) and such odds and ends." Clothing required hours of eye-straining sewing and arm-wearying washing each week. Holes necessitated darning and hems had to be moved up or down, seams in and out *ad infinitum* as garments were repaired or adjusted for each growing child, every expanding adult. Esther Burr might picture herself the reluctant "Taylor," in November 1755, "altering old Cloths which is very hard work." The making and mending of servants' clothing was also within the domain of many housewives. Sarah Logan Fisher was busy on 20 February 1786 putting her little bound girl's clothes in order and an evening a month later mending "My Negro Girl Amy's Summer Cloathes"; while Martha Ogle Forman was relieved to finish "cutting out the people's shirts," from seventy-five yards of linen, in April 1825. These seasonal wardrobe adjustments proved almost overwhelming to many. Ellen Birdseye Wheaton was distraught with the staggering amount of summer sewing yet ahead of her in April 1850. She had begun her work the second week of March with the fervent hope of completing it before the summer heat. Yet the making and altering of children's shirts and dresses had left her "almost bewildered," and the task not yet completed; "it seems at times," she despaired, "as tho' it could never be done." Some were fortunate enough to secure the services of a mantuamaker, or tailoress, at these times. It was with considerable discouragement, however, that Harriet Silliman depicted herself at home in New Haven in November 1828, "very busy for the last ten days with mantua makers, sweetmeats & house cleaning, and am anticipating at least as many more busy days with more cleaning more mantua making and tayloring."[3]

The production of textiles remained very much a part of rural life far into the nineteenth century, and many an early-twentieth-century chronicler affectionately recalled the whirr of the wheel and the thump of the loom. A Scotsman traveling in Virginia and North Carolina in 1823 commented on the ubiquitous reverberation of the weaving loom and commended the large armoires and chests filled with napery and bed linens of home production. The linen closet became a standard by which to

Sewing (Miss Jones). Watercolor by John Lewis Krimmel. Sketchbook, c. 1819. The Winterthur Library: Joseph Downs Collection of Manuscripts and Printed Ephemera. Sewing demands were staggering to many; though the stitches need be infinitesimal in scale, they seemed infinite in number

Ironing. Watercolor by John Lewis Krimmel. Sketchbook, c. 1819. The Winterthur Library: Joseph Downs Collection of Manuscripts and Printed Ephemera. The tables have been spread with clean ironing cloths and the task is well under way. Bare feet and open windows might mitigate the heat of this weekly chore

gauge a housewife's proficiency and promise in all things. Quality and quantity were each important, and literature of the late eighteenth century and early nineteenth century is replete with the imagery of a snow-white abundance. Susan Augusta Fenimore Cooper conjured up the image of a farmhouse in which the presses and cupboards were "overflowing with blankets, white and colored flannels, colored twilled coverlets for bedding, besides sheets, tablecloths, and patched bedquilts, all their own work." And when Henry Wadsworth Longfellow chose a capsule image of Evangeline's merit and virtue, he led the reader to her chamber:

> Simple that chamber was, with its curtains of white, and its clothes-press
> Ample and high, on whose spacious shelves were carefully folded
> Linen and woollen stuffs, by the hand of Evangeline woven.
> This was the precious dower she would bring to her husband in
>   marriage,
> Better than flocks and herds, being proofs of her skill as a housewife.

Most homes, however, both North and South, displayed a miscellany of homespun and purchased yard goods. Mary Walkley Beach, who was born in 1824, said that her mother left off spinning linen for underwear, buying cotton for undergarments, when she was quite young, but continued to make tablecloths and towels for some time after.[4]

All this linen and cotton had to be regularly washed and ironed, onerous tasks dreaded by most housewives. A variety of skeletal washing machines had been available from the late eighteenth century. Anna Bowen Mitchell wrote from Georgia in 1793, asking Lydia Bowen Clark of Providence how she liked her "washing *jinny* . . . if it succeeds well I will have one for now it takes generally the whole time of one servant to wash . . . I *allow* four days—but—something or other generally happens to retard the business." We do not know Mrs. Clark's response, but Martha Ogle

Kitchen Scene. Watercolor by John Lewis Krimmel. Sketchbook, 4 July 1819. The Winterthur Library: Joseph Downs Collection of Manuscripts and Printed Ephemera. The stove appears to be in its aestival storage position, obliging as a table, in this July view. In the arctic depths of winter, however, it might well enhance the meager heat of the open fireplace. The scale of the iron pots and the stooping posture of the figure at the hearth imply that a strong back and mighty muscle were needful to the cook; and the flowing skirt, so near the fire, suggests that celerity of action was a further requisite. Observe the lineup of flatirons on the shelf above the cupboard

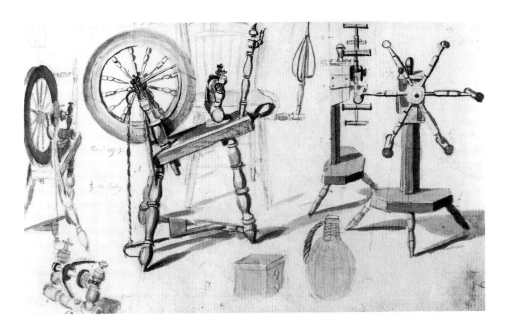

Forman was delighted with the washing machine her husband bought her in September 1832. We can only imagine what pleasure or pain might have been meted out by the musical washing machine mentioned in a New York City newspaper in 1798, "which performs several favorite airs, during the operation of purifying the foul linen. This, one may suppose will prove a useful profection [perfection]: as the persons thus occupied, may be charmed with their work, by a succession of harmonious strains: and the sense of labor, through a repetition of 'Water parted from the Sea,' may be relieved by 'My Chloe left me in the suns.'" Most washing, however, was performed by hand, without music, and there were often the attendant duties of making soap, hauling water from the river or the rain barrel, and bringing it to a boil. Soap was usually made in cool weather—a task redolent of evil-smelling fats and lye and one fraught with some anxiety, as the quality of the product could not be predicted. James Parker of Shirley, Massachusetts, must have been relieved to be able to record on 28 February 1772, "my wife made sope, had very good Luck," for Faith Breckenridge of Meriden, Connecticut, recalled that "if the soap 'came' properly, great was the jubilation thereat; and if not (and sometimes the most skillful soap-maker failed), it had to be put up with like other misfortunes."5

The wash was attended to weekly, although such adversities as sickness or seasonal housecleaning could mean it might accrue over some two to three weeks. It is difficult to determine the regularity with which bed, table, and personal linens were changed, but the heat of the American summer seems to have accelerated the frequency. *The Practical Housekeeper* (1855), for example, advised, "Be very particular to change your sheets and pillow cases once a week in winter, and twice in summer if very hot weather." Foreign observers often commented on the bright, white cleanliness of Yankee shirts, but a New York farmer modestly explained in May 1824 that the linen *had* to be washed every week or it "would rot and tare with the sweat like wet paper"; and Thomas Chaplin of St. Helena Island, South Carolina, found 27 June 1845 "the hottest day I think I have ever felt, almost perspired to death. Changed my linen about four times." John Harrower, a Scottish schoolmaster in Virginia in August

1774, commended the cleanliness of the linens: "They wash here the whitest that ever I seed for they first Boyle all the Cloaths with soap, and then wash them, and I may put on clean linen every day if I please." Such an abundance of clean linen was not easily achieved, however. Servants were often lax in laundry detail. When Caroline Dustan went to close up her Manhattan kitchen the evening of 12 December 1857, she was horrified to see the "flannels laying all wet in a heap, colored clothes in soak—& bushel of cinders on the hearth." That maid lasted one week. Maria Silliman Church was one of the fortunate few, for although she fretted in September 1833 that it was difficult to keep her crawling son sweet and clean, she did have—at least temporarily—an obliging good washer, who "never complains of a large wash," and a nice ironer. In town, the wash could be sent out. In fact, Elizabeth Drinker, having exchanged the heat of Philadelphia for the comforts of her country house in July 1794, was interested to observe her help busy with the laundry, for "washing at home is a new business to me, having been in the practice ever since we were married of putting out our washing." Yet sending out the wash often meant delays. Twelve-year-old Sally Cary of Virginia wrote with self-righteous indignation in 1772 (one can almost see her, hands on hips, foot stomping), "on thursday the 2nd of jan margerry went to washing and brought all the things in ready done on thursday the 9th of the same month I think she was a great while about them a whole week." Further, it was no guarantee of quality and many a housewife complained of having to do the wash over on its return.[6]

The theater for washing might be down by the river, under the quince bushes, over in the washhouse, or out in the kitchen with the brass or copper kettle at center stage. The multioperational process might involve soaking, washing in suds, boiling in strong suds, stirring with a clothes stick, and then transferring the clothes to another tub of water, scouring the spots, rinsing, wringing, immersing in bleaching or bluing water, and wringing again. Some fabrics were then stiffened with starch, and all, having been subjected to five complete baths, were carried out to the lines to be pegged firmly against the wind. That is, with luck, for there were those inevitably disastrous, waterlogged weeks when many a housewife might moan with Elizabeth Porter Phelps of Hadley, Massachusetts, "never dried the clothes till Sat."; or when the whole soppy heap had to be dried indoors and Sarah Logan Fisher would grumble, "had the Cloathes to dry by the Fire, which is very troublesome." A clothesline in the garret, such as Humphrey Devereaux had in Marblehead in April 1774, might circumvent the problem of rainy weather. Clotheslines of horsehair or twisted sea grass were to be wiped clean before being hung up for use and taken down when the clothes were brought in. Henry Wansey in Boston, Harriet Martineau in New York, and William Tallack in Philadelphia all commented on the urban use of an apparatus for drying linen on the roof—at a height that might have appealed to the Connecticut chap who well-nigh beheaded himself on a negligently left-out clothesline one murky night and fumed, "We are just as ready as anybody to see the funny side of a thing, but we have ceased to observe anything amusing in being unexpectedly sawed across the neck, or rasped across the face, by a clothes-line." *The Practical House-keeper*, which considered six dozen to be the requisite number of clothespins, reminded housewives in 1855 to "have your clothesline brought in as soon as done with, pins gathered in your basket." Clotheslines and clotheshorses, baskets and pins, irons and ironing boards abound in the inventory listings of colonial kitchens. Sarah Trecothick's Boston kitchen was admirably outfitted in 1749 with "a hair Cloathes

Hanging Out the Wash. Ink sketch by Michele Felice Corné. c. 1800. The Newport Historical Society, Newport, Rhode Island. Mothers were often called upon to combine the chore at hand with that of child care. A babywalker allowed this mother freedom to hang up her wash, although the child does not appear to fully endorse the solution. Clotheslines of hemp or horsehair were to be wiped clean before being hung up for use. They would be brought in with the dry clothes and stowed away in the kitchen

Line," "an Iron Box heaters & Grates," and "folding Board & horse for Cloathes." Clotheshorses were desirable supports for the freshly ironed items, for ironing followed washing as the night the day. A privileged few owned a mangle to smooth and shine the endless yards of table linen and bed linen, but most housewives relied on sad—i.e., solid—irons, or flatirons, a number of which were essential to ensure that one of these weighty stove- or hearth-heated affairs was always in readiness. Eliza Leslie suggested that there be at least three for each ironer, and four for that doleful solitary sufferer. Anne Gertrude Sneller reminisced without nostalgia, "The heavy flatirons were heated over a very hot fire, and the combined temperatures of fire and irons on a July day called for grim endurance. When I learned that flatirons were once called sadirons, I assumed that the name reflected the ironer's state of mind." Even when the ironing was completed, the play had not concluded, for the theater must be scrubbed, the ironing table scoured. Then, perhaps, the finished ironing on the clotheshorse or about the kitchen might be "satisfying to eyes and pride."[7]

Linen and cotton cloth and clothes were carefully bleached as well. Eliza Leslie suggested that white clothes be spread on the grass in the sun for two or three days after washing, being brought in at night lest they should be mildewed by the evening damp; and when a New Englander, Catherine Henshaw, "took a delightful walk up in the orchard" one early spring day in 1804, shortly before her sister's marriage, there was "Ruthie's diaper which is whitening on the last snowbank that is to be seen." Further south, John Jay Janney said that Virginia housewives were equally meticulous and would spread their muslin on the grass, frequently sprinkling it with a watering

Shake Hands. Oil on canvas, by Lilly Martin Spencer. 1854. Ohio Historical Society, Columbus. Strong arms and capable hands were much in demand in the kitchen. Before the arrival of electric appliances, butter creaming, raisin stoning, spice grinding, lemon squeezing, cream whipping, dough kneading, sugar pounding, coconut grating, and egg frothing must all be done by hand. Luckily some, such as the artist who conceived this portrait, maintained a sense of humor through it all

pot while the sun was shining. When William Wirt arrived at a friend's house in Norfolk in 1803, he, too, could attest to the notable Virginia housewife, for in his chamber "the toilet, the mattresses, the musqueto curtains are all white as snow and Sweet as a rose."[8]

Many women worked long and hard to present all furnishings to advantage. Not only were the linens snowy white, owing to judicious laundering and bleaching, but the pewter was scoured until it shone like silver and the furniture buffed bright, while doors, floors, and walls were subjected to the same vigorous rubbing. When the prince de Broglie took tea with Mrs. Robert Morris in Philadelphia in 1782, he was intrigued not only by her own neat appearance but by the "curiously bright" brass locks and hinges and the doors and tables, which were of "a superb mahogany, and beautifully polished." Mary Vial Holyoke portrayed herself at home in Salem in the 1760s scouring chambers, pewter, and furniture brasses; and in 1819 Harriet

Sowing for Diphtheria. Wood engraving. 1881. The Bettmann Archive, New York. This print expresses the growing concern for sanitation in the second half of the nineteenth century and also suggests the physical endurance requisite to perform such daily household duties as drawing, carrying, using, and disposing of heavy pails of water. Beyond the clothesline is a privy—a common backyard fixture throughout the period examined in this book. Foreign visitors commented upon the cleanliness of American privies. A Frenchman who in 1788 denounced the "disgusting habits" of his kinsmen, whose plumbing arrangements often offended one's sense of decency and sense of smell, contrasted the American custom of siting in the middle or corner of the garden, some thirty to forty yards from the house, "a very clean and often even attractive structure specifically designed for this purpose." Scrupulous Martha Ogle Forman, of Cecil County, Maryland, kept her outhouse regularly whitewashed and even took the trouble on 14 April 1821 to plant round it "a Cherokee rose, a monthly Honeysuckle, a jesamin, the hundred-leaf rose, the Rose of Casi, the sweet scented Shrub and the Spanish broom"

Bradley of Watertown, Connecticut, spent hours similarly scouring brasses and cleaning house, evaluating her stint as a dutiful daughter on October 2, "Ironed, washed floor—'Count that day lost.'" Parlors and bedchambers were to be tidied daily and cleaned *thoroughly* once a week—meaning airing, sweeping, scrubbing, dusting, and polishing. Metal and wooden wares were to be cleaned every Saturday.[9]

China and carpets, curtains, and upholstered furniture received equal attention. The housewife herself might wash the delicate breakfast china and fragile lampshades every morning, and sweep the parlor carpet, scattering it with "well-squeezed" tea leaves to lay all dust and give a slightly fragrant scent to the room.

Carpets were to be regularly turned (turned over or rotated) to ensure even wear—a square carpet could theoretically be changed eight times, a circular one indefinitely. Maria Silliman Church divulged her upbringing among the intelligentsia when she wrote that she had all her carpets "to make over and *tergiversate*"; and Alicia McBlair Lloyd of Wye House in Talbot County, Maryland, was delighted to find that "the colors are as fresh as ever," when she turned her dining-room carpet in October 1836. Carpets were also moved from room to room in a further attempt to prolong their life. It must have been difficult at times to remember which carpet was where, for as one housewife wrote her mother, "I have put my matting in your room upstairs. The woolen one which was up there is in the south parlor . . . and the carpet which was in there is in the parlor." Curtains were taken down seasonally to protect them from summer sun and dust, while sofas and upholstered chair seats were safeguarded with slipcovers—often year-round.[10]

A primary duty of the housewife was to preserve and maintain all these family possessions through a skillful regulation of the household and wise economy. Many diaries and journals were, in part, tools of reference that facilitated smooth management by helping the housewife ascertain or remember when a certain product was purchased, used up, or replenished; when the help was paid; where things were stored. Mary Vial Holyoke's diary is filled with such statistics of inventory control as "Began loaf of sugar," or "Began the firkin of butter, weight 77 lbs." Martha Ogle Forman reminded herself on 9 November 1825 that she had "filled both my sugar boxes, the old box holds 7 lb, but I put 6½. The second holds 9 lb." And when Caroline Dustan went to hang up the parlor curtains in November 1856, she was hindered by not being able to find the pins—so we are not surprised that when she took them down again in May, she meticulously recorded, "I shook folded & put away front and back

Scrubbing the Floor. Watercolor by Baroness Hyde de Neuville. c. 1810. The New-York Historical Society, New York City. From Norfolk, Virginia, M.L.E. Moreau de Saint-Méry observed that the floors were scrupulously scrubbed as the ultimate demonstration of cleanliness, while Anne Royall reported from Fredericksburg that every morning a servant rubbed the floor with brush and wax until it was slippery as glass

[parlor] curtains pins &c in trunk." If an item could not be found, there was a good chance it had been taken, and a wise housewife kept all valuables, including textiles, silver, porcelain, and household supplies, under lock and key. Rooms, cupboards, closets, and chests were fitted with an enormous variety of trustworthy locks, and the keys that dangled from the housewife's chatelaine or weighed heavily in her pockets or jingled in the basket she carried were a symbol of her control over the entire household. When Anna Maria Thornton, wife of architect William Thornton, returned home from a morning of shopping in Georgetown in August 1800, she found a somewhat disgruntled husband and guest waiting for her to admit them to the parlor, for which she had the key and which she had undoubtedly locked as a precautionary measure. Eleanor Putnam said that the paradigmatic Salem housewife "regarded her cupboards as the inner and most sacred portion of her trust." It was no easy task even to keep the keys counted and polished, and "as for losing one, or forgetting which was

which, that would indicate a mind so utterly frivolous that one could hardly conceive of it." Many could draw a complementary picture of the southern housewife, keys at her side. "Everything needed for the daily use of all the people on the plantation was kept rigidly under lock and key," observed a Yankee girl who had gone South to tutor the Henderson children in Virginia; and Mrs. Henderson, who toted her keys in a stout leather basket which she suspended from her waist or hung on her arm, "not only carried the keys of all the pantries, closets, drawers, and chests inside the Mansion, but of all the store-houses outside."[11]

Although burglary does not seem to have posed much of a problem in the country, where doors and windows were left open at night, it was an urban dilemma. Diaries written in eighteenth- and nineteenth-century Philadelphia and New York are filled with references to robberies, some armed. Doors and shutters of urban homes were to be securely fastened at night, and Robert Roberts advised locking the front door at dusk "to prevent any one coming in and stealing coats, cloaks, hats, &c as this very often is the case in a city." Roberts stressed that security was *the* most important part of a servant's duty and that it was essential to see that the evening fires and lights were safely out and all doors and windows secured before retiring. Nonetheless, colonial documents abound with references to silver stolen from the parlor buffet, the pantry, and the sideboard—three likely places to find silver. Perhaps this is one reason why one frequently reads about plate cached in an upstairs chamber. Bostonian Daniel Johonnot secreted his silver in his best front upper chamber in June 1750; and fellow townsman Thomas Parker kept some of his in the front chamber in 1782; while Stephen Greenleaf secured 188 ounces of plate in an iron-clasped chest in his handsomely furnished southeast chamber in 1795. When robbers broke into Sidney George Fisher's Philadelphia home in 1858, they ransacked the house; but, fortunately, "in the entry upstairs is a closet in which all the silver in common use is put every night. It escaped. There is also a linen closet there, in which two chests of silver are kept. It was not opened." Samuel Canby Rumford said that at his Wilmington, Delaware, home in the second half of the nineteenth century, "after each evening meal all silverware was gathered together and carefully packed in a special basket in which were compartments of different sizes, the tea pots and other more bulky pieces being wrapped in flannel bags before going into their designated location. This basket was carried to Mother's room and pushed well under her bed, where it remained until she set it out into the hall on the way to her bath the following morning." Sam Lawson's query in Harriet Beecher Stowe's *Oldtown Folks*—"Do you know where Mis' Kittery keeps her silver nights?"—is significant.[12]

In-house petty thievery was a major problem at home in early America, and the finger was usually pointed at the help. Store closets invited knavery if they were not locked up and monitored. Patsy Jefferson promised her father, "nothing comes in or goes out without my knowledge and I believe there is as little wasted as possible." Homes devoid of a mistress were particularly vulnerable even if a daughter or daughter-in-law tried to assume responsibility. As a widower, Landon Carter was often peeved with the inadequacies of a resident son and daughter-in-law at his Virginia plantation, Sabine Hall. In 1770 he wrote with scorn and exasperation, condemning the latter for refusing to manage the storeroom prudently, as such a chore would be "below the dignity of a princess"; "I laughed at the care we then experienced in Milk, butter, fat, sugar plumbs, soap, Candles, etc. Not one of these innumerations lasted my family half the year. New soap was obliged to be made in

June. Fat gone by July. Sugar continually bought in and old expended plumbs a large barrel of 300 weight. . . . All gone. No body knows how." Lydia Maria Child advised in 1832 that linens and spoons be counted occasionally "that those who use them may not become careless." Patsy Jefferson had demonstrated just such wise economy years before, writing to her father from Monticello in January 1791, "Not relying much in the carefullness of the boys particularly when left to them selves I took an account of the plate china &c. and locked up all that was not in imediate use. . . . The spoons &c. that are in use are counted and locked up night and morning so that I hope to keep them all to gather till your return." When Caroline Dustan washed her own breakfast cups and silver on 13 May 1861, she found a silver teaspoon missing, though all had been there the day before. The maid, whom she was certain had taken it, departed three days later, bidding them "good bye & hoped we would find the *spoon.*" Anxiety over servant thievery and neglect was one reason why American housewives often washed their own fine breakfast wares. The scene of action was often the back parlor, after the maid had brought in a little wooden piggin filled with boiling-hot suds. Maria Silliman Church pictured herself with her mother-in-law in 1831 washing "the breakfast and tea things (including the knives and silver forks) in the parlor," and nine years later she wrote her sister at home on Whitney Avenue in New Haven, "How I wish I could look into the parlor in the avenue this morning—perhaps you have just finished washing the breakfast things as I have." Ruth Huntington Sessions of Massachusetts recalled that after breakfast her mother went through the daily dishwashing task considered indispensable "to an average New England family regime. It was understood that the lady of the house washed her breakfast glass and silver at least, and generally china also, with her own hands." This personal attention, which helped reduce breakage and loss, was not just a Yankee nicety; Margaret Hunter Hall observed and condemned the same practice in Savannah in 1828, and Eliza Chinn Ripley of New Orleans could remember her mother doing the same every morning in the 1830s.[13]

The internal theft of silver was not always restricted to such small items as a single teaspoon. Alice Colden Wadsworth reminisced in 1819 about the family silver that had once stood on a New York sideboard during her youth: "One morning my Mother going into the parlor as usual saw the sideboard entirely stript. The value of the silver was upwards of a thousand dollars." A couple of servants who were strongly suspected left shortly thereafter. China, too, had to be secured. Housewives sometimes kept their fine china upstairs, perhaps also to protect it from thievery and careless hands. Abigail Adams had a "China closet above stairs" at Quincy in 1790; and while Philadelphian Catherine Chew kept her common china and glassware in the pantry closet in 1831, she stored several sets of blue India china, a tea, dessert, and dinner set in the then-popular white and gold, and cut glass in two closets on the third story. The practice was so pervasive by 1837 that Eliza Farrar felt obligated to inveigh against its impracticality: "The best dinner-set is often kept in the closet of a spare chamber; so piles of plates and arms full of dishes are seen walking down stairs on company days, and walking up again the day after." All china was to be regularly accounted for, and housewives tallied their china when they cleaned out their china closet, at least once a year. Martha Ogle Forman "cleaned out the china closet and counted all our China" on 26 October 1818, five days after she had "examined all my thread. Counted all my sheets and pillow cases."[14]

Textiles were to be regularly counted, an arithmetical tabulation that became increasingly complex with incremental quantities of bed linens and table linens. *The Workwoman's Guide* (1838) observed that "gentleman's families generally have three and sometimes more qualities of sheeting," for guests, family, child, and servant use, and although the quantity of sheets depended upon the number of bedsteads, there should be an average of three sheets or two pairs for each bed. These were to be folded, matched, and stored in closets rather than in drawers, as the former were less likely to be damp. Elizabeth Ellicott Lea reminded her readers in 1845 that one should have a book in which to record all the linens and towels, which were to be counted at least once a month and were to be marked in sewing thread or indelible ink with the name of the family or the initials of the master and mistress and identification numbers. A sheet might thus be marked in a corner with a cryptogram like

J.L.C.
B.
3
.35

which could decode to John and Lucy Capewell, best sheets, third pair, 1835. *The Workwoman's Guide* recommended attaching the inventory listing of the contents, together with their numbers and mark, to the door of the closet or cupboard itself, and, with a little less rigor than Mrs. Lea, felt that an annual thorough accounting was sufficient. Marking textiles facilitated the identification of stolen goods and expedited their retrieval. The *Columbian Herald,* for example, alerted Charlestonians in July 1796 to the loss during a recent fire of two fire buckets full of "table cloths, sheets, pillow-cases, towels, men's and children's shirts—all of which are marked with the initials of the Christian name and the surname Reeves in full." Marking might also help family members find and identify things. In response to a request from her mother, Anne Eliza Clark Kane was sorry to report in December 1811, "I have taken all your Blankets out of the trunks and find but two pr of new ones—one pr markd Clark No 2 with green and one pr No 4 with yellow . . . these are every one I can find in the House the one you mention markd Clark with red no where to be found." Also, these markings helped with inventory control, told a housewife or chambermaid at a glance, in a pre-prefitted age, which linens belonged to which bedstead, and expedited making the bed, for the marked end of the sheet was always to be at the head.[15]

These cloth goods of home and commercial manufacture were valuable in both monetary assessment and time expended on them, so prudence and wise economy indicated that they be stored in bolted closets, locked chests, and padlocked trunks. We have already seen some of the bureaus, wardrobes, presses, trunks, high chests, and chests on chests in the chambers and the upper hall. An eighteenth-century nicety practiced by English cabinetmakers and upholsterers such as Thomas Chippendale was to line the drawers of chests and the sliding shelves of presses, unless constructed of cedar, with marbleized paper to promote cleanliness and deter insects. It is no surprise, therefore, to find the custom followed in America. Press paper and marble paper were advertised along with blue, cartridge, brown, and writing paper in 1753 in Boston, where cabinetmaker George Bright, "esteemed the neatest workman in town," billed Jonathan Bowman for a pair of mahogany "buroe tables" in August 1770, the charges covering such fine details as "Lineing the Buroe Table Draws with Marble paper." Fortunately, one of these bureau tables survives, with a scrap of its

marble paper, in the collection of the Society for the Preservation of New England Antiquities. Camphor, shredded tobacco, cracked black pepper, aromatic herbs, dried rose leaves, and lavender were also scattered in drawers and trunks as preventatives to insect damage. One source in 1851 had the heady anti-bug suggestion of storing woolens in an empty hogshead that had held whiskey, exposing them to the air when unpacked in the autumn "till the odour of the whiskey has gone off." One might own camphor-wood chests, and from the seventeenth century American cabinetmakers had lined drawers with white cedar as an effective deterrent to moths. Joshua Brookes commented that the upper rooms of New York houses in the 1790s "are very often hot in summer and smell strong of the cedar as they are often used as a storage room";

Sighting the Enemy. Wood engraving by F. S. Church. 1875. The Bettmann Archive, New York. To many children, the attic and the kitchen were the truly important rooms in the house, with some rather insignificant ones, such as parlor, dining room, and bedchamber, taking up room in between. Attic treasures such as a rope and pulley, spyglass, and costumes help explain such partiality. For the housewife, the attic promoted good housekeeping below by obliging as the storage hold for all outmoded or out-of-season items. Observe the hair-covered trunk of the type often found in bedchambers and the tin-and-wood foot stove in the foreground

and in the third story at Captain Whann's new house in New Orleans in 1860, there was "a cedar closet, lined with shelves, wherein to keep clothing free from moths." Tobacco-scented trunks and whiskey-laced hogsheads crammed with clothing or out-of-season curtains and yard goods were often stashed in the garret. John Innes Clark of Providence could boast of a whole room full of trunks packed with all kinds of textiles, including "1 Trunk containing window & Bed Curtains" in 1808; and in 1811 John C. Howard's Boston "Trunk Room" was filled with tablecloths, napkins, breakfast cloths, kitchen towels, sheets, and pillowcases.[16]

Conscientious housewives knew exactly where all their textiles were—or were supposed to be. Abigail Adams could write from Philadelphia to her sister in 1799, concerning some items she had left behind in Quincy, and ask her "to look in my large Hair cloaths Trunk which stands in the Garret for my white Lutestring Gown & coat which is trimd with silver, and for a Napkin in which is a plain Muslin Gown Embrodered with silk." When William Wirt had trouble finding some infants' clothing his wife had asked him to retrieve from the "upper Press" and "mammoth trunk," at home in Richmond in 1812, she wrote back with some irritation specifying, "The *babys flannel petticoats* I thought you would find in the trunk so particularly described in my memorandum 'as setting in the antechamber with the piece torn loose on the top' they I believed were spread out to the right of the trunk with other flannels, & sprinkled with tobacco." Stored textiles were to be regularly inspected, shaken out, and aired, although even then there might well be insect damage. Caroline Dustan spent 25 August 1864 uneventfully airing blankets and rearranging them on shelves, but Anne Eliza Clark Kane, despite the luxury of a trunk room, morosely penned in October 1811, "to-morrow I shall have all my blankets shaken I find they are eat into holes through and through by the moths."[17]

The dry, musty, herb-scented garret promoted cleanliness by obliging as an ample storehouse for all kinds of outmoded, outgrown, outsize, and out-of-season items. Boxes and bags of candles, feathers, and liquor were stored here year round, to be crowded in summer by the addition of fire screens, paper-wrapped andirons, dismantled stoves, trunks of bed hangings and curtains, chests of winter clothing, and rolled-up carpets. Children's furniture—cribs and a "blue-roofed cradle that had sheltered ten blue-eyed babies," a rocking horse "with real horse-hair mane and tail," might fill one corner, while a cumbersome weaving loom, tape looms, spinning wheel, and flax wheel commandeered another. A clothesline hung taut against one end, while scented herbs—thyme, catnip, thoroughwort, sage, pennyroyal, and balm—and perhaps a labyrinth of dried pumpkins, peaches, and apples hung in festoons all the way across the raftered roof.

But cleanliness was not easy to achieve at home in early America. Servants were indifferent, streets were muddy and dusty, and water might freeze within inches of a roaring fire. The *desire* for cleanliness among upper-class and middle-class Americans from 1750 to 1870 seems, however, to have been real. It is evident in the enormous quantity and variety of brooms and dustpans, brushes, and mops listed in merchants' inventories, enumerated in the account books of those ordering supplies from abroad, and vaunted in newspaper advertisements. It is evident in the widespread use of casters for tables, chairs, chests, and bedsteads so that they might not only be moved about dexterously but be easy to clean under and around; in the varnished walls, glossy paints, glazed chintz, and waxed floors, all of which prolonged cleanliness or facilitated cleaning. In the eighteenth century, the coveted cleanliness was prescribed in part by an esteem for pleasurable and polite surroundings, inoffensive to eye and nose alike, and by a moral obligation to promote the health of the family by effectually preventing dust and dampness and providing a soul-satisfying order. As the eighteenth century advanced, ventilation and air circulation became increasingly important, and by the final decade the demand was for rooms not only clean but "sweet," as the emphasis shifted from genteel politeness to a healthful, lung-strengthening, nose-gratifying airiness. By 1854 a lady of Massachusetts, who described herself as "a grandmother," claimed that she could not "recall the time when agreeable odors, faint and sweet, but not strong, and the sight of pure white linen and white wax candles, were not delightful to me. From childhood, cleanliness and order have been essential to my comfort." In 1855 it was pronounced that "without cleanliness we cannot expect to be healthy," and in the second half of that century the stress would shift once again to include not only a desire for airy, well-ventilated rooms but a demand for sanitary, germ-free apartments.[18]

The relativity of cleanliness, however, is difficult to assess. One cannot help but ponder the implications of Maria Silliman Church's request in April 1842 for a dark dress which she could wear as much as her sister "used to hers, without its looking soiled"; or of Phebe Ann Beach Lyman's gift to her sister, in October 1839, of a dark frock—which she hoped would save her making one, but if not it could be washed and laid by as "it is very dirty, for I have worn it ever since I have been here." Nonetheless, in 1837 Eliza Farrar had stressed the importance of doing one's housework in a tidy, washable dress with a clean apron over it, and an unsoiled apron or pinafore was regarded by many as indispensable feminine garb from girlhood. Thomas Jefferson warned his daughter Patsy in 1783 that she was not to wear her clothes until the dirt was visible to the eye; and when he told this eleven-year-old, "above all things and at all times let your clothes be neat, whole, and properly put on," he addressed the mandate that a girl or woman be neat and clean in dress. It was a cleanliness requisite not only in costume but in "Persons and Houses"; in, as John Adams enumerated in

Height of Cleanliness. Illustration by David Claypoole Johnston in *Scraps #6* (1835). The Winterthur Library: Printed Book and Periodical Collection. This cartoon censures over-zealous cleaning. Indeed, foreign observers often commented upon the exceedingly tidy aspect of town and village homes in this comfortable new nation. One Frenchman exulted that neatness and cleanliness were to be seen everywhere in Boston, and a Polish visitor approvingly surveyed the "greatest cleanliness" of Philadelphia apartments

1761, "Teeth, Necks, Hair, Perspiration and Respirations, Kitchens and even Parlors." Adams went so far as to hypothesize and hyperbolize, "My own Daughters, whenever they shall grow to Years of Discretion, I am determined to throw into a great Kettle and Boil till they are clean, If I ever find them half as nasty as I have seen some." The expressed aim of female neatness at this time was not womanly well-being or self-esteem but male approbation. "Nothing," avowed Adams, "is so disgustful and loathsome to me, and almost all our sex are of my mind, as this Negligence." "Nothing," seconded Jefferson as he wrote to Patsy in 1783, "is so disgusting to our sex as a want of cleanliness and delicacy in yours. I hope, therefore, the moment you rise from bed, your first work will be to dress yourself in such a style, as that you may be seen by an gentleman without his being able to discover a pin amiss." Here was another key ingredient in the recipe for feminine neatness—person and apartments must be clean throughout and at all times. This insistence on an all-inclusive cleanliness is a leitmotiv that runs through household manuals, juvenilia, fiction, and parental advice to daughters. A nursery rhyme summed it up:

> Be cleanly and polite at home,
> Then you're prepared if friends should come;
> Make it your habit to be clean,
> No matter then by whom you're seen.

Enos Hitchcock's inestimable, though fictional, Mrs. Charles Worthy was never ashamed to have any part of her house visited and adjudged for cleanliness, as she was guided by the maxim that "to know the true character of the mistress of the house, you must go into her garret and cellar." And about 1785 a concerned father warned his daughter with this didactic scene:

> True Cleanliness is the same throughout. How often have I been diverted at going into a family of Females to see some run one way and some another like a parcel of Mice at the opening of a Closet Door, & dare not make their appearance 'til they had adjusted their Dress, and made themselves *fit to appear in Company.* Dean Swift made it a practice when he went to visit a female acquaintance always to run into the Back rooms, up Chamber & all over the House to convince himself of the Cleanliness of the Mistress, for he wisely concluded that the room in which he was received would be prepared for the purpose.[19]

The back-country hut and forest-shrouded cabin had condemnation aplenty heaped on them, but observers of the American scene generally admired the neatness and cleanliness of town and village homes in New England and the Middle Colonies. It seemed to Johannes Still, who emigrated from Switzerland in the 1820s and settled on the mid-Atlantic coast, that this concern for cleanliness was carried far enough to become "almost a vice. Every week the houses are scrubbed from top to bottom and not just with water and sand but with soap." By the close of the eighteenth century, the reflective polish of the looking glass had become a metaphor for fastidious housekeeping. Félix de Beaujour was convinced that in America it was "impossible not to admire the polish of the furniture, and even the extreme cleanliness of the floors"—a mirror brightness which Louis de Robertnier in 1780 found enabled "anyone to look at himself anywhere." Indeed, the ultimate compliment to a housewife might be that her mahogany, silver, pewter, and brass emulated the very looking glasses in their luster. Little Louisa Jane and Caroline Trumbull of Worcester, Massachusetts, spent a Saturday in January 1832 helping their mother clean the andirons and the door-latch—which they did so well "as to see your face in it"; in July 1774 a not-easily-satisfied John Adams was entirely happy with Mrs. Eustis's "very neat house" in Portland, Maine, where the "desk and table shine like mirrors." And in the fiction of the time we can admire that aptly named Mrs. Worthy's best room, where beside the window "stood a large maple table, which for its bright polish resembled the looking glass which hung over it."[20]

The farther south all these chroniclers went, the more their approbation diminished. Although they saw much through the prejudicial eyes of those opposed to slavery, yet innumerable observers wrote that the standards of cleanliness were lower where many of the household duties were performed by slaves. During a visit to South Carolina in the 1790s, the duc de La Rochefoucauld-Liancourt maintained that despite the glut of help, "yet the houses are not preserved so clean on the inside as in the northern states," and Robert Sutcliff concurred: "I was sometimes ready to think that the more slaves there were employed about a house and plantation, the more disorder appeared." But everything was clean and comfortable when fastidious Margaret Hunter Hall came to call at Mr. Skirving's South Carolina plantation in 1828; and Anne Royall's comment from Virginia that the floors were rubbed *every* morning with brush and wax until they were "as slippery as glass," or Letitia Burwell's depiction of the matinal buffings at her Virginia plantation in the 1850s, where "every inch of mahogany was waxed and rubbed to the highest state of polish, as were also the floors, the brass fenders, [and]irons, and candlesticks," suggests that all southern housekeeping cannot be condemned.[21]

John Lambert and Patrick Shirreff catalogued New England virtues as cleanliness, order, comfort, and "oeconomy"; while Frances Wright found that cheerfulness, cleanliness, and comfort distinguished Philadelphia; and Félix de Beaujour esteemed the salient qualities of all Americans to be "the love of freedom, of industry, of order, and of cleanliness." Polishing, scouring, sweeping, washing, sewing, and guarding were unvaried duties that stretched minutes into hours, hours into days, days into months, and months into years. When Maria Silliman Church wrote home on 2 July 1833, she apologized for the monotony of her life; she had no incidents to relate, "nothing but the daily dog-trot routine of domestic duties." But in a few months she would be busy enough preparing the house for winter, for the burden of year-round repetitive tasks was enormously complicated by the supplementary demands of winter and summer. To these we will look next.[22]

■ CHAPTER EIGHT ■
THE QUEST FOR
COMFORT:
*Housekeeping Practices
and Living Arrangements
the Year Round*

Foreign observers had nothing nice to say about the extremes of the North American climate. The duc de La Rochefoucauld-Liancourt was dismayed to find the cold incomparably stronger and more protracted in America than in Europe in the same latitude—the heat more intense, more oppressive, and more insupportable. From steamy Philadelphia in August 1769, with the thermometer reading ninety-five degrees and everyone panting with the heat, Alexander Mackraby would marvel that "the mad people will marry in spite of it." Come January, the equivalent cold had not frozen his wit: "The intense heat of last summer overpowered me, and the cold we have already this winter seems to exceed all recollection or idea, as well as it does all endurance. I had almost spoiled my letter with a lump of black ice, which hung from my pen just now. I am going to attend an electrical lecture. We'll try if that spark can touch me, and if it does I will dance it to a blaze at the assembly to night." One foreign officer in New York in 1780 turned to liquor to give temporary respite from these desperate extremes in America, where "You always have to drink, either to get warm, or to get cool, or for protection against the evil mists,—or because you get no letters." But all agreed that there was no sure antidote.[1]

Summer heat was excessive from Maine to Mississippi. To the duke of Saxe-Weimar Eisenach in Boston, "the full moon looked like a glowing coal in the heated atmosphere"; and to Lady Emmeline Stuart Wortley, the Albany sky was "like a great turquoise roof *on fire*." Julian Niemcewicz "breathed in flame" in Portsmouth, New Hampshire, while Tyrone Power was convinced that the morning dew had been boiled the day before and not had time to cool. And the cold! "But what shall I say of the weather?" puzzled Sarah Eve from near Philadelphia in February 1773. "We have had 'very cold,' 'extremely cold,' 'excessive cold,' and 'exceeding cold' . . . none of these separately is sufficient to convey the idea of the temperature of this day—it needs more than the superlative degree, it would take a super-superlative degree if there is such an one, for it is very extremely excessive cold."[2]

European visitors generally found New World houses better suited to warm weather than cold weather. With their slight wooden frames, abundant doors and windows, spacious rooms, and lofty ceilings, American homes were airy and cool all summer long but drafty enough in winter. It seemed to Margaret Hunter Hall in Cayuga, New York, in 1827, that the houses were built "expressly for summer, without the slightest reference to the six months' winter that they suffer." It was yet worse in the South, for, as the duke of Saxe-Weimar Eisenach pointed out, "one suffers no where so much from cold as in a warm climate, since the dwellings are well calculated to resist heat, but in nowise suited to repel cold." J. B. Dunlop shivered in Georgia in February 1811, as the temperature plummeted from a noontime high of sixty degrees to an evening low of twenty-nine—"the effect of so sudden a change was more sensibly felt than the coldest day in Scotland and the houses being ill

How Cold! Oil on academy board, by Charles Markham. 1873. Private collection. Arctic cold slowed the fingers, congealed the blood, tried the spirit, and confined one to the fireside. Indeed, the rigors of the North American climate seemed abusive to foreign visitors, who found both winter frosts and summer blasts debilitating. Temperature extremes often kept Americans seasonally housebound, and it is to these indoor habits and want of exercise that Europeans ascribed the delicate health of pallid-faced Yankees. Observe the hanging map, a wall decoration that might be found in sitting room, study, and hallway alike

calculated to shelter one from its piercing blast—I think I never felt anything so cold." Lieutenant Francis Hall nearly froze in South Carolina, where he found all the houses built of scantling and "penetrable at every crevice; while from the usual mildness of the weather, doors have become altogether released from the duty of being shut." Landscape architect Frederick Law Olmsted confirmed that the very idea of closing a door or window to exclude cold air had not reached the South by 1854, and "from the time I left Richmond, until I arrived at Charleston, I never but once knew a servant to close a door on leaving a room, unless he was requested at the moment to do so."[3]

Winter was despotic—strutting in "like a peremptory bandit." All knew that this season would bring discomfort and hindrance. William Dunlap ruefully acknowledged that Winter had at last mounted his throne in January 1806: "He has cast his white robe o'er his shoulders and shook his glassy sceptre over us in terrorum. I hate him heartily." Housewives agreed, dreading the severe weather, as it seemed to make everything twice as difficult to get on with. Many duties had to be performed if the house and family were to withstand the exacting rigors of winter. Summer clothing was stored and winter items were readied. Stockings, flannels, double (layered) gowns, petticoats, shirts, trousers, and jackets all had to be altered or fabricated—and at a season when the ever-shorter days impeded needlework. There were also many accessories to assemble if one were to stymie Jack Frost. Anne Eliza Clark, when a schoolgirl in Medford, Massachusetts, thanked her mother for the yarn mitts, which were "of great service to me when I sweep my chamber and make my bed," and artist Ruth Henshaw Bascom spent 16 December 1801, in Norfolk, Virginia, making herself "a pair of nankeen mittens to wear in the house." When Charles Carroll of Annapolis ordered a "Light Gray full Bob Wigg" from London in September 1751, he stipulated that it be "full Large in the Head & Deep and well Cover'd with Hair as too thin will not do for Cold weather." Eighty-seven years later, a balding Samuel Breck went to the hairdresser to get "a crown piece of false hair" to "keep the head warm and comfortable." But even dressed in full bob wig and wrapped in a Falstaffian rotundity of flannels and furs, one often found it impossible to keep warm. Rebecca Smith complained from Philadelphia in September 1792 that even though she was in the midst of the flurry of fall cleaning, "up and down and in all the rooms of the house," yet she could scarcely keep from freezing. And Anne Jean Lyman recalled the drafty days at Brush Hill in Milton, Massachusetts, when she and her sister, "wore our great coats in the house half the time . . . and even then could not have been warm without the active employments that kept us constantly busy."[4]

The cellar must be replenished with apples and late vegetables packed in sawdust or sand. Pigs had to be killed—the worst job of the year, according to one housewife—sausages made, and barrels of pork and ham put down. Pies were baked in quantity to be kept frozen in the storeroom, the garret, the guest chamber, or the closed-up parlor. Far into the nineteenth century, many housewives were obligated to spend cold fall days making soap and candles. Maria Silliman Church was relieved to be able to report on 22 January 1834 that she had "now completed all the winter jobs of sausages, pork, putting down hams, making candles, & mince pies." Once the family was provided with winter clothing and provender, the house must be outfitted. New England diaries portray the autumn ritual of banking or "blocking up" the house with leaves or seaweed. Doors were battened, and windows sealed by papering, pasting, or covering them with baize. Alice Izard decided not to have her windows papered in South Carolina in November 1814 as she did not expect a severe winter and rather liked fresh air even in the coldest weather; while William Wirt awaited his sister-in-law's last-minute instructions as to which windows she wished "blinded" with green baize in January 1813, "as tis a work of ten minutes only." Leather had been used in England to weatherstrip doors from the mid-eighteenth century, and the practice was advocated here far into the nineteenth century. An invoice of goods to be sent from London to a merchant in Williamsburg, Virginia, in January 1772, for example, included nine dozen of "yellow Gilt" and nine dozen of "White Silverd" leather "listing" for doors, along with nails to match, to secure both. Eliza Leslie was yet suggesting the use of leather listing in 1840. Catharine Beecher recommended nailing tightly against a door either fabric caulking or strips of wood covered with baize. Mrs. Leslie also remarked that in the North most of the windows were made with double sashes to prevent drafts of cold air, and when Christopher Gore pictured his family at home in Waltham, Massachusetts, in December 1816, they were busy "putting our House in a state for Winter Quarters by some Double Windows, repairing Stoves & making Flues for the Smoke." Double doors might further foil wintry blasts. In December 1825 Ellen Randolph Coolidge assured her grandfather Thomas Jefferson that she was staying warm in Boston, where "the houses are well built, with double doors, small close rooms, stoves and whatever contributes to keep out the general enemy, the intense cold; great stores of wood and other fuel are timely laid in." Indeed, the rise of the sun was often accompanied by the ring of the ax as fuel

The Dining Room on Christmas Eve. Pencil drawing by Lucy Ellen Merrill. c. 1870. Historical Society of Old Newbury, Newburyport, Massachusetts. Garlands of greens were used at parties or special celebrations to decorate pictures, lamps, and chandeliers. In this Christmas scene, they trace about the windows and around the corner buffet and even demarcate each place at table. Observe the candles on the tree and the presents festively stacked before each place setting

Bowery Theatre, New York. Drawing by Charles Burton, engraved by H. Fossette. 1831. I. N. Phelps Stokes Collection, The New York Public Library; Astor, Lenox and Tilden Foundations. New York engraver Alexander Anderson described himself walking down the Bowery to look for a stove on 14 October 1799, and here some thirty-two years later is just such an assortment set up for display across from the Bowery Theatre. These relatively light-weight affairs were set up for the winter months and dismantled in the spring

supplies were readied. Fifteen to fifty cords of wood met a family's needs for a year. Impoverished Jane Mecom told her brother, Benjamin Franklin, that she endured a Boston winter with twelve cords, "as we keept but won Fire Exept on some Extroidenary ocations"; but Abigail Adams, with a family of eighteen at Richmond Hill, wrote from New York that she burned forty to fifty cords a year, "as we are obliged to keep six fires constantly, & occasionally more." La Rochefoucauld-Liancourt remarked that Charlestonians used an anomalous amount of wood because "the intense heat of the summer renders the human frame so sensible to cold, that . . . five or six months together, they keep fire in the rooms; and . . . to the best of my information, one family uses more wood in that town than two families in Philadelphia."[5]

Stoves were much more economical in the consumption of wood or coal, and when Peter Clopper advertised "New-Invented Pennsylvania Stoves," in New York in 1761, he expounded on their virtue as being "remarkable for making a Room Warm and comfortable with very little Wood." Pennsylvania inventories show a widespread acceptance of these Franklin fireplaces and close (airtight) stoves in the second half of the eighteenth century; elsewhere, however, stoves were not in general use until the early years of the nineteenth century, at which time a common compromise seems to have been an airtight stove in the hall and an open fire in the parlor. Catharine Beecher still found the Franklin stove the most agreeable for a parlor in 1841, as it combined the advantages of the frugal stove and genial open hearth. When A. J. Downing drew plans for a truly economical cottage in 1850, he included no fireplaces but only flues for stoves, though he admitted this to be "a mode of warming which we regret to see growing so popular in this country, since we think it consults economy at the cost of both health and cheerfulness. If we were building this cottage, therefore, we would have an open grate or fire-place in the living-room or parlor." Nonetheless, an airtight stove was often put up each fall to be dismantled in the spring and stashed away in the capacious garret or distant shed. Caroline Dustan implies that hers was stored upstairs, perhaps in the garret, for she mentions that her maid "brought down stove" on 22 October 1862. James Bailey didn't care where his was stored but he knew it was an infernal nuisance to put up and take down, and those endless stovepipe pieces were a remorselessly provoking puzzle that never joined up right no matter how you studied them, tried them, jammed them together—"You begin to think the pieces are inspired with life, and ache to kick them through the window." The wood-fueled or coal-stoked furnace, with its tributary hot-air pipes, had arrived in modern, fashionable homes by the 1830s and would incur the wrath and damnation of household reformers, travelers, and social commentators for the remainder of the century. Yet whether they baked, were half-stewed and parboiled, suffered thin faces, pale skin, and unenergetic temperament, or breathed in fifty-seven hogsheads of bad air every twenty-four hours, Americans were determined to try to keep warm. Samuel Eliot Morison said that at his late-nineteenth-century Boston home the hot-air furnace only reached the second floor anyway; in that era, urban homes were generally heated by the furnace in the cellar and supplementary grates burning anthracite coal in the parlors and chambers.[6]

Supplies of coal and wood were no guarantee of comfort during the depth of winter, however. Harriet Beecher Stowe warned that "whoever touched a door-latch incautiously, in the early morning, received a skinning bite from Jack [Frost]"; and Harriet Martineau could recall those December mornings in America when, even with an anthracite-coal fire in your chamber, "everything you touch seems to blister your fingers with cold." "My fingers are so cold I can scarce hold a pen" is a sentence that fills eighteenth-century and nineteenth-century letters from both North and South. Even Landon Carter's clock protested the piercing cold of the Virginia winter in 1776—"except when the chaffing dish is kept under it, it hardly goes." Ink, water, and wine froze regularly and hard liquor on occasion. Burdened with a houseful of guests for Christmas week in 1755, Esther Burr groaned from Princeton, New Jersey, "Extream cold and all the Ink in the House froze up—and with all a good deal of company, [so] that I have had time for nothing heardly." In New York City in January 1829, James Stuart found it "difficult to preserve the body in sufficient warmth, even wrapped in two suits of clothes, and every one kept on stockings and flannel garments during night. The ink froze in my pen in lifting it to the paper from an ink-horn, placed within the fender in front of a good fire." Maria Silliman Church apologized for the illegibility of a letter she was writing on 18 December 1835, but "the cold weather has frozen all colour out of the ink, and made it so *thin* besides that it is like writing with water"—she finished that letter in pencil. A year later her sister Faith complained from the Church home that, even with a stove in the office below, a pipe-fed sheet-iron drum in the entry upstairs, and open wood fires, "it freezes every where, with a fire in the hearth things will freeze in the sideboard and with the largest fire we can make in my room, water will freeze within six feet of it." She further pointed out the difficulty—in fact, the impossibility—of scrubbing anything clean under such circumstances. Anna Maria Thornton monotonously incanted, "Cold & Clear froze in the house," throughout the winter of 1800 in Washington; and Caroline Dustan would do the same in New York in the 1850s and 1860s, specifying on 19 December 1856, "water in Mamma's & my wash bowl freezing thick as half a dollar," and on 26 December 1857, "*pitcher frozen solid* in bedrooms." Well might household manuals offer suggestions on how to prevent water from freezing in lead pipes in winter once town homes began to luxuriate in running water. At a Virginia home in 1795, "the wine was constantly frozen in the bottle, the very cheese cakes and jellies were stiff frozen in the pantries." Benjamin Pickman of Salem would record on 17 February 1816, "Madeira wine froze in the closets." In that town a year later, Margaret Holyoke would marvel that "Strong vineagar & spirit & water" were frozen in a closet by the chimney in which there was a Franklin stove, and in Boston on a chilly Christmas Day in 1778, William Tudor's gill of New England rum froze on a shelf in the pantry.[7]

When the cold arrived in earnest, families moved inside, where, Caroline King tells us, "people lived and moved and had their being in one room in winter." From frigid New York in January 1782, Rebecca Rawle Shoemaker admitted, "Our room is very comfortable, & I seldom go out of it." The apartment selected for the winter sitting room was small in size — "we live in the little room now," wrote Mary Guion in December 1801. Anne Grant commended the cozy winter parlor in the back section of a mid-eighteenth-century Albany home, which "afforded a refuge to the family during the rigours of winter, when the spacious summer rooms would have been intolerably cold"; and Fanny Appleton Longfellow pictured her family in January 1851, "driven out of the big library by the cold . . . to the snug study, where we feel more cozy and comfortable." Sitting-room doors were closed, the family hermetically sealed. Emily Dickinson could portray this insular nature of the hibernal family for her brother one snowy November day in 1851, when "it grew so cold that we gathered up all the quinces, put up the stove in the sitting-room and bade the world good-by." This spatial constriction, uncomfortable though it may have been, ensured the survival of the family as a social unit. Looking back from the threshold of the twentieth century on the subsequent loss of geographic intimacy within the family, William Davis wrote, "I know no greater change within my lifetime than that exhibited by the lessening influence of home. It has been brought about, partly by the disintegrating effect of civilized life, which with new means of heating and lighting, has scattered the members of a family, leaving no fireside to gather around."[8]

Within the cramped intimacy of the winter sitting room, the family clustered in a tight little band around the fireplace or stove. Eliza Farrar remonstrated against this sedentary fender-hugging in 1837, but Ann White Smith of Norton, Massachusetts, vouched in 1790 that the weather was so monstrous cold one couldn't move a yard from the fire. In *Oldtown Folks*, Harriet Beecher Stowe evoked those "extremely cold days, when a very forest of logs, heaped up and burning in the great chimney, could not warm the other side of the kitchen; and when Aunt Lois, standing with her back so near the blaze as to be uncomfortably warm, yet found her dish-towel freezing in her hand, while she wiped the teacup drawn from the almost boiling water." Outrageous hyperbole? Not when William Bentley tells us in January 1810 that on the side of his chamber farthest from a brisk fire the thermometer read "16 below freezing." Nor when Thomas Chaplin writes from South Carolina in January 1857 that the thermometer is down to 20 degrees in the house at eight in the morning and that everything is frozen hard, including eggs, milk, and ink, and that every piece of crockery that water was left in overnight is cracked. Nor when Faith Silliman Hubbard, at home in Hanover, New Hampshire, claims that "the tea kettle froze solid in the cooking stove where there was *fire raked up!*" No wonder early Americans delighted in a reviving cup of boiling-hot tea.[9]

Stoves and fireplaces provided only pockets of heat, which were ineffectual in

Fire Light. Long Island, New York. Pencil sketch by William Sidney Mount. 1847. The Museums at Stony Brook, Stony Brook, New York; bequest of Mr. Ward Melville, 1977. This family huddles close to the fire, the baby holding up her hands to its welcome warmth. It was indeed difficult to keep little children warm in the depths of winter and particularly crawling infants, who had to endure not only a cold floor but low-clinging drafts warming the body all over. Charlotte Taylor, who was born in Virginia in the opening years of the nineteenth century, said that her face and back were never warm at the same time. Ralph Waldo Emerson was grateful for a temperate spell in January 1835: "We are all glad of warm days they are so economical & in the country in winter the back is always cold." Fire screens were essential to block drafts, hold in heat, or insulate the body from too much heat, as one had to sit pretty nearly in the fire for warmth. In promoting his down-draft iron fireplace in 1744, Benjamin Franklin had argued against open wood fires because "the cold Air so nips the Backs and Heels of those that sit before the Fire, that they have no comfort, 'til either Screens or Settles are provided." But these tall-backed forms, he maintained, were costly, encumbered the room, and darkened the fireside. Yet Eliza Leslie insisted in 1840 that "where there is a grate or an open stove, fire-screens are indispensable to comfort, and no room should be without one"; and Catharine Beecher continued to advocate their use well into the second half of the nineteenth century. While convalescing in Boston in February 1772, twelve-year-old Anna Green Winslow could complacently write in her diary, "Everybody says that this is a bitter cold day, but I know nothing about it but hearsay for I am in aunt's chamber (which is very warm always) with a nice fire, a [foot] stove, sitting in Aunt's easy chair, with a tall three leav'd screen at my back, & I am very comfortable." John Buttolph, a Boston wine cooper, owned a "Green Screen 5 leaves" in 1750, and John Hancock had two fire screens and four hand screens in his Boston parlor in 1794. These hand-held screens and small standing screens on poles, called pole screens, were also used pervasively in an attempt to distribute the heat of the fire evenly, although they were not always effective. Eliza Leslie reminded housewives in 1840 not to forget hand screens in furnishing a room, and suggested that these "be large enough to shade the face completely, and may be made very handsome by a young lady of good taste and well skilled in drawing." She pointed out that fire screens not only shielded a lady's face from the excessive heat of the fire but guarded her silk dress from being discolored by the same intensity.[10]

Smoke contributed to the discomfort and disadvantage of open fires. Nancy Tilghman and her friends spent a "stupid silent Afternoon in a bitter cold Room, which smoak'd so monstrously that they came home half blind, and almost frozen," in Maryland in 1785. Anne Eliza Clark Kane, who often complained of malfunctioning chimneys at home in Providence, pictured herself driven out of her room by smoke on a windy Christmas Eve in 1811 and retreating to the study, where she hoped to arrange some books; but smoke again prevented her from seeing across the room, so she was finally obliged to seek refuge in the nursery, "where I am now writing but my eyes are full of tears from the effects of the smoke and I can hardly see my paper." As the nursery, too, was so murky with smoke that she felt "perfectly blind," she soon concluded the letter.[11]

Small tin-and-wood foot stoves fitted with an iron dish of glowing coals were used for additional warmth in pew and parlor alike. Samuel Kelly observed their use by the New York ladies at church in 1791 and added, "These stoves are also used during severe winter by the females in their dwellings, each person having one." This little amenity was introduced to the New World by the Dutch and was, therefore, used primarily in regions where they had settled. Benjamin Prat of Suffolk County, Massachusetts, kept "One Tea Foot Stowe" in his hall chamber in 1763, but the fact that he was "late of the City of New York" is significant. Often pictured beneath a lady's foot in paintings of early Dutch interiors, these stoves were considered a

Keeping Warm. Long Island, New York. Sketch by William Sidney Mount. c. 1840–68. Whereabouts unknown. Courtesy The Museums at Stony Brook, Stony Brook, New York. Beneath the foot of this lady is a foot stove—a wood-framed box with pierced tin sides—into which one would place a pan of hot coals. They were used at first in areas settled by the Dutch but by the opening years of the nineteenth century had found favor in settlements both North and South. Popular for warming toes at home and at church, these were considered a feminine amenity

feminine piece of furniture. Hans and Sylis Bergen of Hempstead, New York, owned "a woman's Stove" in 1726, and a century later a Scotsman traveling through the States referred to "dutch female warming stoves." Samuel Goodrich pronounced them "effeminate luxuries"; and after walking two and a half miles to church one freezing December day in 1819, Theodore Dwight declared his toes "comfortably bitten"—"which excited much sympathy; & I came near suffering the indignity of having a girl with gold beads offer me a *stove.*" By the early nineteenth century, this convenience was found both North and South. Margaret Bayard Smith pictured herself at home in Washington on 19 January 1817, "half frozen, with my back close to the fire and a foot stove beneath my feet." By 1840 Eliza Leslie would maintain that no house should be without them, and in 1857 Caroline Dustan left her "Ma' in sitting room with foot stove . . . & small fire of chips in stove." Alexander Anderson's "Ma" must not have had one, for he spent the evening of 19 May 1794 doctoring "Mama who had discover'd a blister on her leg, which I suspect was caus'd by a smoothing Iron, which she had heated and wrapped up in a cloth, to warm her feet."[12]

In preparation for the widely divergent temperatures of winter and summer, the house was subjected to a biannual housecleaning of calendrical immutability. William Bolling of Goochland County, Virginia, noted in his diary on 14 May 1827, "Summer Establishment. Took up our carpets, put down oil cloth and commenced our summer establishment altho' the weather is but little like it"; and he dutifully updated the routine on 19 October, "Winter Establishment. Took up oil cloth and spread carpets on our floors, tho' the weather did not call for it."[13]

These housecleanings were of almost herculean proportions, often leaving the female members of the family exhausted despite any extra help they might have been able to secure. "Your mother has been somewhat complaining from over work in cleaning the house for the summer, but is again mending," one father advised his son on 24 May 1848. Deborah Norris Logan pictured herself unwillingly caught between "the war of the elements in the reign of chaos called house cleaning"; while Emily Dickinson shuddered, "House is being 'cleaned.' I prefer pestilence." Caroline King rather liked these thorough cleanings at her childhood home in Salem, for then her father's high, obscuring bookcases were pulled out from the wall—once again revealing the scenic wallpaper (probably by Zuber et Compagnie of Alsace), with its Swiss views of Alps and villages, a lively fair, and gaily dressed peasants dancing—"And I remember the glee with which we eagerly slipped behind them and greeted our Swiss friends once more." As a boy, Stephen Walkley thought it strange that his mother and sisters got so very tired because "house cleaning was great fun for Jonny and me, except whipping carpets, lugging all the chairs out in the sun and then back again, and cleaning the cellar." But as he grew older, Stephen undoubtedly joined the bastion of husbands who thoroughly despised the ritual. Harriet Beecher Stowe mused that one season of thorough housecleaning would prove the enormous fallibility of the crusading treatises that propounded the similitude of the sexes.[14]

Lizzie Wonderly teased her fiancé in October 1862, "We have been busy, turning the house upside down which, I suppose, you are exceedingly fond of 'knowing that all gentlemen are.'" Eliza Leslie suggested that the whole business might be deferred or anticipated by a week or so "if there is a prospect of the master of the family having business to take him from home at the period so uncomfortable to all gentlemen"; and Benjamin Franklin Perry thanked his wife for availing herself of his absence to whitewash and clean house as "I do not like such business at all, at all."[15]

Men confessed to hating the confusion. Francis Hopkinson said that if you had ever witnessed the hurry, bustle, confusion, and noise of a house-raising or a ship launching you could have some idea of this cleaning match. Samuel Canby Rumford attributed male disapprobation not only to the confusion during the process but to the impossibility of finding anything at its conclusion. They also condemned the breakage—"An able arithmetician hath made a calculation . . . and proved that the losses and destruction incident to two white-washings are equal to one removal and three removals equal to one fire." But an even more important factor was the wound to male pride, for a "husband, however beloved, becomes a perfect nuisance during this season of female rage." Men were not only unwanted, they were unattended at these hectic times, and a husband knew he was in trouble when his wife appeared, turban around her head, soot on the face, and "nothing in the countenance indicative of love, sweetness, or dinner." Worst of all, however, was the feeling of impotence—a husband lay defenseless before an advancing knight-errant who, suited in an armature of broom and brush, cloth and wash, seized her biannual right to torment her husband, took the reigns of government into her own hands, and determined "what you must wear, where you may sit down, what you may touch, what rooms are usable, what days of the week are home days, or endurable days." The desire for spotless cleanliness might be commendable, but Henry Ward Beecher had had enough. He pined for "a morsel of dirt as a luxury! How good dust looks! A ploughed field with endless dirt,—all hail! The great sentence itself, which consigns man finally to dust again, becomes a consolation!"[16]

Duties common to both the fall and the spring purgations included sweeping chimneys, washing windows, dusting wallpaper, cleaning paint, whitewashing walls, organizing closets, and scouring floors. Carpets and curtains were either brought out or put away according to the dictates of the season. Fall housecleaning might commence as early as September and continue into December. Esther Burr turned her New Jersey house "up-side-down" to clean on 8 September 1755, while Mary Guion of Westchester, New York, spent the week of 16 October 1803 similarly employed. In Hadley, Massachusetts, Elizabeth Porter Phelps had her rooms whitewashed on 7 December 1783, and Elizabeth Oswald Chew of Philadelphia made sure this work was begun by mid-September 1816. Summer ornaments were discarded from fire-places and grates, and stoves were set up.[17]

The surge in textile manufacturing in the late eighteenth century and early nineteenth century meant that more and more housewives had curtains to hang each autumn, sofas to dress in dark, soot-resistant garb, and carpets to put down. The latter were in general use by the 1830s—a certain boon in the typically drafty American house—and all who could purchase or make one did, for heat retention as well as visual enhancement. Upstairs, downstairs, on the stairs, many of these carpets were stretched tightly and secured with tacks—the thousands of which must have seemed overwhelming to those housewives who hammered them in every fall and pried them loose each spring. Maria Silliman Church spent 20 November 1839 "getting my parlor cleaned and stretching & nailing the carpet," and the next day feeling "stiff & sore and *jaded.*" Catharine Beecher suggested placing little pieces of kid beneath the tacks to protect the carpet and facilitate extraction, recommending as well the use of a "carpet fork." Martha Ogle Forman was delighted when in January 1817 her husband purchased her "a little carpet crowbar," which she found "excellent for taking tacks out of the carpet." In some households, particularly during the second half of the nineteenth century, woolen carpets were not removed for the summer months but simply untacked each spring and fall, shaken out, and replaced.[18]

There was considerable controversy over what should be spread beneath the carpet. Anne Gertrude Sneller could remember a heavenly scent of tiny branches of cedar wafting out from under the ingrain carpets at her home near Cicero, New York, in the late nineteenth century. There might also be the less subtle bouquet of tobacco and cracked black pepper, which *The Kitchen Directory and American Housewife* (1844) recommended sprinkling beneath the carpets if there was any evidence of moths, together with a bed of straw, which "will make them last longer, as the dirt will sift through." Little Catherine Havens described the thin, big-figured carpet in her sister's mid-nineteenth-century best parlor with straw underneath—"to make it soft I guess." This was a room not easily forgotten by a child, for it was here, on the mantelpiece, recalled Catherine, that an elderly spinster in the family kept little pieces of wax with which to stick in her missing teeth when company came to call. Elizabeth Ellicott Lea agreed that carpets would wear better with straw underneath, but cautioned that they must be well tacked down lest the straw take fire. Mrs. M. L. Scott disagreed in 1855, ordering, "Do not lay straw under your carpet if you wish to save them," and recommending that "large sheets of coarse paper are far better, and should always be used." Catharine Beecher objected to straw on the grounds that the lumpy surface would make the carpet wear unevenly, and suggested smooth straw matting as an alternative padding. In the second half of the nineteenth century, summer straw matting was often left *in situ* year-round although, as Samuel Canby Rumford reported, with the approach of autumn the matting would again be covered up with carpeting, "even including the narrow piece up the center of the front stairs." Eliza Leslie agreed that matting was better than straw but preferred that drugget (a coarse, durable cloth also used in the dining room as a crumb cloth) be laid on the floor beneath the carpet. Caroline Dustan swept her front parlor on 7 November 1856 and "put down druggets for winter." Mrs. Dustan could have laid her druggets either under or over the carpets, as the latter practice was recommended for rooms in constant use. These were to be taken up when there was company. A third alternative was to use the druggets alone, as carpeting, "and when of a handsome brown or marone colour," allowed *The Workwoman's Guide* (1838), they "look exceedingly well." Baize was also used to protect vulnerable areas or the entire carpet. There was "A Carpet of Blue Bays to cover" Aaron Burr's "Elegant Turkey carpet" in 1797; and when Margaret Izard Manigault rented a Philadelphia house in October 1807, she was relieved that "the house is clean & it is completely covered with green baize—& I hope it will be warm." Anne Eliza Clark Kane wrote from New York that everyone "put down thick double width green baize by the door," and in that city in December 1832 Richard Loins had "A Carpet & Rug & Greene Baize" in his front room. This layered look was quite common, for the carpet was frequently guarded not only by green baize but by just such a small rug—"supposed in these Days a Necessary Article to lay before the hearth over a good Carpet," explained Williamina Cadwalader in December 1801. Lydia Bowen Clark's brother had advised her of this fashion in March 1799, when he sent from London four rugs as "they are used here by every lady to preserve the carpet about the fire place."[19]

Curtains were often hung in November. It was a frustrating and precarious—sometimes life-threatening—undertaking. Christopher Vail of Norwich, Connecticut, wrote his grandson on 15 September 1836, "Your Grand Ma . . . has been an Invalid for a week or two back caused by standing on a table to put up a curtain the table tipt up with her & brought her down to the floor table Croc[k]ery & all"; and Caroline Dustan fell off a ladder while struggling with her curtains in November 1860. It is not surprising, therefore, that a little boy from Danbury, Connecticut, is said to have thought "that 'household gods' are what his pa uses when he puts up curtain fixtures." Bed curtains were hung at the same time and required yet more patience, more stamina, and more expertise. Some of these elaborate hangings were very complicated affairs indeed, and *The Workwoman's Guide* advised that all best-bed and parlor draperies, at least, "should be put up by regular upholsterers, as it requires much correctness of eye, added to taste and knowledge of the prevailing fashion." Account books reveal that many urban wives availed themselves of this professional assistance. But Esther Burr struggled on alone in Princeton, New Jersey, on 6 September 1755, "puting up Beds and no body to help me and it is a good deal of work to pin up two beds"; while on rural Long Island a miserable Mary Cooper was "att home a lone fixing up my bed" on 13 November 1768, though she was "very unwell and tired almost to death." Emily Barnes recalled helping her aunt hang a bedstead in the 1840s, wrestling with "dimity curtains, trimmed with broad, netted fringe, while we found it still more difficult to arrange the blue silk canopy overhead."[20]

Once draped, the bedstead and its mountainous feather bed might offer some refuge from the cold. "I sought my bed quite early this evening," wrote John Quincy Adams on 8 October 1787, "I cannot study now for want of a fire." But going to bed was not always a satisfactory solution. George Channing remembered those mornings in the 1790s when, "owing to a scant supply of bedcovering, I had to jump to the floor; and, by swinging my arms backwards and forwards, after the fashion of wood-sawyers, for a few minutes, I got into a glow." Harriet Beecher Stowe would write of those old-time bedchambers "that never knew a fire, where the very sheets and blankets seemed so full of stinging cold air that they made one's fingers tingle; and where, after getting into bed, there was a prolonged shiver, until one's own internal heatgiving economy had warmed through the whole icy mass." "Delicate people," she added, "had these horrors ameliorated by the application of a brass warming pan."

Warming pans were important not only in heating the sheets but in obviating the dangers of damp beds, and by 1750 they were regularly found in colonial kitchens, where they were polished and maintained, as well as in chambers. Nonetheless, George Channing recalled that at home in Newport, Rhode Island, they were only used in cases of sickness or by stealth; and a Frenchman in rural New England in 1797 observed that a warming pan was a luxury almost unknown—if the natives could not borrow one for a sick person, they would heat two pine boards before the fire, "and by keeping them alternately heating and cooling they contrive to make a very good substitute." Hot soapstones superseded warming pans in the second half of the nineteenth century, and bottles of hot water were also tried but were ineffectual in rooms where the temperature hovered around thirty degrees. James Glen, the English governor of South Carolina between 1743 and 1756, narrated an anecdote of a young man in his family who habitually slept in a room without a fire, and who one night "carried Two Quart Bottles of hot water to Bed, which was of Down and covered with English Blankets; the Bottles were between the Sheets; but in the Morning they were both split to Pieces, and the water solid lumps of Ice." But perhaps the quintessential picture of the early American bedchamber in winter comes from the felicitous pen of Caroline King. The setting was Newburyport, Massachusetts; the date January 1834; the temperature outside "ten below."

> The room was furnished with white painted furniture, the dimity drapery of windows and bed were white, the straw matting on the floor was white, while from the four windows, solid and sparkling with frost, but without shades, icy little draughts of air seemed to blow in upon us from all directions. A great woodfire blazed on the open fireplace, but it did not seem to make the least impression on the frosty air of the room, where every breath looked like a puff of smoke. The great white bed stood like a snowdrift, crowned with a thick white "comforter" or "blessing" as we called the "down puff" of those days. After I had hastily made my preparations for bed, Aunt Nanny brought in a shining brass warming pan, filled with glowing coals, which she moved swiftly up and down between the polished icy cold sheets of the bed, leaving behind, beside the grateful warmth, a smell of just-going-to-be-scorched linen, which is inseparable from my memory of that old-time luxury. I was not used to a feather bed, and I thought I should never stop sinking into that soft nest of down, and after Aunt Nanny had administered a glass of hot wine whey, and covered me up to my eyes, I soon fell into a peaceful slumber, unconscious of Jack Frost or Jack Zero, being only once disturbed in the course of the night, by a dim consciousness that Aunt Nanny was piling wood on the fire. But in the morning I fully realized what a cold night I had passed through. The pail of water which was standing on my hearth had frozen solid during the night, and I gladly accepted Aunt Nanny's offer of dressing in her room where there was a stove, and where I could at least move my poor benumbed fingers.[21]

Sleep was sometimes no easier during the fiery side of the trial. In fact, Emily Dickinson, who "verily *baked* in bed," in Amherst, Massachusetts, in June 1851, was determined to "adopt a method of keeping up all *night* which having never *tried* I think will turn out nicely!" But one can be sure that with the return of the warm

Wyck. Philadelphia. Pencil drawing by Charles A. LeSueur. 12 August 1824. The Wyck Association, Germantown, Philadelphia. When the weather got hot, a through hall with open doors at either end provided a breezy respite, and here the family might gather for eating, playing, conversing, reading, or working. Light open chairs with cane seats would further enhance summer comfort. Wyck still stands today in Fairmount Park, Philadelphia

Martha Washington and Her Granddaughter Eliza Custis. Mount Vernon, Virginia. Drawing in pencil, pen, and ink, by Benjamin Henry Latrobe. July 1796. The Maryland Historical Society, Baltimore. The Washington family has moved to the airy comfort of the piazza in this summertime view. In his journal narrative of this visit to Mount Vernon, Latrobe commented upon neither the salubrity of the air, nor the beauty of the prospect down to the Potomac, nor the fragrance of the tea, for his attentions were entirely diverted to the classical beauty of Eliza Custis. To him, she appeared to be everything that the chisel of Phidias had aimed at but could not attain

weather the whole family was delighted to reopen doors and windows and burst out of their confinement in that cramped winter sitting room. Caroline Dustan exulted on 14 June 1859, "Sashes all raised up & down stairs." It was now possible to spread out over a greater part of the house with comfort, and bedchambers might provide a seasonal privacy for reading and writing. Sarah Anna Emery, who studied with her aunt, was delighted to welcome spring, for "with the warmer weather Aunt Betsy transferred our work to her chamber, where it escaped the espionage of the curious eyes and gossiping tongues that during the winter had at times been excessively annoying." Airiness and coolness would be the gauges of comfort for the next few months, and the family adjusted their living arrangements accordingly. The summer parlor was often more spacious than its hibernal counterpart, as large, airy rooms with a plenitude of doors and windows, lofty ceilings, and limited furnishings augured well for summer contentment. Those roomy double reception rooms offered refresh-

ing possibilities. "I hastened from my chamber, as usual of late," wrote Margaret Cary from New York on 3 August 1819, "to find a cool seat in the front parlor, with the folding-doors thrown open to make a draught through."[22]

The spacious and lofty through hall was a zephyr-cooled spot in summer, and in Philadelphia Samuel Breck commended his as "a fine open space for every breeze that blows" in July 1825. To this hallway many families resorted as soon as the cold season was over, transforming it into the summer sitting room, dining room, game room, and music room. Anne Grant pictured the through hall at The Flats, near Albany, "which in summer admitted a stream of air peculiarly grateful to the languid senses. It was furnished with chairs and pictures like a summer parlour. Here the family usually sat in hot weather." Lucy Breckinridge's sobriquet for the much-frequented center hall at her Virginia home in 1864 was "our 'omnibus.'" Indeed, in the South these breezeways could be used the greater part of the year. Joseph Holt

Foot of Dey Street, detail of *Hudson's River, Dey Street*. New York City. Drawing in watercolor and pencil, by Baroness Hyde de Neuville. c. 1810. The New-York Historical Society, New York City. On a summer's evening one might expect to see New Yorkers assembled in groups in their hallways or seated on their stoops enjoying the panorama of the street

Ingraham was surprised to eat dinner in New Orleans in December "in a hall open on two sides for ventilation, even at this season of the year."[23]

Just as the family had seated itself as close to the fire as possible all winter, it now moved to windows and doorways to breathe in cool air. Sarah Logan Fisher portrayed herself at home in Philadelphia on 21 July 1790, "very pleasantly at the Door with my dear children, a beautiful moonlight Night"; and Fanny Appleton Longfellow pictured her family in Newport, Rhode Island, in August 1852, typically sitting after breakfast "about the hall door, looking over green fields to the sea." Residents of the Middle Colonies were only too happy to escape the heat and blind-shrouded obscurity of their dwellings at sunset, crowding into the cooling streets to walk about and to visit their acquaintance. Indeed, it appeared in summer Philadelphia at dusk "as if some grand spectacle was to be exhibited, for not a street or alley was there, but what was in a state of commotion." When not mingling in this crowd, citizens might survey the scene from porch and stoop—"which as a *mother* I think expose girls too early to the acquaintance of men," remonstrated Ann Head Warder, an English Quakeress visiting in Philadelphia.[24]

From the eighteenth century, piazzas further extended the breezy comforts of halls and stoops, offering yet another cool retreat throughout the day and evening. They also shielded apartments within the house from the sun's scorching rays, and that they were effective in this we read in Alice Izard's letter concerning The Fold, the

View along the East Battery, Charleston. Oil on canvas, by S. Barnard. 1851. Yale University Art Gallery, New Haven; Mabel Brady Garvan Collection. Southern homes with their spacious, lofty rooms, large windows, and expansive piazzas were much more comfortable in summer zephyrs than in wintry gusts. Everything was done to encourage a free flow of air. According to one observer, open windows, doors opposite each other, and multistoried piazzas were the luxuries preferred by rich Charlestonians to the ornaments of gilding and painting

South Carolina home of her son and daughter-in-law, who had "taken their abode up stairs, which she prefers greatly to the dark rooms below. The Piazza overshades them so much as to make them too dark for dressing or working." In Charleston, John Lambert observed that almost every house was furnished with balconies and verandas, some of which occupied the whole side of the building from top to bottom—a gallery for each floor. John Drayton specified that these piazzas were generally attached on the south side, and Joseph Holt Ingraham said that in these southern-fronted galleries the Mississippians, as well as the South Carolineans, "wash, lounge, often sleep, and take their meals." Like the hall, the piazza was often furnished with Windsor furniture, which when it was first introduced via England in the early 1700s was regarded as particularly suited to outdoor seating. Andrew Gautier offered Windsor chairs "fit for Piazza or Gardens" in New York in April 1765, and there were thirty Windsor chairs on the piazza at Mount Vernon in 1800. Benches abounded and tables were regularly moved outside to the piazzas for warm-weather patterns of living. Sarah Logan Fisher carpeted her piazza with a painted floor cloth imported from England. Both the duke of Saxe-Weimar Eisenach and Joseph Holt Ingraham commented on the use in New Orleans galleries of large curtains, which were "festooned in massive folds" and "dropped along the whole length of the balcony in a summers afternoon, not only excluding the burning rays of the sun, but inviting the inmates to a cool and refreshing *siesta*" in the netted hammocks that swung in these piazzas. Venetian blinds and lattices extending between piazza pillars served the same function. Margaret Hunter Hall was somewhat equivocal in her opinion of this practice, observing that some of the deep verandas about Charleston houses "are fitted the whole way round with Venetian blinds, but altogether the houses look very pretty."[25]

Piazza blinds not only regulated light and heat but deterred insects, a problem of far greater magnitude on this side of the Atlantic than in Europe. Refuse and animals attracted flies and mosquitoes; standing water and large tracts of woodland were fertile breeding grounds. "The mosquitoes *so plenty*," fretted Caroline Barrett White in Jersey Hook in June 1857, "I counted one hundred in Julia's parlor tonight," while Martha Ogle Forman's walls were "literally covered" in August 1820 with what Landon Carter had called "Vile Musketoes . . . as plenty as bees in a hive," in September 1764. These "Liliputian lancers" proved the last straw for many, particularly at night, and swearing aplenty was heaped upon them. "But, oh! immortal gods," cussed Tyrone Power in 1833, "how they did hum and buzz! and how I did fume, and slap, and snatch, and swear." Summer heat compounded the discomfort, and the necessity of keeping doors and windows closed at night to exclude these winged pests made the heat more unbearable and sleep more difficult. A further inconvenience was the necessity of extinguishing all illumination: "as Othello says, 'put out the light, and then—' for if you do not, you will find yourself eaten up by mosquitoes (whom the candle has attracted to your room)"; or spend the night as Mary Gould Almy did in August 1778 in "frightful dreams and broken slumbers, listening to the noise of a fly, or mosquito, as they hummed around the candle."[26]

Some twenty yards of mosquito netting or pavilion gauze enveloped beds (and even cribs), offering some relief. To the Honorable Amelia Murray in New Orleans, these pavilions looked "like a transparent bonnet-box," and to Benjamin Henry Latrobe in the same city, they "resembled a kind of box without a bottom." According to Latrobe, they were "made of either coarse open canvass, French lino (which are the best), silk, open and figured Gauze (which are the most handsome), and most frequently of check Muslin which are I believe the cheapest." A New York newspaper offered "green Musqueto Neeting" in February 1768, while a wide chromatic variety had been available in Charleston from the 1740s. Robert Pringle mentioned that blue and green were the colors "best liked," but one could also have purchased white, pink, white spotted, checked green, green and blue, green and white, striped or spotted pavilion gauze. Borders gave a pavilion a nice finishing touch, and Charleston inventories suggest a colorful assortment: dark green with red calico border, light green with chintz border, thread pavilion with lace linen border, or lawn with calico border. Settees were also shrouded. In Samuel Naeve's Philadelphia parlor in September 1774 there was "a large Couch with a Cover of Check a Frame & Gause Hangings"; and Janet Schaw penned a fuller picture when she described her summer surrounds in North Carolina in the 1770s, where the heat, the mosquitoes, the bugs, and the ticks were increasing daily: "The curtains of our beds are now supplied by Musquetoes' nets. Fanny has got a neat or rather elegant dressing room, the settees of which are canopied over with green gauze, and on these we lie panting for breath and air, dressed in a single muslin petticoat and short gown." Indeed, in the Deep South, ladies might not only seek refuge beneath a rainbow of pavilions but enswathe themselves in gossamer armor. Harriet Martineau observed in New Orleans that "many ladies are accustomed, during the summer months, to get after breakfast into

a large sack of muslin tied round the throat, with smaller sacks for the arms, and to sit thus at work or book, fanning themselves to protect their faces. Others sit all the morning on the bed, within their moscheto-curtains."[27]

None of these measures were foolproof, of course, and James Stuart was only one of many to confess, "although this might perhaps be owing to my want of skill in the use of the curtain . . . I, again and again, while at New Orleans, found that the enemy had broken through the protecting curtain, and had not left me altogether uninjured." Eliza Leslie argued against the use of netting, except where absolutely necessary, because it impeded the free circulation of air around the bed and was highly flammable, and because a few stray mosquitoes would inevitably contrive to get in the net anyway.[28]

Fabrics that were hopefully believed to deter insects around the bed could also be found at the window as blinds or screens. "Green muskito netting for Bed Curtains or Blinds for Windows" was advertised in Annapolis on 26 July 1759, and "wide yellow canvas for window screens" was touted on 23 June 1760 in Boston—where Benjamin Goldthwait had two window screens in a bedchamber in July 1782. Charles Bagot, the British minister in Washington, advised his successor, Stratford Canning, on the eve of Canning's departure for America in 1819: "I took out a great quantity of mosquito netting, but I never had occasion to use mosquito curtains. You may as well take out a piece or two, to make blinds with, which you may put against the windows when they are open in Summer evenings and you have a light in your room. They serve to keep out the myriads of bats, beetles, and devils, which then assail you." Thomas Fessenden advocated the use of screens of millinet for bedchamber windows in 1826, and Thomas Webster recommended screens of black net in 1845. Isaac Weld suffered much from mosquitoes the first night he slept in what is now Whitehall, New York, in the 1790s, "notwithstanding that the people of the house, before we went to

bed, had taken all the pains possible to clear the room of them, fumigating it with the smoke of green wood, and afterwards securing the windows with gauze blinds." Many teary-eyed, smoke-choked survivors of this procedure regretted that it was "a remedy pretty nearly as bad as the disorder."[29]

William Hugh Grove mentioned some "Wire and some Gause blinds which keep out the flyes but admit the air," when traveling in Virginia in 1732; and Thomas Jefferson used wire screening both at the President's House in Washington and at Monticello, yet wire screening was not much used in early America. Isaac Conro advertised "brass wire wove fit for pantries and da[i]ries to keep out flies," in New York in October 1770, but although wire workers enjoyed a ready market for screens at dairy, springhouse, and cellar windows, references to other residential screening is sparse. When used within the house, wire screening was typically fitted into folding frames. J. C. Loudon would write in 1833 that "the very fine wire cloth now applied as inside blinds, might, we think, in some cases be advantageously placed outside," and in 1851 Gervase Wheeler would again recommend that all doors and windows in southern homes at least "be provided with folding-frames, lightly made, and covered with netting, either of wire, gauze, or muslin"; interior folding screens remained the norm, however. A major prejudice against any kind of screening—fabric or wire—was the belief that it would diminish air circulation. Fabric was preferred to wire screening, when any was used at all, because it was more easily obtained and installed, impervious to disfiguring rust, and much less expensive.[30]

Once inside, winged pests could be poisoned, trapped, or kept moving by overhead spring-driven fans, hand-held palmetto fans, ostrich feathers and peacock feathers, and fly brushes. Nineteenth-century household guides also provided abundant recipes for fly poisons. At his early-nineteenth-century home near Baltimore, Richard Parkinson used a substance called "fly-stone" mixed with water and sugar, which proved so effective that "it was necessary to sweep the room repeatedly in the

A Covered Painting; or, Fruit Piece. Oil on wood panel, by Raphaelle Peale. c. 1818. Courtesy Frank S. Schwarz and Son, Philadelphia. If one was not supplied with gauze covers to protect viands from flies and other winged pests then a piece of cheesecloth might be laid over the food. Another strategy was to lure flies away from the table by suspending above it a clump of fly-attracting, feathery asparagus greens

Ripe Melons. Oil on canvas, by John F. Francis. c. 1850. The Shearson Lehman Brothers Collection. Sweet, refreshing watermelon was a summertime treat enjoyed in both town and country, North and South, from the opening years of the eighteenth century

course of a day, during which times several handfulls were poisoned." One of the most frequently cited nonpoisonous concoctions was a blend of black pepper, brown sugar, and cream, which was to be stirred well and set about on plates—a certain way to trip humans if not entrap flies. Moreau de Saint-Méry had seen saucers of vitriol set about for the same purpose and also observed the use of "a sort of chandelier or garland of very white paper to attract flies" and keep them off the walls and ceiling. "This paper," he continued, "must be changed often; for it quickly becomes black and disgusting." Included in Royall Tyler's sketch of a fictional eighteenth-century parlor were two pendant, paper fly cages, which "zigzaged into every shape angular and rotund"; and in 1845 Thomas Webster was yet recommending that flypaper, "formed of papers of various colors cut out fancifully, in order to render them somewhat ornamental as well as useful," be hung from the kitchen ceiling, as "flies seem to incline to settle more on suspended objects than on any other." James Forbes had "two Fly Cages" at home in New York in August 1781, where Elbert Haring also had "2 Tormentors"—which we will hope were for flies—in his kitchen. John Jay Janney described the fly traps in use in early-nineteenth-century Virginia: "One was a glass tumbler filled nearly full of soap suds, with a slice of bread with a hole in the center and the under side covered with molasses, and laid in the tumbler. Another was two shingles tied together at the thick end, hung up by a string and smeared with molasses. When covered with flies, clap them together." Mrs. Leslie also recommended the latter rather brutal trap in 1840, and by the 1870s this snare had evolved into sticky flypaper, sometimes to the "discomfiture of family cats" as well as to the demise of flies. Samuel Eliot Morison firmly believed that "if you have never seen a lively kitten mixing it up with a sheet of 'Tanglewood' flypaper, you have really missed something in life."[31]

Fans, brushes, feathers, and punkah boards kept flies from alighting on dinners and diners alike and provided a gratifying breeze as well. Nathalie Boyer's mother, who was born in the early nineteenth century, "had a horror of flies, but she would also have no screens at the windows . . . fearing to keep out the air." In the dining room of their summer house outside Philadelphia, therefore, the flies were kept stirred up by a little servant girl waving "a large peacock-feather flybrush," a dual-purpose brush that not only kept the flies active but also reinforced table manners, for, as Nathalie remembered, "on occasions if any of the grown children put their arms on the table or took a bone in their fingers, the flybrush would be taken from the little blackie by my mother and the offender would get a gentle rap on the head or shoulder." Overhead fans replaced servants waving feathers and fans as the nineteenth century advanced. Samuel Canby Rumford recalled a fan with arms like squash rackets that hung above their dining table in Wilmington, Delaware, and these "arms passing just before the nose of a boy were surely very tempting, and it is not at all surprising that upon those occasions when we [boys] were having meals alone we experimented with the number and sizes of pieces of bread that each arm would carry around and bring back to the sender."[32]

Anne Royall was disgusted to sit down to a dinner in Saratoga, New York, where swarms of flies covered every dish, and in genteel dining rooms all provisions were covered with gauze fabric. Many a diner took his seat at a veiled table. Net removed and gourmands seated, they might enjoy several amenities peculiar to summer dining. One of these was ice, the liberal supply of which has astonished our British guests since the late eighteenth century. "Those who have never visited warm climates," wrote Robert Sutcliff from Philadelphia in 1806, "can scarcely conceive how pleasant the use of ice is, for various purposes of the table, in the summer season." As the ice-export industry became well established in the nineteenth century, southerners who had struggled to keep their icehouses full with local supplies, sometimes resorting to ineffectual snowballs, were relieved to be able to purchase northern ice in huge and solid masses. One visitor to the South, grateful for this abundance, was regaled with the sight of "ice in the water-jug, ice on the lump of butter, ice in the wineglass, and icecream for dessert." Watermelon was also a favorite summer dessert from early times. To a Swiss traveler in Virginia in 1702, this fruit seemed "very refreshing in the hot summer because of its cool, sweet juice"; and to Ann Head Warder, taking her first bite in Philadelphia in July 1786, it tasted like sweetened snow. The experience could be bittersweet, however, as noted in the *Pennsylvania Gazette* on 26 July 1797: "The very incautious practice of throwing the rinds of watermelons on the foot paving, has been more than once lamented. A lady in consequence of treading her foot on a rind last Friday evening, in Fifth Street, received a fall which fractured the bone of one of her arms in a shocking manner." But watermelon remained popular in Philadelphia, New York, and New England, and after refreshing herself with watermelon one summer evening near Boston, Harriet Martineau enjoyed being "capriciously lighted home by fireflies" to bed.[33]

Summer slumber was often disturbed not only by flies and mosquitoes but by other creeping, crawling, biting invertebrates. Bedbugs or "buggs," as they were familiarly called, reveled in bedstead joints, curtain folds, and beds filled with feathers or straw unless the housewife kept constant vigil. Liquor, pearl ash, mercury, sassafras bark, camphor, tobacco, lamp oil, lard, and even cucumber juice were resorted to in an oft-losing battle with these nocturnal pests. "Oh, blast the bedbugs & Mosquitoes," cursed a rather whimsical pedlar on his trek through New England in 1853, "I wonder if there is any country where they don't live. It must be a happy place—I wonder if Job was ever troubled with them." Cockroaches joined the offense. Philip Fithian told of a live trap at Nomini Hall in Virginia: "Tom the Coachman came in with a wood Terripin which he brought to be a resident in our Room to catch the Bugs & Cockroaches." Then there were the four-legged vertebrates, or rats. Eliza Ann Summers had for a lullaby in her homely Hilton Head chamber in 1867 the syncopated rhythm of great rats lumbering across the floor with potatoes. "We take 3 or 4 pair of shoes to bed with us every night," she wrote, "and when we hear the rats we sit up in bed and throw the shoes at them." At home in New York, Susan Augusta Fenimore Cooper said that the "number of *rats* was really alarming! I remember distinctly their running over the bed in which I slept." Others vividly recalled being bitten by rats—a particular danger for little children who slept close to the floor in trundle beds. Recipes to rid a room of the smell of a dead rat were common in household manuals. Up in Angelica, New York, the Church family was "over run and *literally run over*" with mice—"one or two to half a dozen in my room every night . . . on and *in* our *beds*." Traps were a help. *The New Family Receipt-Book*, published in New Haven in 1819, touted a "Mouse Trap, by which forty or fify Mice may be caught in a Night." Maria Silliman Church caught a paltry nineteen the first two nights after she employed the presumably more modest New Haven traps her brother sent her in 1836. (Cats were popular pets at home in early America.) But things could get yet worse, as John Harrower discovered at Colonel Dangerfield's home near Fredericksburg, Virginia, in August 1774: "Last night after I hade put out the Candle and gone to bedd I was obliged to get up again & put on my Cloaths and sit up all night by reason of a snake having got under my Pillow, which made me afraid I having no light to clear the bedd of him."[34]

April, May, and June might well find the housewife turban-wound and soot-

Great Cry and Little Wool. Illustration by David Claypoole Johnston in *Scraps* #3 (1832). The Winterthur Library: Printed Book and Periodical Collection. Summer slumber was made difficult not only by the heat of the chamber and the sting of the mosquito but by the bite of the bedbug. In combat against the latter it was recommended that one wash the bed joints once a week in soap and water and completely dismantle the bedstead each spring for thorough investigation. John Henry Belter, the New York City cabinetmaker, entered a patent for a bed in 1856; its improvements were that it came apart quickly for cleaning or for dismantlement in case of fire and it was composed of layers of wood pressed so tightly into a mold that there were no interstices in which bugs or germs might prosper. Three years earlier, Eliza Leslie had advised that, above all things, one must avoid telling one's hostess that insects had been discovered in the bed, "a circumstance that may chance sometimes to happen even in the best kept houses"

faced once again, eradicating the smoky traces of winter fires and mustering her defenses against spring dust and summer pests. Maria Silliman Church regretted that her father planned to visit her in April, as "it is too early to whitewash and clean house and we have not cast off our winter's smoke and dirt." Caroline Dustan had both her parlors "put in summer costume" by 20 May 1859, and Lavinia Dickinson could look approvingly into her sitting room on 16 June 1853 and see it "all ready for summer" and looking "quite refreshing." To Caroline Barrett White, though tired from cleaning in May 1857, her parlor looked "so nice and clean that I feel repaid for my labor"; but Sarah Logan Fisher, after days of papering and painting in April 1785, wrote with considerably less equanimity, "troublesome work indeed, the pleasure afterwards of being nice, hardly pays for the trouble."[35]

Spring cleaning was, indeed, often more thorough than the fall preliminaries. One was supposed to start at the top and work down, and the many-storied verticality of urban homes compounded the trouble. It was vain to try to seek retreat or seclusion during these topsy-turvy days. Alexander Anderson verbally portrayed himself driven from room to room by the relentless whitewash brush every May in the 1790s; while Laura Wirt found her aunt's home in Buckingham County, Virginia, so thoroughly turned upside down in May 1820 as the family tackled spring cleaning and prepared for a wedding, "that I find it impossible to read or sew—there is not one quiet room in the house—every one is filled with negro men or women, taking down, & putting up bedsteads, rubbing furniture—cleaning locks; scouring, dry rubbing the floors, clatter, clatter, clatter—what a din!"[36]

Trunks were emptied of clothing, rooms stripped of furniture, and all was carted outside to air. The architectural elements were whitened and brightened, floors polished, chimneys swept, and fireplaces cleaned and adorned for summer. Stoves vanished. Furniture was then subjected to the dust cloth, and closets were cleaned, as china, silver, and glassware came under the dominance of the washcloth. "Wednsday, and Thursday, and Fryday, all up in Arms a cleaning House, white-washing, rubing

Tables, cleaning silver, China and Glass, etc. And poor I am almost tired out of my senses," wailed Esther Burr in late June 1755. And with the increasing number of personal possessions, what had taken three to seven days in the eighteenth century might demand two to three weeks in the nineteenth.[37]

Women's diaries portray the seasonal imperative of taking the window curtains down each spring and rehanging them in the fall. Anne Eliza Clark Kane said that she took the curtains down in one room in May 1811, "as in summer the room looked better without any." Eliza Leslie gave further reasons in 1840: "It is not a good custom to keep the curtains up during the summer, as it fades them, and covers them with dust; besides which they seem to increase the heat of the rooms, and impede the free entrance of the air." She suggested that venetian blinds and linen shades were best for summer windows. Curtains, therefore, were shaken out, brushed of dust, aired for a day, and folded neatly with camphor or tobacco into clean white sheets or tablecloths, which were then pinned or sewn closed and stored—preferably in a trunk reserved for curtains. When an inventory of Thomas Roach's New York estate was taken on 31 May 1798, there was "1 Trunk containing Bed & Window Curtains," while Dolley Madison kept her "Front Parlor curtains" seasonally in "the Press in the Chamber." Caroline Dustan "shook, folded & put up parlor curtains with tobacco" in May 1856, and in May 1865 noted, "I put up our woolen curtains in the curtain trunk." By that year, parlor windows might well be veiled in outside blinds, inside shades, muslin "sheers," and woolen curtains. Only the woolen curtains would be stored: the muslin under-curtains would be washed, bleached, starched, ironed, and rehung.[38]

As we have seen, bed curtains were also taken down for the summer and rehung in the fall. Eliza Leslie, however, did not approve of naked bedsteads and suggested that "in summer, after the curtains are taken down and put away, it is well, on a high post bedstead, to have a tester and top-valance of dimity or white muslin; otherwise the bare posts and top-rail will look naked and ungainly. There should also be a white foot-valance to correspond." William Hugh Grove divulged that in 1732 Virginians had told him that they washed their bed curtains every two weeks, "but the truth is they seldom use any in Summer nor Testers or Head boards because of the Chintzes or Buggs which are plenty."[39]

For this reason it was recommended that bedsteads be washed at the joints once a week, but springtime, after the curtains had been taken down, offered a particularly propitious moment to do a thorough job. "A *most effectual* remedy against bugs is to have all the bedsteads in the house taken down every spring," wrote Eliza Leslie, "and after washing the joints with cold water and brown soap, to have the whole bedstead completely varnished (even on the inside of the joints) with varnish procured from a cabinet-maker; or getting a cabinet-maker's man to come and do it." Account books and newspaper advertisements confirm that cabinetmakers and upholsterers readily obliged in pulling down and putting up bedsteads, searching crevices, and slathering mysterious potions, which they also offered for sale separately. Many housewives, however, had no such help, and we can be sure that Messrs. Gilman and Jackson of Portsmouth, New Hampshire, addressed an attentive audience when they advertised in the *Ladies Miscellany* in May 1804 a new patent bedstead that could be put up and taken down in little more time "than for doing the same by the leaves of a dining table." Indeed, the "1 Bed Wench" accompanying a turned-post bedstead in a Charleston chamber was undoubtedly no such delightful thing, but a common bed

View of the Langdon House. Hyde Park, New York. Oil on canvas, by Johann Hermann Carmiencke. 1856. Courtesy Berry-Hill Galleries, New York City. John Jacob Astor had this house built for his daughter Dorothea Langdon in the 1840s. Despite its impressive provenance, someone has transgressed the accepted rules of color gradation. As Calvert Vaux warned in his *Villas and Cottages* (1864), if the shutters were painted the same color as the rest of the house, a blank, uninteresting effect would be produced; for when the blinds were closed, which was generally the case, the house would appear to be without any windows at all. Rather, Vaux suggested painting the house four different tints, one for the roof trim, verandas, and other woodwork; another for the main walls; a third, not markedly different from the other woodwork, for the frames of the venetian shutters; and a fourth, the darkest, for their movable slats

wrench or bed key to facilitate dismantling. Cedar beds, rising in four-posted defiance against the propagation of bugs, were further testimony to a housewife's defenses.[40]

Next, tacks had to be pried out, carpets taken up, shaken clean, aired, and stored for the summer or relaid after a lusty beating out on the lawn. "The parlor carpets have been taken up & put down again & none of us killed," marveled Lavinia Dickinson in May 1852, displaying considerably better spirits than fellow housewife Sarah Wister, who complained on 10 May 1861, amid the chaos of spring cleaning:

Was busy the whole day literally in superintending & assisting putting away carpets putting up curtains &c. The servants despite their lofty pretentions are just as incompetent as if they had never lived in a house in their life, & so inattentive that they forget your orders while you are speaking & disobey them under your eyes. This is my first experience in house cleaning, & unless I secure some servant who can overlook & direct it before the autumn I think it will probably be among my last for I have not the physical strength for it nor the moral serenity.

Carpets were rolled and wrapped in the same manner as the curtains and stowed somewhere upstairs, perhaps in a carpet chest on the third floor, perhaps in a garret storeroom, where Aaron Burr had three Turkey carpets and a small green and white one in the summer of 1797. Josiah Bumstead & Son, Boston purveyors of wallpaper, in 1848 advertised carpet paper "for keeping out moths and otherwise preserving a carpet to a good old age." In 1837 Frances McDougall had recommended paper as a shroud in which to pin up curtains for the summer months, although papering up the curtains and furniture does not appear to have been done in America to the extent that it was in England.[41]

A painted floor cloth might be tacked down, but straw matting was the universal favorite, for it just seemed to breathe cool comfort, and Maria Silliman Church contentedly pictured herself "sitting in the south parlor which looks quite pretty, and cool with the matting and light cover to the sofa."[42]

Pictures and looking glasses were to be divested of winter smoke and flyspecks. Prudence Smith alarmingly recommended in her *Modern American Cookery* (1831) that paintings be rubbed with an admixture of common salt and stale urine "till they are quite clean," then bathed in a freshet of clean water. Robert Roberts rather approved of washing flyspecks from looking-glass plates with a splash of gin and he also subscribed to the oft-quoted recipe for washing gilded frames with water in which onions or leeks had been boiled. Gilded frames and paintings might be varnished to resist the attacks of flies.[43]

Dust was a major problem in spring and summer. "I open my window and it fills the chamber with white dirt. I think God must be dusting," mused Emily Dickinson in March 1873. All upholstered furniture was, therefore, garbed in light cotton or linen covers, which were easily washed and cool to sit on. These were usually loose-

Cat and Kittens. Oil on millboard, by an unknown American artist. c. 1872–83. National Gallery of Art, Washington, D.C.; gift of Edgar William and Bernice Chrysler Garbisch. Straw matting was the favorite floor covering for summer parlors, lending its golden tints and its subtle but perceptible scent to the aura of the room. Edges might be bound in red or green leather, alternatively in wide cotton or linen binding

Mrs. William Cooper (Elizabeth Fenimore Cooper). Cooperstown, New York. Watercolor by George Freeman. Summer 1816. The New York State Historical Association, Cooperstown. Elizabeth Fenimore Cooper, mother of the celebrated author James Fenimore Cooper, had moved, most unwillingly, from Burlington, New Jersey, to Cooperstown, New York, with her husband and children in 1790. She suffered keenly the privations of this rural outpost, but was undoubtedly somewhat reconciled to her situation after the completion of her new home, Otsego Hall, in 1799. Here she is portrayed in the hall during the summer of 1816 with plants flourishing in a large array of tubs before the windows. Indeed, Mrs. Cooper was characterized by a granddaughter as being partial to flowers, a great reader of romances, and a marvelous housekeeper. True to meticulous summer housekeeping are the curtainless windows, the slipcovered settee, and the gauze-enveloped chandelier, thereby protected from flies

Mrs. A. W. Smith's Parlor. Broad and Spruce streets, Philadelphia. 1853. Watercolor by Joseph Shoemaker Russell. Private collection. Observe the fireplace opening closed with a fireboard for the summer months, the chairs, which have been drawn to the open windows, the small scale of the bouquets on mantel and stand, and the obviously gas-fed lamp. The pained expression of the upright gentleman on the couch offers no endorsement of the comfort of American sofas

fitting and blousy in appearance, although the Charleston cabinetmaker Thomas Elfe offered a choice of "tight or loose cases" for upholstered chairs in 1751. Eliza Leslie recommended handsome chintz, but approved stout brown linen covers in rooms little used, so that, as Harriet Beecher Stowe wrote with pardonable hyperbole, "all the articles of furniture had their covers, made of cold Holland linen, in which they looked like bodies laid out,—even the curtain-tassels had each its little shroud." Gilded objects were also swathed in muslin, gauze, or tissue paper. The protective covering was to be tied on lamps and chandeliers with ribbons of the same color and secured around picture frames and looking glasses with small pins. Eliza Leslie considered gauze the least effective, as it was apt to split, admitted dust, and could only serve one season, but it was in great demand. George Washington purchased gauze "to cover pictures & glass" during his second term as president, and in the ballroom of the Governor's Palace in Williamsburg in the summer of 1770 were "3 glass lustres with 6 branches each & gauze covers" together with "2 large paintings of the King and Queen gauze covers." Samuel Kelly observed black gauze over all the looking glasses in Philadelphia during the summer of 1790, and Martha Ogle Forman covered a family portrait with "green gause" in July 1826. Sarah Wister of Philadelphia showed herself to be a notable, though captious, housewife on 18 May 1861, when she "went to market before breakfast, & spent the rest of the morning in counting clothes, adding accounts, giving out stores & finally in covering the pictures and looking glasses in the parlour with rose coloured net to protect them from flies & dust, a task which should have been done by the servants at least a week ago." Muslin dyed yellow with turmeric and milk or yellow cambric were favored, as they could be used two or

Woman Seated at a Piano, Looking into a Mirror. New York City. 1859. Drawing in pencil heightened with tempera, by Thomas Charles Farrer. The Pierpont Morgan Library, New York City; gift of Mr. Charles Ryskamp. Thomas Farrer drew this interior while living with the English-born cabinetmaker Edward Meek, whose business and residence were located on West Fifty-second Street. The mistress at the Meeks' home seems to have heeded Lydia Maria Child, who in 1833 had advised her readership that instead of covering up looking glasses with muslin one might cover only the frames with a cheap yellow cambric, which would camouflage with the gilded frame, leaving the glass open for use

Careless Maria. Woodcut from *The Rose Bush; or, Stories in Verse* (New York, n.d.). Old Sturbridge Village, Sturbridge, Massachusetts. Gilded objects of all kinds, including picture and mirror frames, donned summer apparel of muslin, gauze, or tissue paper to protect them from dust and flies. This looking glass appears to be sheathed in muslin or gauze, which would have been secured with very small pins

three years and were not so noticeable if dyed as near to the color of the gilt as possible. Eliza Leslie thought tissue paper to be yet more impervious to dust and particularly admired some she had seen "cut out into large jagged leaves, laid closely over each other, so as to cover completely the gilt frames of mirrors and pictures, and looking like a thick mass of foliage all round."[44]

Brass andirons were also cleaned, rubbed with mutton suet, sprinkled with unslaked lime, done up in muslin and brown paper, and relegated to the garret or, more simply, encased in muslin or tissue paper and left in place. Once again we must

View from the House of Henry Briscoe Thomas. Baltimore. Drawing in pen and black ink, black crayon, and gray wash heightened with white, by an unknown American artist. c. 1841. The Metropolitan Museum of Art, New York City; gift of Mrs. Lydia Bond Powel, 1967. This room has the interior shutters, venetian blinds, and layered curtains censured by Harriet Beecher Stowe for making a house "tight as a box." At least the blinds are raised, the curtains back, the window open, so that the family songster may enjoy his privileged perch with its view down to the mills at the mouth of the Patapsco River

forgive Mrs. Stowe her taste for exaggeration, for she used it in *Oldtown Folks* to capture the essential image of all those enshrouded summer parlors across eighteenth- and nineteenth-century America.

> We had our best room, and kept it as cold, as uninviting and stately, as devoid of human light or warmth, as the most fashionable shut-up parlor of modern days. It had the tallest and brightest pair of brass andirons conceivable, and a shovel and tongs to match, that were so heavy that the mere lifting them was work enough, without doing anything with them. It had also a bright-varnished mahogany tea-table, over which was a looking-glass in a gilt frame, with a row of little architectural balls on it; which looking-glass was always kept shrouded in white muslin at all seasons of the year, on account of a tradition that flies might be expected to attack it for one or two weeks in summer. But truth compels me to state, that I never saw or heard of

North Parlor of Dr. Whitridge's, Tiverton, Rhode Island, 1814. Watercolor by Joseph Shoemaker Russell. c. 1850. Old Dartmouth Historical Society, New Bedford, Massachusetts. For an open fireplace in summer, there was nothing prettier than a large hearth jar filled with the blooms of the season. The pictures over the desk appear to be schoolgirl works wrought in watercolor on paper or silk on satin

a fly whose heart could endure Aunt Lois's parlor. It was so dark, so cold, so still, that all that frisky, buzzing race, who delight in air and sunshine, universally deserted and seceded from it; yet the looking-glass, and occasionally the fire-irons, were rigorously shrouded, as if desperate attacks might any moment be expected.[45]

Once the andirons were put up and the hearth cleaned, the parlor fireplace remained inviolate until fall, regardless of the weather. May was often cold and damp, and housewives east of New York were urged to delay their spring cleaning till June, but one might as well have asked the birds to stay building their nests. Harriet Silliman and her family sought refuge by the office fire one chilly May week in 1836, the parlor stove having been dismantled. Others crept furtively to the kitchen to warm themselves, while Mary Boardman Crowninshield and Elizabeth Wirt each resorted to foot stoves. "Have we not shivered with cold all the glowering, gloomy month of May," grumbled Christopher Crowfield, "because the august front-parlor having undergone the spring cleaning, the andirons were snugly tied up in the tissue paper, and an elegant frill of the same material was trembling before the mouth of the once glowing fireplace." Baron de Montlezun nearly froze in Virginia one frigid September day in 1816, and concluded his host must belong "to that school of thought which for nothing in the world could bring itself to removing from their icy fire-place the fan-shaped paper of the screen which must, at any price, decorate it until a certain fixed day in November or December." Many closed their fireplaces for the summer months with wooden fireboards, which could be decoratively, and often imaginatively, painted or covered with wallpaper squares specifically designed for this purpose. Transparent paintings stretched on a frame were also used. When illuminated from behind by lamps, a fine night-view of a great eruption of Vesuvius or Alpine

The Children of Commodore and Mrs. John Daniel Danels. Albemarle Street, Baltimore. Oil on canvas, believed to be by Robert Street or Francis Martin Drexel. c. 1826. The Maryland Historical Society, Baltimore. With the temperature hovering in the mid-nineties, no one ventured outside who was not impelled to do so. It was a morning ritual to open all doors and windows, closing the louvered doors and the shutters before them. All light but that absolutely necessary for domestic business was thereby excluded. Many homes, according to one observer, were kept so dark that on going into them from the street it was impossible to perceive who was there until one's eyes grew accustomed to the gloom. Notable in this Baltimore parlor are the neoclassical wallpaper, large pier glass, handsome carpet, and baize table cover, and also the lively grain and high polish of the mahogany furniture and marble fireplace surround

scenery by moonlight would cast a romantic glow about the evening parlor. Eliza Leslie believed that for the admission of air, no fireboard was superior to those in the form of venetian shutters, opening in the middle.[46]

"Still," she continued, "for an open fire-place in summer, there is nothing better than a large handsome jar to stand on the hearth, well filled with fresh flowers, relieved against a background of long and spreading cedar or pine twigs." Sarah Logan Fisher intended to ask Captain Bell to bring back from the East Indies "a large handsome china Jar suitable to stand in a Chimney in summer, or under a China Table in Winter, perhaps about two feet high"; and eighteenth-century Charleston inventories suggest that the sweet scent of local flowers emanated from hearths throughout the warm seasons of the year. Charles Carleton Coffin wrote that in early New Hampshire "in summer, green pine boughs adorn the fireplace, and fill the room with fragrant odors." Asparagus fern was arranged about the fireplace and suspended from the walls and ceiling not only as decoration, but to attract the flies, thus keeping them off the whitewashed walls and gilded frames. When Alexander Anderson took an early morning stroll in New York City on 2 July 1796, he "got some asparagus at the market and fix'd it up in my room to coax the flies away from my maps & pictures"; and Samuel Kelly had been regaled on entering "a pleasant, white-limed parlour" in Philadelphia in 1790, with the sight of "bunches of asparagus hung up here and there near the ceiling to attract the flies from dirting the nice white walls, and being fresh and green with red berries, had a cool and neat appearance."[47]

Anne Grant, who lived in Colonel Schuyler's upstate New York home in the 1760s, observed that "the rooms were merely shut up to keep the flies, which in that country are an absolute nuisance, from spoiling the furniture. Another motive was, that they might be pleasantly cool when opened for company." The darkened room became the nineteenth-century housewife's primary mode of attack in a final all-out offensive against summer heat and flies. Her arsenal was far better stocked than had been her eighteenth-century predecessor's, for the Industrial Revolution had enabled the upholsterer to come armed with yards upon yards of damask, cord, tassel, lace, muslin, and canvas with which to block out flies and light, and there was a new artillerist on the scene—the maker of venetian blinds. In 1827 Margaret Hunter Hall would commend the typical American summer sitting room, "covered with mats instead of carpets, and most effectually kept cool by the outward air and light being excluded." Twenty years later, however, Alexander Mackay worried that these darkened windows were successful in excluding not only "every particle of light, but also every breath of air, the families melting, in the meantime"; and by 1873 Catharine Beecher would be pleading with housewives to shut out flies "with wire netting in open windows, and also doors of the same" because "it costs much less than ill health" from closed and mournfully darkened rooms.[48]

Keeping house was exhausting year-round. It demanded strength and stoicism. We can be reasonably confident that, having faithfully followed the biblical injunction to "set thine house in order," the early American housewife, "fatigued to death both mind and body," was only too happy to end her day and light her way to bed, whether to face the chilling frost of winter or the stifling heat of summer.

One of the very first trials to a little girl's temper was the lesson that she wasn't supposed to have much of a temper at all. Passions of all kinds were suspect in the Enlightenment world of the eighteenth century, when moderation, whether in interior decor or personal conduct, was the measure of esteem. "Let thy countenance be moderately chearful, neither laughing nor frowning," counseled *The School of Good Manners* in 1794. Anger was considered the most mischievous passion and the one most needful of restraint, particularly in girls. From Paris in 1785, a solicitous Thomas Jefferson wrote his seven-year-old daughter Maria, then staying with an aunt in Virginia, "never suffer yourself to be angry with any body," and when she arrived in France two years later to join her older sister Martha at school, Jefferson asked Martha to help him "teach her never to be angry." Discontent, fretfulness, or anger bespoke selfishness and ingratitude to God for the mercies that he had bestowed, so a girl learned early that she must suppress these negative humors with silent effort or dispel them with cheerful good spirits. Because a woman's good temper was considered crucial to the happiness of the domestic circle, every mistress of a family must strive to be cheerful. "There is nothing which has a more abiding influence on the happiness of a family," intoned Catharine Beecher and Harriet Beecher Stowe in 1869, "than the preservation of equable and cheerful temper and tones in the housekeeper." To be always pleasant and content with one's lot in life is not easy at seven or seventy-seven, but females strove hard throughout their lives to achieve this ideal. When twelve-year-old Louisa Jane Trumbull of Worcester, Massachusetts, scribbled in her diary that 29 January 1834 had been a particularly happy day, she felt it was in part "because I have tried to be as pleasant as I possibly could and I think I have succeeded tolerably well."[1]

Further, a female must be tractable—sharing of herself, her time, her possessions: "give your playthings to those who want them," Jefferson told little Maria in 1785. And sixteen years later he encouraged his granddaughter Ellen Wayles Randolph to be "a very good girl, never getting angry with your playmates nor the servants, but always trying to be more good humored and more generous than they." Once grown, these girls must continue to be "Virtuous, Sensible, good-natured, complaisant, complying, & of a Cheerful Disposition." John Brown would "Begg Beceash and Intreat" his roving son in 1782 to marry a woman of the best family and well educated, "*but above all* let the Lady be of a Vertuous Carrector and an agreeable Disposition, a Calm and Unruffled Temper tho Spritly and Agreeable." That many New England wives achieved this amiable amalgam we hear from Timothy Dwight, who believed "a gentle and affectionate temper, ornamented with sprightliness and gilded with serenity," to be their natural character.[2]

A wife's easy, tractable disposition was a principal ingredient in a successful marriage during those years when success was measured by peace and tranquillity.

"Harmony in the married state is the very first object to be aimed at," wrote Jefferson: "Nothing can preserve affections uninterrupted but a firm resolution never to differ in will." The burden was often on the wife: "A difference with your husband ought to be considered as the greatest calamity," James Madison, bishop of Virginia, warned his recently married daughter in 1811, ". . . it is a demon which must never be permitted to enter a habitation where all should be peace, unimpaired confidence, and heartfelt affection." It seemed to Benjamin Rush, writing his fiancée on 15 November 1775, that the clue to conjugal happiness was a "sympathy" between husband and wife in eight different areas: religion, tempers, understandings, sentiments, tastes, opinions, manners, and animal love. The sympathy of tempers "excludes anger—resentment—& peevishness in every shape," and the sympathy of manners meant "the mutual politeness between married people. Although it confers no real happiness, yet it is the best vehicle for it." It was courtesy that enabled a wife, as the mechanic in the marriage, to smooth connubial relations.[3]

The same politeness must distinguish the relations between mistress and maid, mother and daughter, brother and sister. "Quarrel not nor contend with thy brethren or sisters, but live in love, peace and unity," directed *The School of Good Manners.* This emphasis on courtesy underscores the early American definition of self in its relation to others: each individual was a small part of a much larger unit—the family—and must contribute to the cohesion of the whole. Abigail Adams regretted the necessity of dismissing an able servant because of her temper, but "I must, or I shall never have a quiet family," Mrs. Adams allowed, for she "keeps the whole House in disorder, and gives a bad name to the whole Family"; and Maria Silliman Church knew the time had come to take a firm hand with her little daughter Maria in October 1839, for "she shows so much naughty *temper* and petty tyranny that she quite destroys the *peace* of the little community."[4]

For there to be comfort and social peace at home it was also essential that the housewife establish and maintain regularity and order. In 1808 Anne Grant would look back on her years in the Schuyler household during the 1760s and applaud Catherine Van Rensselaer Schuyler, whose "household affairs, ever well regulated, went on in a mechanical kind of progress." Indeed, many housewives were as successful in imposing order on their often disorderly lives as Enlightenment gardeners were in bringing geometric precision to a defiantly irregular landscape, and their families moved with time-clock invariability through a metered pace of days. In April 1819 Margaret Cary commended the regularity that reigned at her brother's New York home, where they breakfasted at seven, dined at three, and "at ten o'clock exactly Henry rings for the three flat candlesticks, and we all separate." Abraham Ridgely assured his mother in February 1786 that he was happy as a boarder in Dr. Anderson's household, as "his family is under such good regulation, & every thing is conducted so cleaverly . . . we have our meals nearly at the same hour every day; nine o'clock is our bed time, & day light our time of getting up."[5]

When Anne Shippen wrote her schoolgirl daughter in 1777, "You may be sure you improve in proportion to the degree of ease with which you do any thing," she addressed another virtue of the good housewife. Sarah Anna Emery could picture Grandmother Little sewing at her Newburyport window, the morning duties done and dinner put over the fire to boil, and Harriet Beecher Stowe would describe a fictional inestimable housewife seated every afternoon "at her shady parlor-window behind the lilacs, cool and easy, hemming muslin cap-strings, or reading the last new

Detail of *The Artist's Family* by Benjamin West (see page 1). Many were the conflicting claims on a woman's time and spiritual reserves. Housewifery, child care, health, servants, and hospitality all imposed rigorous demands on her. Fortunate indeed was the woman who found peace on this earth

book." Both had accomplished their tasks in good time, without bustle and confusion, and seemingly without effort. That worthy Mrs. Schuyler, too, who regulated her household "in the most judicious manner, so as to prevent all appearance of hurry and confusion," was a great manager of her time and "always contrived to create leisure hours for reading," retiring "to read in her closet" once her morning chores had been quickly dispatched. Such unruffled ease in manner and person was extolled for its effect in diffusing a calm serenity over all and because it bespoke control. Robert

Roberts told other servants that "you must not seem to be in the least confusion, for there is nothing that looks so bad as to see a man in a bustle or confused state."[6]

A hushed quietude was an additional domestic desideratum. When Sidney George Fisher, yet a bachelor, conjured the image of the quintessential ideal home in 1841, the salient features were regularity, neatness, order, cleanliness, and silence. Servants were to move about as noiselessly as possible in shoes that did not squeak or creak. Ellen Rollins recalled her grandmother's placid farmhouse in the 1840s, where "there was no hurry, no bustle, no rattling of dishes"; and in *Uncle Tom's Cabin* Harriet Beecher Stowe evoked that old-time "air of order and stillness," the "wide, clean rooms, where nothing ever seems to be doing or going to be done, where everything is once and forever rigidly in place, and where all household arrangements move with the punctual exactness of the old clock in the corner."[7]

The compact nuclear family, living in cheerfulness, selflessness, and courtesy in the hushed, calm atmosphere of a neat, well-regulated home, had become the beau ideal by the early 1800s. But the ideal and the real were often far apart. Those women who achieved even a modicum of these desiderata deserve our esteem, for the obstacles in their path seem overwhelming to us today, as they did to many of them at the time.

Perhaps the deepest font of anxiety to the early American housewife was the uncertainty and instability in every aspect of her life. Health, family, domicile, fortune, and servant help—all were equivocal. And there were additional vicissitudes peculiar to America that further taxed mind and body. In 1841 Catharine Beecher summarized the fluidity and permutations that both invigorated and complicated American life, which proved particularly perplexing to the housewife:

> Every thing is moving and changing. Persons in poverty, are rising to opulence, and persons of wealth, are sinking to poverty. The children of common laborers, by their talents and enterprise, are becoming nobles in intellect, or wealth, or station; while the children of the wealthy enervated by indulgence, are sinking to humbler stations. The sons of the wealthy are leaving the rich mansions of their fathers, to dwell in the log cabins of the forest, where very soon they bear away the daughters of ease and refinement, to share the privations of a new settlement.

Maria Silliman Church was one of those "daughters of ease and refinement" who followed a husband to a primitive settlement, and who strove long and hard to maintain a contented spirit in the wilderness "new country" of Allegany County, New York, where "one endures more trials, and finds a more niggardly reward . . . than anywhere that the lot of refined or educated people is ordinarily cast." "I often think," she despaired, "of what dear Aunt said to me 'Strive for a quiet spirit'—but indeed there is every thing in Allegany to oppose it."[8]

Adding up the members of her household in December 1777, Elizabeth Drinker had "but 9 Persons in our Family this winter; we have not had less than 13 or 14 for many years past." The American family from 1750 to 1870 was a complex and ever-changing affair. Although the nuclear grouping was the ideal, the extended family—with servants, relatives, and boarders amplifying the neat nuclear number—was often the real social unit throughout the eighteenth and nineteenth centuries. When William Wirt, who was born in 1772, went as a schoolboy to board with Major

Samuel Wade Magruder of Montgomery County, Maryland, he shared the house with "not less than twenty white persons," including children, apprentices, an English schoolmaster, and other boarders, and there were always additional visitors. "It was, in fact, an active, bustling, merry, noisy family, always in motion, and often in commotion," summarized Wirt. Catherine Robbins, the youngest of seven children on an early-nineteenth-century Massachusetts farm, similarly characterized her family as "a large and confused one." "I assure you," she elaborated, "the providing for numbers, caring for the house, nursing the sick, and receiving friends (which went on all the time), with a great many changes, and coming and going both in parlor and kitchen, made an establishment which required skill and industry and activity to carry on with any comfort to the members of it."9

The opportunities for discord were rife at home in early America. The prevalence of early death contributed to the frequency of remarriage, and mates, stepparents, and stepchildren struggled to rethink and rework relationships—always striving, against the odds, for harmony. Various relatives periodically swelled the family circle. Because of the endemic insufficiency of servant help in America, an unmarried sister often came to assist a sibling who was trying to cope with a house and young family. Faith Silliman came to Triana to lighten the burden for her sister Maria Silliman Church, whose home it was, and when Faith married, the next youngest, Henrietta, went to Hanover, New Hampshire, to help her; and it is probable that when Henrietta was wed, sister Julia was ready to come when needed. That this was not always a felicitous arrangement we hear from Alexander Anderson, who in 1798 "took an opportunity at bed-time, to mention to my wife the impropriety of her sister Helen's further stay with us." Mrs. Anderson became so upset that sister Helen was allowed to remain. On occasion, there might be a widowed father on the scene, and often a widowed mother came to reside for at least part of the year, perhaps dividing her time between her children. A housewife might not only have to adjust to changes in family composition but to rethink and to reorganize the use and furnishings of her rooms to accommodate these tenants and their possessions. When Mary White's mother came to live with her in West Boylston, Massachusetts, in the fall of 1838, the new arrival moved

Portrait of Job Hill and His Family. Watercolor and pencil on paper, by Caroline Hill. New Hampshire. 1837. Courtesy Peterborough Historical Society, Peterborough, New Hampshire. Solidarity is here suggested not only in the intimate, shoulder-to-shoulder grouping of this family around the sitting-room table (in this case, one of the tripod-based, tilt-top tea tables) but in the genealogical "family register" proudly displayed on the wall. Commonly worked in either watercolor on paper or silk on canvas, these family registers, or records, came into fashion in the late eighteenth century, giving decorative expression to the growing perception of the family as a private, close-knit domestic unit that was at once fragile and unique

into the east room, and Mary's diary entries for 17 and 18 October reveal the scenario: "Mr. Ball went to Westboro for my mother's furniture and returned at night. I removed our sideboard to the west room. Put my mothers furniture in the East room." Innumerable are the eighteenth-century letters and nineteenth-century reminiscences in which a resident grandmother plays a prominent role. Many of these older women were of invaluable assistance in caring for the grandchildren—dressing them, giving them their lessons, playing with them, nursing them when ill, and sitting with them at bedtime. But all and any of these living arrangements could be detrimental to family peace. With "many things to fret perplex and afflict me," including her father's increasing senility, Sarah Connell Ayer unbosomed herself to her diary in September 1825: "My father is unwell, and so childish and unreasonable that I know not how to act towards him, as it seems as though he was determined not to be pleased with anything I did for him. He often utters sentiments before my children which it is improper for them to hear, and which grieves me to the heart." Caring for the aged was so considerable a domestic concern that Catharine Beecher and Harriet Beecher Stowe devoted a chapter to the subject in their *American Woman's Home* (1869).[10]

Another frequent source of discord was the necessity of living in the home of parents or parents-in-law until financially independent. Elizabeth Foote Washington seems to have entered into her marriage in 1779 fully cognizant of the potential dangers ahead. About that time she acknowledged, "as there is a probability of my living in Houses not my own for Sometime—may the divine goodness assist me, so that I may study to live in pease & friendship with the family where I live." But a 1784 diary entry suggests that she had not found uninterrupted peace while boarding out, as she expressed the fervent wish that *when* she got to housekeeping on *her own,* her

The Talcott Family. Probably in or near Hamilton, New York. Drawing in watercolor, pencil, and gold paint, by Deborah Goldsmith. 1832. Abby Aldrich Rockefeller Folk Art Center, Williamsburg, Virginia. Diaries, letters, and pictorial evidence from the years between 1750 and 1870 confirm that a grandparent was often an integral part of the domestic circle and that the true nuclear family, composed only of mother, father, and children, was by no means the universal unit. Observe the sprightly striped "Venetian" carpeting, the cricket, and the clothespress with its brass hardware (simulated by the artist in gold paint). It was the housewife's responsibility to care for and maintain all the textiles that might fill such a piece. Inventory listings that particularize drawer contents attest that the quantities were often very large

family would be conducted in great peace, health, and quietness. Mary Guion's only objection to marrying Samuel Brown was the obligation to live with his parents. She did marry him, however, in 1807, after a lengthy courtship. An equivocal entry in her diary a couple of years later suggests that some of her fears had been realized: "In our family perfect harmony prevails but liveing with a family many unpleasant things will and does arise for his parents have arived to a state of old age and considerably childish and fretful." Emotions, finances, children, health, and possessions were all triggers for tension. Frances Bowen Moore's arrival at her husband's family home was anything but promising, and a letter to her sister in 1790 provides documentation for the displacement and discord that could arise so easily at home in early America.

> I have but little yet [in the way of furnishings] till Mr. Moore's mother moves. I have no room to put any thing of mine. She thought hard of my having her bed taken away and putting my own in its place, I did not wish to use her bed when I had one of my own:—she took a conceit that I thought hers *not good enough* for me—it is true my bed is much the handsomest, but that was not my motive for putting it up. If she is hurt at such trifles, I am sure we could never have lived happily together, however I will try to do my duty, and then I shall have nothing to reproach myself with.[11]

Obligations of hospitality weighed heavily on the housewife. Family composition might have to be adjusted at any moment to allow for the care of widowed, orphaned, or infirm kin. Home was also hospice. Martha Sellers admired her mother's warm heart and open sympathies, but when she welcomed a recently widowed daughter and

Chamber Maid. Watercolor by Baroness Hyde de Neuville. c. 1810. The New-York Historical Society, New York City. Servants were a major source of anxiety in this land of opportunity, where no one served anyone for long. The absence of a servant class meant that it was often the girl down the street or the miss across town who came to serve till she saved up enough money to move on

a gaggle of grandchildren into the already complex Sellers household in July 1855, Martha grumbled, "we girls are getting pretty tired of it." Martha Sellers was the ninth child. Because of the large size of many families and the wide age span between the oldest and the youngest siblings, younger daughters often had to put up with the disruptive visits of older siblings and the antics of nieces and nephews.[12]

Then there were the formal and informal visits to be paid and received. The constant expansion and contraction of the family circle with the arrival and departure of guests was perplexing. "Aunt Harriet has been added to our family the last few days, and Sally came yesterday," wrote Mary Lee of Boston in September 1838, confessing that "this perpetual fluctuation in our family circle is somewhat annoying to me." It was, in fact, physically and mentally exhausting to have a house "crowded with company," as Esther Burr complained in July 1756, with "no soul to help me but Harry and my young sister that is with me." Furthermore, the constant social demands overruled convenience and were disruptive to family routine. Anne Eliza Clark Kane of Providence wrote with anguish of a terrible ten days in October 1813, during which a daughter lay dangerously ill while a constant string of guests dribbled in, abided, and finally departed, seemingly unconcerned for the welfare of mother or child—"had not my Child begun to get better I should have gone crazy," sighed a weary Mrs. Kane. Town residents in particular suffered from the sheer quantity of visiting. Harriet Manigault pictured her family in Philadelphia one January evening in 1815 "quite alone until 8 o'clock, & had just observed how pleasant it was to pass an evening quite alone *some times*, when a carriage stopped at the door." At home in Newark, New Jersey, with a bad headache and a vast deal of company in February 1755, Esther Burr wailed, "I am almost wore out and tired of *staying* here, for living I cant call it. Tis all tumult and confusion, going and coming, tis this, that, and every body. O for some calm retreat, far from the busy World!" This supplication for asylum would again be murmured in 1811 by Anne Eliza Clark Kane, who was very anxious "to get some where in the Country [for] this kind of life I do not love and cannot any longer put up with [as] I neither do my duty to myself or my Children but while one lives in a small town there is no avoiding it."[13]

But seclusion in the country could inflict yet another heartbreak—loneliness. Solitude became a grievous complaint as families scattered across the vast expanse of nineteenth-century America, interspersing miles of forest between soul mates. It was this privation of family support and congenial society in the silent world of rural America that bequeathed to us today so many diaries, journals, and letters replete not only with details of the day-to-day but with the confessional unbosoming of tired, perplexed, yet resolute women. The possibility of never seeing friends and relatives again compounded and prolonged the anguish of these separations. Preparing to assume a teaching post in the West in 1846, Lucy Larcom confessed, "I said positively that I should soon return, but underneath my protestations I was afraid that I might not. The West was very far off then,—a full week's journey. It would be hard getting back. Those I loved might die; I might die myself. These thoughts passed through my mind, though not through my lips." Uncertainty crowded in upon every aspect of life. As Samuella Curd bade adieu to her Virginia family in 1860, to travel out to Missouri with her husband, she despaired. "As the last sound of good night fell on my ears, I could but ask, will we? can we ever meet thus again? and a voice within whispered, *never!*" The ruggedness of the roads precluded facile travel over even incidental distances, so that although Harriet Silliman, depressed about her lack of

Kitchen Interior. Oil on canvas, by Thomas Hicks. 1865. Collection of the IBM Corporation, Armonk, New York. Out-of-fashion furniture was found in secondary rooms throughout a house. This once high-style Philadelphia Queen Anne armchair has been demoted to propping open the door of an old kitchen. Its leather seat is time-worn, its splat broken, its left arm crudely repaired, but its inherent elegance of line is intact and it is as much an accepted, time-honored member of the household as the elderly lady and the great open fireplace, of which we see a small portion

help and other domestic vexations at home in New Haven, wished for the comforting company of her sister in Hartford, that she might have someone with whom "to converse about my troubles," yet it was not possible. The early American wife and mother was often forced to internalize her anxieties.[14]

Servants—or the lack thereof—were indeed a dilemma that threatened to turn all housewives into misanthropes. American architects modified their house plans according to the number, or deficiency, of servants, and Catharine Beecher and Harriet Beecher Stowe could yet proclaim domestic service "the great problem of life here in America," in 1869. To have good help never defined a blissful continuum but a momentary interval that was always threatened with dissolution. You held your breath. "Miss Becky desires to know how I like My New Servant, which I hired," wrote Elizabeth Graeme from Philadelphia in 1767. "She seems sober and Modest, but I have had so much trouble about Servants that I hate to enter on the theme; for if I had Not my Father, and the Children I hate Housekeep[ing] so much that I Never would encumber my Self with it in any degree; for I find it a very great Tryal to the temper." Often there was no help at all. John Bill observed in 1827, during his tour through the States, that "a large House without Servants is an anomely I apprehend rarely to be met with but in America," and Henrietta Silliman conceded that in Hanover, New Hampshire, it was fashionable to be without a girl. Others found help but concluded, " 'there is none good, no not one.'" Purchased, hired, indentured, foreign-born, native-born, married, with children, childless—all were tried and all were found thankless, dirty, impudent, thieving, drunk, haughty, or presumptuous. "We have tried them all round," muttered Alexander Mackraby in Philadelphia in 1769, "and this is the sum total of my observations, 'the devil take the hindmost.'" A treadmill of finding, hiring, training, and losing help was time-consuming, futile, and depressing—"with respect to domestics," moaned Maria Silliman Church, "continual change appears to be our unchanging condition." Inexperienced servants required training and surveillance, though the housewife often resented time so expended. Caroline Dustan's new cook said she had never made coffee, nor seen a beet or cut up a chicken, and was considered beyond training. Faith Silliman Hubbard hired one woman so slothful she refused to scour the parlor floor with anything but the sweep of a broom, and another so enthusiastic that she had a regular bonfire going in the parlor by half past five every morning—Faith's husband threatened to dose this one with a pile of opium. Elizabeth Drinker's new maid invited a friend to lodge with her without asking permission, while Peter Neilson's Irishman "came 'right' into the parlour, and going over to the sideboard, lifted a large decanter of spirits, and walked out, saying 'he wished to *treat* a *boy* or two who were in the kitchen!'" Two of the Churches' girls left in a sniff because the house was locked up at ten in the evenings, while Faith Silliman Hubbard's maid went off because she couldn't sit at the table or in the family pew, and Caroline Dustan's because she didn't like the kitchen or the looks of the house. And when the Breckinridges wanted the evening lights gotten, there was no one to get them because the girls had instead gotten religion—"We all agreed that religion had a singular effect and hoped the rest of the servants would wait until after supper to get it." Nabby Higgins, the hired girl in Harriet Beecher Stowe's *Poganuc People*, insisted on using the front door as she had "heard the subject discussed among other girls." Indeed, as Faith Silliman Hubbard further elucidated, "These things are talked over among the different girls in the village & if at one house they are permitted liberties that are not allowed at others, it causes dissatisfaction." Neighbors had to cooperate in many ways.[15]

Also, servants were destructive. "Peg burnt my new dining-room carpet—being always drunk," repined Martha Blodget in 1796, while Caroline Dustan could tally the lid of a butter crock, a lampshade, and a range cover against her maid's three-week rampage. Martha Jefferson Randolph asked her father to pick up some glassware for her in Washington as her pantry was once again depleted of glasses, tumblers, and wineglasses; and a Creole's quick reaction upon seeing a Yankee's collection of generations-old India china was, "Oh, but they did not have a Christophe."

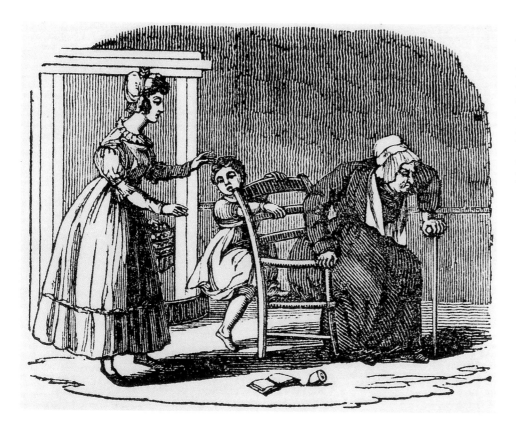

Charleston cabinetmaker Josiah Claypoole promised to "warrant his work for 7 years, the ill usage of careless servants only excepted." Perhaps the chaste aspect of early American furniture was in part an adaptation to these native conditions. The proverbial dearth of help and the carelessness of those who did serve mandated a solid, plain style free of "superfluous carving," with "no work that will harbor dust"; and when Charles Carroll of Carrollton ordered girandoles and a pair of pier glasses from England in 1771, he knowingly insisted that the carving "be of a solid kind," for he had found by experience that slight carving could withstand neither the rigors of the climate nor the abuse of the servants.[16]

Those who lived on farms and plantations had the additional problem of rude field hands who swore before the children, tracked mud (or worse things) into the house, and ate illimitable amounts of food. Catherine Robbins said that it was not unusual for them to hire eight or ten men in summer, "which complicated the housekeeping very much"; and Maria Silliman Church regularly boarded eight to twenty-two hearty men and fretted at not being able to make butter because those titans drank the milk up. In June 1831, Sarah Clarke Whitings, trying to recover from childbirth in Litchfield, Connecticut, complained that the warm weather, together with a large family of seven men, "has been too much for my feeble health to bear up under. . . . we have this morning dismissed four and we all feel the relief."[17]

The anxieties of childbirth and the demands of child care were complicating to many a housewife's schedule. There has been much excellent demographic work done recently that traces a falling birthrate throughout the eighteenth and nineteenth centuries. But few mothers from 1750 to 1870 could claim to have borne the number of children they would have had by choice. Some had too few, but the majority

complained of too many. A large family of children seemed inevitable; Abigail Swett was not being completely facetious in 1822 when she told a correspondent that a mutual friend was "again as 'women wish to be who love their lords' and as women will be whether they wish it or not." At home with two small children in April 1756, Esther Burr fretted about the present and worried about an almost certain future— "When I had but one Child my hands were tied, but now I am tied hand and foot. (How I shall get along when I have got ½ dzn. or 10 Children I cant devise.)" Annie Crowninshield Warren was not thankful for her Thanksgiving Day gift of a fifth daughter in 1851, "as my house was very small"; and Fanny Appleton Longfellow was depressed by the prospect of another child in October 1853, because "I find children such a responsibility as they grow older, and so difficult to manage rightly, that I shrink from further duties beyond my capacities." As conscientious and involved mothers, these women worried about the feasibility of giving each child its due as the little troop expanded while their own capabilities stayed the same. "I find a great accumulation of cares growing out of my new acquisition," wrote Anne Jean Lyman

The Proud Mother. Oil on canvas, by an unknown American artist. c. 1810. National Gallery of Art, Washington, D.C.; gift of Edgar William and Bernice Chrysler Garbisch. Mothers, then as now, rejoiced in their children, loved them, worried about them, and were constantly amazed at how much care just one child demanded

in 1823, after the birth of her tenth child, "and I do not find proportionate increase of talents for the demand."[18]

Although the statistics were increasingly on their side, all these women were concerned about the critical nature of childbirth itself. They were present when neighbors delivered, they paid the traditional lying-in, or "sitting-up," visit, they shared the same nurses: in all these ways they knew the intimate details of every birth in town and the lesson they came home with was—nothing is certain. Sarah Logan Fisher, whose diaries are filled with references to the untimely death of friends in childbed, wrote in August 1785, pregnant herself, "This day John Bayards Wife Buried who had Died in Child Bed[;] so many lately have been taken off in that situation, that it is an awfull consideration to those who expect to be in that way." When Abigail Adams advised her husband of a similar instance, she could add with first-hand authority, "Every thing of this kind naturally shocks a person in similar circumstances. How great the mind that can overcome the fear of Death!" Recently, Roger Schofield and other scholars have postulated that as their chances of surviving delivery improved, women did not evaluate the dangers of childbirth in isolation but relative to the dangers of dying from other causes. Primary source materials do not substantiate this premise. Although women feared death in many guises for their husbands and children, the dread of their own demise in childbed far outweighed their dread of dying in any other manner. And although many tried to be rational, to cheat apprehension and anxiety, endeavoring to face their confinement with equanimity, realism, faith, and cheerful good spirits, yet it was a troublesome and not always successful effort. Whether the danger was real or imagined, the apprehension was genuine, and to many it was deep, obsessive, and prolonged. Louisa Park, who expected to deliver in April 1800, wrote her distant husband in January, "Anticipation looks no further forward than spring—and from that I turn with horror. . . . I have always from the first had a presentiment that I should never live to see May, and it grows stronger every day—at present, it appears an absolute certainty." Mrs. Park was safely delivered of a son, Joseph Warren, on 19 April, but she, and many of her sisterhood, spent many months in a world of anxiety, considering everything to be uncertain "so long as a certain event intervenes." This trepidation did not necessarily diminish with subsequent pregnancies, and in some cases was even intensified. Maria Silliman Church weighed the odds against her as she faced her sixth confinement, "I have done well so often, that I cannot but think that this time I may not be so fortunate." And she confessed to suffering a nervous alarm which intensified with each successive confinement: "When I know the event is at hand, I am seized with such agitation, and utter depression of spirits, that I almost faint from this effect, and this continues until all is over. I can summon no resolution to meet what is inevitable, and find no support to my spirits from any source whatever." Mrs. Church ultimately went through nine anxiety-ridden yet successful deliveries over a twenty-year span and died at the age of seventy, in 1880, with six of her children still living. Given the choice, she would not have had nine children. Although expectant mothers were repeatedly admonished not to worry, they did, and their worst fears were often realized. On Christmas Day 1857, Sidney George Fisher was astonished to see his perpetually energetic and always-cheerful sister-in-law "depressed, even to agitation and constant weeping. She thinks she will not survive her confinement, which is to come in May, & that this is the last Christmas she will pass with her family." Sarah Ann Fisher died of puerperal fever that May. Thomas Jefferson, who had lost his wife to the rigors of childbearing, tried to allay the nervous alarm of his daughter Maria as she neared her third confinement, and encouraged her to "have good spirits, and know that courage is as essential to triumph in your case as in that of a soldier." Courageous or not, Maria Jefferson Eppes died in that childbed.[19]

The probability of pregnancy was in itself restrictive, as one could not plan ahead—a sustained dilemma that persisted throughout one's childbearing years. In March 1757 Esther Burr could not do much more than contemplate a trip north to Boston in the autumn, as "I suppose it may be possible enough that I may not be in Circumstances proppor [proper] for Traveling, tho' nothing of that yet." And pregnancy was restrictive—house-binding because the medical dictates of the day, and often the weather, proscribed outdoor exercise for those with child. The piazza was a welcome alternative. "I have been a good deal confined to the house of late, as thaws have rendered the walking intolerable and find my piazza a great comfort, as I can pace there in nearly all weather with dry feet," wrote a grateful Fanny Appleton Longfellow in December 1843, pregnant with her first child. After the birth, the lying-in period was disquieting and disruptive to family routine, particularly if

The New Baby. Woodcut from [Jane Taylor], *Rhymes for the Nursery* (Boston [1837]). The Winterthur Library: Printed Book and Periodical Collection. This mother peeks out from behind the curtains of her tent bed to apprize the newest member of the household — a frequent enough scene in the bedchambers of early America. Four weeks was the standard interval between delivery and a full resumption of household duties. Pre-delivery discomfort or post-delivery complications could keep a mother chamber-bound much longer

mother or child was not doing "bravely." The constant arrival and departure of well-wishers paying their obligatory sitting-up visits were addling to the household, exhausting to the new mother, and, according to Esther Burr, often uncomfortable to the visitor as well, for when she fulfilled her obligation at a neighbor's home on 7 August 1755, she found "a house full of people (as there always is as soon as a woman is a Bed) and a deal of confusion, and I had not much comfort, but wished my self at home 10 times in half an hour."[20]

Many new mothers kept to their bedchamber for a month while older children ran up and down stairs and got into all kinds of mischief, servants slacked off, and housekeeping was neglected. Fanny Appleton Longfellow was rather relieved to escape the bustle of her household for a few weeks and confessed one month after the birth of daughter Edith that she felt "no haste to leave my pleasant chamber." Others were only too glad to burst out of those confines. "Little baby is now a month old and I am emancipated from my bed room," wrote Maria Silliman Church in March 1834, following the birth of her second child, though when she stepped into the kitchen she found that things had "got into such a condition that I feel as if I should fly until I can get them cleaned and regulated." Complications after delivery could keep a mother confined much longer. Because of her own and her son Aaron's indisposition following his birth on 6 February 1756, Esther Burr was not able to get about again until April, and when she did she found "All in confusion," and spent 20 April "setting the House a little in order for it hant been done to any purpose since I Layin." Once a mother, a woman was certainly confined, and often for years to come, as the difference in the ages of the firstborn and lastborn could span more than two decades. At the age of forty-six, in 1829, Mary Lee of Boston wrote a Newburyport friend, regretting that "I cannot think of visiting you probably for many years, for as my children are some of

Rollo. Engraving from Jacob Abbott, *Rollo Learns to Read* (New York, 1839). Women's letters are filled with complaints about the difficulty of writing amid the distracting noise and constant interruptions of children. Here young Rollo asks his mother's help in his vain attempt to push the ponderous rocking chair near the fire so that his father may have a comfortable seat upon his momentary arrival

them the children of my old age, I have still some time to look forward before the younger ones will be out of leading strings"; and Elizabeth Dorsey of Elk Ridge, Maryland, regretted in 1787 that it would probably never be possible for her to visit her sister in Dover, Delaware, again, for "I am so tyed down by the trouble of children and servants that I seldom leve them one half day in six months."[21]

Generations of mothers have each in turn been astonished at the work generated by even one child. Harriet Silliman would equivocate that baby Henrietta was playful and pleasant, the delight of the whole house, but kept her constantly occupied and confined; and Mrs. Silliman's daughter Maria Silliman Church would gasp eleven years later, "Baby begins to know me and doesn't like to go to any one else,—so that some days I dont get an hour for my work." The limitless demands of both child care and housework found many a mother hoping to cut corners by accomplishing both at the same time—cooking, sewing, weaving, spinning, writing with baby nearby or even in arms. Telling pairs in inventories include a spinning wheel and cradle or a loom and crib. That none of these combinations promoted productivity we hear from Lucy Clark Allen of Northborough, Massachusetts, in her delightful 1819 soliloquy on the timelessness of maternal vexations.

After I have spent sufficient time in the morning attending to my domestic affairs, I go and find my *sewing-work* and go into the parlor. I set the baby on the carpet, with playthings enough around her to amuse any reasonable being half a day at least; but I have scarcely found my needle and threaded it before the little rogue is pulling herself up by my clothes, or creeping into some mischief or other, and, after trying various methods to amuse her, I put her into a new place away from me. By and by she cries with cold fingers and toes. Then I must carry her to the fire and warm her and dry her and feed her, and it is no exaggeration to say that I take her up for various purposes twenty times in a day.

And where is my work all this time? When I go to sit down to it, my thimble is under one chair, my scissors under another, my needle is lost or stuck into a far distant part,—for I sometimes have to jump in a pretty great hurry,—and by the time I have collected all my materials together, down it must go again.[22]

Mothers were indeed concerned about keeping their children warm, particularly crawling infants, in the typically cold, drafty American house; and also about keeping them safely away from fires and stoves—a very real threat at home in early America. In mild weather, babies were sometimes tied in chairs for short periods of time to keep them out of mischief and to free a mother's arms. But this resort was not feasible in freezing weather, for as one mother presented the problem, "it is difficult to write with her in my arms, and it is too cold to tye her into a chair; even before the fire, it hardly thaws."[23]

A mother's role as teacher to her children was of paramount importance in the Victorian era, but it had been acknowledged long before. Thomas Jefferson could say with admiration that his daughter Martha, the mother of a dozen children, had "made their education the object of her life"; and Mary Guion, who was extremely sensitive about her own lack of formal education, was determined that if she ever became a mother, her first care would be for the education of her children, "which I

Interior Scene. Boston. Oil on canvas, by Jane Stuart. c. 1835. Collection Mr. and Mrs. Joseph A. McFalls. In this handsome interior, a mother has momentarily set aside her sewing tasks to hear her son recite his lessons. In the late eighteenth century, a growing awareness of the malleability of a child's mind placed an additamentary obligation on mothers and fathers to become both dedicated and successful teachers. Parlor lessons commenced when the children were yet babies, and because of either the lack of a school or parental disapproval of a teacher or classmates, or perhaps the uncertain health of the child itself, they might need to continue for years to come. Such lessons were continually being disturbed for one reason or another, concentration and consistency were well-nigh impossible, and many a mother would have willingly given up this duty had there been alternatives

should consider as a very Essential part of my duty towards them." Throughout the second half of the eighteenth century there had been a growing awareness of the malleability of a child's mind, and this perception placed a supplementary obligation on a mother to be a dedicated and successful pedagogue. Sitting rooms and bed-chambers obliged as schoolrooms as well. Mary Palmer Tyler recalled with pleasure her childhood days in the 1780s when her mother had called "us to our daily lessons, reading and writing, (for we were mere babies when we began) in her chamber overlooking the sea," with its white muslin bed and window curtains and the soft pine floor scoured as white as could be. One senses an element of urgency in these precipitous attempts to teach facts, figures, skills, and values to little children hardly more than babbling toddlers. They perhaps suggest a mother's recognition of her mortality—the uncertainty of her life—coupled with the belief that no one could instill values and virtues as effectively as a natural mother could; these lessons might be a mother's most important bequest. "Favor is deceitful, beauty is vain, property precarious," Sarah Livingston Jay warned her daughter Maria in December 1794, "but mental & personal accomplishments death only or sickness can deprive our families off [*sic*] & if you should live until your family should be first instructed by you, your virtues will survive in them here, & in yourself meet the promised reward." The education of children brought all kinds of additional anxieties to the housewife. Often there were no good schools nearby, which meant that one had either to send children away to school—which caused many to express the anguish of separation from their little ones—or to teach them at home—which caused others to bemoan their own deficiencies as instructors or to regret the impossibility of continuity in this teaching. Although mothers might spend hours tutoring their children, household duties, servant ineptitude, illnesses, and other interruptions simply would not permit a consistent schedule, much to a mother's chagrin. For mothers of large families, of course, the demands of nursing, caring for, and teaching children were stretched out over many years. As family membership and the resultant duties grew larger and more complex, the aging mother's energies and cheerful good spirits ebbed little by little. Harriet Silliman pondered whether her low spirits were due to being "either more tired by domestic cares and vexations than formerly, or else I have more of them." The elder Palmer children assumed housework duties so that their mother might be freed to instruct the younger siblings. But all mothers were not so fortunate. To many it seemed ever more difficult to maintain a strictly scheduled, calm household.[24]

Housework seemed to grow apace with every other obstacle. In the course of the eighteenth and nineteenth centuries, houses expanded and possessions multiplied, but there were few new amenities to counterbalance these incremental encumbrances. Servants remained as ineffective, and although the sewing machine and kitchen range were important advancements, there were no revolutionary inventions to speed housework. Nonetheless, these women strove hard. To the question What did the early American housewife hope for in life? one might respond that her chief pleasure and her main ambition lay in doing her duty well. How regrettable, therefore, that the goal and the means were often far apart. A wife and mother was often not able to complete a task to her satisfaction because there were so many scattering demands on her time. Maria Silliman Church vouched that she did not ask for exemption from care and constant occupation, but only for time and opportunity to do her duty well. With what despair, therefore, she faced the winter of 1839: "I see so much coming upon me. With the care of my baby, the instruction of John and Bennie, my family cares, and the making so many little garments as they will all require—it appears to me as if I could never get on with it and do my *duty* in *any thing*." Time seemed to her to be the scarcest commodity in the world. Household tasks were either so trivial or so great that even after completion it seemed that nothing had been accomplished, and the demands these women placed on themselves made guilt a significant problem. Harriet Beecher Stowe, despite all she did as a wife, mother, and professional author, was "constantly pursued and haunted by the idea I don't do anything"; while in 1818 one Mrs. Cleveland, with "not only the care of the farm, the accounts to keep both private & family, the government of family concerns," could "rise early & retire late, yet I accomplish little of any thing." Indeed, the scope of many housewives' responsibilities seemed excessive. Sidney George Fisher was concerned that his sister-in-law's debility was in part owing to her "too great a charge in their large establishment and the way it is kept up; house, children, garden, farm, all are directed by her." Although Harriet Beecher Stowe might voice the accepted tenet that "she who hath faculty is never in a hurry, never behindhand," these wives and mothers, including herself, were often in a hurry and usually behindhand. Further, the very nature of household tasks precluded finiteness, and that the dilemma of the uncompleted task was exacting on body and depressing to the spirit is colorfully illustrated by the ruminations of a fictitious New York farm wife.

> Now when a man ploughs a field, or runs up a line of figgers, or writes a serming, or kills a beef critter, there it is done—no more to be done over. But sposen a woman washes up her dishes clean as a fiddle, no sooner does she wash 'em up once, than she has to, right over and over agin, three times three hundred and 65 times every year. And the same with the rest of her work, blackin' stoves, and fillin' lamps, and washin' and moppin' floors, and the same with cookin'. Why jest the idee of paradin' out the table and teakettle 3 times 3 hundred and 65 times every year is enough to make a woman sweat. And then to think of all the cookin' utensils and ingredients—why if it wuzzn't for principle, no woman could stand the idee, let alone the labor, for it haint so much the mussle she has to lay out, as the strain on her mind.

Nothing ever seemed to be finished. Mary Beth Norton, in her insightful study of women in Revolutionary America, has pointed out that notable housewifery was an inadequate prop for female self-esteem as it was regarded as an end in itself, rather than as a means to a more significant end. Even so, many women would have been content if they could only have seen their duties performed properly and to completion. It was the impossibility of doing one's duty well that made Harriet Silliman feel "as if I were good for nothing," which suffered Sarah Logan Fisher to feel "unequal," which underlay Mrs. Cleveland's concern for her own "deficiencies," and which plunged Maria Silliman Church into gloom because she meant to do right, "and yet somehow, nobody seems to fall so far short."[25]

A particularly perplexing problem to the early American housewife was the infeasibility of commanding any uninterrupted time. Concentration was impossible; one's thoughts must always be scattered. "The pleasure of writing a letter in *peace*, and *doing no other thing* at the same time, is what I hardly ever know," complained one, setting the stage for the picture that Harriet Beecher Stowe drew of herself in 1850, shortly after the birth of her fifth child: "Since I began this note I have been called off at least a dozen times; once for the fishman, to buy a codfish; once to see a man who had brought me some barrels of apples; once to see a book-man; then to Mrs. Upham, to see about a drawing I promised to make for her; then to nurse the baby; then into the kitchen to make chowder for dinner; and now I am at it again," though she knew that nothing but her "deadly determination" would ever enable her to write—"it is rowing against wind and tide." Elizabeth Wirt would attempt to write a letter in April 1819 amid children scolding, "*slamming* the door," "jumping about with the keys," and talking "in a *loud key*"; while a rattled Martha Jefferson Randolph would have to beg her father's indulgence in January 1804, and beg him "to recollect, that I write amidst the noises and confusion of six children interrupted every moment by their questions, and so much disturbed by [their] pratling around me that I catch my self repeatedly writing [their words] instead of my own thoughts." The desire for private time, time to be alone in silence, was strong for many. Maria Silliman Church would have given "more for one quiet hour every day, than for almost anything else which could be named"; and Mary Cooper would rejoice on 23 October 1768 to have "the blessing to be quite alone, without any body greate or small." Ellen

Portrait of Mrs. William Frazer. Oil on canvas, by William Clarke. 1798. The Historical Society of Delaware, Wilmington. Though private space was often desired, it could not always be had indoors. In the warm weather, however, a silent garden or solitary grove might offer sanctuary for rest and contemplation

Curiosity. Oil on canvas, by Christian Mayr. 1833. Courtesy Frank S. Schwarz and Son, Philadelphia. Many were the challenges to privacy at home in early America. One mischievous miss, living with her maternal grandparents and their ten daughters in early-nineteenth-century Massachusetts, recalled that she and her younger aunt felt it was their *duty* to find out and relate all the love secrets of the older girls — either by hiding behind a door or curtain or by peeping through the keyhole

Birdseye Wheaton wondered whether this longing after quiet was a natural trait or the result of an "overtasked state of the nervous system." It was perhaps a combination of the two, but it was a desire shared by much of her sisterhood. Those who could claim a moment of solitude found it physically refreshing and mentally restorative. Evenings offered a mother the best opportunity for completing tasks without interruption; "I find the evening, (as Mama always told me I would if I ever was a mistress of a family) my best time to sew," admitted Maria Silliman Church in November 1833. And the blissful quiet made it a consecrated moment. "The evening is a blessed time it is still when they are asleep," exulted one exhausted mother, while another echoed, "I am so happy when the children get away to bed, that I feel like prolonging the hour of quiet, to a great length."[26]

Private space was also coveted at home in early America. In 1754, Edward Shippen of Lancaster, Pennsylvania, extolled the sweetness and refreshing pleasure enjoyed by a man and his wife spending their evenings alone. "And for my part rather than be deprived by my very best friends of such a pleasure sometimes, I should chuse to retire into our Chamber privately that even our own Servants should not know where to find us out." Locked doors enhanced privacy by refusing entrance and securing possessions from the untoward scrutiny of others. When Gold Selleck Silliman collapsed in his Connecticut chamber one July evening in 1790, his frightened wife—in her haste to summon help—locked, rather than unlocked, their chamber door, assuming that it was in its wonted locked position; and Charles Carroll of Carrollton wished for a dead bolt that could be maneuvered from a bed, ordering in March 1773, "1 Falling Latch or Bolt for a Bed Chamber Door with a line & Pulleys—and a handle to pull at a Beds head." Sometimes a small room offered sanctuary. Esther Burr and a friend were grateful to escape a babbling crowd of people and slip "into a room by our selves a little while"; and Mary Guion's sister called her into "a little room" that she might confide in her in July 1801. The garret was Lucy Larcom's usual retreat "when I wanted to get away by myself with my books or my dreams." And a fortunate few had a little room or closet of their own, often off a bedchamber, for reading, writing, and reflection. Louisa May Alcott was delighted to get "the little room I have wanted so long," in March 1846, and placing her workbasket and desk by the window, and breathing in the pleasant scent of the dried herbs that filled her room, she reveled in the knowledge that "it does me good to be alone." Not only could a person find solitude in such a closet but one's writings—one's privacies, as Esther Burr termed her most intimate correspondence—would be secure from the curious gaze and meddling touch of others. Had Mary Guion had a closet for her private writings, she would not have had to suffer the distress she experienced the evening of 4 February 1805: "I had no sooner retired last night and put out my candle than I recolected my writing I had left on the stand by the fire, how did I feal at that moment for it was so very cold I could not thinck of going down after it and I knew the boys would like to read it when they got up to make a fire in the morning." Abigail Adams wrote with envy in August 1776 of the "convenient pretty closet" in her aunt's chamber. It had a window that looked out on the flower garden and was lined with bookshelves and a desk, where Abigail, during her visit with this aunt, could "write all my Letters and keep my papers unmollested by any one. I do not covet my Neighbours Goods," she insisted, "but I should like to be the owner of such conveniances. I always had a fancy for a closet with a window which I could more peculiarly call my own." Determined to strive for a happy marriage, Benjamin Rush wrote his fiancée, Julia Stockton, in December 1775, advising her that he had "had a few shelves put up in a closet in your bed chamber, into which I am removing all such books as are commonly read by your sex, and have called it Julia's library. I have appropriated one shelf for paper & an inkstand only, which are never to be touched by any body's fingers but your own."[27]

A garden might also offer seasonal refuge. When the family circle became large and noisy or when sorrows overcame her, Mary Guion would steal out into the peach orchard, the grove, the garden, to read, to write, to indulge herself in a hearty fit of weeping. Yet with the return of the piercing cold she could "no more amuse myself in a flower garden or Solitary grove but spend my whole time in the house till that pleasing Spring once more returns." The silent garden and the solitary grove were important in more than a visual sense at home in early America. The desire for private time, the longing for private space, were real to eighteenth-century and nineteenth-century Americans. But company, children, servants, cold weather—all were impedi-

The First, Second and Last Scenes of Mortality. Preston, Connecticut. Embroidery in silk on silk, by Prudence Punderson. c. 1778–83. The Connecticut Historical Society, Hartford. Childhood is here symbolized by the baby in the cradle; maturity by the lady, presumably Prudence Punderson herself, at work on her round table; and the final stage by the appropriately initialed casket on the drop-leaf table below the pedimented pier glass, which has been muffled in white cloth. Looking glasses and pictures were sometimes shrouded in their own white winding sheet following a death in the family. Prudence married in 1783 and died nine months later

ments that might foil circumvention, making privacy something that was often unattainable.28

When Grace Growden Galloway went to her neighbor's house in search of comfort and tea one very cold and gloomy November afternoon in 1778, she found instead the unnerving confusion of a family of five boisterous children, and "what with their Opening & shuting ye doors & the Noise they Made in the rooms threw everything into confusion . . . I cou'd hear Nothing for ye bawling round me." When Nancy Tilghman called on Mrs. Robert Wright in Chestertown, Maryland, for tea and warmth in 1785, she was instead treated to a cold room and the lively tableau of "Miss Caroline and master Bob who were fighting on the carpet, during the whole visit." When Alexander Anderson took tea at Dr. Davidson's in New York City in February 1795, he had, in addition to good tea and fine sweetmeats, "the noise of the children and the impertinence of a young goat, who made a forcible entry in to the room." It is not surprising, therefore, that when David Warden visited Mrs. Mason at home along the Potomac River, he found vigorous twin boys "tumbling on the carpet of the saloon full of joy and merriment." The "air of order and stillness" had evaporated! The early American home was, in fact, often alive and aloud with jubilant children plowing, "driving team—haw! gee! whoa!," shooting arrows down the stairs, or playing menagerie, wild horses, bear and lion, and, on occasion, a *"gentle mother scolding."* "I often think of what you have got to come to if you live long enough," Sarah Clarke Whitings wrote to a friend who was expecting her first child in 1832, "and if you do not occasionally feel a little like *scold[ing]* then you and yours will be different from me and mine." The boisterous noise and frolicsome play of lively children was distracting, even deeply disturbing, to women who had been brought up to admire quietude and order and to abhor noise and confusion. Even their daughters—when not augmenting the chorus with their own clamor—would complain. Fourteen-year-old Laura Wirt might wish in 1817 that her two-year-old sister Agnes "would hush[;] we have been trying to stop her tongue ever since I began to write [and] she puts me out." And thirteen-year-old Louisa Jane Trumbull of Worcester, Massachusetts, was delighted to report in her diary in February 1835 that she would soon be going to stay with an aunt in Greenfield for about a month. "I wish much to go," she confided, "for I am sick of the noise and crying of our little children and glad shall I be to go there where in the quiet of Aunt Susan's family I shall for a short time at least escape that noise which is daily and hourly made by each child." We can be sure that there was precious little quiet on those rainy and snowy days when a houseful of energetic children left mothers light-headed with their noise. In fair weather there were the "safety valves of open doors & windows" and the resource of romping outdoors in the yard or frolicking on the piazzas, which did, indeed, reverberate with the running feet and lively laughter of children.[29]

There was a silence, however, a silence dreaded above all: "Every tramper that ever tramped is abroad but the little feet are still," grieved Ralph Waldo Emerson over the untimely death of his little Waldo. There was but one certainty at home in early America, and that was the uncertainty of life itself. "Experience learns us to be always anxious about the health of those whom we love," wrote a chastened and saddened Thomas Jefferson in 1787. Although statistics document an ever-increasing life expectancy for Americans between 1750 and 1870, yet there were few families that did not frequently renew acquaintance with the grim reaper. The pall of death was omnipresent: at home, next door, intoned from the pulpit in the roll of the week's dead, heard from one's bed as the bells tolled the count, indicating whether it was man, or woman, or child who had last been taken. And totalitarian death was no snob. Accidents, epidemics, malnutrition, and primitive medical practices claimed rich and poor, young and old.[30]

Health was not a given in early America. Eliza Farrar would warn in her *The Young Lady's Friend* (1837) that a girl should be ready at any moment to attend her parents, her siblings, her friends, as "there is no possession more uncertain than that of health, and since the young and vigorous are liable, as well as the aged and the infirm, to be laid upon the bed of sickness." A woman was connected by duty to neighbors, servants, and kin—any one of whom might need to be cared for at any time—and she was expected to spend many hours sitting by or "watching" at a sickbed, for to be " 'a good watcher' was considered one of the most important of womanly attainments." Catharine Beecher readily acknowledged in 1849 that the state of health in this nation was such that a woman, with the care of a large family, "seldom passes a week without being called on to know what shall be done for some one who is indisposed." It was indeed difficult to keep everyone well. Landon Carter's plaintive lament in 1770—"It is impossible in such a large family of Children and grand Children, but some of them may be indisposed"—was echoed by Mary Minor Anderson, the mother of eight, about 1858: "It seems almost impossible to have all well at the same time." And Laura Wirt jubilantly told her grandmother in May 1818 that "for *once*, I can say that *all* of the children are well at *one* time." Contagious diseases might take weeks to make the rounds. Elizabeth Wirt tried to keep her younger children out of daughter Laura's chamber, where she lay ill with scarlet fever in 1819, "but it is to late to avoid the contagion if there be any—They have all been there repeatedly—particularly on yesterday to see the *Leeches* applied to her neck." And the servants might be affected. The transmission of illnesses between the "Big House" and the slave quarters complicated the life of the southern housewife, relegating her to weeks of nursing duty when a contagious disease struck.[31]

Lucy Clark Allen maintained that she almost looked forward to an occasional mild sickness in her family, "for, amid the hurry and confusion in which I live, I feel often the need of a *resting-spell*, and a time and place for retreat and meditation, which the sick-chamber affords me." But the fatigue and sleeplessness that accompanied a more serious illness took its toll on the maternal watcher who, like Esther Burr, "almost got to be as bad as the Child." As diligent nursing was the most effective medicine, mothers sat up night and day with ailing children, often never undressing or going to bed for a week at a time. Sarah Livingston Jay told her husband, John, in the fall of 1790, that she had not left their daughter's bedside for an hour since diphtheria had been diagnosed a week before, despite the nauseating smell peculiar to the disease, while Elizabeth Wirt was so exhausted running up two flights of stairs to care for Laura during that scarlet fever episode, and then back down to put away 250 shad, that she found herself "scarcely able to sit up—and [I] am sore from the crown of my head to the sole of my feet."[32]

The physical exhaustion, however, was nothing compared with the anxiety, for death trod closely behind sickness, and just how closely no parent could be sure. When Sarah Livingston Jay wrote her husband in February 1779 to advise him that their son had been seriously ill, she confided that "during his indisposition my suffering I think was little inferior to his as he was only affected by immediate pain & not by the apprehension of future consequences." The threat of loss was a constant. "Every moment of my life is embitered by the aprehensions of losing her," murmured Martha Jefferson Randolph as she nursed her eldest through her first major illness in 1792, and when dysentery struck the family in 1803, particularly threatening nine-year-old Ellen, Martha asked her father to judge of her feelings "at seeing her escaping from me so rapidly." She, herself, could only "reflect with horror upon that week that no language can paint." When little Hatty Hubbard was similarly seized in September 1839, her mother also felt "that we might have to part with her and I need not say that it has been a week of great anxiety." Letters and diaries are regularly punctuated

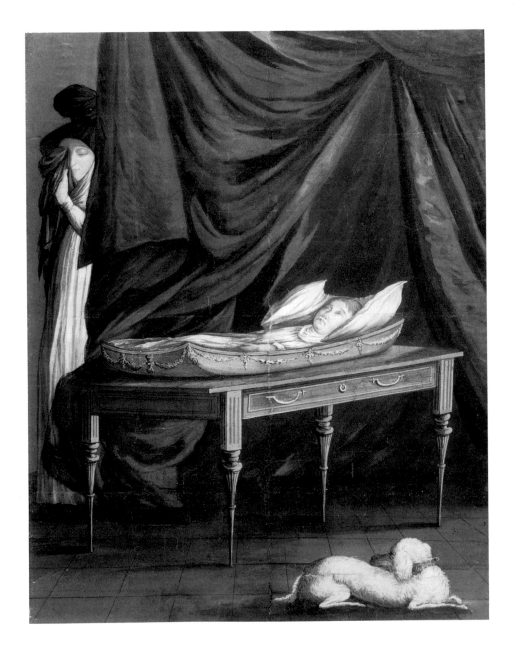

Death of William. Watercolor attributed to Michele Felice Corné. c. 1800. On deposit with Essex Institute, Salem, Massachusetts. It was often the mother herself who bathed her deceased children and prepared them for the grave, taking small comfort in the fact that none but loving hands had touched them

Dr. Philemon Tracy. Oil on paper mounted on board, by an unknown American artist. c. 1790. National Gallery of Art, Washington, D.C.; gift of Edgar William and Bernice Chrysler Garbisch. Uncertainty was one of the most trying aspects of early medicine. No one, not the well-intentioned doctor, nor the distraught family, nor the concerned neighbors, knew just how closely death might follow in the wake of illness. Here the concerned doctor mentally clocks the patient's pulse rate

with the three-word conditional phrase—"if he lives." It is expressed in an unselfconscious, natural way, such as "The scarlet merino frock will fit Sam—if he lives"; or, "In three years if Johnny lives he will be old enough for school." The provisional aspect of life subconsciously wove itself into one's pattern of thought. Abigail Adams thought her grandson "dead for ten minuts" in July 1797, while in December 1777 Sarah Logan Fisher walked up to comfort Cousin Sally Emlen, who had sent word that her child was dying, "but found it rather better on my getting there, tho' very Ill." Mrs. Fisher could say of her own child in February 1794, "this day [a] week [ago] we thought her very low and had not much hopes"; while Faith Silliman Hubbard, and hundreds of other thankful mothers, would echo, "my dear little boy's life which a week ago seemed sorely threatened has been spared." Every one of these children lived, but their parents had struggled through agonizing, exhausting days and nights trying to resign themselves to the loss of their child. The strain was exacting in its variableness, for hope succeeded despair, which rose in hope, which plunged in despair. Mary Guion's brother was thought imminently dying for eight weeks in 1804, as both he and his family vacillated between pious resignation and tentative optimism; and little Aaron Burr was so ill in October 1756 that for three

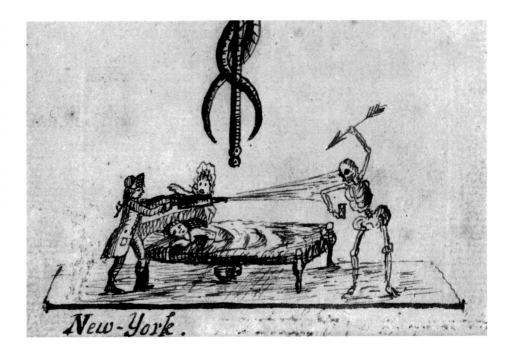

A Medical Cartoon. Ink sketch by Alexander Anderson. c. 1792–95. The New-York Historical Society, New York City; Anderson Papers. Alexander Anderson, physician and artist, scribbled this vignette on the cover of his textbook, *A Medical Grammar.* It illustrates the contemporary belief that the most effective weapon against the grim reaper was purging—purging the body of all foul humors. Here, the clyster is defiantly aimed at the insatiate archer rather than at an already weakened patient

nights his parents were told he could not survive till morning. Although he would show signs of improvement, he then would grow considerably worse, so that his mother was faced with "the greatest tryal that ever I meet with in my life." Baby Aaron had hovered on the "borders of Eternity," but others would cross over. Louisa Park went through the same "sleepless nights—the fatiguing days—the quick succession of hopes and fears," the horrible trauma of watching her baby suffer while not being able to relieve him, but Joseph Warren Park died in April 1801, one year after that birth his mother had so dreaded. "How could I endure it—much less, compose myself—but by believing him gone to perfect rest and happiness—there to wait for his father and mother," asked his anguished mother. Pious resignation to God's purpose was the ideal way to cope with death, a conviction that the child had gone to a happier home the chief solace. But it was not easy. As Mary Fish Noyes walked to the grave of her firstborn in 1759, her father sought to console her with the conviction that though these were melancholy steps, yet "the path of glory leads through the grave and it is well worth while to undergo the pains of bearing and of parting with children if thereby we people the redeemers kingdom for of such the kingdom consists," and yet she could but feel "like a bullock unaccustomed to the yoke." Sarah Logan Fisher wondered "how can I come at Resignation, as I ought," following the death of her "dearest Billy" in September 1780, and her diary portrays a grieved mother vacillating for months between feeling "calm & composed which is a Mercy," or endeavoring "to keep my mind quiet but Alass almost in vain."[33]

As the Enlightenment world of reason eased into the Romantic world of emotion, children came to be appreciated as enjoyable innocents who not only enhanced the affectionate family group but who were, in fact, the adhesive that bonded it together. These "rivets of affection," these "dear pledges which bind us to one another and to life itself," were at the very center of family life. How, then, could they be easily spared? As each child was studied for its own unique qualities, it became all the more difficult to accept the silence of a once-prattling tongue, the abandonment of a once-favorite toy. To Benjamin Silliman, his little Trumbull, who died before his fifth birthday in 1818, was "a child of the most attractive traits, lovely and beautiful, serious, considerate, and affectionate, but with a slight air of pensiveness, which added to the interest of his character." To Ralph Waldo Emerson, his little Waldo, who "decorated for me the morning star, & the evening cloud," had been "a boy of early wisdom, of a grave & even majestic deportment, of a perfect gentleness."[34]

When thirteen-year-old Mary Perkins of Jaffrey, New Hampshire, stitched a mourning sampler in 1829, she recorded the deaths of three siblings by an "Insatiate archer," who

> could not once suffice
> Thy darts flew thrice
> and thrice our peace was slain.

Repetitive losses were particularly trying to family solidarity and parent equanimity. Sarah Connell Ayer ended her journal in October 1811, preoccupied with household duties and preparations for the birth of her first child. In September 1815 she resumed writing, tersely recording the ordeal of the intervening years. "Since closing my last journal, I have been the mother of four children, which now lay side by side in the grave-yard." The threat of epidemics remained very real from 1750 to 1870, and many of the women whose diaries and letters are quoted in this book were intimately acquainted with families who had lost three or four children at a time, causing each of these mothers to worry in turn for the safety of their own. The incremental strain was appalling. "Oh my Brother she was Every thing to me," moaned Jane Mecom to Benjamin Franklin after the death of her daughter in October 1765. "Sorrows roll upon me like the waves of the sea. I am hardly allowed time to fetch my breath. I am broken with breach upon breach, and I have now, in the first flow of my grief, been almost ready to say, 'What have I more?' But God forbid, that I should indulge that thought, though I have lost another Child. God is sovereign and I submit." Parents who mustered the strength to cope with the death of one, even several, children, were not always able to do the same for yet another. When William Wirt's eldest son died at the age of nineteen, in 1824, Wirt sought to bolster his wife's morale. "What can we do, if you suffer yourself to sink under the sorrow that afflicts you? Let us bear up and endeavour to fulfill our duty to our surviving children . . . May God bless you, and breathe into your bosom peace and cheerful resignation!" But when their sixteen-year-old daughter died seven years later, he was simply overcome with grief and turned increasingly away from the mundane, seeking solace in religion.[35]

The ironic lesson of life on earth was that "this world *is* no home"; and Abigail Adams, with a heart made sore by repeated affliction, knew well enough that "if any thing can effectually wean & detach us from this world, it is the loss of those who render Life pleasant and agreable to us." There is much evidence suggesting that the loss of children did effectually wean some parents of their desire to live. "I have often implored the almighty to release by death a poor mesirable creature that had not a wish this side of the grave," wrote Rachel Campbell in July 1799. "All my desire was to be intered in the same Tomb with a darling Son I had lost the fall before." Manasseh Cutler mentioned a friend who had been in declining health for several months, owing to the loss of her little son in 1803, and Williamina Ridgely pictured another mother that same year who, though once "gay as a bird," was now so deeply depressed by the death of her only son that it did not seem possible she would ever regain her spirits. To Susan Dabney Smedes it seemed that her mother never rallied after the loss of her eldest son to yellow fever in 1853. She remained cheerful, even smiling in the presence of the family, "but it was not the bright look that we had known before, and whenever she was found after being alone for even a few minutes it was seen that she had been bathed in tears." Mrs. Dabney gradually sank deeper and deeper into depression. She "began to say that she was tired of bringing up her young children. 'I do not bring them up as I did the others,' she said. 'I am not able to do it.'"[36]

A move or a trip was often prescribed for persistent depression. Having lost her husband and daughter, one mother took her two sons and moved away from their Boston home, where "each fold of the bed curtains held some past sorrow which could never be dispelled; and objects on which my eyes had so long rested during their melancholy vigils, were inseparably imbued and associated with that wretchedness." Benjamin Silliman, his spirits drooping and his health failing after Trumbull's death, planned a trip to Canada with his brother-in-law, while Richard Adams of Richmond, Virginia took his wife to New Kent County, in 1771, "to divert her thoughts by a little change & getting into better air," a month after a son's death, which had shocked the whole family, "particularly his poor Mama."[37]

Time was, of course, the great natural healer, but diaries make clear the longevity of mellowed grief as parents calculated, "Henry would have been 23, Elizabeth 14," or, "this day is eleven years since my dear son Isaac departed this life." Or, as softly murmured by Henry Wadsworth Longfellow in verse,

> Day after day we think what she is doing
> In those bright realms of air;
> Year after year, her tender steps pursuing,
> Behold her grown more fair.[38]

Even when death had not yet struck, its shadow loomed large and threatening. "Blessed be God," wrote Margaret Cary of Massachusetts, in 1762, "we are yet a family not broken up by death. . . . I know not what another year may be to us; it may be the parting year." The legacy that transient life bestowed upon the early American family was an abiding anxiety. Even happiness was bittersweet and suspect, for it might be shattered at any moment. Sarah Logan Fisher, contentedly surrounded by her husband and children in December 1778, hoped to be grateful for "the Blessing & favour of being united together & of having two such sweet pledges of our mutual Love," but worried, "it seems a Happiness almost too exquisite to last." She timorously wondered on New Year's Day 1786, "shall I, dare I, hope, to be favored this Day twelvemonth, with all those dear domestic Blessings, that bind us so strongly to Life[?]" Maria Silliman Church felt "all the time, as if we were *too* happy and too much favored in our children, and am looking for some cloud to sadden the prospect"; while Faith Silliman Hubbard weighed the odds against her. "It is fourteen years next month, since death has entered our immediate circle, can we hope to be much longer spared[?]"[39]

Fear was everywhere, and humanity was not kind. Sarah Logan Fisher was upset in January 1779 because a friend had said "my Happiness to[o] great to last," and in 1782 spent another January day reflecting on an acquaintance's sinister prognosis

Family Record

Married
Mr. John Giles
to Miss Susan
Baldwin Mar.
15. 1787

Married
Mr. John Giles
to Miss Mary
Adams April
6. 1789

Mrs.
Susan Giles
Died Oct. 17 1788
Aged 24 y. 5 m.
25 d.

Daniel Giles
Born Feby. 28. 1790
Married Sept. 23. 1813
Do. May 31. 1827

When
we
shall reach
That
destin'd
coast
O'er
life's rough
ocean
driven
O may
We meet
No Wand'rer
lost
A
family
in heaven

Joel Giles
Born April 9. 1799
Died Aug. 28. 1800

John Giles
Born Novr. 11. 1791
Died Sept. 12. 1800

Polly Giles
Born Decr. 18. 1801

Samuel Giles
Born June 24. 1793
Died Aug. 22. 1800

Joel Giles
Born May 6. 1804

Abner Giles
Born March 16. 1795
Died Aug. 22. 1800

John Giles
Born March 3. 1806

Susan Giles
Born Aug. 25. 1797
Died May 8. 1798

Dea. John Giles
Died Aug. 24. 1825
Aged 62 y. 9 m. 20 d.

Mrs. Betsy S.
Giles Wife of
Capt. Danl. Giles
Died Novr. 28.
1823 Aged
35 y. 6 m.

Giles Family Register. Embroidery in silk on linen, by Mary (Polly) Giles, Groton Female Seminary, Groton, Massachusetts. c. 1825. Formerly collection Theodore Kapnek. The demographics of this family history are, sadly, not unique. John and Mary Giles of Townsend, Massachusetts, lost their only daughter, Susan, as a baby in 1798. Then, in late August and early September 1800, they lost their sons John, Samuel, Abner, and Joel, all probably victims of an epidemic such as dysentery or a childhood disease such as diphtheria, measles, or scarlet fever. One child survived, their first-born son, ten-year-old Daniel. The first child born after this tragedy was the seamstress who stitched this tale of woe

"that my dear little Son Billy would not be continued to us becauce he is so very fine a Child." Mr. Babcock predicted that Walter Church wouldn't grow up because "that child is too handsome to live"; and the inhabitants of Hanover made a great wonderment of little Hatty Hubbard, who weighed less than eleven pounds at three months, "and one lady feared we would not *raise her* she was so small."[40]

Parents struggled to keep their affections loose, to look upon their children as blessings only lent. Having lost her first child little more than a year before, Mary Fish Noyes welcomed the birth of a son in February 1761, but "with different eyes did I look on him," she acknowledged. "I always viewed him as mortal, and mine no longer than God pleased to lend him, and every night I felt thankful that he was alive." Minerva Rodgers tasted of the same bitter draft when her firstborn died in 1808, and when a second son arrived a year later, she thought he resembled "his poor little brother but I do not feel as if I should ever take the same pride in him. I am afraid to place my affections too strongly on him least he should not be spared to me." Fanny Appleton Longfellow's "remaining blessings" seemed dearer to her than ever after the loss of a baby daughter, "though I feel I can never henceforth call them mine, and at first saw nothing in their faces but the awful Shadow which had entered our home. I am calmer now, and mean to enjoy them as long as they are granted to me." Thus, even natural maternal affection was a source of anxiety to the early American mother. Margaret Morris struggled desperately "to live loose" of her infant son, "and not to let my natural affection make me desirous of his life," in 1760; while Samuella Curd, a century later, would aspire not to cling too much to her baby daughter, "for we are not permitted to make idols & keep them," yet, she had to admit, "Patty is as sweet as possible & pats the cakes sweet enough to eat her up." Many found it difficult, in fact impossible, to keep "loose." Maria Silliman Church admitted that son Walter was "an *idol*," and son Benjamin a really "*perfectly beautiful* child as beautiful as any little cherub you ever saw in canvas. . . . He is his father's idol almost." Esther Burr said her husband found their baby daughter "good to kiss," and a strong "temptation to him, to spend two [*sic*] much time with her—he does love to play with her dearly." Eighteenth-century and nineteenth-century accounts are buoyant with the delight parents took in their children. Yet, always nagging at this natural affection was the omnipresent fear that the child might die. Harriet Silliman worried that her son Benjamin was "too much a favorite with the whole family, I feel as if we were all in danger of loving him too much"; and her daughter Maria would, in turn, "tremble to think how devoted all our hearts are" to her own son. William Wirt was afraid he loved his "precious" Laura "with too much tenderness, and when I indulge the sentiment, there is a melancholy, which mingles with it; that fills my eyes—I fear this is no good omen—Heaven spare my babe."[41]

The fragility of life and the constant threat to the dissolution of happiness underline the words that Thomas Jefferson penned Mrs. Francis Eppes in 1785. He expressed his contentment at hearing that her family and his little Maria, who was boarding with them, were well: "Every information of this kind is like gaining another step, and seems to say we 'have got so far safe.'" Life was a steep and exacting ladder, its ascent often precarious, and the higher one climbed the greater the burden of cares one had to tote along, the lesser the chances of tranquillity or happiness.[42]

A woman's myriad ties to immediate family, more distant kin, servants, and friends meant that she could hardly look for anything like uninterrupted tranquillity. Nor could she expect to be supported in her endeavors by a reassuring sense of confidence and security—for all was uncertain. And though life itself was rushed and melodramatic, she must play her part with composure and equanimity, concealing her own feelings, if necessary, for the benefit of others. The belief that all was preordained and ordered for the best by a judicious God sustained some. But the frequent headaches, the nervous complaint, the neat, compact script that gradually deteriorates into scrawls and dashes, betray many, many more. The lot of the early American housewife was indeed a very great trial to the temper. Surrounded by ailing children, and in shock over the recent death of an infant daughter, wearied in brain and sick at heart, Fanny Appleton Longfellow was astonished when Julia Ward Howe appeared "*à cheval*," wishing for the *intense* in life. "What more can she desire," queried the knowing Mrs. Longfellow, "than the extremes of joy and suffering in domestic life?"[43]

■ CHAPTER TEN ■
"IT SHALL BE
PROCURED AGREEABLE
TO YOUR LIKING":
*Husband and Wife
as Consumers*

"I am an honest Tradesman, who never meant Harm to any Body. My Affairs went on smoothly while a Batchelor." Thus Benjamin Franklin, alias Anthony Afterwit, prefaced his diatribe on the rocky shoals of wedlock with a shopper for a wife. It all began, innocently enough, when his bride replaced an old-fashioned looking glass with a much handsomer one. But this venial refinement proved the catalyst in an impetuous spree of spending. "Accordingly the Glass was bought, and hung against the Wall: But in a Week's time, I was made sensible by little and little, *that the Table was by no Means suitable to such a Glass.* And a more proper Table being procur'd, my Spouse, who was an excellent Contriver, inform'd me where we might have very handsome Chairs *in the Way;* And thus, by Degrees, I found all my old Furniture stow'd up into the Garret, and every thing below alter'd for the better."[1]

One hundred and thirty-three years later, Harriet Beecher Stowe, alias Christopher Crowfield, penned a comparable picture of female consumer extravagance in her *House and Home Papers.* The trigger this time was a new piece of Brussels carpet purchased for the parlor. The bright, untrodden rug made the furniture look dull and shabby, and Mrs. Crowfield and her daughter felt obliged to reupholster every piece to comparable splendor. Next, the windows must be enswathed in billowing yards of curtain stuffs to protect the now-resplendent goods from the deleterious effects of the sun; and in this penumbral parlor the vanquished husband was no longer permitted to light the fire, or smoke his pipe, or read his newspaper (even if he could see) for fear of deranging the pristine surroundings.[2]

Through hyperbole, Franklin and Stowe addressed a truth that transcended time: ladies cherish nice possessions and harbor strong consumer aspirations. Letters, diaries, and account books all reveal that although a husband was often the principal purchaser of furnishings for the eighteenth-century home, a wife had a share in these decisions, and that from the 1790s she gradually became the primary consumer of household goods.

The speech, costume, cuisine, architecture, furniture, and furnishings of these American couples were English. It seemed to a French officer in Boston in 1781 that Americans lived "absolutely in the English manner"; as Henry Wadsworth Longfellow expressed it, Americans were "English under another sky." While strolling on the Boston Common in 1797, John Bernard, a comic actor and an astute observer, could scarcely believe that he had not been "whisked over to St. James's Park; and in their houses the last modes of London were observable in nearly every article of ornament or utility." This influence was suffusive. "Before the Revolution, all our ideas of elegance had been derived from England, and, at this period, the country had not thrown off this allegiance," wrote Sarah Anna Emery of the early-nineteenth-century citizens of Newburyport, Massachusetts. "English style and mode of life were affected by our gentry, in their spacious mansions, well-stocked wine cellars, heavy family coaches, superb horses, and liveried servants." Parisian taste would launch a struggle for parity in the early 1800s, but by then London had been the great font of American fashion for nearly two hundred years.[3]

A knowledge of the latest London styles was acquired in several ways. The importation of British goods was frequent and pervasive. Also, many of the cabinet-makers, upholsterers, and silversmiths whose shops lined the streets of American towns were "lately from London," bringing with them taste, training, and templates, and often stylish goods as well. As master craftsmen they bequeathed to American apprentices and journeymen generations-old skills learned first in London or Liverpool, in Troutbeck or Hawkshead, in Easton-on-the-Hill or Hutton le Hole. The allure of vanity and the thirst for novelty meant that those "lately from London" would be assured a receptive clientele on this side of the Atlantic. One cabinetmaker revealed his marketing astuteness when he advertised his newly invented patent window sunshades in the *Charleston City Gazette* in October 1795. First, he made sure to say he came from the fountainhead—"from London." Then, to a conservative public he offered the snob appeal of a product acclaimed by the British bon ton—"The utility of this invention has been fully proved by the approbation of all persons of taste, and the encouragement given by the people of property in England." And, finally, his local contacts were impeccable—"a specimen of which [sunshades], may in the course of a few days be seen on the house of the hon. John Rutledge."[4]

The intimacy of these early towns and the frequent rounds of visiting meant that all were familiar with both the exterior and the interior of every neighbor's domicile. Nothing escaped the scrutiny of the curious at home in early America. When Anna Maria Thornton drank tea with Mr. and Mrs. Lands in Washington in January 1800, she cast an admiring eye over the handsome curtains and elegant looking glasses that had just arrived from Scotland. And Margaret Izard Manigault was delighted when Mr. and Mrs. Ogilvie moved in across the street from her in Charleston in February of that same year: "They are very rich, & just arrived from London, where they saw a great deal of company & lived in a very fashionable style. Their house is completely furnished, & in the most elegant manner. And she gives me particulars of all the pretty little inventions which have lately appeared."[5]

In the same letter, Mrs. Manigault asked her correspondent if she had subscribed to any journals for some account of what was new and out of the common way. British and, to a lesser extent, French design books, journals, and ultimately catalogues enlightened craftsmen, merchants, and consumers alike. By the opening years of the nineteenth century, many lending libraries subscribed to fashion magazines, and the well-to-do might do so on their own. Mrs. Manigault said she "should like of all things to be able to do so." Female correspondence was of inestimable importance in the dissemination of fashion and goods. Via the post, fashion advice traveled westward across the Atlantic and then through a radiate network of New World "reporters." Kinship and friendship bonds set geographic hurdles at naught, and women often bypassed nearby cities and market towns in favor of a distant but trusted contact. In November 1755, Esther Burr, a Massachusetts girl who had followed her husband, the president of the College of New Jersey, to Newark, wrote to a girlhood friend in Boston requesting some practical information. "I want to know how a body may have some sorts of Household stuff—What is the price of a Mehogane [mahogany] Case of Drawers . . . in Boston, and also a Bulow [bureau] Table and Tea Table and plain Chairs with Leather bottoms and a Couch covered with stamped Camblet or China [popular furnishing fabrics], all of that wood." She also wanted a fashion update from

The Samuels Family. Possibly Philadelphia. Oil on canvas, by Johann Eckstein. c. 1800. Museum of Fine Arts, Boston; Ellen Kelleran Gardner Fund. This family is surrounded by the comforts of affluence. Observe the fashionable haircloth-covered furniture, the squab on the sofa, the chimney garniture, and the sconce glass, to which a candle would be fitted at candlelighting time. According to the season, this was often just before or after tea time. Though the long days of summer meant that one enjoyed this repast by natural light, the shortened days of winter would ensure that the gilded rims of teacups and saucers, the polished silver tea wares, and the shining mahogany table would glitter in the light of candle or lamp. As was characteristic of the period, the diverse elements of the Samuelses' tea service— teapot, cream pot, sugar bowl, cups, and saucers—do not match

Detail of a painted tin tea tray from America or England. c. 1790. Lynn Historical Society, Inc., Lynn, Massachusetts. According to tradition, the scene on this tray depicts Ebenezer Breed of Lynn, Massachusetts, being introduced to an English merchant by William Roach of New Bedford, Massachusetts. The interior in which these men of business stand could as easily be American as English, offering yet more evidence that in their costumes, customs, and furnishings, early Americans were English

251

The Tea Table. Wood engraving by Alexander Anderson in [Arnaud Berquin], *The Looking-Glass for the Mind; or, Intellectual Mirror* (New York, 1804). Special Collections, Baker Library, Dartmouth College, Hanover, New Hampshire. A looking glass, a silk dress, a mahogany tea table, a porcelain tea set—this was the stuff consumer dreams were made of. And anyone might dream in the new nation

this sophisticated, urban friend: "I should be glad to know what is most fashionable—wheather to have looking Glasses or sconcers [sconces] for a Paylor [parlor], and what for a Chamber." Mrs. Burr had recently been in New York City, "driving about York streets like mad," and Philadelphia was close at hand, but she had implicit faith in the taste and judgment of her New England friend. Perhaps she was doing some comparative shopping. Or, perhaps, being a native of Northampton, Massachusetts, she preferred the Boston regional expression to that of New York or Philadelphia and hoped ultimately to commission some Boston pieces. For although the American decorative arts had an English nucleus, the final product was tempered by distinct local preferences. When Eliza Wainwright visited Manhattan in 1831, she confided in those at home in Boston that she did "not like New York furniture as well as ours . . . it is too *shiny & showy* for my taste."[6]

Because of such regional fancy, eighteenth-century and early-nineteenth-century brides often acquired many of their dowry goods at home before following their husbands afar. The tables, bedsteads, chests, chairs, carpets, curtains, china, silver, and accessories that these girls brought to their new homes must have elicited the curiosity and sometimes piqued the envy of the neighbors; and these goods were unquestionably effective not only in diffusing fashion but in disseminating local distinctions. As a young bride in New York in 1809, Anne Eliza Clark Kane of Providence was pleased to be able to report that her "Salem furniture is arrived and is much admir'd." And it is probable that on occasion a neighbor might try to have something similar made locally or to send for the same. Maria Silliman Church wrote her family in New Haven to say that her mother-in-law was so taken by the doilies, which numbered among the innumerable dowry items Maria had brought to Angelica, New York, that she "would like some of them, say three dozen."[7]

The possessions of others were a constant frame of reference. William Wirt wondered whether his wife wanted her easy chair like Mrs. Tazewell's or like her mother's; Harriet Silliman told daughter Maria that their new coal grate was of the same description as Mrs. Whitney's but more ornamented. Faith Silliman Hubbard found Mrs. Brown's Hanover home as handsome as Mr. Skinner's New Haven residence and thought her father should get bookcases like Mr. W. Hillhouse's and that her mother might have her mantels marbleized like the one in Mr. Whitney's breakfast room. All these possessions might also be the cause of envy. Mary Boardman Crowninshield wanted her husband to be sure and acquaint her with all the details of Commodore and Mrs. John Rodgers's home in April 1815, and asked with some concern, "Is the furniture handsomer than ours?" Emulation was a constant goad to the consumer; and the feminine desire for tea and its equipage fully illustrates the thrust of emulative spending at home in early America.[8]

Anthony Afterwit's wife, having been "entertain'd with *Tea* by the Good Women she visited, we could do no less than the like when they visited us; and so we got a *Tea-Table* with all its Appurtenances of *China* and *Silver*." Several months after Boston artist John Smibert ordered a silver teapot for his wife in 1743, he acknowledged receipt of the pot and gave his London agent proof of its local acclaim: "I hope youl excuse the trouble I now give you, occasioned by the Tea Pott you sent which is admired by all the Ladies and so much that in behalf of one of them (who I assure you has great merit) I Must beg the favour of you to send such another one of the same fashion and size." One way or another, every woman contrived to have tea wares. Elizabeth Bleecker McDonald could simply walk out in New York City in September 1800 and buy a "Tea-Pot, Sugar Pot, and Milk Pot at Mr. Peter's," but others had to be more resourceful. Elizabeth Duché had displayed her determination in 1739 when she procured her tea tongs from Philadelphia silversmith Joseph Richardson with a combination of cash, goods (25 pounds of rice) and services (washing his linen). It seemed to Claude Robin by the 1780s that there was not a single American, regardless of where he or she lived, who did not drink tea out of china cups and saucers. When John Newton recalled life at home in early-nineteenth-century Marlboro, Vermont, he could say that "everything was of the simplest and plainest style, with one exception—my mother had a china tea set"; and though Ann Biddle Wilkinson obligingly followed her husband to Frankfort, Kentucky, she was not willing to be deprived of certain amenities that had graced her refined girlhood in Philadelphia. She therefore wrote to her father, John Biddle, in that city in 1788, hoping that he would not think her extravagant "if I ask for a Dozen Blue & White China Cups & Saucers, if tis possible to pack them Securely, we have been so very unfortunate as to break every one of ours, & I do not like Queens ware to drink Tea out of, *Provided I can get any others*, necessity Compels me to use them now & I could sooner drink it out of a Gourd than go without." And by the 1820s, Anne Royall, traveling through what is now West Virginia, was astonished to see loads of crockery, teacups, and such things being purchased by people who lived twenty, thirty, or even fifty miles distant. They "put them in the saddle-bags or tie them up in a kerchief: and a woman will think nothing of setting them in her lovely lap, holding them with one hand and the reins of an unruly horse in the other, and set out for home."9

The quest for these tea accoutrements reflected in microcosm new philosophical and economic precepts evolving during the second half of the eighteenth century. Before the 1780s, those with money owned fine possessions and those without did not. But in the course of the late eighteenth century and the first half of the nineteenth century, what had been enjoyed by the few—mahogany furniture, brilliant textiles, fragile china, colorful wallpaper, sweetened tea, and gorgeous gowns—came to be regarded as the inalienable right of the many. The marquis de Chastellux worried in 1786 that in America "such is the general equality of condition that those things which everywhere else would be regarded as luxuries are here considered necessities. So it is that the salary of a workingman must not only provide subsistence for his family, but also comfortable furniture for the home, tea and coffee for his wife, and a silk dress to put on every time she goes out." In an earlier era, immutability had been important. The Enlightenment paterfamilias expected his house and his household goods to be not only serviceable in his lifetime but suitable for future generations— thus the frequent directive to the craftsman that the work be neat, be strong, be "made to endure." For furniture strengthened with solid woods, bracing stretchers, and through tenons the patron was willing to pay extra because these features promised durability. By the close of the eighteenth century, "in the latest taste" was challenging "made to endure" as the measure of esteem. This changing perception was in part due to the acceleration evident in all aspects of life, to the growing influence of feminine persuasion in the retail market, to the vaulting ambition of the many, and to the unprecedented quantity of goods that the Industrial Revolution made available. Astute artisans realized that the way to wealth was to produce more goods at a lower price, either by discovering a more expeditious method of producing them or by compromising former high standards of quality. The resultant influx of goods in a then-novel range of price and quality gave buoyant elasticity to the retail market. Some ate with pewter forks, others with silver; some walked on list carpeting, others on Brussels; some sat on painted pine chairs, others on polished mahogany—but everyone was an owner. Thus, one dinner guest at a Philadelphia wedding in 1791 might casually remark on what she perceived to be the comparable similarity of the table decoration to her own: "eight silver candlesticks with spermaceti candles were substituted for our brass and tallow, Mrs. S.'s elegant table china for the queen's-ware, which was all the difference." By the 1840s and for the remainder of that century, manuals and journals would be filled with advice on how to furnish the home for "next to nothing," for it was preferable to have a toilet table of even the most rudimentary kind—a crude piece of pine dressed up in the best breadths of a cast-off frock—than to have none at all.[10]

Shops proliferated in the course of the eighteenth century as ambitious manufacturers, ever-expanding trade routes, and better transportation supplied more products for a growing market. By 1795 Thomas Cooper found New York and Philadelphia shops as well stocked with every article of European comfort as the shops of any English town; while the duc de La Rochefoucauld-Liancourt maintained that these urban stores were even as well furnished as those in Paris and London. Both agreed that the prices were far higher in America than in Europe—Cooper calculating that if one added one-third more to the British price of such luxury items as pictures, pier glasses, and carpets, one would have the full American price. A veritable profusion of goods spilled out of these emporiums. When Sarah Logan Fisher walked down the streets of New York City in May 1785, the great display of goods at the doors and windows made the scene appear to her "like a Fair"; while to a Scotsman strolling along Broadway in 1821, the colorful fabric wares billowing about the shop doors resembled jubilee flags. In mid-nineteenth-century Boston, Lady Emmeline Stuart Wortley found "a multitude of stores teeming with goods of every description, which are actually running over from their crammed and loaded shelves and counters, and often blockade the foot-pavements." To her it looked as if it had rained silks, calicoes, and cottons as the very sidewalks were turned into counters, or perhaps "as if some of the richly-laden ships, had by some magic, been carried into the heart of the town, and wrecked almost on the door-steps of the stores."[11]

Many of these retail stores lining the principal streets of American towns were located on the lower floors of dwellings, for the residential and commercial areas of eighteenth-century and early-nineteenth-century towns and cities were one and the same. Often a family shop occupied the whole ground floor of a house and sometimes a downstairs front room—or it might be next door. It is perhaps Sarah Anna Emery's catalogue listing of the buildings along Water Street in early-nineteenth-century Newburyport, Massachusetts, that best encapsulates the intermixture.

Below was Humphrey Cook's hatter's shop, and that of Thomas Lord; David Moody and Thomas Moody had malt houses, Mrs. Richardson a milliner's shop, Joseph O'Brien's house and store, the Harrod house, and Joseph Brown, auctioneer. John Hart's tavern, Benjamin Appleton's hatter's shop, Marm Seward's boarding house, a boarding house kept by Hannah Prime, Joseph Toppan's house and dry goods store, Stephen Gerrish & Son's house and dry goods store, John Greenough, hatter, Clement Star, house and shop, T. & A. Wheeler, grocery and boarding house, Benjamin H. Toppan, coppersmith, Timothy T. Ford's house and dry goods store, and Capt. Dunlap's house and shop.

Of course, this commingling meant that street noises and trade smells were daily details of domestic life. The din of halloing draymen, bellowing auctioneers, and rattling carts assailed the ear as the odor of steaming pine tar, brewing hops, and stewing animal glue bedeviled the nose. "We have a Windsor chairmaker next door to us," wrote Elizabeth Drinker, at home in Philadelphia on 24 June 1806, "who I think, by the smell, is boiling varnish this day." This same proximity would have

Portrait of Mrs. Reuben Humphreys. East Granby, Connecticut. Oil on canvas, attributed to Richard Brunton. c. 1800. The Connecticut Historical Society, Hartford. Anne Humphrey Humphreys was the wife of the superintendent of Newgate Prison in East Granby, and it must have been with considerable pride that she sat for this portrait, surrounded by the tangible evidences of worldly success. Observe the enameled cloak pins decoratively supporting the looking glass from below. Perhaps Mrs. Humphreys had heeded the advertisement of the Hartford cabinetmaking firm of Kneeland and Adams a few years earlier, offering an elegant selection of looking glasses and a good assortment of "China faced" cloak pins with which to hang them

made it impossible for the residents not to know what was for sale in the shops, and by 1800 innovative display techniques offered retailers the opportunity to show off the multiplicity of their wares to the greatest advantage.[12]

Larger-paned windows in bright glass-fronted shops had first appeared in eighteenth-century London and were subsequently introduced into all the British provinces, including America. Having observed that the greater part of New York houses had shops in them, Joshua Brookes went on to contrast their appearance in 1798, when "they generally had windows or fronts like private houses," with their modern aspect in 1803, by which time "a great many were altered into handsome shop windows." Savvy retailers displayed their wares enticingly, lighting them at night with oil lamps or gaslights to ensnare the passerby. Anne Royall penned a picture of these captivating displays in Philadelphia in 1826.

The windows are low, large, and project into the streets some distance. These windows (or the most of them,) are from eight to eleven or twelve feet wide, and from four to six feet high. Some are filled with the most splendid plate, glass and china ware; some with caps, ruffs, bonnets and ribbons; others with liquid medicine, contained in vast glass bottles of every colour, and look exceedingly beautiful at night. The windows have different rows of shelves on the inside, from the bottom to the top, and upon these shelves the articles are disposed. But it is at night that the wealth and splendor of Philadelphia appears to the best advantage; the windows being lighted with numerous lamps and gas-lights, which, with the lamps in the streets, and the lustre of the glittering wares in the windows, present a scene of astonishing beauty.[13]

These refined techniques of urban display had no impact in the hinterlands. The ludicrous medley of disparate wares at that omnium-gatherum known as the country store raised the risibles of many who came to survey the American scene. To one with a flair for alliteration, just such a store "presented a grotesque collection of almost every article under the Sun, either useful, or ornamental, consisting of Drapery, frocking, Stationery, Grocery, Hardware, Tin-Ware, Toys, Tapes & other Small Ware, Hats & Bonnets, Boots, and Shoes, Brushes, & Blacking, Lamps- Lanthorns & Looking-Glasses, Saws, Spits, & all sorts of Spirits, Pitch-forks, & Toasting-forks, Besoms, & Watch-ribbons, Physic and Mops, Ropes & Rattletraps—Horse-gearing, & maps, Mugs, Mouse-traps—almanacks & Fiz-gigs." Despite the daunting profusion, the quality of products available to the rural family was often inferior—many a crateful of mismatched, seawater-stained, and outmoded wares was foisted upon the unsuspecting provincials. Shrewder customers with personal contacts in towns and cities might order long distance. An additional perplexity to the country consumer was the absence or shortage of cash at a time when shopkeepers were becoming increasingly unwilling to accept the barter system of exchange. Julian Niemcewicz observed that in Hartford, Connecticut, "every house is either a workshop or a store," and that on the signboards which hung outside indicating the nature of the business within, "there is always an addition in big letters: 'Cash in hand.'" When times were hard in Angelica, New York, shopkeepers were unwilling to accept the local commodity—lumber—in trade, demanding cash, a situation that caused Maria Silliman Church much anxiety. Other store owners were more obliging, at least when times were favorable, and many an eighteenth-century farmhouse and plantation was furnished with the most recent crop of cotton or the last sledgeful of lumber. Alicia McBlair Lloyd of Wye House, near Easton, Maryland, intended to pay for her carpet when the grain went up to be sold in 1836. Maria Silliman Church was able to buy twenty dollars' worth of household goods in Geneseo, New York, in 1835, "paid for in *lumber!*" and in September 1849 she purchased a bedstead and bureau from a New York City cabinetmaker named Woodruff *"for lumber."*[14]

An early and overt suggestion of women's awakening consumer aspirations was in the matter of dress and toilette. By the early 1770s Anne Hulton, the sister of the commissioner of customs at Boston, could write from that city, "We follow the fashions in England & have made great strides in Luxury & Expence within these three years Esp[ly] in that of Dress & the young Ladies seem as smart as those we left in England." To many observers of post-Revolutionary mores, this extravagant female

dress—silks, gauzes, laces, and feathers—contrasted sharply with republican manners and simply furnished homes. Perhaps this dichotomy illustrates the overzealous foray of women into an enormously expanding retail market. Initially, it would have been natural for them to direct their attention to fabrics and toilette as costume had long been an accepted arena of female expenditure. But as home furnishings became increasingly available in a wide variety of form, material, and price, many women diverted their attention thither, and by the mid-nineteenth century we hear less about extravagant dress and more about luxurious parlors.[15]

A cursory perusal of surviving bills of sale addressed to women during the late eighteenth century and early nineteenth century suggests just how accustomed upper-class and middle-class women were to going in and out of shops to purchase home furnishings, and letters and journals corroborate the evidence. When William Osgood and William Duer were appointed to procure a house and furnish it for a reception for George Washington in New York in 1789, they "pitched on their wives as being likely to do it better." Mrs. Osgood's niece was delighted when she toured the finished product, which "really did honour to my Aunt and Lady Kitty" in its elegant furniture "and the greatest quantity of plate and china that I ever saw before, [and] the whole of the first and second story is papered and the floors covered with the richest kind of Turkey and Wilton carpets." Wives had always had some purchase power. When a ship from London docked at Leeds, Virginia, in September 1774, it had aboard not only Robert Carter's dashing black and pea-green coach, for which he paid £120, but Mrs. Carter's imports of "about 30£ value in plate in a pair of fashionable Goblets; Pair of beautiful Sauce-Cups; & a Pair of elegant Decanter-holders." As long as the purchases were commensurate with family frugality they would be tolerated.[16]

When Charles Carroll of Annapolis wrote to his son, Charles Carroll of Carrollton, and his daughter-in-law, Molly, in 1772, taking note of the orders and bills that flowed freely between his son's home and London and the consequential arrival of plate and furniture, he expressed a wish that *Molly* not be extravagant, not order any "Superfluities." "Enjoy your fortune, keep an hospitable table," this concerned father

advised the young couple, "but lay out as little money as possible in dress, furniture, and show of any sort; decency is the only point to be aimed at." Anthony Afterwit's wife, like Christopher Crowfield's, had trespassed not in buying goods but in the extravagance of her purchases. "Had we stopp'd here, we might have done well enough," conceded Afterwit following the purchase of the looking glass, table, and chairs, but before the acquisition of the tea equipage, clock, and fine prancing mare. Afterwit then assumed the role of disciplinarian, disposing of his wife's extravagances while she was out visiting, and replacing them with a milk cow, spinning wheel, knitting needles, and an hourglass—icons of the notable housewife. "I have reserv'd the great Glass, because I know her Heart is set upon it," he craftily observed. "I will allow her when she comes in, to be taken suddenly ill with the *Headach,* the

Stomach-ach, Fainting-Fits, or whatever other Disorders she may think more proper; and she may retire to Bed as soon as she pleases: But if I do not find her in perfect Health both of Body and Mind the next Morning, away goes the aforesaid Great Glass . . . to the Vendue that very Day." A comparable, nonfictional, scene had been enacted along the banks of the James River in Virginia earlier in the eighteenth century. Among the London letters delivered to William Byrd at Westover on 14 June 1709 was an invoice of things sent for by his wife, "which are enough to make a man mad. It put me out of humor very much." And the following day as he sat at dinner, the ship captain brought him "also some goods for my wife, to an extraordinary value." Two weeks later Byrd noted in his diary, "I made an invoice of the things that my wife could spare to be sold," while she, poor thing, "was in tears" about her cargo. Mrs.

Byrd had taken the initiative and ordered the goods without her husband's knowledge, either because she thought it was right to do so or because she hoped to get away with it, but she erred in incurring costs to an "extraordinary" value, thereby jeopardizing the whole shipment. Moderation was all-important.[17]

Early American fiction is lively with lampoons of female consumer extravagance; but women's letters rather show them to have been conscientious, astute, knowledgeable, discriminating shoppers who were concerned about both quality and value. Eliza Wainwright wrote from New York in 1831 asking her brother to enquire about the price of a full set of Canton china in Boston, "for I cannot like the Liverpool—whereas the other will do at all times & never looks amiss." For thirty-three dollars she could get in Manhattan a set of "a *handsome* blue, not dingy as they sometimes are," and she wished him to advise if she might do as well in Boston, "if so I should save expence & risk of sending." Margaret Izard Manigault was delighted with a set of fancy chairs in "a modern handsome shape," which an aunt had procured for her in New York in 1811. When they arrived at home in Charleston, Mrs. Manigault found these white chairs with their gold Grecian decoration not only pretty but, at four dollars each, "wonderfully cheap compared to those in Philadelphia." And she quickly determined that "when I want chairs again in Philadelphia, I shall certainly send to New York for them!" A thrifty Sarah Waring went to Charleston cabinetmaker Thomas Elfe in April 1774 to exchange her double chest of drawers for a better one; while a frugal Deborah Franklin was delighted with the "quite new" carpet which she bought "cheap for the goodness." In November 1809 Anne Eliza Clark Kane wrote to her sister in Providence, asking her to send to Boston immediately for a large carpet and some Brussels stair carpeting of dark, rich coloring as she could not get them for equal value in Manhattan, where both fashion and price were wrong. New England women seem to have been particularly fastidious in their selection of carpets—to the point that Boston merchant John Doggett threw up his hands in exasperation in 1828, conceding that at least in the matter of rugs, "the taste of Boston people is very peculiar and difficult to please." So the taste in carpets apparently also had a regional expression, and an editorial in a British newspaper could yet perceive in the 1870s that "a pattern which sells readily in New York is frequently unsaleable in Boston, and vice versa."[18]

Carpets and many other household furnishings and supplies were often purchased at auction in both rural and urban America from 1750 to 1870, the bidders being male and female alike. A Philadelphian stated in 1836 that it had been "a general custom for wives & widows to attend at auction stores, then called vendues, and purchase goods for their shop supplies." Often the entire contents of a house were dispersed in this way—a valuable source for looking glasses, curtains, and so forth. John Barker Church was pleased with the stair rods, copper teakettle, and large Brussels carpet that he purchased at the auction of a neighbor's earthly goods in Angelica, but his exhausted wife, Maria Silliman Church, vowed, "If I were a *fairy* I would transform the carpet into a good *cook* and *nurse*." Both new and used goods were sold in this way. The forthcoming sale of a cargo off the barque *Adiona* titillated the consumer instincts of several Salem, Massachusetts, ladies in the summer of 1815. When Mary Boardman Crowninshield wrote her husband in June concerning the two little couches "which will just fit our recesses," she expressed her intention "to have [them] if they don't go too high," even though Mrs. White also wanted them very much. Further, she was determined to have "and suspect Aunt Silsbee is determined

Elizabeth Denison. Oil on canvas, by the Denison Limner. c. 1790. National Gallery of Art, Washington, D.C.; gift of Edgar William and Bernice Chrysler Garbisch. This young woman, with her frizzed hair and frilled dressing table, her nodding plumes and artificial flowers, could serve as a metaphor for Americans' undisciplined urge for personal possessions and fantastic finery, which struck foreign observers of the late-eighteenth-century scene as being singularly inappropriate to the Spartan civic ideals of a republic. Benjamin Franklin was similarly dismayed by his daughter's request for plumes and lace, but quickly regained enough composure coolly to suggest that for plumes she need but look about the poultry yard, and as for lace she might wear her clothes till the holes showed through

to try for the globes although she knows you wrote to have them but I shall try for them—for you *will* give me one thousand dollars worth of pretty things won't you? You will never miss it . . . and what is money for, but to gratify ourselves in what we think useful." Through the lighthearted, teasing tone of this letter one can visualize Mrs. Crowninshield balancing accounts and weighing expense against worth and need.[19]

Silverware offers additional evidence of the housewife's concern for both style and economy. Anna Rawle wrote her mother from Philadelphia in 1783 saying that she had shown a local silversmith (one of the Richardsons) "an old fashioned tankard and cup which he says will make a handsome coffee pot," and she offered to have them converted if her mother approved, for "in their present form they are useless, being of an uncommonly antique appearance." A receipt from Philadelphia silversmith Joseph Lownes to a Miss Bailey testifies not only to yet one more effort at economy,

Trade card for Ball and Price Plain and Fancy Blind Factory. New York City. Lithograph. c. 1835. The New-York Historical Society, New York City; Bella C. Landauer Collection. Merchants recognized a feminine influence behind much consumer spending and from the late eighteenth century addressed women more openly in their advertisements and portrayed them more freely on their trade cards

but to the ever-increasing size of tea services, for when she purchased coffee, tea, water, and cream pots, a sugar dish, and a slop bowl, she turned in a silver teapot weighing twenty-two and a half ounces, thereby reducing her bill by $33.37.[20]

Women seem to have been especially pleased when they were able to pay for incidentals or even luxury items with money they had earned themselves. Martha Ogle Forman was proud to lay down a chamber carpet that had arrived from Baltimore in November 1818, for she had "bought it with my butter money." Twenty-two years later she noted that her husband had opened a package from Philadelphia containing "the box with my blue foot tub, mugs, and 4 china candlesticks and one china quill inkstand and 12 finger glasses, amber color, bought with butter money." A New England girl in 1860 thought she might resort to mill work in a year or two so that she might "get some money to buy a piano as I dont see much prospect of haveing one unless I do work for the money and I want one very much."[21]

These women knew exactly what they wanted. When Rebecca Rawle Shoemaker ordered a tea set of Nankin china in 1785, she wanted the cups to have handles, and she also wished for a set of cream ware or "Queens ware" with a green edge—not a blue rim, which would look "too much like delph [delft]." Further, they would not be satisfied with substitutions or faulty work. Shortly after her marriage, Anna Maria Thornton purchased furniture, glass, silver, cutlery, jewelry, and china in Georgetown. When some of these goods were delivered to her Washington home on 8 May 1800, she was "much disappointed in the Wedgewood Ware & think them very dear—the des[s]ert service is pretty but not such as I expected, as they were not limited in the price," and the knives and forks were rusted. A week later she made her decision as to what to do with these unsatisfactory wares: "Sent to George Town a basket containing nearly half the dinner Set and all the des[s]ert set except four [compotes] and two baskets with stands, to be put into Mr. Whann's Store for Sale. They came too high—as they did [not] answer my wishes—and I found by washing that the Gilding was not burnt in but only burnished." Martha Jacquelin of York, Virginia, had been equally irritated by the impractical fireplace utensils sent to her by John Norton & Sons of London, and she wrote to Norton's in August 1770, "the Tongs, Shovels, and Pokers are too heavy for me to lift; and you know wee burn wood in kitchens here; I have therefore taken the liberty to send them back." A wife's disapproval might well preclude the use of an object at home. Rebecca Rawle Shoemaker was somewhat nonplussed when her husband sent her from London a Wedgwood tea set that apparently was ornamented with putti, and she wrote him with delicacy in April 1784, acknowledging that the pieces were "uncommon & very curious," but "we thought the little creatures should have been *cloathed.*" A month later she fully implied that these offending wares had been banished from her tea table, yet "if the little creatures on the teapots had been a little dressed, if it had been only a thin mantle, thrown over them, we could have introduced them more freely into company without fear of hurting any person's delicacy."[22]

These tea wares that Mrs. Shoemaker found so embarrassing had been purchased at Josiah Wedgwood's showroom on Greek Street in London while her husband was abroad. By the close of the eighteenth century, such showrooms offered one further emporium for the urban housewife—and for her husband. On display was a multiplicity of ready-made goods, and purchasing was presented as a social event. That business and amusement were to go hand in hand is documented by contemporary prints depicting ladies and gentlemen admiringly strolling through these attrac-

Detail of *The Shop and Warehouse of Duncan Phyfe* by John Rubens Smith (see page 19). Surviving bills of sale, receipts, letters, journals, and account books from the late eighteenth century on suggest that upper-class women and middle-class women were very much at ease wandering in and out of shops purchasing home furnishings

tive surroundings. The showroom was in a sense the commercial recognition of a long-established fact—purchasing for the home was an experience shared by husband and wife.

When John Barker Church wrote to his bride-to-be, Maria Silliman, in March 1831 concerning progress on their future home, Triana, he urged, "If you meet with any [floor] plan that pleases you, I wish you would send it on as it may perhaps be in time & of a nature to adopt." Correspondence between couples who were building a house suggests that husbands were more closely involved with floor plans at these initial stages, but room usage was never static at home in early America. And with the passage of years it was the wife who oversaw the evolution of that plan—rethinking, adjusting room use to the momentary comfort, convenience, and safety of an ever-changing family. Elizabeth Wirt was most unhappy with the floor plan at her

Broadway, New York. View from the corner of Canal Street north past Niblo's Garden. Aquatint by Thomas Hornor and John Hill. 1836. The Henry Francis du Pont Winterthur Museum, Winterthur, Delaware. Commerce, commerce, commerce was the cry of the many and the preoccupation of the multitude in democratic America. The enthusiasm with which it was embraced and the staccato rhythm with which it animated urban life are here readily apparent

Richmond, Virginia, home and wrote her husband in 1812 concerning the changes she desired—which included a more convenient dining room, with improved access to the out kitchen and pantry, and a roomier, safer nursery for her growing family. When he replied suggesting alternative solutions for the nursery, she fired back a peppery note, implying that she was the one to know best and making it clear that she intended to have her way. Four years later she was yet complaining of the inconvenience of this house, wishing for a commodious, comfortable one "in which the chambers at least were drawn together by immediate communication"—an axis which many young mothers would have seen the merit of. Further, as the family circle continued to expand, it seemed to her that the house was bursting at the seams and she wrote Wirt with anything but the esteemed equanimity: "With my family of eight young children I *must* have a more commodious dwelling. . . . It is not worth while to talk to me about Building & building—let me have present comfort—and the next wife may be welcome to the rest." And just in case she had not made her point emphatically enough, she demonstratively reiterated, "I tell you again Husband—I am so anxious upon this same subject of getting better accommodated—so harassed and fretted by others—that at this moment I do not suppose there is a more unquiet being in the state. And I could *almost* wish me and mine were in a better world." In his answering letter, William Wirt ignored the mood but gave his wife permission to negotiate the purchase of a house that she had mentioned as available. This she did not do as there were inconveniences here as well—the servants' quarters were under the house and over the icehouse, locations which she felt were too close, an intrusion on family privacy. A year later, as the family prepared to move to Washington, Mr. and Mrs. Wirt wrote back and forth concerning room usage, furniture, carpets, curtains, and colors, and the convenience of this new home seems to have soothed the ruffled spirits of one harassed wife and mother.[23]

Women were recognized connoisseurs in the large and often-confusing world of textiles, and early letters give ample evidence that husbands sought their wives' advice in the selection of cloth goods. Bed hangings, curtains, and upholstery fabrics were chosen together, although before women actively entered the retail market it was often the husband who actually placed the order. Among the items Sir William Pepperrell of Piscataqua ordered from England in December 1737 was a set of bed curtains, which "My wife would Chuse ... Should be of a Crimson Couler, if Fashionable." When William Franklin wrote to his London factor in 1765 ordering yellow silk and worsted damask curtains to be hung in festoons to match some yellow damask chairs and furniture in his Burlington, New Jersey, dining room, he specified that his wife "desires you will employ Mr. Timothy Golding upholsterer in Brewer Street near Golden Square, as she is acquainted with him and thinks he will do it in the best and most reasonable manner when he knows it is for her." That same year, Deborah Franklin wrote her husband, Benjamin, who was in London, assuring him that he might use his own taste in selecting curtains for their Philadelphia home, "or as we talked before you went away." David Spear of Boston wrote his fiancée, Marcy Higgins, in February 1787, asking her to inform him of her choice of color in the copperplate covering for their lolling chairs, and at the same time advising, "If you recollect, my Dear, you mentioned purple, but Scarlet is the most fashionable and airy." The decision ultimately rested with Marcy, nonetheless, and he urged her to let him know speedily what she would have "and it shall be procured agreeable to your Liking."[24]

Wives were important instigators and collaborators in the purchase of carpets as well. "If you meet with a Turkey Carpet I should like it," Deborah Franklin delicately suggested to that distant husband, and he happily obliged, sending her in April 1766, "a large true Turkey Carpet" for their dining parlor. When George Washington commissioned a large carpet to accord with the furniture in the blue parlor at Mount Vernon in 1797, he suggested that he would prefer a Wilton to Scotch carpeting. Mrs. Washington, however, had advised him there was a different kind much in use, and if this were not more expensive than the Wilton, or but slightly so, he would have it sent. Charles Carroll of Annapolis had obviously discussed the need for painted floor cloths with his wife, for accompanying an order in 1767 were her packing instructions to the shippers in London that the paint might not be chipped off in transit. And David Spear told Marcy Higgins that his father and the painters had all approved the pattern this young couple had designed for a painted carpet, and assured her that his father had commissioned it for them.[25]

David also wanted Marcy's advice about wallpaper. He was perfectly knowledgeable about certain fashions, mentioning the prevalent taste for a plain blue or green paper with a very wide and bold border at the chair rail, but he was perplexed by the plethora of choices. "There are a great variety of Fashions; I am totally at a loss what Kind to get." Indeed, it is easy to comprehend his befuddlement in a land of plenty if one considers advertisements such as that of Thomas and Caldcleugh in the Baltimore *Federal Gazette* on 29 May 1801, boasting a stock of more than two hundred patterns. David Spear gracefully extricated himself from the quandary by turning the whole matter over to Marcy. John Barker Church told Maria Silliman that he wished her by all means to select the paper for their house, as she would be "the best judge with regard to the *quality*." And by the time John Gale married Sylvia Lyon of Colchester, Vermont, in 1858, he had given "Sylvia the money to get the paper & she got it to suit herself."[26]

During the summer of 1800, Elizabeth Bleecker McDonald frequently met her new husband at his Manhattan office and they went together "to look at some Chairs," "to look for Carpeting," "to look for Paper," or "to see about a Picture." In rural areas, young couples might have to travel farther afield, but they, too, often selected their "outfitting" together. In November 1796 Thankful Phelps married Charles Hitchcock of Northampton, Massachusetts, and several months later they "set out for Springfield to get furniture"; and five months after Mary Guion was wed to Samuel Brown in Westchester, they went to New York City to buy theirs. Others, such as Marcy Higgins and David Spear, were able to plan ahead and had their home almost entirely furnished by the date of the wedding. Phebe Crowell and John Fanning Watson conferred during their engagement, and she obligingly told him in March 1812 that her ideas concerning their furniture coincided exactly with his. Watson then went ahead and ordered maple chairs with white rush seats, which he knew "cannot but please you," commissioning as well a sideboard and a sofa, upon which sofa he blissfully envisioned himself "pressing thee to my bosom, while I cheer thyself & me with the events of the pressing day." In 1826 Elijah Colburn and Sarah Belknap pondered whether it would be better for her to purchase her wedding furniture in her future setting of Dunstable (now Nashua), New Hampshire, or in her hometown of Framingham, Massachusetts. Although it certainly would be easier not to have to transport heavy furniture, Elijah worried that Sarah would not approve of the quality of work available in Dunstable—ready-made pieces sent up, probably from Salem or Boston, for quick distribution. The selection was quite large of all but mahogany pieces, which would have been too expensive for this kind of venture. There were, when he wrote, perhaps twenty or thirty bureaus, chairs, etc., which at first glance looked very good. But upon closer examination even the best were not particularly fine, and these were purchased as soon as they were brought in by a public undoubtedly delighted by this novel supply. Paying tribute to Sarah as a discriminating consumer, Elijah worried that "the best of it would not suit you very well. It is not good custom work, it is made for sale."[27]

The populist cry for "cheap" that lay behind some of these new marketing ventures was heard ever more stridently in the democratic scramble for goods in the 1820s and 1830s, pitting merchant against merchant, cabinetmaker against cabinetmaker, merchant against auctioneer. John Doggett complained repeatedly that auctions were hurting his carpet sales as they attracted the bargain hunters, and when he placed an order for carpets of lively color on dark grounds with Gregory Thomson & Co. of Kilmarnock, Scotland, in June 1827, Doggett asked that they "not cost with you more than 1/6 [$1.60] the yard," as "it is very important for us to have an article in our Store which can be sold less than our neighbors, for the appearance of selling *Cheap* is what will Call Custom to our place." Appearance was all-important and much was not in fact what it appeared to be. S. and J. Rawson, Jr., cabinetmakers in Providence, Rhode Island, in the late 1820s and 1830s argued against the pieces produced for distribution at auction right on the paper label they attached to their furniture: "Knowing the deception in work made for auction, we trust that if people would examine for themselves, and compare the work and pieces, that business, so destructive to all good work, and deceptive to the public, would have an end." Indeed, the perspicacious Alexis de Tocqueville, who came to study American penitentiaries in 1831 and left to measure the success of the American experiment in democracy in a seminal book, observed that "the handicraftsmen of democratic ages not only endeavor to bring their useful productions within the reach of the whole community, but strive to give all their commodities attractive qualities that they do not in reality possess." Elijah Colburn's quick analysis of ready-made venture furniture, which brought more furniture into the homes of more people, corroborates de Tocqueville's analysis of the democratization of the American arts. Elijah Colburn and Sarah Belknap felt fortunate that there were still cabinetmakers working with customers on a commission or "bespoke" basis—the "good custom work," which he had mentioned to her. So it was decided that Sarah would bespeak her furniture of the Framingham cabinetmaker Samuel Warren. Consequently, she wrote her fiancé on 14 May 1826 to say that her father had that morning purchased chairs and "spoke to Mr. Warren for Bureau Tables Bedstead & other necessary furniture so you will not be under the necessity of purchasing anything more except a Looking-glass & perhaps shall see you before you purchase it." The carpet she would buy in Dunstable, as there was not a good selection in Framingham, but she wanted to see Elijah concerning this. Sarah's final letter before setting out for this New Hampshire town intimates that she was going to be a notable housewife. Having sent her goods on, she wanted Elijah to hang the paper curtains as soon as they arrived, "as they will prevent the sun's fading the carpet." He was to lock all the drawers and take charge of the keys until she arrived. And would he please have the bed tick sufficiently well stuffed with straw that her counterpane might "hang well."[28]

Merchants in home furnishings increasingly turned their attention to the ladies. Early-nineteenth-century trade cards were engraved with inviting views of well-dressed women selecting goods in amply stocked shops, newspaper and journal advertisements courted the feminine persuasion, and household manuals offered hints to women on becoming perspicacious consumers (something many of their grandmothers and mothers had each in turn been before them). Husbands became increasingly willing to leave decorative details to their spouses, although from 1750 to 1870 they remained the family comptrollers and as such were assured veto power over any purchase deemed superfluous or extravagant.

When Benjamin Rush tallied those requisites for a harmonious marriage in 1775, they included a sympathy of tastes. "When we consider how many objects of taste in building—furniture—gardening—& books of entertainment engage the minds of married people, it will appear to be of great importance that there be a strict uniformity in them." If there was not always uniformity in taste, and there often was not, then there might at least be an understanding between husband and wife. David Spear hoped that his plans for their future home had met with Marcy's approval, "but if it does not; I beg you will not be backward in letting me know it, but speak your mind freely, and be assured I shall not take it amiss." Personal correspondence from 1750 to 1870 gives ample evidence that husbands and wives did speak their minds freely and were frank with each other in many matters of domestic concern, including interior decor. Architecture, floor plans, furniture, pictures, carpets, curtains, colors, and costs were sometimes a source of anger and discord, but in the most felicitous marriages these issues were debated and mutually determined. The decoration of houses was a collaborative effort at home in early America.[29]

NOTES

In the notes, short titles have often been used for works cited in full in the bibliography. The date when a book was first published is sometimes followed by the date of a reprint or new edition, and in such cases the page number refers to the reprint or new edition. Institutions and collections frequently mentioned in the notes have been identified by the following abbreviations:

AAS American Antiquarian Society

BFP Beach Family Papers, Rare Books and Manuscripts Division, The New York Public Library; Astor, Lenox and Tilden Foundations

BFP-LC Barnard Family Papers, The Library of Congress, Manuscript Division

CCSCI Charleston County, South Carolina, Inventories, Museum of Early Southern Decorative Arts

CFP Chew Family Papers, The Historical Society of Pennsylvania

CPP Connecticut Probate Packets, Connecticut State Library

DFP Dwight Family Papers, Rare Books and Manuscripts Division, The New York Public Library; Astor, Lenox and Tilden Foundations

FSHP Faith Silliman Hubbard Papers, Dartmouth College, Baker Library, Special Collections

HSP The Historical Society of Pennsylvania

INYC Inventories of Estates, New York City and Vicinity, 1717–1844, The New-York Historical Society, Manuscript Collection

JICP John Innes Clark Papers, Manuscript Collection, The Rhode Island Historical Society

LC-MD The Library of Congress, Manuscript Division

L-PL Lee-Palfry Letters, The Library of Congress, Manuscript Division

MSCP Maria Trumbull Silliman Church Papers, Rare Books and Manuscripts Division, The New York Public Library; Astor, Lenox and Tilden Foundations

NYHS-MC The New-York Historical Society, Manuscript Collection

NYPL Rare Books and Manuscripts Division, The New York Public Library; Astor, Lenox and Tilden Foundations

NYSI New York State Manuscript Inventories after 1800, The New-York Historical Society, Manuscript Collection

OSV Old Sturbridge Village Research Library

RFC Rodgers Family Collection, The Library of Congress, Manuscript Division

RFP Ridgley Family Papers, Delaware State Archives

RIFP Ralph Izard Family Papers, The Library of Congress, Manuscript Division

SCPC Suffolk County, Massachusetts, Probate Court

SFP Silliman Family Papers, Manuscripts and Archives, Yale University Library

SLJ Sarah Livingston Jay Letters, Rare Book and Manuscript Library, Columbia University

WFP Wadsworth Family Papers, Manuscripts and Archives, Yale University Library

WL-JD The Winterthur Library: Joseph Downs Collection of Manuscripts and Printed Ephemera

WP Wainwright Family Papers, Rare Books and Manuscripts Division, The New York Public Library; Astor, Lenox and Tilden Foundations

WWP William Wirt Papers, ms. 1011, Maryland Historical Society Library

CHAPTER ONE

1. "Singularly bright and lovely": "Letters from New York, No. II," *The New Monthly Magazine*, vol. 26, no. 105 (September 1829), p. 280. William Tallack, *Friendly Sketches in America* (London, 1861), p. 85. James Fenimore Cooper, *Notions of the Americans Picked Up by a Travelling Bachelor* (1828; New York, 1963), vol. 1, p. 143.

2. [Captain Thomas Hamilton], *Men and Manners in America* (Edinburgh, 1833), vol. 1,

pp. 13–14. On fresh paint, white seams between bricks, see Sarah Mytton Maury, *An Englishwoman in America* (London, 1848), p. 163. John M. Duncan, *Travels through Part of the United States and Canada in 1818 and 1819* (New York, 1823), vol. 1, pp. 28–29. James Stuart, *Three Years in North America*, 2d ed. (Edinburgh, 1833), vol. 1, p. 23. Mrs. Lydia Maria Child, *Letters from New York*, 10th ed. (New York, 1849), pp. 23–24.

3. Quoted in Avrahm Yarmolinsky, *Picturesque United States of America, 1811, 1812, 1813; Being a Memoir on Paul Svinin . . .* (New York, 1930), pp. 39–40. Thomas Twining, *Travels in America One Hundred Years Ago* (New York, 1894), p. 44. Louis Auguste Félix, baron de Beaujour, *Sketch of the United States of North America at the Commencement of the Nineteenth Century, from 1800 to 1810* (London, 1814), p. 76.

4. "Gay and *riant*": "Letters from New York, No. I," *The New Monthly Magazine*, vol. 26, no. 104 (August 1829), p. 133. Duncan, *Travels*, vol. 1, p. 94.

5. Julian Ursyn Niemcewicz, *Under Their Vine and Fig Tree: Travels through America in 1797–1799, 1805*, trans. and ed. Metchie J. E. Budka (Elizabeth, N.J., 1965), p. 36. John Shaw, *A Ramble through the United States, Canada and the West Indies* (London, 1856), p. 9. Charles Dickens, *American Notes* (1842; Oxford, 1957), p. 71. "The little Toys": [?] Brickenden, "A Journal of My Proceedings in America in 1833," LC-MD. Ann Maury, quoted in Anne Fontaine Maury, ed., *Intimate Virginiana: A Century of Maury Travels by Land and Sea* (Richmond, Va., 1941), p. 165. D[avid] Wilkie, *Sketches of a Summer Trip to New York and the Canadas* (Edinburgh, 1837), p. 236.

6. Emilie Cowell, *The Cowells in America: Being the Diary of Mrs. Sam Cowell during Her Husband's Concert Tour in the Years 1860–1861*, ed. M. Willson Disher (London, 1934), pp. 11, 21. Mrs. Anne Royall, *The Black Book*, vol. 1 (Washington, D.C., 1828), p. 254; and [Mrs. Anne Royall], *Sketches of History, Life and Manners, in the United States by a Traveller* (New Haven, 1826), p. 253.

7. Peter Neilson, *Recollections of a Six Years' Residence in the United States of America* (Glasgow, 1830), p. 306. On buzzards, see also

John Drayton, *Letters* (Charleston, S.C., 1794), p. 91; and Mrs. Anne Royall, *Mrs. Royall's Southern Tour*, vol. 2 (Washington, D.C., 1831), p. 8. [Chevalier de Bacourt], *Souvenirs of a Diplomat: Private Letters from America during the Administrations of Presidents Van Buren, Harrison, and Tyler* (New York, 1885), p. 157. On the New York law of 1731, see Esther Singleton, *Social New York under the Georges 1714–1776* (New York, 1902), p. 13. Joshua Brookes journal 1798–1803, typewritten transcript, NYHS-MC.

8. "Hair-covered trunks": C. D. Arfwedson, *The United States and Canada in 1832, 1833, and 1834* (London, 1834), vol. 1, pp. 41–42. John J. Sturtevant, "Recollections of a Resident of New York City from 1835 to 1905," typewritten transcript of a journal, NYPL. [Bacourt], *Souvenirs*, p. 157.

9. On street traffic, see Samuel Dexter Ward, Jr., "Journal of a Tour to New York and Other Places in the Summer of 1842," NYHS-MC. The insomniac was the Chevalier de Bacourt: *Souvenirs*, p. 157.

10. Abigail Adams, *New Letters of Abigail Adams, 1788–1801*, ed. Stewart Mitchell (Boston, 1947), p. 194. Baron Ludwig von Closen, *The Revolutionary Journal . . . 1780–1783*, trans. and ed. Evelyn M. Acomb (Chapel Hill, N.C., 1958), p. 226. *New Orleans Picayune*, quoted in Cowell, *Cowells in America*, pp. 68–69.

11. Peter Kalm, *The America of 1750*, ed. Adolph B. Benson (1770; New York, 1966), vol. 1, p. 34. *Facts for the People, or Things Worth Knowing* (Philadelphia, 1851), p. 6. "With as much painful caution": Francis Hopkinson, *The Miscellaneous Essays and Occasional Writings* (Philadelphia, 1792), vol. 2, p. 159. Royall, *Southern Tour*, vol. 2, p. 86. New Orleans sidewalks: Vincent Nolte, *Fifty Years in Both Hemispheres; or, Reminiscences of the Life of a Former Merchant* (London, 1854), p. 298.

12. Elizabeth Drinker, *Extracts from the Journal of Elizabeth Drinker, from 1759 to 1807 A.D.*, ed. Henry D. Biddle (Philadelphia, 1889), pp. 184–85. "Laughed so much": Sarah Ridg diary, typewritten transcript, entry in March 1809, LC-MD. J. B. Dunlop journal 1810–11, NYHS-MC. John Davis, *Travels of John Davis in the United States of America 1798 to 1802*, ed. John Vance Cheney (Boston, 1910), vol. 1, p. 123. Royall, *Southern Tour*, vol. 2, p. 30. Frederick Van Wyck, *Recollections of an Old New Yorker* (New York, 1932), p. 61. Cowell, *Cowells in America*, pp. 48, 50.

13. Faith Wadsworth to Eliza Sebor, 3 January 1830, WFP. Maria Silliman Church to Henrietta Silliman, 22 October 1838; and Church to Faith Silliman, 6 June 1833, MSCP. Caroline A. Dustan diary, 5 and 7 January 1859, NYPL. Salomon de Rothschild, *A Casual View of America: The Home Letters of Salomon de Rothschild 1859–1861*, trans. and ed. Sig-

mund Diamond (Stanford, Calif., 1961), pp. 91–92. Catharine E. Beecher, *A Treatise on Domestic Economy* (1841; New York, 1977), p. 373. Henry A. Shute, *The Real Diary of a Real Boy* (Boston, 1903), p. 22. George Combe, *Notes on the United States of North America* (Philadelphia, 1841), vol. 1, p. 205.

14. Ebenezer Parkman, *The Diary of Ebenezer Parkman 1703–1782*, ed. Francis G. Walett (Worcester, 1974), p. 74. Maria Silliman Church to Faith Silliman Hubbard, 22 January 1842, MSCP.

15. Drayton, *Letters*, p. 91. [Royall], *Sketches*, p. 155. Sturtevant, "Recollections." Caroline Howard King, *When I Lived in Salem, 1822–1866* (Brattleboro, Vt., 1937), p. 23.

16. Drayton, *Letters*, p. 69. Sarah Logan Fisher diary, September 1778, HSP. [Margaret Bayard Smith], *A Winter in Washington* (New York, 1824), vol. 1, p. 7.

17. Sarah Logan Fisher diary, September 1778, 9 September 1779, 30 July 1786, 18 July 1790. Emily R. Barnes, *Narratives, Traditions, and Personal Reminiscences* (Boston, 1888), p. 267. Alfred Frankenstein, *William Sidney Mount* (New York, 1975), p. 102.

18. Manasseh Cutler, *The Life, Journals and Correspondence*, ed. William Parker Cutler and Julia Perkins Cutler (Cincinnati, 1888), vol. 1, pp. 267–68. Thomas Jefferson, quoted in Sarah N. Randolph, *The Domestic Life of Thomas Jefferson*, 3d ed. (Charlottesville, Va., 1947), p. 185. On the availability of Windsor furniture in New York, see Rita Susswein Gottesman, *The Arts and Crafts in New York, 1726–1776* (New York, 1938), pp. 113–14.

19. Minard Lafever, *The Young Builder's General Instructor* (Newark, N.J., 1829), p. 157. A[lexander] J[ackson] Downing, *The Architecture of Country Houses* (1850; New York, 1969), pp. 44, 34. Harriet Beecher Stowe [Christopher Crowfield, pseud.], *House and Home Papers* (Boston, 1865), pp. 278–79.

20. Charles Carroll of Carrollton letterbook, 8 October 1771, 15 October 1791, Arents Collections, New York Public Library; Astor, Lenox and Tilden Foundations. Miss [Eliza] Leslie, *The House Book* (Philadelphia, 1840), p. 183. Mrs. M. L. Scott, *The Practical Housekeeper and Young Woman's Friend* (Toledo, Ohio, 1855), p. 208.

21. Jean Pierre Brissot de Warville, *New Travels in the United States of America, 1788*, ed. Durand Echeverria (Cambridge, Mass., 1964), p. 256. Edward Ringwood Hewitt, *Those Were the Days: Tales of a Long Life* (New York, 1943), p. 5. One denigrator was Israel Acrelius: *A History of New Sweden; or, The Settlements on the River Delaware* (Philadelphia, 1874), p. 157. Mrs. A. L. Webster, *The Improved Housewife; or, Book of Receipts*, 20th ed. (Hartford, 1854), p. 207.

22. John Blott, quoted in Alfred Coxe

Prime, *The Arts and Crafts in Philadelphia, Maryland and South Carolina 1721–1785* (1929; New York, 1969), p. 275. Johann David Schoepf, *Travels in the Confederation (1783–1784)*, trans. and ed. Alfred J. Morrison (New York, 1968), vol. 1, p. 60. Eliza Ripley, *Social Life in Old New Orleans* (New York, 1912), p. 77. Downing, *Architecture of Country Houses*, p. 403.

23. King, *When I Lived in Salem*, p. 83. James Smithwick estate inventory, 3 December 1779, docket book 81, SCPC. Faith Silliman Hubbard to Harriet Silliman, 27 November 1837, FSHP.

24. M.L.E. Moreau de Saint-Méry, *Moreau de St. Méry's American Journey, 1793–1798*, trans. and ed. Kenneth Roberts and Anna M. Roberts (Garden City, N.Y., 1947), p. 269. *Facts for the People*, p. 7. Mary Palmer Tyler, *Grandmother Tyler's Book*, ed. Frederick Tupper and Helen Tyler Brown (New York, 1925), pp. 61–62. "The Old Clock on the Stairs," in *Favorite Poems of Henry Wadsworth Longfellow* (Garden City, N.Y., 1947), p. 392.

25. Jane Haines, quoted in Sandra MacKenzie Lloyd, "Wyck," *The Magazine Antiques*, August 1983, p. 280. Phebe Ann Beach Lyman to Mary M[atilda] Beach, 21 February 1842, BFP.

26. John Hancock estate inventory, 28 January 1794, docket book 93, SCPC. Philip Vickers Fithian, *Journal and Letters . . . 1773–1774*, ed. Hunter Dickinson Farish (Williamsburg, Va., 1945), p. 52. Ellen H. Rollins [E. H. Arr, pseud.], *New England Bygones* (Philadelphia, 1880), p. 36.

CHAPTER TWO

1. Catharine E. Beecher, *Letters to Persons Who Are Engaged in Domestic Service* (New York, 1843), p. 225. Letitia M. Burwell, *A Girl's Life in Virginia before the War* (New York, 1895), p. 147.

2. [Mrs. Anne Royall], *Sketches of History, Life and Manners, in the United States by a Traveller* (New Haven, 1826), p. 59. [Eliza Ware Farrar], *The Young Lady's Friend* (Boston, 1837), p. 210. Ellen Birdseye Wheaton, *Diary*, ed. Donald Gordon (Boston, 1923), p. 236.

3. On moving furniture, see Susannah Whatman, *The Housekeeping Book of Susanna Whatman 1776–1880*, ed. Thomas Balston (London, 1956), p. 35. Miss [Eliza] Leslie, *The House Book* (Philadelphia, 1840), p. 177. Catharine E. Beecher, *A Treatise on Domestic Economy* (1841; New York, 1977), p. 340.

4. Rebecca Rawle Shoemaker to Anna Rawle, 4 June 1783, "Letters and Diaries of a Loyalist Family of Philadelphia. Written be-

tween the Years 1780 and 1786," typewritten transcript, HSP. Andrew Johnston estate inventory, 7 March 1764, CCSCI (1763–71). Edward Everett Hale, *A New England Boyhood* (1893; New York, 1927), p. 6.

5. George G. Channing, *Early Recollections of Newport, R.I., from the Year 1793 to 1811* (Newport, R.I., and Boston, 1868), p. 252. Harriet Beecher Stowe, *Oldtown Folks* (1869; reprinted in *Stowe: Three Novels*, ed. Kathryn Kish Sklar, New York, 1982), chapter 6, p. 946.

6. Esther Edwards Burr, *Journal . . . 1754–1757*, ed. Carol F. Karlsen and Laurie Crumpacker (New Haven, 1984), p. 268. Ferdinand M. Bayard, *Travels of a Frenchman in Maryland and Virginia*, 2d ed., trans. and ed. Ben C. McCary (1798; Williamsburg, Va., 1950), p. 47. Mrs. Basil Hall, *The Aristocratic Journey . . . 1827–28*, ed. Una Pope-Hennessy (New York, 1931), pp. 63, 81.

7. Margaret Pardee Bates, ed., "Some Letters of Mary Boardman Crowninshield," *Essex Institute Historical Collections*, vol. 83 (April 1947), p. 132. Harriet Silliman to Maria Silliman Church, 22 May [1836], SFP. George Hepplewhite, *The Cabinet-Maker and Upholsterer's Guide*, 3d ed. (1794; New York, 1969), p. 23. Thomas Twining, *Travels in America One Hundred Years Ago* (New York, 1894), p. 128. Mrs. Samuel Harrison Smith, *The First Forty Years of Washington Society*, ed. Gaillard Hunt (New York, 1906), p. 343.

8. The sufferer is quoted in Alan Trachtenberg, ed., *Democratic Vistas 1860–1880* (New York, 1970), p. 133. Hall, *Aristocratic Journey*, p. 282. Abram C. Dayton, *Last Days of Knickerbocker Life in New York* (New York, 1882), p. 27.

9. On the chromatically harmonious parlor, see Leslie, *House Book*, p. 188. Stephen Greenleaf estate inventory, 13 February 1795, docket book 93, SCPC.

10. John Parkinson, quoted in Alfred Coxe Prime, *The Arts and Crafts in Philadelphia, Maryland and South Carolina 1721–1785* (1929; New York, 1969), p. 224. Paint colors for parlor walls: ibid., p. 279.

11. Mary Hill Lamar, quoted in John Jay Smith, ed., *Letters of Doctor Richard Hill and His Children* (Philadelphia, 1854), pp. 197–98.

12. Lamar, quoted in Smith, ed., *Letters of Doctor Hill*, p. 198. Benjamin Backhouse estate inventory, 16 December 1767, CCSCI (1763–71).

13. Ebenezer Thayer estate inventory, quoted in Abbott Lowell Cummings, *Rural Household Inventories . . . 1675–1775* (Boston, 1964), p. 120.

14. Stowe, *Oldtown Folks*, chapter 4, pp. 915–16.

15. "Shine and glister": Gertrude Z. Thomas, *Richer Than Spices* (New York, 1965), p. 79. Lydia Howard [Huntley] Sigourney,

Sketch of Connecticut, Forty Years Since (Hartford, 1824), pp. 46–47.

16. Frances M. Trollope, *Domestic Manners of the Americans*, ed. Donald Smalley (1832; New York, 1949), p. 281. Sarah Anna Emery, *Reminiscences of a Nonagenarian* (1879; Bowie, Md., and Hampton, N.H., 1978), p. 108. "Diminutive, thin-legged, wheezy piano": Dayton, *Last Days*, p. 28. A[lexander] J[ackson] Downing, *The Architecture of Country Houses* (1850; New York, 1969), p. 429. "A kettle in disguise": Mark Twain, *Life on the Mississippi* (1883; reprinted in *Mark Twain, Mississippi Writings*, ed. Guy Cardwell, New York, 1982), chapter 38, p. 458.

17. "There warn't no bed": Mark Twain, *Adventures of Huckleberry Finn* (1885; reprinted in *Mark Twain, Mississippi Writings*, ed. Guy Cardwell, New York, 1982), chapter 17, p. 723. Samuel Bolles estate inventory, 24 April 1813, CPP (1641–1880). Abbott Lowell Cummings, *Bed Hangings: A Treatise on Fabrics and Styles in the Curtaining of Beds 1650–1850* (Boston, 1961), p. 2. Ellen H. Rollins [E. H. Arr, pseud.], *New England Bygones* (Philadelphia, 1880), pp. 51, 46.

18. Charles Carroll of Carrollton letterbook, 9 February 1784, Arents Collections, New York Public Library; Astor, Lenox and Tilden Foundations. Francis J. Grund, *The Americans in Their Moral, Social and Political Relations* (1837; New York, 1971), p. 47.

19. James Fenimore Cooper, *Notions of the Americans Picked Up by a Travelling Bachelor* (1828; New York, 1963), vol. 1, p. 144. Sir Charles Lyell, *A Second Visit to the United States of North America* (New York, 1849), vol. 2, p. 248.

20. On the profusion of chairs, stands, and tables in the drawing room, see Downing, *Architecture of Country Houses*, pp. 201, 437–38. J[ohn] C[laudius] Loudon, *An Encyclopaedia of Cottage, Farm, and Villa Architecture and Furniture* (1833; London, 1853), p. 797.

21. Downing, *Architecture of Country Houses*, pp. 429, 423. Loudon, *Encyclopaedia*, p. 797.

22. Charles Carroll of Carrollton letterbook, 26 October 1771. Faith Silliman to Harriet Silliman, 1 April 1836, MSCP.

23. Faith Silliman to Harriet Silliman, 1 April 1836, MSCP. Elizabeth Wirt to William Wirt, 1 December 1817, WWP. John M. Duncan, *Travels through Part of the United States and Canada in 1818 and 1819* (New York, 1823), vol. 2, p. 279. Trollope, *Domestic Manners*, p. 339. Isabella Lucy (Bird) Bishop, *The Englishwoman in America* (London, 1856), p. 355.

24. Harriet Manigault, *Diary . . . 1813–1816*, ed. Virginia and James S. Armentrout, Jr. (Rockland, Maine, 1976), p. 4. Lady Emmeline Stuart Wortley, *Travels in the United States, etc.,*

during 1849 and 1850 (New York, 1851), p. 53.

25. Thomas Colley Grattan, *Civilized America*, 2d ed. (London, 1859), vol. 1, p. 104. Smith, *The First Forty Years*, p. 244.

26. Andrew L. Winton, "Why We Collect Fairfield County, Connecticut, Antiquities," *Old-Time New England*, vol. 34, no. 2 (October 1943), p. 22. Russell Lynes, *The Domesticated Americans* (New York, 1957), p. 140.

27. Elizabeth Drinker, *Extracts from the Journal of Elizabeth Drinker, from 1759 to 1807 A.D.*, ed. Henry D. Biddle (Philadelphia, 1889), p. 185. Emily Johnston DeForest, *James Colles, 1788–1883: Life and Letters* (New York, 1926), p. 215.

28. Elizabeth Wirt to William Wirt, [13?] December 1812, WWP. John Rattray estate inventory, [1761], CCSCI (1756–63). Rebecca Rawle Shoemaker to Anna Rawle, 4 June 1783, quoted in "Letters and Diaries of a Loyalist Family." Mabel L. Webber, ed., "The Thomas Elfe Account Book, 1768–1775," *The South Carolina Historical and Genealogical Magazine*, vol. 36, no. 4 (October 1935), p. 122. Charles Carroll of Carrollton letterbook, 16 October 1772. Benjamin B. French to Mary [Richardson?], 4 November 1838, Library of Congress, Benjamin B. French Collection.

29. M[arianne] C. D. Silsbee, *A Half Century in Salem* (Boston and New York, 1887), pp. 41–42.

30. Thomas Burling estate inventory, 29 April 1833, NYSI. Loudon, *Encyclopaedia*, p. 302.

31. On the use of green silk in European libraries, see Peter Thornton, *Authentic Decor: The Domestic Interior 1620–1920* (New York, 1984), pp. 128–29. Thomas Sheraton, *The Cabinet-Maker and Upholsterer's Drawing-Book*, 3d ed. (1802; New York, 1970), pp. 97, 102, 151, 200. George Smith, *George Smith's Collection of Designs for Household Furniture and Interior Decoration*, ed. Charles F. Montgomery and Benno M. Forman (1808; New York, 1970), p. 19. Faith Silliman to Benjamin Silliman, 15 February 1836, MSCP. Caroline Howard King, *When I Lived in Salem, 1822–1866* (Brattleboro, Vt., 1937), p. 144.

32. Thomas Tilestone estate inventory, 17 October 1794, docket book 93, SCPC. Mrs. Elizabeth [Buffum] Chace and Lucy Buffum Lovell, *Two Quaker Sisters*, ed. Malcolm Read Lovell (New York, 1937), p. 7.

33. Dr. John Nacy estate inventory, 15 October 1776, CCSCI (1771–76). David Hatch estate inventory, 22 September 1794, docket book 93, SCPC. James Townsend Leonard estate inventory, 14 February 1833, NYSI. Lucy A. Beach to a sister, 15 February 1851, BFP.

34. Andrew Sigourney estate inventory, 14 December 1762, docket book 65, SCPC. Ebenezer Simmons estate inventory, 20 December 1763, CCSCI (1763–71). Anne Eliza[beth]

Clark to Lydia Bowen Clark, 1790s, JICP.

35. Downing, *Architecture of Country Houses*, p. 423. Harriet Beecher Stowe, quoted in Lyman Beecher, *Autobiography, Correspondence, etc., of Lyman Beecher, D.D.*, ed. Charles Beecher (New York, 1865), vol. 1, p. 527.

36. John Peirce estate inventory, 30 September 1794, docket book 93, SCPC. *Godey's Magazine and Lady's Book* (1850), pp. 152–53. Rutherford B. Hayes, *Diary and Letters of Rutherford Birchard Hayes*, ed. Charles Richard Williams (Ohio State Archaeological and Historical Society, 1922), vol. 3, p. 5. Polly Bennett, quoted in Edgar deN. Mayhew and Minor Myers, Jr., *A Documentary History of American Interiors* (New York, 1980), p. 128.

37. Captain John Indicott estate inventory, 26 November 1750, docket book 44, SCPC. [Martha Sellers], *M.S.: The Story of a Life*, ed. Frances Sellers Garrett (Philadelphia, 1901), p. 6. Louisa Crowninshield Bacon, *Reminiscences* ([Salem, Mass.], 1922), p. 22.

38. Newburyport parlor: Emery, *Reminiscences*, p. 32.

39. Mrs. Anne Royall, *The Black Book*, vol. 1 (Washington, D.C., 1828), p. 77. [Austin T. Foster], *A Grandfather's Reminiscences, 1822–1900* (Hartford, [1922]), p. 7. Miss [Eliza] Leslie, *The Behaviour Book: A Manual for Ladies*, 3d ed. (Philadelphia, 1853), p. 33.

40. Harriet Beecher Stowe, *The Minister's Wooing* (1859; reprinted in *Stowe: Three Novels*, ed. Kathryn Kish Sklar, New York, 1982), chapter 10, pp. 621–22. Eliza S. M. Quincy, *Memoir of the Life of Eliza S. M. Quincy* (Boston, 1861), p. 89. Ebenezer Storer estate inventory, 16 March 1807, docket book 105, SCPC. John Hancock estate inventory, 28 January 1794, docket book 93, SCPC. Silsbee, *Half Century*, p. 41. Joseph Cutler estate inventory, 18 December 1806, docket book 105, SCPC.

41. David Nelson Beach, *Beach Family Reminiscences and Annals* (Meriden, Conn., 1931), p. 193. Susan Augusta Fenimore Cooper, quoted in James Fenimore Cooper, *Correspondence*, ed. James Fenimore Cooper (New Haven, 1922), vol. 1, pp. 14–15. Loudon, *Encyclopaedia*, p. 315. Joshua Brookes journal 1798–1803, typewritten transcript, NYHS-MC. [Jacob Abbott], *Cousin Lucy's Conversations* (Boston, 1842), p. 19.

42. Beach, *Beach Family*, p. 193. Susan I. Lesley, *Recollections of My Mother, Mrs. Anne Jean Lyman of Northampton* (1886; Boston, 1899), p. 90.

43. Faith Silliman to Maria Silliman Church, 5 November 1831; and Harriet Silliman to Faith Silliman and Maria Silliman Church, 5 February 1836, SFP. Sarah Logan Fisher diary, December 1786, HSP.

44. Joshua Brookes journal, February 1799. Rattray estate inventory, CCSCI (1756–63). Mrs. Ann Air estate inventory, 13 May

1764, CCSCI (1763–71). Emery, *Reminiscences*, p. 29.

45. Deborah Logan, quoted in Penelope Franklin, ed., *Private Pages: Diaries of American Women 1830s–1970s* (New York, 1986), pp. 458–59. Salty old parrot: Eleanor Putnam, *Old Salem*, ed. Arlo Bates (Cambridge, Mass., 1889), pp. 98–100.

46. Chace and Lovell, *Two Quaker Sisters*, p. 8. Connecticut girl: Member of the Beach family to a sister, Plantsville, Conn., 15 June 1855, BFP.

47. Cooper, *Notions*, vol. 1, p. 151. [Isabella Trotter], *First Impressions of the New World on Two Travellers From the Old* (London, 1859), p. 190.

48. Beecher, *Autobiography, Correspondence*, vol. 1, p. 124. William McKoy, quoted in John F. Watson, *Annals of Philadelphia and Pennsylvania* (Philadelphia, 1887), vol. 2, p. 550. John Trumbull, *The Autobiography of Colonel John Trumbull, Patriot-Artist, 1756–1843*, ed. Theodore Sizer (New Haven, 1953), p. 5.

49. Emery, *Reminiscences*, p. 222. John Jay Janney, *John Jay Janney's Virginia*, ed. Werner L. Janney and Asa Moore Janney (McLean, Va., 1978), p. 84. Hall, *Aristocratic Journey*, p. 45. Victorian parlor: Twain, *Life on the Mississippi*, chapter 37, p. 460. Twain, *Huckleberry Finn*, chapter 17, pp. 724–25.

50. Silsbee, *Half Century*, p. 20. Mary Palmer Tyler, *Grandmother Tyler's Book*, ed. Frederick Tupper and Helen Tyler Brown (New York, 1925), pp. 68–69.

51. Jane Margaret Craig, quoted in Nicholas B. Wainwright, "Andalusia, Country Seat of the Craig Family and of Nicholas Biddle and His Descendants," *Pennsylvania Magazine of History and Biography*, vol. 101, no. 1 (January 1977), p. 24. Downing, *Architecture of Country Houses*, p. 429. Maria Silliman Church to Harriet Silliman, 13 October 1833; and Silliman to Church, 4 March 1835, MSCP.

52. [Sellers], *Story of a Life*, p. 7. Barnes, *Narratives*, p. 251. "At ½ past nine": Anna Quincy Thaxter Parsons, journal (original manuscript: Elizabeth Margaret Carter Papers, Essex Institute Manuscript Collections, Salem, Mass.), quoted in "A Newburyport Wedding One Hundred and Thirty Years Ago," *Essex Institute Historical Collections*, vol. 87 (October 1951), p. 318.

CHAPTER THREE

1. [Anne Grant], *Memoirs of an American Lady* (London, 1808), vol. 1, p. 171. Robert Sutcliff, *Travels in Some Parts of North America in the Years 1804, 1805, and 1806* (Philadelphia, 1812), p. 263.

2. On American and English dining rooms in general, see John Fowler and John Cornforth, *English Decoration in the Eighteenth Century* (Princeton, N.J., 1974), pp. 66–68; Mark Girouard, *Life in the English Country House: A Social and Architectural History* (New Haven, 1978), p. 203; and Clifford E. Clark, Jr., "The Vision of the Dining Room: Plan Book Dreams and Middle-Class Realities," in Kathryn Grover, ed., *Dining in America 1850–1900* (Amherst, Mass., and Rochester, N.Y., 1987), pp. 142–72. Mrs. Samuel Harrison Smith, *The First Forty Years of Washington Society*, ed. Gaillard Hunt (New York, 1906), pp. 327–28.

3. The English visitor is quoted in Charles Lockwood, *Bricks and Brownstone: The New York Row House, 1783–1929* (New York, 1972), p. 14. "Monotonous procession": Ruth Huntington Sessions, *Sixty-Odd: A Personal History* (Brattleboro, Vt., 1936), p. 21. On the well-appointed dining room, see Robert Kerr, *The Gentleman's House*, 2d ed. (London, 1865), p. 91; Thomas Sheraton, *Thomas Sheraton's Cabinet Dictionary*, ed. Charles F. Montgomery (1803; New York, 1970), vol. 2, p. 218; George Hepplewhite, *The Cabinet-Maker and Upholsterer's Guide*, 3d ed. (1794; New York, 1969), p. 24; George Smith, *George Smith's Collection of Designs for Household Furniture and Interior Decoration*, ed. Charles F. Montgomery and Benno M. Forman (1808; New York, 1970), p. xiii; and A[lexander] J[ackson] Downing, *The Architecture of Country Houses* (1850; New York, 1969), p. 404.

4. The first step: Catharine E. Beecher, *A Treatise on Domestic Economy* (1841; New York, 1977), p. 353. Miss [Eliza] Leslie, *The House Book* (Philadelphia, 1840), p. 176. Thomas Jefferson, quoted in Rodris Roth, "Floor Coverings in 18th-Century America," *United States National Museum Bulletin 250* (Washington, D.C., 1967), p. 25. Leslie, *House Book*, p. 177. Martha Ogle Forman, *Plantation Life at Rose Hill*, ed. W. Emerson Wilson (Wilmington, Del., 1976), pp. 94, 152, 211. Beecher, *Treatise*, p. 350.

5. "Stand firm": Beecher, *Treatise*, p. 353. Edward Augustus Kendall, *Travels through the Northern Parts of the United States in the Years 1807 and 1808* (New York, 1809), vol. 1, p. 327. Faith Silliman to Harriet Silliman, 20 February 1837, FSHP.

6. Sarah Anna Emery, *Three Generations* (Boston, 1872), p. 119. Robert Adam, quoted in Fowler and Cornforth, *English Decoration*, p. 67. François Alexandre Frédéric, duc de La Rochefoucauld-Liancourt, *Travels through the United States of North America in the Years 1795, 1796, and 1797* (London, 1799), vol. 4, p. 589. Robert Waln, Jr., *The Hermit in America; or, A Visit to Philadelphia*, ed. Peter Atall, 2d ed. (Philadelphia, 1819), p. 113. "Bacchus to Venus": M.L.E. Moreau de Saint-Méry, *Moreau de St. Méry's American Journey*

1793–1798, trans. and ed. Kenneth Roberts and Anna M. Roberts (Garden City, N.Y., 1947), p. 54. Eliza Farrar, quoted in Helen Sprackling, *Customs on the Table Top* (Sturbridge, Mass., 1958), p. 20.

7. For a discussion of the specifics of American table settings, see Louise Conway Belden, *The Festive Tradition: Table Decorations and Desserts in America, 1650–1900* (New York, 1983). On the theme of prosperity and abundance, see David M. Potter, *People of Plenty* (Chicago, 1954); see also, La Rochefoucauld-Liancourt, *Travels*, vol. 4, pp. 586–87; William Cobbett, *A Year's Residence in the United States of America* (1818; New York, 1969), pp. 351–52; and [Captain Thomas Hamilton], *Men and Manners in America* (Edinburgh, 1833), vol. 2, p. 5. Rosalie Calvert, quoted in William D. Hoyt, Jr., ed., "The Calvert-Stier Correspondence, Letters from America to the Low Countries, 1797–1828," *Maryland Historical Magazine*, vol. 38, no. 2 (June 1943), p. 134. Caroline Howard King, *When I Lived in Salem, 1822–1866* (Brattleboro, Vt., 1937), p. 25. Advertisement for "new invented chaffing dishes," quoted in Rita Susswein Gottesman, *The Arts and Crafts in New York, 1800–1804* (New York, 1965), p. 210. Dr. Alexander Hamilton, *Gentleman's Progress: The Itinerarium of Dr. Alexander Hamilton, 1744*, ed. Carl Bridenbaugh (Chapel Hill, N.C., 1948), p. 40.

8. Robert Roberts, *The House Servant's Directory* (1827; Waltham, Mass., 1977), p. 53. Leslie, *House Book*, p. 260. Catharine Sedgwick, *Home* (Boston, 1837), p. 28. Philip Hone, *The Diary of Philip Hone 1828–1851*, ed. Allan Nevins (New York, 1936), p. 300.

9. On white tablecloths, see Catharine E. Beecher, *Miss Beecher's Housekeeper and Healthkeeper: Containing Five Hundred Recipes for Economical and Healthful Cooking; also, Many Directions for Securing Health and Happiness* (New York, 1873), p. 109. Marquis de Chastellux, *Travels in North America in the Years 1780, 1781, and 1782*, ed. Howard C. Rice, Jr. (Chapel Hill, N.C., 1963), vol. 1, p. 132. Isabella Beeton, *Mrs. Beeton's Book of Household Management* (1861; London, 1982), p. 963.

10. Leslie, *House Book*, p. 255. Charles Bagot, quoted in Samuel Eliot Morison, "Charles Bagot's Notes on Housekeeping and Entertaining at Washington, 1819," in *Publications of the Colonial Society of Massachusetts. Transactions 1924–1926* (Boston, 1927), p. 443. *An Inventory of the Contents of the Governor's Palace Taken after the Death of Lord Botetourt* (Williamsburg, Va., 1981), p. 18. Advertisements for clear starching and mangling appeared, for example, in *Maryland Journal and Baltimore Daily Advertiser*, 29 April 1791; *South Carolina Gazette*, 18 December 1794;

and *Charleston City Gazette and Advertiser*, 20 September 1798; see Prime Cards, Winterthur Library, Winterthur, Del. "A woman may do as much": advertisement by Hercules Courtenay in *Pennsylvania Packet*, 13 June 1774; see Prime Cards. Forman, *Plantation Life*, p. 65. King, *When I Lived in Salem*, pp. 22–23, 25.

11. Two white cloths: *The Domestic's Companion* (New York, 1834), p. 23. Henry Barnard, quoted in Bernard C. Steiner, ed., "The South Atlantic States in 1833, As Seen by a New Englander; Being a Narrative of a Tour Taken by Henry Barnard," *Maryland Historical Magazine*, vol. 15, no. 4 (December 1918), p. 320. Mrs. Sarah J. Hale, *Mrs. Hale's Cook Book* (Philadelphia, [1857]), pp. 496–97. Sarah J. Hale, *Manners; or, Happy Homes and Good Society All Year Round* (Boston, 1868), p. 272.

12. Henry Barnard, quoted in Steiner, ed., "South Atlantic States," p. 319. Smith, *The First Forty Years*, p. 69. Letitia M. Burwell, *A Girl's Life in Virginia before the War* (New York, 1895), p. 54. *Domestic's Companion*, p. 21. Beecher, *Miss Beecher's Housekeeper*, p. 109.

13. Absence of napkins: Oscar Handlin, ed., *This Was America* (Cambridge, Mass., 1949), p. 157; Charles H. Sherrill, *French Memories of Eighteenth-Century America* (New York, 1915), p. 106; Baron Ludwig von Closen, *The Revolutionary Journal . . . 1780–1783*, trans. and ed. Evelyn M. Acomb (Chapel Hill, N.C., 1958), p. 50; and Jean Pierre Brissot de Warville, *New Travels in the United States of America, 1788*, ed. Durand Echeverria (Cambridge, Mass., 1964), p. 347. The Frenchman who remarked on American table settings is quoted in John C. Milley, ed., *Treasures of Independence: Independence National Historical Park and Its Collections* (New York, 1980), p. 88. "Capital wines": E. W. Balch, ed., "Narrative of the Prince de Broglie, Part IV," *Magazine of American History*, vol. 1, no. 6 (June 1877), p. 379. *Facts for the People, or Things Worth Knowing* (Philadelphia, 1851), p. 7. Maria Foster Brown, quoted in Harriet Connor Brown, *Grandmother Brown's Hundred Years, 1827–1927* (Boston, 1929), p. 58. Franklin Butler Van Valkenburgh, *Grandpapa's Letter to His Children*, comp. and ed. Charles H. Vilas (1899; privately reprinted, 1978), p. 106. Forman, *Plantation Life*, pp. 67, 63.

14. Frances M. Trollope, *Domestic Manners of the Americans*, ed. Donald Smalley (1832; New York, 1949), p. 299. Bernhard Karl, duke of Saxe-Weimar Eisenach, quoted in Thomas D. Clark, ed., *South Carolina: The Grand Tour 1780–1865* (Columbia, S.C., 1973), p. 98.

15. "Excerpts from the Day-Books of David Evans, Cabinet-Maker, Philadelphia, 1774–1811," *Pennsylvania Magazine of History and Biography*, vol. 27, no. 1 (1903), p. 50. Dean A. Fales, Jr., "Joseph Barrell's Pleasant

Hill," in *Publications of the Colonial Society of Massachusetts*, vol. 43 (Boston, 1966), p. 384. Louisa Crowninshield Bacon, *Reminiscences* ([Salem, Mass.], 1922), p. 21. Chairs placed back after use: *Domestic's Companion*, p. 21. Roberts, *House Servant's Directory*, p. 61. Kerr, *Gentleman's House*, p. 94.

16. Mabel L. Webber, ed., "The Thomas Elfe Account Book, 1768–1775," *The South Carolina Historical and Genealogical Magazine*, vol. 37, no. 4 (October 1936), p. 152; and vol. 38, no. 4 (October 1937), p. 132. On what was put on the serving table, see Roberts, *House Servant's Directory*, p. 51; and *Domestic's Companion*, p. 25. J[ohn] C[laudius] Loudon, *An Encyclopaedia of Cottage, Farm, and Villa Architecture and Furniture* (1833; London, 1853), p. 800. John Ball estate inventory, 18 April 1765, CCSCI (1763–71). Roberts, *House Servant's Directory*, p. 51.

17. Benjamin Bass estate inventory, 27 September 1819, docket book 117, SCPC. Hepplewhite, *Cabinet-Maker*, p. 6.

18. "John Singleton Copley's Houses on Beacon Hill, Boston," *Old-Time New England*, vol. 25, no. 3 (January 1935), p. 88. Leslie, *House Book*, pp. 250–51. Thomas Sheraton, *The Cabinet-Maker and Upholsterer's Drawing-Book*, 3d ed. (1802; New York, 1970), p. 366. Kerr, *Gentleman's House*, p. 93.

19. George G. Channing, *Early Recollections of Newport, R.I., from the Year 1793 to 1811* (Newport, R.I., and Boston, 1868), pp. 248–49. Laura Richards, *Stepping Westward* (New York, 1931), pp. 3–4. [Charles] H. Haswell, *Reminiscences of New York by an Octogenarian (1816 to 1860)* (New York, 1896), p. 70. Julian Ursyn Niemcewicz, *Under Their Vine and Fig Tree: Travels through America in 1797–1799, 1805*, trans. and ed. Metchie J. E. Budka (Elizabeth, N.J., 1965), p. 36. The Marylander is quoted in "Buchanan Family Reminiscences," *Maryland Historical Magazine*, vol. 35, no. 3 (September 1940), p. 264.

20. Sheraton, *Cabinet-Maker*, p. 364. "A closet to hold utensils": Loudon, *Encyclopaedia*, p. 800. Moreau de Saint-Méry, *Journey*, p. 266.

21. Baron Axel Klinkowström, *Baron Klinkowström's America 1818–1820*, ed. Franklin D. Scott (Evanston, Ill., 1952), p. 128. Moreau de Saint-Méry, *Journey*, p. 266. "Study neatness": Roberts, *House Servant's Directory*, pp. 48–49. Josiah Quincy, "Journal of Josiah Quincy, Junior, 1773," in *Proceedings of the Massachusetts Historical Society*, vol. 49 (Boston, 1916), p. 446.

22. Richly hued sideboard: see Blackie and Son, *The Victorian Cabinet-Maker's Assistant* (1853; New York, 1970), p. 10. *Domestic's Companion*, p. 24. Roberts, *House Servant's Directory*, p. 50. *Domestic's Companion*, ibid. "When a gentleman does honour": Kerr, *Gentleman's House*, p. 93. Loudon, *Encyclopaedia*,

p. 800. Roberts, ibid., p. 49. Sheraton, *Cabinet-Maker*, p. 363. Anne Eliza Clark Kane to Lydia Bowen Clark, 26 January [1803–4?], JICP.

23. Patricia Holbert Menk, "D. M. Erskine: Letters from America, 1798–1799," *The William and Mary Quarterly*, 3d ser., vol. 6, no. 2 (April 1949), p. 272. On the vast display, see Carole Shammas, "The Domestic Environment in Early Modern England and America," in *The American Family in Social-Historical Perspective*, ed. Michael Gordon (New York, 1983), p. 125; and Dwight P. Lanmon, "The Baltimore Glass Trade, 1780 to 1820," in *Winterthur Portfolio 5*, ed. Richard K. Doud (Charlottesville, Va., 1969), pp. 15–48. E. W. Balch, ed., "Narrative of the Prince de Broglie," p. 379. Alice Izard to Margaret Izard Manigault, 16 May 1814, RIFP.

24. Bernhard Karl, duke of Saxe-Weimar Eisenach, *Travels through North America, during the Years 1825 and 1826* (Philadelphia, 1828), vol. 2, p. 64. Miss [Eliza] Leslie, *The Behaviour Book: A Manual for Ladies*, 3d ed. (Philadelphia, 1853), p. 325. Florence Hartley, *The Ladies' Book of Etiquette and Manual of Politeness* (Boston, 1873), p. 916.

25. "Great purple raisins," "enriched by cream": King, *When I Lived in Salem*, pp. 26–27. Quincy, "Journal of Josiah Quincy, Junior," p. 446. Samuel Breck, *Recollections of Samuel Breck*, ed. H. E. Scudder (London, 1877), p. 111.

26. Robert Adam, quoted in Fowler and Cornforth, *English Decoration*, pp. 67–68. Mrs. William Parkes, *Domestic Duties*, 3d American ed. (New York, 1829), pp. 173–74.

27. Smith, *George Smith's Collection*, p. xii. The order placed by Charles Carroll, the Barrister of Mount Clare, is quoted in Michael S. Trostel, "Mount Clare," *The Magazine Antiques*, February 1979, p. 345. Julia Ward Howe, *Reminiscences, 1819–1899* (Boston, 1900), p. 44.

28. Kerr, *Gentleman's House*, p. 91. Sidney George Fisher, *A Philadelphia Perspective: The Diary of Sidney George Fisher Covering the Years 1834–1871*, ed. Nicholas B. Wainwright (Philadelphia, 1967), p. 207. "During dinner": Thomas Walker, *The Art of Dining; and The Art of Attaining High Health* (Philadelphia, 1837), p. 40. Leslie, *House Book*, pp. 260–61. "It is extremely uncomfortable": Hartley, *Ladies' Book*, p. 89.

29. Walker, *Art of Dining*, pp. 39, 53, 101. Roberts, *House Servant's Directory*, pp. 177, 48. Margaret L. Brown, "Mr. and Mrs. William Bingham of Philadelphia," *Pennsylvania Magazine of History and Biography*, vol. 61, no. 3 (1937), p. 304. Alexis Soyer, *The Modern Housewife or Menagere* (London, 1849), p. 391.

30. *Inventory of the Contents of the Governor's Palace*, pp. 6, 11. Roberts, *House Servant's Directory*, pp. 65–66.

CHAPTER FOUR

1. "To be constructed": Harriet Beecher Stowe, *Poganuc People* (1878; Hartford, 1977), p. 166.

2. On the efficient kitchen, see T[homas] Webster and Mrs. [William] Parkes, *The American Family Encyclopedia of Useful Knowledge* (New York, 1856), p. 801; and Isabella Beeton, *Mrs. Beeton's Book of Household Management* (1861; London, 1982), p. 25.

3. "Greatest possible results": Harriet Beecher Stowe, *The Minister's Wooing* (1859; reprinted in *Stowe: Three Novels*, ed. Kathryn Kish Sklar, New York, 1982), chapter 2, p. 536. On the Rice family kitchen, see Mary A. Livermore, *The Story of My Life* (Hartford, 1899), p. 46. A[lexander] J[ackson] Downing, *The Architecture of Country Houses* (1850; New York, 1969), p. 121.

4. Faith Silliman Hubbard to Harriet Silliman, 23 June 1837, FSHP. Peter Neilson, *Recollections of a Six Years' Residence in the United States of America* (Glasgow, 1830), p. 194. "Kitchen Triton": S. G. Goodrich, *Recollections of a Lifetime; or, Men and Things I Have Seen* (New York, 1856), p. 84.

5. George G. Channing, *Early Recollections of Newport, R.I., from the Year 1793 to 1811* (Newport, R.I., and Boston, 1868), pp. 239–40. Edmund Soper Hunt, *Reminiscences* (Boston, 1907), p. 47. Caroline Howard Gilman [Clarissa Packard, pseud.], *Recollections of a Housekeeper* (New York, 1834), p. 17. Catharine E. Beecher, *A Treatise on Domestic Economy* (1841; New York, 1977), p. 323. Gervase Wheeler, *Rural Homes; or, Sketches of Houses Suited to American Country Life* (New York, 1851), p. 165. Stowe, *Minister's Wooing*, chapter 2, p. 536.

6. Jonathan Davis estate inventory, quoted in Abbott Lowell Cummings, *Rural Household Inventories . . . 1675–1775* (Boston, 1964), p. 188. A clock in or near the kitchen: Beecher, *Treatise*, p. 367; and [Frances Harriet Whipple McDougall], *The Housekeeper's Book* (Philadelphia, 1837), p. 33. "Old worn hourglass": Leonard Withington, *The Puritan: A Series of Essays* (Boston, 1836), vol. 1, p. 15. Abigail Adams, *New Letters of Abigail Adams 1788–1801*, ed. Stewart Mitchell (Boston, 1947), p. 50. Polly Bennett, quoted in Edgar deN. Mayhew and Minor Myers, Jr., *A Documentary History of American Interiors* (New York, 1980), p. 128.

7. Neilson, *Recollections*, p. 194. John J. Sturtevant, "Recollections of a Resident of New York City from 1835 to 1905," typewritten transcript of a journal, NYPL. Sarah Trecothick estate inventory, 8 March 1749, docket book 43, SCPC. Beecher, *Treatise*, p. 366. Miss [Eliza]

Leslie, *The House Book* (Philadelphia, 1840), pp. 183, 228. Robert Donald Crompton, ed., "A Philadelphian Looks at New England—1820: Excerpts from 'Journal of a Journey by Sea from Philadelphia to Boston' by William Wood Thackara, 1791–1839," *Old-Time New England*, vol. 50, no. 3 (January–March 1960), p. 59. Harriet Beecher Stowe, *Uncle Tom's Cabin* (1852; reprinted in *Stowe: Three Novels*, ed. Kathryn Kish Sklar, New York, 1982), chapter 13, p. 162. Sarah Anna Emery, *Reminiscences of a Nonagenarian* (1879; Bowie, Md., and Hampton, N.H., 1978), p. 10.

8. "Neat look": Catharine E. Beecher and Harriet Beecher Stowe, *The American Woman's Home* (1869; Hartford, 1975), p. 371. Martha Ogle Forman, *Plantation Life at Rose Hill*, ed. W. Emerson Wilson (Wilmington, Del., 1976), p. 429. Elizabeth E[llicott] Lea, *Domestic Cookery* (1845; facsimile of the 1853 edition, as *A Quaker Woman's Cookbook*, ed. William Woys Weaver, Philadelphia, 1982), p. 199. Astonished sojourner: *Things as They Are; or, Notes of a Traveller through Some of the Middle and Northern States* (New York, 1834), p. 91. Susan Fenimore Cooper, *Rural Hours* (1850; Syracuse, N.Y., 1968), p. 107. Flypaper: M.L.E. Moreau de Saint-Méry, *Moreau de St. Méry's American Journey, 1793–1798*, trans. and ed. Kenneth Roberts and Anna M. Roberts (Garden City, N.Y., 1947), p. 325. "For all the men": Theodore Dwight to Abigail Dwight, 30–31 December 1819, DFP.

9. Wheeler, *Rural Homes*, p. 26.

10. All quotations are from Robert Roberts, *The House Servant's Directory* (1827; Waltham, Mass., 1977), pp. 157–58, 176.

11. On timing the cooking of a roast, see Miss Prudence Smith, *Modern American Cookery* (New York, 1831), p. 28. On gauging the temperature of a brick oven, see Mrs. E[sther] A[llen] Howland, *The New England Economical Housekeeper and Family Receipt Book* (Worcester, 1845), p. 45. "For its 'keeping' quality": Hunt, *Reminiscences*, p. 19. Lasting "till March": Lyman Beecher, *Autobiography, Correspondence*, ed. Charles Beecher (New York, 1865), vol. 1, p. 27.

12. Elizabeth Watters to Lydia Bowen Clark, 21 February 1803, JICP. Cooper, *Rural Hours*, p. 106. Faith Silliman Hubbard to Benjamin and Harriet Silliman, 12 August 1837, FSHP. Caroline A. Dustan diary, 9 January 1861, NYPL.

13. Catherine Chew inventory, 18 May 1840, CFP. Beecher, *Treatise*, p. 374. G. M. Towle, *American Society* (London, 1870), vol. 1, p. 268.

14. Eliza Ripley, *Social Life in Old New Orleans* (New York, 1912), p. 43. Leslie, *House Book*, p. 235.

15. Thomas Tilestone estate inventory, 17 October 1794, docket book 93, SCPC. John

Guerard estate inventory, 30 May 1764, CCSCI (1763–71).

16. Philip Freeman estate inventory, 12 November 1782, docket book 81, SCPC.

17. Joseph Edward Flower estate inventory, 17 February 1757, CCSCI (1756–63). Theodore Dwight to Abigail Dwight, 30–31 December 1819, DFP. Ebenezer Pierpoint estate inventory, quoted in Cummings, *Rural Household Inventories*, p. 220. Cornelius Bennett estate inventory, 25 May 1784, INYC. Beecher, *Treatise*, pp. 309–10. Saturday-night bath: Ethel Ambler Hunter, "We Were Not Poor," *Old-Time New England*, vol. 35, no. 3. (January 1945), p. 49.

18. William T. Davis, *Plymouth Memories of an Octogenarian* (Plymouth, Mass., 1906), p. 281. Deacon Enoch Little, quoted in Charles Carleton Coffin, *The History of Boscawen and Webster, from 1733 to 1878* (Concord, N.H., 1878), p. 185. Beecher, *Treatise*, pp. 367, 371. Roberts, *House Servant's Directory*, p. 178. Joseph Gooch estate inventory, quoted in Cummings, *Rural Household Inventories*, p. 236. On the dresser and its shelf rails, see J[ohn] C[laudius] Loudon, *An Encyclopaedia of Cottage, Farm, and Villa Architecture and Furniture* (1833; London, 1853), pp. 294, 297. "And the pewter plates": see "Evangeline," in *Favorite Poems of Henry Wadsworth Longfellow* (Garden City, N.Y., 1947), p. 323.

19. Nathaniel Saltonstall, quoted in Robert E. Moody, ed., *The Saltonstall Papers, 1607–1815* (Boston, 1972), vol. 1, p. 542. "As neat as a table": Mrs. Sarah J. Hale, *Mrs. Hale's Cook Book* (Philadelphia, [1857]), p. 489. Livermore, *Story of My Life*, p. 45.

20. Roberts, *House Servant's Directory*, p. 178. Jean Pierre Brissot de Warville, quoted in Charles H. Sherrill, *French Memories of Eighteenth-Century America* (New York, 1915), p. 106. Mrs. Anne Royall, *The Black Book*, vol. 1 (Washington, D.C., 1828), pp. 255, 148.

21. Ruth Huntington Sessions, *Sixty-Odd: A Personal History* (Brattleboro, Vt., 1936), p. 25. See also Eleanor Putnam, *Old Salem*, ed. Arlo Bates (Cambridge, Mass., 1889), p. 74. "Queer little Chinamen," "bright-colored labels": Caroline Howard King, *When I Lived in Salem, 1822–1866* (Brattleboro, Vt., 1937), pp. 109–10.

22. James Smithwick estate inventory, 3 December 1779, docket book 81, SCPC. On Helen Davis's parrot, see Katharine Minot Channing, *Minot Family Letters 1773–1871* (Sherborn, Mass., 1957), p. 135.

23. "Heart of the house": Elinor Stearns, "A Kitchen of 1825 in a Thriving New England Town," *Old-Time New England*, vol. 13, no. 3 (January 1923), p. 125. Livermore, *Story of My Life*, p. 47. Ellen H. Rollins [E. H. Arr, pseud.], *New England Bygones* (Philadelphia, 1880), pp. 37, 38.

CHAPTER FIVE

1. John Jay Janney, *John Jay Janney's Virginia*, ed. Werner L. Janney and Asa Moore Janney (McLean, Va., 1978), p. 40. *A Journal by Thos. Hughes for His Amusement, & Designed Only for His Perusal by the Time He Attains the Age of 50 If He Lives so Long*, ed. E. A. Benians (Cambridge, 1947), p. 26.

2. "The Passing of the Spare Chamber," *Atlantic Monthly*, vol. 83, no. 495 (January 1899), p. 140. "The family Zeraphim": [Anne Grant], *Memoirs of an American Lady* (London, 1808), vol. 1, p. 165. Caroline Howard King, *When I Lived in Salem, 1822–1866* (Brattleboro, Vt., 1937), p. 185.

3. For details of the components of the well-made bed, see Audrey H. Michie, "Charleston Upholstery in All Its Branches, 1725–1820," *Journal of Early Southern Decorative Arts*, vol. 11, no. 2 (1985), p. 46. King, *When I Lived in Salem*, p. 186.

4. Maria Foster Brown, quoted in Harriet Connor Brown, *Grandmother Brown's Hundred Years, 1827–1927* (Boston, 1929), p. 31. John J. Sturtevant, "Recollections of a Resident of New York City from 1835 to 1905," typewritten transcript of a journal, NYPL.

5. Joshua Brookes journal 1798–1803, typewritten transcript, NYHS-MC. Maria Silliman Church to Harriet Silliman, 4 November 1831, 11 June 1832, MSCP. Silliman to Church, 27 November 1831, SFP.

6. S[amuel] G[riswold] Goodrich, *Recollections of a Lifetime* (New York, 1856), p. 80. Miss [Eliza] Leslie, *The House Book* (Philadelphia, 1840), p. 66. "My grandparents' geese": quoted in Steven J. Zeitlin, Amy J. Kotkin, and Holly Cutting Baker, eds., *A Celebration of American Family Folklore, Tales and Traditions from the Smithsonian Collection* (New York, 1982), p. 125. Eagle Furniture Warehouse, Boston, receipt on printed billhead, 27 December 1830, WL-JD. Leslie, *House Book*, p. 66. Elizabeth E[llicott] Lea, *Domestic Cookery* (1845; facsimile of the 1853 edition, as *A Quaker Woman's Cookbook*, ed. William Woys Weaver, Philadelphia, 1982), p. 212. Care of tick and feathers: *The Workwoman's Guide* (1838; Guilford, Conn., 1986), p. 175.

7. Massachusetts girl: King, *When I Lived in Salem*, p. 186. Mrs. Basil Hall, *The Aristocratic Journey . . . 1827–1828*, ed. Una Pope-Hennessy (New York, 1931), p. 51. Catharine E. Beecher, *A Treatise on Domestic Economy* (1841; New York, 1977), p. 361. Florence Hartley, *The Ladies' Book of Etiquette and Manual of Politeness* (Boston, 1873), p. 61.

8. Elizabeth Drinker, *Extracts from the Journal of Elizabeth Drinker, from 1759 to 1807 A.D.*, ed. Henry D. Biddle (Philadelphia, 1889), p. 32. Goodrich, *Recollections*, p. 80. *The Amer-*

ican Housewife (New York, 1841), p. 121. Ellen H. Rollins [E. H. Arr, pseud.], *New England Bygones* (Philadelphia, 1880), p. 49. Andrew Buni, ed., "Rambles among the Virginia Mountains: The Journal of Mary Jane Boggs, June 1851," *Virginia Magazine of History and Biography*, vol. 77, no. 1 (January 1969), p. 84. Miss [Eliza] Leslie, *The Behaviour Book: A Manual for Ladies*, 3d ed. (Philadelphia, 1853), p. 13. Nicholas Ridgely, quoted in Mabel Lloyd Ridgely, ed., *The Ridgelys of Delaware and Their Circle* (Portland, Maine, 1949), pp. 177–78.

9. Inverted tumbler: Robert Roberts, *The House Servant's Directory* (1827; Waltham, Mass., 1977), pp. 110–11. Benjamin Franklin, *The Papers of Benjamin Franklin*, ed. Leonard W. Labaree, vol. 6 (New Haven, 1963), p. 365.

10. [Jane Taylor], *Rhymes for the Nursery* (Boston, [1857]), p. 17. Margaret Manigault to Alice Izard, 6 October 1814, RIFP. Beecher, *Treatise*, p. 361. "Should not take cold": Elizabeth Wirt to William Wirt, 22 November 1813, WWP.

11. Anne Newport Royall, *Letters from Alabama, 1817–1822*, intro. and notes by Lucille Griffith (1830; University, Ala., 1969), p. 111. Thomas Twining, *Travels in America One Hundred Years Ago* (New York, 1894), p. 31.

12. Alexander Anderson, "Diarium Commentarium Vitae Alex. Anderson," typewritten transcript of a journal, 1793–99, NYHS-MC (original manuscript: Rare Book and Manuscript Library, Columbia University). A[nthony] F. M. Willich, *The Domestic Encyclopedia; or, A Dictionary of Facts and Useful Knowledge* (1802; 2d American ed., Philadelphia, 1821), vol. 1, p. 175.

13. Plunket Fleeson's bill: Nicholas B. Wainwright, *Colonial Grandeur in Philadelphia: The House and Furniture of General John Cadwalader* (Philadelphia, 1964), pp. 40, 42–43.

14. Sarah Anna Emery, *Reminiscences of a Nonagenarian* (1879; Bowie, Md., and Hampton, N.H., 1978), p. 6. On the colors of bed hangings, see *Workwoman's Guide*, p. 192; and *Hand Book of Practical Receipts; or, Useful Hints in Every Day Life* (New York, 1860), p. 107. Mrs. William Parkes, *Domestic Duties*, 3d American ed. (New York, 1829), p. 182. Dorothy Dudley, quoted in *The Cambridge of 1776: Wherein Is Set Forth an Account of the Town, and of the Events Witnessed: With Which Is Incorporated The Diary of Dorothy Dudley* (Cambridge, Mass., 1876), p. 78.

15. William T. Davis, *Plymouth Memories of an Octogenarian* (Plymouth, Mass., 1906), p. 483. King, *When I Lived in Salem*, pp. 186–87. William Dunlap, *Thirty Years Ago; or, The Memoirs of a Water Drinker* (New York, 1836), vol. 1, p. 71. "William Penn's Treaty" bed hangings: Charles F. Montgomery, *American Furni-*

ture of the Federal Period (New York, 1966), p. 60.

16. Green check, see Abbott Lowell Cummings, Bed Hangings: A Treatise on Fabrics and Styles in the Curtaining of Beds 1650–1850 (Boston, 1961), p. 20; and Edward S. Cooke, Jr., et al., Upholstery in America and Europe from the Seventeenth Century to World War I (New York, 1987), p. 179. Crimson and yellow check: Alice Hanson Jones, American Colonial Wealth: Documents and Methods (New York, 1977), vol. 1, p. 235. Sarah Frazier, "A Reminiscence, West Chester, September 11, 1840," Pennsylvania Magazine of History and Biography, vol. 46, no. 1 (1922), p. 45.

17. On bed-curtain fabric, see Leslie, House Book, p. 307. "Clean appearance": J[ohn] C[laudius] Loudon, An Encyclopaedia of Cottage, Farm, and Villa Architecture and Furniture (1833; London, 1853), p. 337. Willich, Domestic Encyclopedia, vol. 1, p. 174.

18. Mary Guion diary, 21 April 1803, NYHS-MC. Beecher, Treatise, p. 372. Massachusetts girl: [Mrs. A. M. Richards], Memories of a Grandmother (Boston, 1854), p. 43.

19. On the concern over bed curtains, see T[homas] Webster and Mrs. [William] Parkes, The American Family Encyclopedia of Useful Knowledge (New York, 1856), p. 43; and Parkes, Domestic Duties, p. 233. On the ideal chamber, see Mrs. Sarah J. Hale, Mrs. Hale's Cook Book (Philadelphia, 1857), p. 494. "All may endeavour": Parkes, ibid. Beecher, Treatise, pp. 358–59. Mrs. M. L. Scott, The Practical Housekeeper (Toledo, Ohio, 1855), pp. 202–3. A[lexander] J[ackson] Downing, The Architecture of Country Houses (1850; New York, 1969), p. 431. Amelia M. Murray, Letters from the United States, Cuba and Canada (1856; New York, 1969), p. 268. On the trend to reduce or eliminate bed curtains, see Cooke et al., Upholstery, p. 176.

20. Leslie, House Book, p. 307. Beecher, Treatise, p. 361. George Washington, The Writings of George Washington, ed. John C. Fitzpatrick (Washington, D.C., 1931), vol. 2, p. 138. Ibid., pp. 319–20. Franklin, Papers, vol. 7 (New Haven, 1963), p. 382.

21. Anne Eliza Clark Kane to Lydia Bowen Clark, 17 July 1812, JICP. Elizabeth Wirt to William Wirt, 30 April 1820, WWP. "Grandmother": see "Passing of the Spare Chamber," pp. 140–41.

22. Parkes, Domestic Duties, p. 293. Ann Maury, quoted in Anne Fontaine Maury, ed., Intimate Virginiana: A Century of Maury Travels by Land and Sea (Richmond, Va., 1941), p. 206. Minerva Rodgers to Commodore John Rodgers, 14 October 1807, 21 July 1810, RFC. Anne Eliza Clark Kane to Lydia Bowen Clark, New Year's Day 1813, JICP.

23. Loudon, Encyclopaedia, pp. 355, 1087. William Wirt to Elizabeth Wirt, 10 May 1805, WWP. Hext McCall Perry, ed., Letters of My Father to My Mother (Philadelphia, 1889), p. 110.

24. Fanny Appleton Longfellow, Mrs. Longfellow: Selected Letters and Journals . . . (1817–1861), ed. Edward Wagenknecht (New York, 1956), p. 139. Sarah Logan Fisher diary, 30 December 1787, 17 February 1788, HSP. King, When I Lived in Salem, p. 169.

25. Rebecca Rawle Shoemaker to Anna Rawle, 4 June 1783, "Letters and Diaries of a Loyalist Family of Philadelphia. Written between the Years 1780 and 1786," typewritten transcript, HSP. William Hall estate inventory, 15 November 1771, docket book 71, SCPC. William Banford estate inventory, 26 June 1767, CCSCI (1763–71). "Not to be stumbled over": [Eliza Ware Farrar], The Young Lady's Friend (Boston, 1837), p. 130. Benjamin Godin estate inventory, 21 June 1749, CCSCI (1748–56). Hartley, Ladies' Book, p. 61. Leslie, House Book, p. 296. Thomas Tilestone estate inventory, 17 October 1794, docket book 93, SCPC.

26. Anne Eliza Clark Kane to Lydia Bowen Clark, 4 November 1812, JICP. Elizabeth Wirt to William Wirt, 7 [or 8] January 1816, WWP. Emery, Reminiscences, p. 84. Ribton Hutchison estate inventory, 17 October 1753, CCSCI (1748–56). Loudon, Encyclopaedia, p. 322. On the use of easy chairs, see also, Morrison H. Heckscher, In Quest of Comfort (Metropolitan Museum of Art, New York, 1971).

27. [Grant], Memoirs, vol. 2, p. 145. C[aroline] G[ilman] C[urtis], ed., The Cary Letters (Cambridge, Mass., 1891), p. 200. Susan I. Lesley, Recollections of My Mother, Mrs. Anne Jean Lyman of Northampton (1886; Boston, 1899), p. 192. Abigail Adams, New Letters of Abigail Adams 1788–1801, ed. Stewart Mitchell (Boston, 1947), p. 78. Robert Kerr, The Gentleman's House, 2d ed. (London, 1865), p. 131.

28. [Taylor], Rhymes, p. 14. Eliza S. M. Quincy, Memoir of the Life of Eliza S. M. Quincy (Boston, 1861), p. 52. Samuel Canby Rumford, "Life along the Brandywine between 1880–1895," typewritten transcript of a reminiscence, WL-JD. Charles White, A Treatise on the Management of Pregnant and Lying in Women (Worcester, 1793), p. 101.

29. Maria Silliman Church to Faith Silliman, 18 March 1834, MSCP. Sarah Logan Fisher diary, 25 December 1776; 17 August, 3 September 1779; 17, 21 August 1781; 25, 27, 28, 29 August 1783; 25 April 1786. Elizabeth DeHart Bleecker McDonald diary, 20 July, 8 September 1801, NYPL. Elizabeth Wirt to Catharine Gamble, 25 May 1818, WWP.

30. Nathaniel Hawthorne, The American Notebooks by Nathaniel Hawthorne, ed. Randall Stewart (New Haven, 1932), p. 150. Mary Cadwalader Jones, Lantern Slides (Boston, 1937), p.

18. John Billings estate inventory, April 1763, docket book 62, SCPC.

31. Beecher, Treatise, p. 360. John Coles estate inventory, 1 September 1758, CCSCI (1756–63). David Ochterlong estate inventory, 25 April 1766, docket book 65, SCPC.

32. William Young estate inventory, 9 July 1750, docket book 43, SCPC. Ephraim Chambers, Cyclopaedia; or, An Universal Dictionary of Arts and Sciences (London, 1783). Frazier, "Reminiscence," p. 46. Leslie, House Book, p. 301.

33. James Smyth estate inventory, 31 December 1764, CCSCI (1763–71). Faith Silliman to Harriet Silliman, 20 February 1837, FSHP. On the fabrics used for bureau scarves, see Leslie, House Book, p. 299. Workwoman's Guide, p. 182. Boston Gazette, quoted in George Francis Dow, The Arts and Crafts in New England 1704–1775 (Topsfield, Mass., 1927), p. 170. Andrew Oliver's table and oilcloth: Jones, American Colonial Wealth, vol. 2, p. 967.

34. On the continued use of skirted dressing tables, see Martha Gandy Fales, ed., The Curtain-Maker's Handbook (New York, 1979). Emery, Reminiscences, p. 32. Mary Palmer Tyler, Grandmother Tyler's Book, ed. Frederick Tupper and Helen Tyler Brown (New York, 1925), p. 305. Mrs. Anne Royall, The Black Book, vol. 1 (Washington, D.C., 1828), pp. 268–69.

35. Leslie, House Book, p. 300.

36. Leslie, House Book, p. 300. Chinn girls: Eliza Ripley, Social Life in Old New Orleans (New York, 1912), p. 36. James Postell estate inventory, 16 August 1773, CCSCI (1771–76).

37. Willich, Domestic Encyclopedia, vol. 1, p. 160. [Farrar], Young Lady's Friend, pp. 160, 165–66. Two-fold screens: Workwoman's Guide, p. 208. Beecher, Treatise, pp. 360–61.

38. On dressing-room furnishings, see Loudon, Encyclopaedia, p. 802. Peter Delancey estate inventory, [1771], CCSCI (1771–76).

39. Samuel Kempton, quoted in Rita Susswein Gottesman, The Arts and Crafts in New York, 1777–1799 (New York, 1954), pp. 229–30. Catherine Chew inventory, 1 July 1831, CFP. Anne Eliza Clark to John Innes Clark, 20 August 1791, JICP. "Tub, douche, shower": Henry Ward Beecher, Eyes and Ears (Boston, 1863), p. 2. Isabella Lucy (Bird) Bishop, The Englishwoman in America (London, 1856), p. 355.

40. Sidney George Fisher, A Philadelphia Perspective: The Diary of Sidney George Fisher Covering the Years 1834–1871, ed. Nicholas B. Wainwright (Philadelphia, 1967), pp. 240–41. Scott, Practical Housekeeper, p. 208. The "formidable operation" is described in Facts for the People, or Things Worth Knowing (Philadelphia, 1851), pp. 73–74, 46. Kempton, quoted in Gottesman, Arts and Crafts, 1777–1799, p. 230.

[Farrar], *Young Lady's Friend*, p. 166. Leslie, *House Book*, p. 178. Polly Bennett, quoted in Edgar deN. Mayhew and Minor Myers, Jr., *A Documentary History of American Interiors* (New York, 1980), p. 129.

41. Lawrence Shaw Mayo, ed., *America of Yesterday as Reflected in the Journal of John Davis Long* (Boston, 1923), p. 35. Frederick Law Olmsted, *The Cotton Kingdom*, ed. Arthur M. Schlesinger (New York, 1953), p. 145.

42. Louis Philippe, *Diary of My Travels in America, Louis-Philippe, King of France, 1830–1848*, trans. Stephen Becker (New York, 1977), pp. 60–61. Charles Carroll of Carrollton letterbook, 4 November 1796, 9 February 1784, 8 January 1775, Arents Collections, New York Public Library; Astor, Lenox and Tilden Foundations. Thomas Sheraton, *The Cabinet-Maker and Upholsterer's Drawing-Book* (1793; New York, 1972), p. 92.

43. On the fitted roundabout, see Brock Jobe and Myrna Kaye, *New England Furniture: The Colonial Era* (Boston, 1984), p. 361. Sheraton, *Cabinet-Maker*, p. 92.

44. Della Lutes, *Home Grown* (Boston, 1937), p. 95.

45. Bellamy Partridge, *Big Family* (New York, 1941), pp. 201–2. King, *When I Lived in Salem*, p. 185.

46. King, *When I Lived in Salem*, p. 119. Loudon, *Encyclopaedia*, p. 801. Downing, *Architecture of Country Houses*, p. 404. "Are not health, and cleanliness": Henry W. Cleaveland et al., *The Requirements of American Village Homes* (New York, 1856), p. 124. Elizabeth Wirt to William Wirt, 22, 23 September 1818, WWP.

47. "Chambers all without carpets": Goodrich, *Recollections*, p. 79. Ellen H. Rollins [E. H. Arr, pseud.], *New England Bygones* (Philadelphia, 1880), p. 66. Maria Silliman Church to Harriet Silliman, 3 November 1833; Church to Faith Silliman, 8 October 1835, MSCP.

48. "Sleep was a luxury": Goodrich, *Recollections*, p. 80. Ruth Huntington Sessions, *Sixty-Odd: A Personal History* (Brattleboro, Vt., 1936), pp. 25–26.

CHAPTER SIX

1. [Eliza Leslie], *The House Book* (Philadelphia, 1840), p. 4.

2. [John Bill], "Extracts from the Journal of Philo-Jocundus 1827 [and 1828]," typewritten transcript, NYHS-MC. [Janet Schaw], *Journal of a Lady of Quality*, ed. Evangeline Walker Andrews (New Haven, 1921), pp. 146–47. Levi Hutchins, *The Autobiography of Levi Hutchins: with a Preface, Notes and Addenda, by His Youngest Son [Samuel Hutchins]* (Cambridge, Mass., 1865), p. 67. Ulysses Hedrick, *Land of*

the Crooked Tree (New York, 1948), p. 189.

3. Catharine E. Beecher and Harriet Beecher Stowe, *The American Woman's Home* (1869; Hartford, 1975), pp. 365–66. Anne Gertrude Sneller, *A Vanished World* (Syracuse, N.Y., 1964), p. 151. Louisa Jane Trumbull diary, 1 November 1836, Trumbull Family Papers, AAS. Stephen Walkley, quoted in David Nelson Beach, *Beach Family Reminiscences and Annals* (Meriden, Conn., 1931), p. 210. Mary Guion diary, 26 January 1801, NYHS-MC. Maria Silliman Church to Faith Silliman, 10 January 1834, MSCP. Thomas Eliot Andrews, ed., "The Diary of Elizabeth (Porter) Phelps," *The New England Historical and Genealogical Register*, January 1966, p. 62. On mutton tallow, see George G. Channing, *Early Recollections of Newport, R.I., from the Year 1793 to 1811* (Newport, R.I., and Boston, 1868), p. 268. Maria Silliman Church to Faith Silliman, 14 February 1834, MSCP. On tallow candles, see William O'Dea, *Social History of Lighting* (London, 1958), pp. 3, 5, 6. Maria Foster Brown, quoted in Harriet Connor Brown, *Grandmother Brown's Hundred Years, 1827–1927* (Boston, 1929), p. 124. A[nthony] F. M. Willich, *The Domestic Encyclopedia; or, A Dictionary of Facts and Useful Knowledge* (1802; 2d American ed., Philadelphia, 1821), vol. 1, p. 373. Robert Beverley, *The History and Present State of Virginia*, ed. Louis B. Wright (1705; Chapel Hill, N.C., 1947), pp. 137–38. [Schaw], *Journal*, p. 203.

4. John Jay Janney, *John Jay Janney's Virginia*, ed. Werner L. Janney and Asa Moore Janney (McLean, Va., 1978), p. 86. William T. Davis, *Plymouth Memories of an Octogenarian* (Plymouth, Mass., 1906), p. 42. On Boston chandlers Edward Langdon and James Clemens, see "Trades and Occupations in 18th Century New England; Gleanings from Boston Newspapers," *Old-Time New England*, vol. 18, no. 1 (July 1927), pp. 36–37.

5. Anne Newport Royall, *Letters from Alabama, 1817–1822*, intro. and notes by Lucille Griffith (1830; University, Ala., 1969), p. 169. Elisabeth Koren, *The Diary of Elisabeth Koren 1853–1855*, ed. David T. Nelson (New York, 1979), p. 233.

6. Martha Ogle Forman, *Plantation Life at Rose Hill*, ed. W. Emerson Wilson (Wilmington, Del., 1976), pp. 216, 261. The quantity of candles in Humphrey Devereaux's attic is mentioned in Alice Hanson Jones, *American Colonial Wealth: Documents and Methods* (New York, 1977), vol. 2, p. 653. Robert C. Alberts, *The Golden Voyage: The Life and Times of William Bingham 1752–1804* (Boston, 1969), p. 471. On Mrs. Jaques, see Sarah Anna Emery, *Reminiscences of a Nonagenarian* (1879; Bowie, Md., and Hampton, N.H., 1978), p. 35.

7. On the advantages of candlelight, see T[homas] Webster and Mrs. [William] Parkes,

The American Family Encyclopedia of Useful Knowledge (New York, 1856), p. 165. J[ohn] C[laudius] Loudon, *An Encyclopaedia of Cottage, Farm, and Villa Architecture and Furniture* (1833; London, 1853), p. 797.

8. James Silk Buckingham, quoted in Mills Lane, ed., *The Rambler in Georgia* (Savannah, 1973), p. 174. Elizabeth Oswald Chew cashbook, 1814–19, CFP. Catharine Gansevoort, receipt, 3 December 1817, Gansevoort-Lansing Family Papers, NYPL.

9. George J. Cummings, "A Leaf from the Life of a Farmer's Boy Ninety Years Ago," *Old-Time New England*, vol. 19, no. 3 (January 1929), p. 102. Thomas Colley Grattan, *Civilized America*, 2d ed. (London, 1859), vol. 1, p. 106. Maria Silliman Church to the Silliman family, 28 May 1849, MSCP.

10. Webster and Parkes, *American Family Encyclopedia*, p. 202. Nicholas B. Wainwright, ed., "The Diary of Samuel Breck, 1839–1840," *Pennsylvania Magazine of History and Biography*, vol. 103, no. 4 (October 1979), p. 508. Edgar Allan Poe, "Philosophy of Furniture," quoted in *The Magazine Antiques*, August 1977, p. 285. Alexsandr Borisovich Lakier, *A Russian Looks at America: The Journey of Alexsandr Borisovich Lakier in 1857*, ed. Arnold Schrier and Joyce Story (Chicago, 1979), p. 152. Samuel Eliot Morison, *One Boy's Boston 1887–1901* (Cambridge, Mass., 1962), p. 19. Caroline A. Dustan diary, NYPL. "Diary and Letters of George M. Dallas, December 4, 1848–March 6, 1849," *Pennsylvania Magazine of History and Biography*, vol. 73, no. 4 (October 1949), p. 491. Philip Hone, *The Diary of Philip Hone 1828–1851*, ed. Allan Nevins (New York, 1936), p. 233.

11. Mrs. Frances A. ("Faith") Breckenridge, *Recollections of a New England Town* (Meriden, Conn., 1899), p. 142. Robert Roberts, *The House Servant's Directory* (1827; Waltham, Mass., 1977), pp. 27–28, 21. Harriet Manigault, *Diary . . . 1813–1816*, ed. Virginia and James S. Armentrout, Jr. (Rockland, Maine, 1976), p. 7. Mrs. Basil Hall, *The Aristocratic Journey . . . 1827–1828*, ed. Una Pope-Hennessy (New York, 1931), pp. 173–74. Franklin Butler Van Valkenburgh, *Grandpapa's Letter to His Children*, comp. and ed. Charles H. Vilas (1899; privately printed, 1978), p. 68. Catharine E. Beecher, *A Treatise on Domestic Economy* (1841; New York, 1977), p. 304.

12. Hedrick, *Land of the Crooked Tree*, p. 188. Sneller, *A Vanished World*, p. 151.

13. Mary Cooper, *Diary . . . 1768–1773*, ed. Field Horne (Oyster Bay, N.Y., 1981), p. 36. Peggy Rawle diary, "Letters and Diaries of a Loyalist Family of Philadelphia. Written between the Years 1780 and 1786," typewritten transcript, HSP. Elizabeth Drinker, *Extracts from the Journal of Elizabeth Drinker, from 1759 to 1807 A.D.*, ed. Henry D. Biddle (Phila-

delphia, 1889), p. 396. Laura Wirt to William Wirt, 20 November 1818, WWP. Frederick Law Olmsted, *The Cotton Kingdom*, ed. Arthur M. Schlesinger (New York, 1953), p. 146. Daniel Drake, *Daniel Drake, Pioneer Life in Kentucky, 1785–1800*, ed. Emmet Field Horine (New York, 1948), p. 95.

14. Emily Barnes, *Narratives, Traditions, and Personal Reminiscences* (Boston, 1888), p. 61. Virginia Randolph Trist, quoted in Sarah N. Randolph, *The Domestic Life of Thomas Jefferson*, 3d ed. (Charlottesville, Va., 1947), p. 297.

15. Breckenridge, *Recollections of a New England Town*, p. 142. Sarah Ridg diary, typewritten transcript, entry in August 1809, LC-MD. Leslie, *House Book*, p. 158. Caroline Cowles Richards, *Village Life in America, 1852–1872*, ed. Margaret E. Sangster (1908; Williamstown, Mass., 1975), p. 84.

16. Channing, *Early Recollections*, pp. 267–68. Nathalie Robinson Boyer, *A Virginia Gentleman and His Family* (Philadelphia, 1939), p. 185. Drinker, *Journal*, p. 86. Henry A. Shute, *The Real Diary of a Real Boy* (Boston, 1903), p. 84.

17. John Greenleaf Whittier's couplet is from "Snow-Bound," in Wallace Brockway and Bart K. Winer, eds., *Homespun America* (New York, 1958), p. 166. William Fletcher King, *Reminiscences* (New York, 1915), p. 46.

18. Lucy Clark Allen, quoted in Allen children, *Memorial of Joseph and Lucy Clark Allen* (Boston, 1891), p. 39. Eliza S. M. Quincy, *Memoir of the Life of Eliza S. M. Quincy* (Boston, 1861), p. 89. Ebenezer Storer estate inventory, 16 March 1807, docket book 105, SCPC. Royall Tyler, "The Bad Boy," quoted in *The Magazine Antiques*, May 1971, p. 688. Royall Tyler, Sr., estate inventory, 20 December 1771, docket book 71, SCPC.

19. Roberts, *House Servant's Directory*, p. 221. [Frances Harriet Whipple McDougall], *The Housekeeper's Book* (Philadelphia, 1837), p. 187. "Sattin Painting" and satin paper: Rodris Roth, "Interior Decoration of City Houses in Baltimore: The Federal Period," in *Winterthur Portfolio 5*, ed. Richard K. Doud (Charlottesville, Va., 1969), p. 68; and Catherine Lynn, *Wallpaper in America* (New York, 1980), pp. 260–61. John Mifflin, quoted in Nadine Charlotte Luporini, "Lansdowne: A Cultural Document of Its Time," master's thesis (University of Delaware, 1967), p. 56. Orson Squire Fowler, *A Home for All* (New York, 1848), pp. 94–95. Rainbow wallpapers: Lynn, *Wallpaper in America*, pp. 274–75. Louisa Crowninshield Bacon, *Reminiscences* ([Salem, Mass.], 1922), p. 42.

20. Maria Silliman Church to Henrietta Silliman, 28 September 1840, MSCP. Mrs. George Fry, quoted in *The Magazine Antiques*, September 1977, p. 522. "Silver Grounds": Alfred Coxe Prime, *The Arts and Crafts in Phila-

delphia, Maryland and South Carolina 1786–1800* (1932; New York, 1969), p. 285. "Gold, Silver and Cloth Papers": Richard C. Nylander, Elizabeth Redmond, and Penny J. Sander, eds., *Wallpaper in New England* (Boston, 1986), p. 21. "Frosted, spangled and velvet papers": see "Early Paper-Hangings in Boston," *Old-Time New England*, vol. 12, no. 3 (January 1922), p. 117. "Tinsel'd" floor cloths: Roth, "Interior Decoration," p. 44. Sidney George Fisher, *A Philadelphia Perspective: The Diary of Sidney George Fisher Covering the Years 1834–1871*, ed. Nicholas B. Wainwright (Philadelphia, 1967), p. 116.

21. Eliza Bowen Ward to Mary Bowen, 5 May 1791, JICP. Charlotte Chambers to Mrs. James Chambers, 23 February 1795, quoted in *Pennsylvania Magazine of History and Biography*, vol. 20, no. 4 (1896), p. 500. Letter written by an unidentified Pennsylvania woman, 17 November 1810, quoted in *Pennsylvania Magazine of History and Biography*, vol. 22, no. 3 (1898), p. 378.

22. Mrs. William Parkes, *Domestic Duties*, 3d American ed. (New York, 1829), p. 82. Hall, *Aristocratic Journey*, p. 137.

23. Elijah Hunt Mills, quoted in *Proceedings of the Massachusetts Historical Society*, vol. 19 (Boston, 1882), p. 26. Letitia Burwell, *A Girl's Life in Virginia before the War* (New York, 1895), pp. 143–44. Julia Ward Howe, *Reminiscences, 1819–1899* (Boston, 1900), p. 29. "Mrs. B. I. Cohen's Fancy Dress Party," *Maryland Historical Magazine*, vol. 14, no. 4 (December 1919), p. 349. Miss [Eliza] Leslie, *Pencil Sketches; or, Outlines of Character and Manners*, (Philadelphia, 1854), p. 225. Roberts, *House Servant's Directory*, p. 28.

24. Eliza Quincy, quoted in M. A. De-Wolfe Howe, ed., *The Articulate Sisters* (Cambridge, Mass., 1946), pp. 33–34.

CHAPTER SEVEN

1. Emily Dickinson, *Letters of Emily Dickinson*, ed. Mabel Loomis Todd (Boston, 1894), vol. 1, p. 49. Maria Silliman Church to Faith Silliman, 22 November 1831, MSCP. Caroline Howard Gilman [Clarissa Packard, pseud.], *Recollections of a Housekeeper* (New York, 1834), p. 18. "Prickly art": Dickinson, ibid., vol. 2, p. 298. Maria Silliman Church to Faith Silliman, 21 June 1833, MSCP.

2. Dickinson, *Letters*, vol. 1, p. 176.

3. Maria Silliman Church to Harriet Silliman, 27 September 1837, MSCP. Esther Edwards Burr, *Journal . . . 1754–1757*, ed. Carol F. Karlsen and Laurie Crumpacker (New Haven, 1984), p. 165. Sarah Logan Fisher diary, 20 February, [undated] March 1786, HSP. Martha Ogle Forman, *Plantation Life at Rose Hill*, ed. W. Emerson Wilson (Wilmington, Del., 1976),

p. 197. Ellen Birdseye Wheaton, *Diary*, ed. Donald Gordon (Boston, 1923), p. 14. Harriet Silliman to Faith Wadsworth, 4 November 1828, WFP.

4. "Travels in the United States of America in the Years 1821, 1822, 1823 to 1824 . . . by a Scotsman," NYHS-MC. Susan Fenimore Cooper, *Rural Hours* (1850; Syracuse, N.Y., 1968), p. 108. Henry Wadsworth Longfellow, "Evangeline," in *Favorite Poems of Henry Wadsworth Longfellow* (Garden City, N.Y., 1947), p. 328. Mary Walkley Beach, quoted in David Nelson Beach, *Beach Family Reminiscences and Annals* (Meriden, Conn., 1931), p. 195.

5. Anna Bowen Mitchell to Lydia Bowen Clark, 18 May 1793, JICP. Forman, *Plantation Life*, p. 318. Musical washing machine: Rita Susswein Gottesman, *The Arts and Crafts in New York, 1777–1799* (New York, 1954), p. 377. "Diary of James Parker of Shirley, Massachusetts," transcribed by Mrs. Ethel Stanwood Bolton, *The New England Historical and Genealogical Register*, January 1915, p. 15. Mrs. Frances A. ("Faith") Breckenridge, *Recollections of a New England Town* (Meriden, Conn., 1899), p. 140.

6. Mrs. M. L. Scott, *The Practical Housekeeper* (Toledo, Ohio, 1855), p. 202. New York farmer, quoted in "Travels, by a Scotsman." Thomas Chaplin, quoted in Theodore Rosengarten, *Tombee: Portrait of a Cotton Planter, with the Plantation Journal of Thomas B. Chaplin (1822–1890)* (New York, 1986), p. 355. John Harrower, *The Journal of John Harrower, an Indentured Servant in the Colony of Virginia 1773–1776*, ed. Edward Miles Riley (Williamsburg, Va., 1963), p. 56. Caroline A. Dustan diary, 12 December 1857, NYPL. Maria Silliman Church to Harriet and Faith Silliman, 4 September 1833, MSCP. Elizabeth Drinker, *Extracts from the Journal of Elizabeth Drinker, from 1759 to 1807 A.D.*, ed. Henry D. Biddle (Philadelphia, 1889), p. 231. Sally Cary, quoted in Wilson Miles Cary, *Sally Cary, a Long Hidden Romance of Washington's Life* (New York, 1916), p. 60.

7. Thomas Eliot Andrews, ed., "The Diary of Elizabeth (Porter) Phelps," *The New England Historical and Genealogical Register*, January 1966, p. 62 (entry in November 1790). Sarah Logan Fisher diary, January 1789. Humphrey Devereaux, quoted in Alice Hanson Jones, *American Colonial Wealth: Documents and Methods* (New York, 1977), vol. 2, p. 653. On care of clotheslines, see Mrs. William Parkes, *Domestic Duties*, 3d American ed. (New York, 1829), p. 142; and Miss [Eliza] Leslie, *The House Book* (Philadelphia, 1840), p. 9. Henry Wansey, *Henry Wansey and His American Journal, 1794*, ed. David John Jeremy (Philadelphia, 1970), p. 56. Harriet Martineau, *Retrospect of Western Travel*, ed. Joseph J. Kwiat

(1838; New York, 1968), vol. 1, p. 37. William Tallack, *Friendly Sketches in America* (London, 1861), p. 85. Connecticut chap: James M. Bailey, *The Danbury Boom!* (Boston, 1880), p. 185. Scott, *Practical Housekeeper*, pp. 210, 214. Sarah Trecothick estate inventory, 8 March 1749, docket book 43, SCPC. Leslie, ibid., p. 27. Anne Gertrude Sneller, *A Vanished World* (Syracuse, N.Y., 1964), p. 155.

8. Leslie, *House Book*, p. 25. Catherine Henshaw, quoted in Catherine Fennelly, *Textiles in New England, 1790–1840* (Sturbridge, Mass., 1961), p. 11. John Jay Janney, *John Jay Janney's Virginia*, ed. Werner L. Janney and Asa Moore Janney (McLean, Va., 1978), p. 101. William Wirt to Elizabeth Wirt, 28 June 1803, WWP.

9. Prince de Broglie, quoted in *Pennsylvania Magazine of History and Biography*, vol. 2, no. 2 (1878), p. 166. Mary Vial Holyoke, quoted in George Francis Dow, ed., *The Holyoke Diaries, 1709–1856* (Salem, Mass., 1911), pp. 50, 67, 78, 79. Harriet P. Bradley diary, 2 October 1819, OSV. On the specifics of the cleaning round, see *The Kitchen Directory and American Housewife* (New York, 1844), p. 132; Robert Roberts, *The House Servant's Directory* (1827; Waltham, Mass., 1977), pp. 86–89; *The Domestic's Companion* (New York, 1834), p. 11; and Mrs. Sarah J. Hale, *Mrs. Hale's Cook Book* (Philadelphia, [1857]), p. 493.

10. On the housewife's own tasks, see Isabella Beeton, *Mrs. Beeton's Book of Household Management* (1861; London, 1982), p. 990. Maria Silliman Church to Harriet Silliman and Faith Silliman Hubbard, 15 May 1843, MSCP. Alicia McBlair Lloyd to Edward Lloyd, 3 October 1836, Lloyd Papers, ms. 2001, Maryland Historical Society Library. "I have put my matting": Maria Silliman Church to Harriet Silliman, 2 November 1838, MSCP.

11. Mary Vial Holyoke, quoted in Dow, ed., *Holyoke Diaries*, p. 57. Forman, *Plantation Life*, p. 210. Caroline A. Dustan diary, 15 November 1856, 22 May 1857. "Diary of Mrs. William Thornton, 1800–1863," *Records of the Columbia Historical Society*, vol. 10, no. 1 (Washington, D.C., 1907), p. 181. Eleanor Putnam, *Old Salem*, ed. Arlo Bates (Boston, 1889), pp. 68–69. Southern housewife: Janney, *John Jay Janney's Virginia*, p. 93. Yankee girl: Mary A. Livermore, *The Story of My Life* (Hartford, 1899), p. 158.

12. Roberts, *House Servant's Directory*, p. 67. Daniel Johonnot estate inventory, 6 June 1750, docket book 44; Thomas Parker estate inventory, 2 July 1782, docket book 81; and Stephen Greenleaf estate inventory, 13 February 1795, docket book 93, SCPC. Sidney George Fisher, *A Philadelphia Perspective: The Diary of Sidney George Fisher Covering the Years 1834–1871*, ed. Nicholas B. Wainwright (Philadelphia, 1967), p. 297. Samuel Canby

Rumford, "Life Along the Brandywine between 1880–1895," typewritten transcript of a reminiscence, WL-JD. Harriet Beecher Stowe, *Oldtown Folks* (1869; reprinted in *Stowe: Three Novels*, ed. Kathryn Kish Sklar, New York, 1982), chapter 26, p. 1198.

13. Patsy Jefferson, quoted in Edwin Morris Betts and James Adam Bear, Jr., eds., *The Family Letters of Thomas Jefferson* (Charlottesville, Va., 1986), p. 68. Landon Carter, *The Diary of Colonel Landon Carter of Sabine Hall, 1752–1778*, ed. Jack P. Greene (Charlottesville, Va., 1965), vol. 1, p. 359. Mrs. Lydia Maria Child, *The American Frugal Housewife*, 12th ed. (1832; [Worthington, Ohio], 1980), p. 8. Patsy Jefferson, quoted in Betts and Bear, eds., ibid., p. 68. Caroline A. Dustan diary, 13 May 1861. Maria Silliman Church to Harriet Silliman, 4 November 1831; and Church to Henrietta Silliman, 26 January 1840, MSCP. Ruth Huntington Sessions, *Sixty-Odd: A Personal History* (Brattleboro, Vt., 1936), pp. 21–22. Mrs. Basil Hall, *The Aristocratic Journey . . . 1827–1828*, ed. Una Pope-Hennessy (New York, 1931), p. 230. Eliza Ripley, *Social Life in Old New Orleans* (New York, 1912), p. 31.

14. Alice Colden Wadsworth, "A Sketch of my Fathers and Mothers family with a short record of my Parents history and my own," 1819, NYPL. Abigail Adams, *New Letters of Abigail Adams 1788–1801*, ed. Stewart Mitchell (Boston, 1947), p. 52. Catherine Chew inventory, 1 July 1851, CFP. [Eliza Ware Farrar], *The Young Lady's Friend* (1837; Boston, 1859), p. 53. Forman, *Plantation Life*, p. 69.

15. *The Workwoman's Guide* (1838; Guilford, Conn., 1986), p. 181. On the stock of household sheets and their care, see Scott, *Practical Housekeeper*, p. 209. Elizabeth E[llicott] Lea, *Domestic Cookery* (1845; facsimile of the 1853 edition, as *A Quaker Woman's Cookbook*, ed. William Woys Weaver, Philadelphia, 1982), p. 208. *Workwoman's Guide*, p. 187. *Columbian Herald*, quoted in Alfred Coxe Prime, *The Arts and Crafts in Philadelphia, Maryland and South Carolina 1786–1800* (1932; New York, 1969), p. 137. Anne Eliza Clark Kane to Lydia Bowen Clark, 6 December 1811, JICP. Bedlinen marks: Catharine E. Beecher, *A Treatise on Domestic Economy* (1841; New York, 1977), p. 363; and Catharine E. Beecher and Harriet Beecher Stowe, *The American Woman's Home* (1869; Hartford, 1975), p. 370.

16. Marbleized paper: Christopher Gilbert, *The Life and Works of Thomas Chippendale* (New York, 1978), vol. 1, pp. 138, 184, etc. Advertisements for paper, quoted in George Francis Dow, *The Arts and Crafts in New England 1704–1775* (Topsfield, Mass., 1927), p. 29. George Bright's bill: Brock Jobe and Myrna Kaye, *New England Furniture: The Colonial Era* (Boston, 1984), pp. 143–45. Empty hogshead: *Facts for the People, or Things Worth*

Knowing (Philadelphia, 1851), p. 51. Joshua Brookes journal 1798–1803, typewritten transcript, NYHS-MC. Captain Whann, quoted in Emilie Cowell, *The Cowells in America: Being the Diary of Mrs. Sam Cowell during Her Husband's Concert Tour in the Years 1860–1861*, ed. M. Willson Disher (London, 1934), p. 69. John Innes Clark inventory, 1808, JICP. John C. Howard estate inventory, 27 May 1811, docket book 109, SCPC.

17. Adams, *New Letters*, p. 218. Elizabeth Wirt to William Wirt, 8 November 1812, WWP. Caroline A. Dustan diary, 25 August 1864. Anne Eliza Clark Kane to Lydia Bowen Clark, 6 December, 11 October 1811, JICP.

18. An interesting treatment of the whole subject of this paragraph is Richard L. and Claudia L. Bushman, "The Early History of Cleanliness in America," *The Journal of American History*, vol. 74, no. 4 (March 1988), pp. 1213–38. [Mrs. A. M. Richards], *Memories of a Grandmother* (Boston, 1854), p. 33. "Without cleanliness": Scott, *Practical Housekeeper*, p. 203.

19. Maria Silliman Church to Harriet Silliman, 10 April 1842, MSCP. Phebe Ann Beach Lyman to Mary M[atilda] Beach, 26 October 1839, BFP. [Farrar], *Young Lady's Friend*, p. 46. Thomas Jefferson, quoted in Sarah N. Randolph, *The Domestic Life of Thomas Jefferson*, 3d ed. (Charlottesville, Va., 1947), pp. 45–46. John Adams, *Diary and Autobiography of John Adams*, ed. L. H. Butterfield, Leonard C. Faber, and Wendell D. Garrett (Cambridge, Mass., 1961), vol. 1, pp. 193–94. [Jane Taylor], *Rhymes for the Nursery* (Boston, [1837]), p. 107. Enos Hitchcock, *The Farmer's Friend; or, The History of Mr. Charles Worthy* (Boston, 1793), pp. 88–89. Concerned father: fragment of a letter, c. 1780–90, L-PL.

20. Johannes Still, quoted in Robert H. Billigmeier and Fred Altschuler Picard, eds., *The Old Land and the New: The Journals of Two Swiss Families in America in the 1820s* (Minneapolis, 1965), p. 127. Louis Auguste Félix, baron de Beaujour, *Sketch of the United States of North America at the Commencement of the Nineteenth Century, from 1800 to 1810* (London, 1814), p. 150. Louis de Robertnier, quoted in "Rhode Island in 1780," *Rhode Island Historical Society Collections*, vol. 16 (July 1923), p. 69. Caroline Trumbull's assistance: Louisa Jane Trumbull diary, 22 January 1832, Trumbull Family Papers, AAS. John Adams, quoted in Charles Francis Adams, ed., *Familiar Letters of John Adams and His Wife, Abigail Adams, during the Revolution, with a Memoir of Mrs. Adams* (Boston, 1875), p. 11. Mrs. Worthy's best room: Hitchcock, *Farmer's Friend*, p. 102.

21. François Alexandre Frédéric, duc de La Rochefoucauld-Liancourt, *Travels through the United States of North America in the Years 1795, 1796, and 1797* (London, 1799), vol. 2, p.

378. Robert Sutcliff, *Travels in Some Parts of North America in the Years 1804, 1805, and 1806* (Philadelphia, 1812), p. 44. Hall, *Aristocratic Journey*, p. 219. Mrs. Anne Royall, *The Black Book*, vol. 1 (Washington, D.C., 1828), p. 147. Letitia M. Burwell, *A Girl's Life in Virginia before the War* (New York, 1895), p. 43.

22. John Lambert, *Travels . . . in the Years 1806, 1807, and 1808*, 2d ed. (London, 1814), vol. 2, p. 323. Patrick Shirreff, *A Tour through North America* (Edinburgh, 1835), p. 40. Frances Wright, *Views of Society and Manners in America*, ed. Paul R. Baker (Cambridge, Mass., 1963), p. 47. Beaujour, *Sketch*, p. 148. Maria Silliman Church to Harriet Silliman, 2 July 1833, MSCP.

CHAPTER EIGHT

1. François Alexandre Frédéric, duc de La Rochefoucauld-Liancourt, *Travels through the United States of North America in the Years 1795, 1796, and 1797* (London, 1799), vol. 4, p. 552. Alexander Mackraby, quoted in *Pennsylvania Magazine of History and Biography*, vol. 11, no. 4 (1887), pp. 491, 492. The foreign officer is quoted in Ray W. Pettengill, *Letters from America 1776–1779* (Boston, 1924), pp. 230–31.

2. Bernhard Karl, duke of Saxe-Weimar Eisenach, *Travels through North America, during the Years 1825 and 1826* (Philadelphia, 1828), vol. 1, p. 35. Lady Emmeline Stuart Wortley, *Travels in the United States, etc., during 1849 and 1850* (New York, 1851), p. 36. Julian Ursyn Niemcewicz, *Under Their Vine and Fig Tree: Travels through America in 1797–1799, 1805*, trans. and ed. Metchie J. E. Budka (Elizabeth, N.J., 1965), p. 164. Tyrone Power, *Impressions of America during the Years 1833, 1834, and 1835* (1836; New York, 1971), p. 417. "Extracts from the Journal of Miss Sarah Eve, Written While Living near Philadelphia (Northern Liberties) 1772–1773," *Pennsylvania Magazine of History and Biography*, vol. 5, no. 1 (1881), p. 25.

3. Mrs. Basil Hall, *The Aristocratic Journey . . . 1827–1828*, ed. Una Pope-Hennessy (New York, 1931), p. 51. Saxe-Weimar Eisenach, *Travels*, vol. 2, p. 15. J. B. Dunlop journal 1810–11, NYHS-MC. Lieutenant Francis Hall, *Travels in Canada and the United States in 1816 and 1817* (Boston, 1818), p. 240. Frederick Law Olmsted, quoted in Thomas D. Clark, ed., *South Carolina: The Grand Tour 1780–1865* (Columbia, S.C., 1973), p. 265.

4. "Peremptory bandit": John P. Kennedy, *At Home and Abroad* (New York, 1872), p. 182. William Dunlap, *Diary of William Dunlap (1766–1839)* (New York, 1930), vol. 2, p. 367. Anne Eliza Clark to Lydia Bowen Clark, 2

January 1791, JICP. A. G. Roeber, ed., "A New England Woman's Perspective on Norfolk, Virginia, 1801–1802: Excerpts from the Diary of Ruth Henshaw Bascom," in *Proceedings of the American Antiquarian Society*, vol. 88, part 2 (Worcester, 1979), p. 287. "Extracts from Account and Letter Books of Dr. Charles Carroll, of Annapolis," *Maryland Historical Magazine*, vol. 24, no. 3 (September 1929), p. 257. Nicholas B. Wainwright, ed., "The Diary of Samuel Breck, 1834–1835, 1838," *Pennsylvania Magazine of History and Biography*, vol. 103, no. 3 (July 1979), p. 381. Rebecca Smith to Ann Ridgely, 13 September 1792, RFP. Anne Jean Lyman, quoted in Susan I. Lesley, *Recollections of My Mother, Mrs. Anne Jean Lyman of Northampton* (Boston, 1886), p. 53.

5. Maria Silliman Church to Mrs. Daniel Wadsworth, 22 January 1834, MSCP. Alice Izard to Margaret Izard Manigault, 24 November 1814, RIFP. William Wirt to Elizabeth Wirt, 6 January 1813, WWP. Invoice of goods, quoted in Frances Norton Mason, ed., *John Norton and Sons, Merchants of London and Virginia* (1937; Newton Abbott, England, 1968), p. 218. Miss [Eliza] Leslie, *The House Book* (Philadelphia, 1840), p. 322. Catharine E. Beecher, *A Treatise on Domestic Economy* (1841; New York, 1977), p. 347. Christopher Gore to Rufus King, 20 December 1816, quoted in *The Magazine Antiques*, December 1976, p. 1255. Ellen Randolph Coolidge, quoted in Edwin Morris Betts and James Adam Bear, Jr., eds., *The Family Letters of Thomas Jefferson* (Charlottesville, Va., 1986), p. 465. Carl Van Doren, ed., *The Letters of Benjamin Franklin and Jane Mecom* (Princeton, N.J., 1950), pp. 284–85. Abigail Adams, *New Letters of Abigail Adams 1788–1801*, ed. Stewart Mitchell (Boston, 1947), p. 33. La Rochefoucauld-Liancourt, *Travels*, vol. 2, p. 415.

6. Peter Clopper's advertisement, quoted in Rita Susswein Gottesman, *The Arts and Crafts in New York, 1726–1776* (New York, 1938), p. 123. Beecher, *Treatise*, p. 300. A[lexander] J[ackson] Downing, *The Architecture of Country Houses* (1850; New York, 1969), p. 127. Caroline A. Dustan diary, 22 October 1862, NYPL. James M. Bailey, *Life in Danbury* (Boston, 1873), p. 152. Denigrators of the hot-air furnace, see Thomas Colley Grattan, *Civilized America*, 2d ed. (London, 1859), vol. 1, p. 105; and Anthony Trollope, *North America*, ed. Donald Smalley and Bradford Allen Booth (New York, 1951), pp. 141, 178, 196. Samuel Eliot Morison, *One Boy's Boston 1887–1901* (Boston, 1962), p. 41.

7. Harriet Beecher Stowe, *Oldtown Folks* (1869; reprinted in *Stowe: Three Novels*, ed. Kathryn Kish Sklar, New York, 1982), chapter 23, p. 1148. Harriet Martineau, *Retrospect of Western Travel*, ed. Joseph J. Kwiat (1838; New York, 1968), vol. 2, p. 171. Complaints about

Carter's clock: Landon Carter, *The Diary of Colonel Landon Carter of Sabine Hall, 1752–1778*, ed. Jack P. Greene (Charlottesville, Va., 1965), vol. 2, pp. 968, 974, 991. Esther Edwards Burr, *Journal . . . 1754–1757*, ed. Carol F. Karlsen and Laurie Crumpacker (New Haven, 1984), p. 178. James Stuart, *Three Years in North America*, 2d ed. (Edinburgh, 1833), vol. 1, p. 311. Maria Silliman Church to Henrietta and Julia Silliman, 18 December 1835, MSCP. Faith Silliman to Harriet Silliman, 5 February 1836, MSCP. Mrs. William Thornton, "Diary of Mrs. William Thornton, 1800–1863," *Records of the Columbia Historical Society*, vol. 10, no. 1 (Washington, D.C., 1907), pp. 100–105. Caroline A. Dustan diary, 19 December 1856, 26 December 1857. "The wine was constantly frozen": Wilson Miles Cary, *Sally Cary, a Long Hidden Romance of Washington's Life* (New York, 1916), p. 80. Benjamin Pickman, *The Diary and Letters of Benjamin Pickman (1740–1819) of Salem, Massachusetts*, ed. George Francis Dow (Newport, R.I., 1928), p. 206. Margaret Holyoke, quoted in George Francis Dow, ed., *The Holyoke Diaries, 1709–1856* (Salem, Mass., 1911), p. 166. William Tudor, quoted in Fitz-Hugh Smith, Jr., "Some Old-Fashioned Winters in Boston," in *Proceedings of the Massachusetts Historical Society*, vol. 65 (Boston, 1940), p. 276.

8. Caroline Howard King, *When I Lived in Salem, 1822–1866* (Brattleboro, Vt., 1937), p. 190. Rebecca Shoemaker diary, "Letters and Diaries of a Loyalist Family of Philadelphia. Written between the Years 1780 and 1786," typewritten transcript, HSP. Mary Guion diary, 14 December 1801, NYHS-MC. [Anne Grant], *Memoirs of an American Lady* (London, 1808), vol. 1, p. 171. Fanny Appleton Longfellow, *Mrs. Longfellow: Selected Letters and Journals . . . (1817–1861)*, ed. Edward Wagenknecht (New York, 1956), p. 175. Emily Dickinson, *Letters of Emily Dickinson*, ed. Mabel Loomis Todd (Boston, 1894), vol. 1, pp. 98–99. William T. Davis, *Plymouth Memories of an Octogenarian* (Plymouth, Mass. 1906), p. 482.

9. [Eliza Ware Farrar], *The Young Lady's Friend* (Boston, 1837), p. 21. Ann White Smith to Miss Susan Palfry, 9 March 1790, L-PL. Stowe, *Oldtown Folks*, p. 1148. William Bentley, *The Diary of William Bentley, D.D.* (Gloucester, Mass., 1962), vol. 3, p. 492. Thomas Chaplin, quoted in Theodore Rosengarten, *Tombee: Portrait of a Cotton Planter, with the Plantation Journal of Thomas B. Chaplin (1822–1890)* (New York, 1986), p. 685. Faith Silliman Hubbard to Harriet Silliman, 27 January 1840, FSHP.

10. Charlotte Taylor, quoted in Nathalie Robinson Boyer, *A Virginia Gentleman and His Family* (Philadelphia, 1939), p. 31. Ralph Waldo Emerson, *Emerson in His Journals*, ed. Joel Porte (Cambridge, Mass., 1982), p. 136.

Benjamin Franklin, *The Papers of Benjamin Franklin*, ed. Leonard W. Labaree, vol. 2 (New Haven, 1960), p. 424. Leslie, *House Book*, p. 151. Anna Green Winslow, *Diary of Anna Green Winslow, a Boston School Girl of 1771*, ed. Alice Morse Earle (1894; Williamstown, Mass., 1974), p. 23. John Buttolph estate inventory, 10 May 1750, docket book 44, SCPC. John Hancock estate inventory, 28 January 1794, docket book 93, SCPC. Leslie, *House Book*, pp. 152–53.

11. J. Hall Pleasants, ed., "Letters of Molly and Hetty Tilghman, Eighteenth-Century Gossip of Two Maryland Girls," *Maryland Historical Magazine*, vol. 21, no. 1 (March 1926), p. 33. Anne Eliza Clark Kane to Lydia Bowen Clark, 24 December 1811, JICP.

12. Samuel Kelly, *Samuel Kelly, an Eighteenth-Century Seaman*, ed. Crosbie Garstin (New York, 1925), pp. 204–5. Benjamin Prat estate inventory, quoted in Abbott Lowell Cummings, *Rural Household Inventories . . . 1675–1775* (Boston, 1964), pp. 198, 200. Hans and Sylis Bergen estate inventory, 3 February 1726, INYC. "Travels in the United States of America in the Years 1821, 1822, 1823 to 1824 . . . by a Scotsman," NYHS-MC. S[amuel] G[riswold] Goodrich, *Recollections of a Lifetime* (New York, 1856), p. 134. Theodore Dwight to Abigail Dwight, 30–31 December 1819, DFP. Mrs. Samuel Harrison Smith, *The First Forty Years of Washington Society*, ed. Gaillard Hunt (New York, 1906), p. 136. Leslie, *House Book*, p. 321. Caroline A. Dustan diary, 7 September 1857. Alexander Anderson, "Diarium Commentarium Vitae Alex. Anderson," typewritten transcript of a journal, 1793–99, NYHS-MC (original manuscript: Rare Book and Manuscript Library, Columbia University).

13. "Diary of Col. William Bolling of Bolling Hall," *Virginia Magazine of History and Biography*, vol. 44, no. 1 (January 1936), p. 16; vol. 44, no. 4 (October 1936), p. 334.

14. "Your mother": Elizabeth Curtis, ed., *Letters and Journals: Judge William Edmond . . . Judge Holbrook Curtis . . . Judge William Edmond Curtis . . . William Edmond Curtis and Dr. Holbrook Curtis* (New York, 1926), p. 189. Deborah Norris Logan, quoted in Penelope Franklin, ed., *Private Pages: Diaries of American Women 1830s–1970s* (New York, 1986), p. 466. Dickinson, *Letters*, vol. 1, p. 171. King, *When I Lived in Salem*, pp. 118–19. Stephen Walkley, quoted in David Nelson Beach, *Beach Family Reminiscences and Annals* (Meriden, Conn., 1931), pp. 210–11. Harriet Beecher Stowe, *The Minister's Wooing* (1859; reprinted in *Stowe: Three Novels*, ed. Kathryn Kish Sklar, New York, 1982), chapter 34, p. 824.

15. Elizabeth Wonderly to Stewart Brown, 14 October 1862, Wonderly Family Papers, WL-JD. Leslie, *House Book*, p. 336. Benjamin Franklin Perry, quoted in Hext McCall Perry,

ed., *Letters of My Father to My Mother* (Philadelphia, 1889), p. 125.

16. Samuel Canby Rumford, "Life along the Brandywine between 1880–1895," typewritten transcript of a reminiscence, WL-JD. "An able arithmetician," "husband however beloved": Francis Hopkinson, *The Miscellaneous Essays and Occasional Writings of Francis Hopkinson, Esq.* (Philadelphia, 1792), vol. 2, pp. 151, 156. "Nothing in the countenance": James M. Bailey, *The Danbury Boom!* (Boston, 1880), p. 129. "What you must wear," "a morsel of dirt": Henry Ward Beecher, *Eyes and Ears* (Boston, 1862), pp. 171–73.

17. Burr, *Journal*, p. 149. Mary Guion diary, October 1803. Thomas Eliot Andrews, ed., "The Diary of Elizabeth (Porter) Phelps," *The New England Historical and Genealogical Register*, April 1965, p. 140. Elizabeth Oswald Chew cashbook, 1814–19, CFP.

18. Maria Silliman Church to Faith Silliman Hubbard, 21 November 1839, MSCP. Beecher, *Treatise*, p. 340. Martha Ogle Forman, *Plantation Life at Rose Hill*, ed. W. Emerson Wilson (Wilmington, Del., 1976), p. 35.

19. Anne Gertrude Sneller, *A Vanished World* (Syracuse, N.Y., 1964), pp. 42–43. *The Kitchen Directory and American Housewife* (New York, 1844), p. 130. Straw under the carpet was also recommended by Mrs. A. L. Webster, *The Improved Housewife; or, Book of Receipts*, 20th ed. (Hartford, 1854), p. 207. Catherine Elizabeth Havens, *Diary of a Little Girl in Old New York* (New York, 1919), pp. 34–35. Elizabeth E[llicott] Lea, *Domestic Cookery* (1845; Baltimore, 1859), p. 211. Mrs. M. L. Scott, *The Practical Housekeeper* (Toledo, Ohio, 1855), p. 205. Beecher, *Treatise*, pp. 339–40. Rumford, "Life along the Brandywine." Leslie, *House Book*, p. 175. Caroline A. Dustan diary. *The Workwoman's Guide* (1838; Guilford, Conn., 1986), p. 202. "The Furnishings of Richmond Hill in 1797: The Home of Aaron Burr in New York City," *New-York Historical Society Bulletin*, vol. 11, no. 1 (April 1927), p. 17. Margaret Izard Manigault to Mrs. [Alice] Izard, 25 October 1807, RIFP. Anne Eliza Clark Kane to Harriet Clark, undated, JICP. Richard Loins estate inventory, December 1832, NYSI. Williamina Cadwalader to Ann Ridgely, 9 December 1801, RFP. Ephm. Bowen, Jr., to Lydia Bowen Clark, 23 March 1799, quoted in Joseph K. Ott, "John Innes Clark and His Family—Beautiful People in Providence," *Rhode Island History*, vol. 32, no. 4 (November 1973), p. 129.

20. Christopher Vail to Reverend Thomas H. Vail, 15 September 1836, WL-JD. Caroline A. Dustan diary, 22 November 1860. Boy from Danbury, quoted in James M. Bailey, *Life in Danbury* (Boston, 1873), p. 278. *Workwoman's Guide*, p. 192. Burr, *Journal*, p. 148. Mary Cooper, *Diary . . . 1768–1773*, ed. Field Horne (Oyster Bay, N.Y., 1981), p. 3. Emily Barnes,

Narratives, Traditions, and Personal Reminiscences (Boston, 1888), p. 268.

21. John Quincy Adams, *Life in a New England Town, 1787, 1788: Diary of John Quincy Adams* (Boston, 1903), p. 45. George G. Channing, *Early Recollections of Newport, R.I., from the Year 1793 to 1811* (Newport, R.I., and Boston, 1868), p. 254. Stowe, *Oldtown Folks*, p. 1147. Channing, ibid., p. 241. Frenchman in rural New England: "Observations sur les Moeurs &c des Habitants de la Nouvelle Angleterre écrit à New Gloucester, 1797," WL-JD. Chapman J. Milling, ed., *Colonial South Carolina, Two Contemporary Descriptions by Governor James Glen and Doctor George Milligen-Johnston* (Columbia, S.C., 1951), p. 28. King, *When I Lived in Salem*, pp. 192–93.

22. Millicent Todd Bingham, *Emily Dickinson's Home* (New York, 1955), p. 146. Caroline A. Dustan diary, 14 June 1859. Sarah Anna Emery, *Reminiscences of a Nonagenarian* (1879; Bowie, Md., and Hampton, N.H., 1978), p. 28. Margaret Cary, quoted in C[aroline] G[ilman] C[urtis], ed., *The Cary Letters* (Cambridge, Mass., 1891), p. 243.

23. Nicholas B. Wainwright, ed., "The Diary of Samuel Breck, 1823–1827," *Pennsylvania Magazine of History and Biography*, vol. 103, no. 1 (January 1979), p. 89. [Grant], *Memoirs*, vol. 1, p. 165. Lucy Breckinridge, *Lucy Breckinridge of Grove Hill: The Journal of a Virginia Girl, 1862–1864*, ed. Mary D. Robertson (Kent, Ohio, 1979), p. 211. [Joseph Holt Ingraham], *The South-West* (New York, 1835), vol. 1, p. 235.

24. Sarah Logan Fisher diary, 21 July 1790, HSP. Longfellow, *Mrs. Longfellow*, p. 189. "As if some grand spectacle": Isaac Weld, Jr., *Travels . . . during the Years 1795, 1796, and 1797*, 4th ed. (London, 1807), vol. 1, pp. 251–52. Ann Head Warder, quoted in Nancy F. Cott, ed., *Root of Bitterness: Documents of the Social History of American Women* (Boston, 1986), p. 99.

25. Alice Izard to Margaret Izard Manigault, 5 May 1803, RIFP. John Lambert, *Travels . . . in the Years 1806, 1807, and 1808*, 2d ed. (London, 1814), vol. 2, p. 125. John Drayton, quoted in Clark, ed., *South Carolina: The Grand Tour*, p. 22. [Ingraham], *South-West*, vol. 2, p. 98. Andrew Gautier's advertisement, quoted in Gottesman, *Arts and Crafts 1726–1776*, p. 113. The piazza at Mount Vernon: Susan Gray Detweiler, *George Washington's Chinaware* (New York, 1982), p. 176. Sarah Logan Fisher diary, 26 April 1790. Saxe-Weimar Eisenach, *Travels*, vol. 2, p. 80. [Ingraham], ibid., vol. 1, pp. 80–81, p. 232. Hall, *Aristocratic Journey*, p. 210.

26. Caroline Barrett White diary, 13 June 1857, AAS. Forman, *Plantation Life*, p. 107. Carter, *Diary*, vol. 1, p. 278. "Liliputian lancers": Wortley, *Travels*, p. 122. Power, *Impres-*

sions, vol. 1, p. 71. "As Othello says": Alfred Bunn, *Old England and New England, in a Series of Views Taken on the Spot* (1853; New York, 2 vols. in 1, 1969), p. 49. Mary Gould Almy, quoted in Elizabeth Evans, *Weathering the Storm: Women of the American Revolution* (New York, 1975), p. 256.

27. On the quantity of netting required for beds, see Audrey H. Michie, "Charleston Upholstery in All Its Branches, 1725–1820," *Journal of Early Southern Decorative Arts*, vol. 11, no. 2 (1985), p. 57. Amelia M. Murray, *Letters from the United States, Cuba and Canada* (1856; New York, 1969), p. 268. Benjamin Henry Latrobe, *Journals . . . 1799–1820, from Philadelphia to New Orleans*, ed. Edward C. Carter II, John C. Van Horne, and Lee M. Formwalt (New Haven, 1980), vol. 3, p. 307. Advertisement for netting, quoted in Gottesman, *Arts and Crafts 1726–1776*, p. 136. Robert Pringle on blue and green netting, quoted in Michie, ibid., pp. 61–62. For an idea of available netting colors, see inventory of the goods of Robert and Nathaniel Scott, merchants, 29 September 1771, CCSCI (1771–76); and advertisement by Roger Smith, merchant, in *South Carolina Gazette and Country Journal*, 2 August 1774. Netting bordered in contrasting colors is listed, for example, in the estate inventories of Isaac Nichols, 4 March 1768, CCSCI (1763–71), and Mrs. Mary Baker, 28 June 1760, CCSCI (1756–63). Samuel Naeve, quoted in Alice Hanson Jones, *American Colonial Wealth: Documents and Methods* (New York, 1977), vol. 1, p. 191. [Janet Schaw], *Journal of a Lady of Quality*, ed. Evangeline Walker Andrews (New Haven, 1921), pp. 182–83. Harriet Martineau, *Retrospect*, vol. 1, pp. 258–59.

28. Stuart, *Three Years*, vol. 2, p. 196. Leslie, *House Book*, p. 113.

29. *Maryland Gazette* advertisement, quoted in Cecil K. Drinker, *Not So Long Ago; a Chronicle of Medicine and Doctors in Colonial Philadelphia* (New York, 1937), p. 32. *Boston Gazette* advertisement, quoted in George Francis Dow, *The Arts and Crafts in New England 1704–1775* (Topsfield, Mass., 1927), p. 167. Benjamin Goldthwait estate inventory, 23 July 1782, docket book 81, SCPC. Charles Bagot, quoted in Samuel Eliot Morison, "Charles Bagot's Notes on Housekeeping and Entertaining at Washington, 1819," in *Publications of the Colonial Society of Massachusetts. Transactions, 1924–1926* (Boston, 1927), p. 445. Thomas Fessenden, quoted in Jane C. Nylander, "Summer Housekeeping in Early 19th-Century New England," *Early American Life*, vol. 11, no. 2 (April 1980), p. 56. Thomas Webster, *An Encyclopedia of Domestic Economy . . .* (New York, 1845), p. 312. Weld, *Travels*, vol. 1, p. 285.

30. Gregory A. Stiverson and Patrick H. Butler III, eds., "Virginia in 1732: The Travel Journal of William Hugh Grove," *Virginia*

Magazine of History and Biography, vol. 85, no. 1 (January 1977), p. 29. I am indebted to Lucia Goodwin and William Beiswanger for the information on Jefferson. Isaac Conro's advertisement, quoted in Gottesman, *Arts and Crafts 1726–1776*, p. 189. J[ohn] C[laudius] Loudon, *An Encyclopaedia of Cottage, Farm, and Villa Architecture and Furniture* (1833; London, 1853), p. 271. Gervase Wheeler, *Rural Homes; or, Sketches of Houses Suited to American Country Life* (New York, 1851), p. 133.

31. Richard Parkinson, *A Tour in America in 1798, 1799, and 1800* (London, 1805), vol. 2, p. 364. The nonpoisonous fly-bait recipe is given, for example, in H. L. Barnum, *Family Receipts; or, Practical Guide for the Husbandman and Housewife* (Cincinnati, 1831), p. 34; and Mrs. E[sther] A[llen] Howland, *The New England Economical Housekeeper and Family Receipt Book* (Worcester, 1845), p. 95. M.L.E. Moreau de Saint-Méry, *Moreau de St. Méry's American Journey, 1793–1798*, trans. and ed. Kenneth Roberts and Anna M. Roberts (Garden City, N.Y., 1947), p. 325. Royall Tyler, "The Bad Boy," quoted in *The Magazine Antiques*, May 1971, p. 688. Webster, *Encyclopedia*, p. 377. James Forbes estate inventory, 24 August 1781; and Elbert Haring estate inventory, 14–15 December 1773, INYC. John Jay Janney, *John Jay Janney's Virginia*, ed. Werner L. Janney and Asa Moore Janney (McLean, Va., 1978), p. 30. Leslie, *House Book*, p. 112. Morison, *One Boy's Boston*, p. 24.

32. Boyer, *Virginia Gentleman*, p. 176. Rumford, "Life along the Brandywine."

33. Mrs. Anne Royall, *The Black Book*, vol. 1 (Washington, D.C., 1828), p. 21. Robert Sutcliff, *Travels in Some Parts of North America in the Years 1804, 1805, and 1806* (Philadelphia, 1812), p. 181. One visitor to the South: Martineau, *Retrospect*, vol. 1, p. 276. The Swiss traveler was Francis Louis Michel; see William J. Hinke, ed., "Report of the Journey of Francis Louis Michel from Berne, Switzerland, to Virginia, October 2, 1701–December 1, 1702," *Virginia Magazine of History and Biography*, vol. 24, no. 1 (January 1916), p. 34. Sarah Cadbury, ed., "Extracts from the Diary of Mrs. Ann Warder," *Pennsylvania Magazine of History and Biography*, vol. 17, no. 4 (1893), p. 459. News item in *Pennsylvania Gazette*, see Prime Cards, Winterthur Library, Winterthur, Del. Martineau, ibid., vol. 2, p. 183.

34. "Journal of a Peddling Trip Kept by Ebenezer Graves of Ashfield, Massachusetts, Part II," *Old-Time New England*, vol. 56, no. 4 (April–June, 1966), p. 112. Philip Vickers Fithian, *Journal and Letters . . . 1773–1774*, ed. Hunter Dickinson Farish (Williamsburg, Va., 1945), p. 177. Eliza Ann Summers to Sarah Summers, 27 February 1867, quoted in *"Dear Sister" Letters Written on Hilton Head Island 1867*, ed. Josephine W. Martin (Beaufort, S.C.,

1977), p. 36. Susan Augusta Fenimore Cooper, quoted in James Fenimore Cooper, *Correspondence*, ed. James Fenimore Cooper (New Haven, 1922), vol. 1, p. 53. Maria Silliman Church to Harriet Silliman, 13 May 1836; and Faith Silliman to Harriet Silliman, 15 April 1836, MSCP. *The New Family Receipt-Book, Containing Eight Hundred Truly Valuable Receipts . . . Selected from the Works of British and Foreign Writers* (New Haven, 1819), p. 336. John Harrower, *The Journal of John Harrower, an Indentured Servant in the Colony of Virginia 1773–1776*, ed. Edward Miles Riley (Williamsburg, Va., 1963), p. 52.

35. Maria Silliman Church to Harriet Silliman, 21 April 1843, MSCP. Caroline A. Dustan diary, 20 May 1859. Lavinia Dickinson, quoted in Bingham, *Emily Dickinson's Home*, p. 298. Caroline Barrett White diary, 28 May 1857, AAS. Sarah Logan Fisher diary, 18 April 1785.

36. Anderson, "Diarium." Laura Wirt to Elizabeth Wirt, 15 May 1820, WWP.

37. Burr, *Journal*, p. 127.

38. Anne Eliza Clark Kane to Lydia Bowen Clark, 20 May 1811, JICP. Leslie, *House Book*, p. 188. On summer storage of curtains, see Lea, *Domestic Cookery*, p. 207. Thomas Roach estate inventory, 31 May 1798, WL-JD. Conover Hunt-Jones, *Dolley and the "Great Little Madison"* (Washington, D.C., 1977), p. 121. Caroline A. Dustan diary, 28 May 1856, 23 May 1865.

39. Leslie, *House Book*, pp. 307–8. Stiverson and Butler, eds., "Travel Journal of William Hugh Grove," pp. 22–23.

40. Leslie, *House Book*, p. 109. Messrs. Gilman and Jackson's advertisement, quoted in Rita Susswein Gottesman, *The Arts and Crafts in New York 1800–1804* (New York, 1965), p. 161. "1 Bed Wench": John Green estate inventory, [1767], CCSCI (1763–71).

41. Lavinia Dickinson, quoted in Bingham, *Emily Dickinson's Home*, p. 239. Fanny Kemble Wister, "Sarah Butler Wister's Civil War Diary," *Pennsylvania Magazine of History and Biography*, vol. 102, no. 3 (July 1978), p. 296. Aaron Burr's garret storeroom: "Furnishings of Richmond Hill," p. 19. Josiah Bumstead & Son advertisement, quoted in Richard C. Nylander, Elizabeth Redmond, and Penny J. Sander, eds., *Wallpaper in New England* (Boston, 1986), p. 21. [Frances Harriet Whipple McDougall], *The Housekeeper's Book* (Philadelphia, 1837), p. 21.

42. Painted floor cloth: Beecher, *Treatise*, p. 342. Maria Silliman Church to Harriet Silliman, 14 June 1836, MSCP.

43. Miss Prudence Smith, *Modern American Cookery* (New York, 1831), pp. 202–3. Robert Roberts, *The House Servant's Directory* (1827; Waltham, Mass., 1977), pp. 92, 93. Varnish for gilded frames: Mrs. [Sarah Stickney]

Ellis, *Mrs. Ellis's Housekeeping Made Easy* (New York, 1843), p. 103.

44. Dickinson, *Letters*, vol. 2, p. 272. Thomas Elfe's advertisement, quoted in Alfred Coxe Prime, *The Arts and Crafts in Philadelphia, Maryland and South Carolina 1721–1785* (1929; New York, 1969), p. 166. Leslie, *House Book*, p. 345. Harriet Beecher Stowe [Christopher Crowfield, pseud.], *House and Home Papers* (Boston, 1865), pp. 35–36. Leslie, ibid., p. 344. "George Washington's Household Account Book, 1793–1797," *Pennsylvania Magazine of History and Biography*, vol. 30, no. 1 (1906), p. 33. *An Inventory of the Contents of the Governor's Palace Taken after the Death of Lord Botetourt* (Williamsburg, Va., 1981), p. 6. Kelly, *Samuel Kelly, Seaman*, p. 187. Forman, *Plantation Life*, p. 221. Wister, "Sarah Butler Wister's Civil War Diary," p. 299. Muslin and yellow cambric covers for gilded objects: Mrs. [Elizabeth Fries Lummis] Ellet, ed., *The New Cyclopaedia of Domestic Economy and Practical Housekeeper* (Norwich, Conn., 1873), p. 568; and Mrs. Lydia Maria Child, *The American Frugal Housewife*, 12th ed. (1832; [Worthington, Ohio], 1980), pp. 17–18. Leslie, ibid.

45. Care of brass andirons: Leslie, *House Book*, p. 217. Stowe, *Oldtown Folks*, chapter 6, pp. 945–46.

46. Harriet Silliman to Maria Silliman Church, 27 May 1836, MSCP. Margaret Pardee Bates, ed., "Some Letters of Mary Boardman Crowninshield," *Essex Institute Historical Collections*, vol. 83 (April 1947), p. 125. Elizabeth Wirt to William Wirt, 27–28 April 1830, WWP. Stowe [Crowfield, pseud.], *House and Home*, p. 66. Baron de Montlezun, quoted in L. G. Moffatt and J. M. Carrière, "A Frenchman Visits Norfolk, Fredericksburg and Orange County, 1816," *Virginia Magazine of History and Biography*, vol. 53, no. 2 (April 1945), p. 118. Leslie, *House Book*, p. 346.

47. Sarah Logan Fisher diary, [c. 1785]. Charles Carleton Coffin, *The History of Boscawen and Webster, from 1733 to 1878* (Concord, N.H., 1878), p. 177. Anderson, "Diarium." Kelly, *Samuel Kelly, Seaman*, p. 189.

48. [Grant], *Memoirs*, vol. 1, pp. 165–66. Hall, *Aristocratic Journey*, p. 32. Alexander Mackay, *The Western World* (London, 1849), vol. 1, p. 135. Catharine E. Beecher, *Miss Beecher's Housekeeper and Healthkeeper: Containing Five Hundred Recipes for Economical and Healthful Cooking; also, Many Directions for Securing Health and Happiness* (New York, 1873), p. 198.

Chapter Nine

1. *The School of Good Manners* (Boston, 1794), p. 15. Thomas Jefferson, quoted in Edwin Morris Betts and James Adam Bear, Jr., eds., *The Family Letters of Thomas Jefferson* (Charlottesville, Va., 1986), pp. 29, 36. Catharine Beecher and Harriet Beecher Stowe, *The American Woman's Home* (1869; Hartford, 1975), p. 212. Louisa Jane Trumbull diary, 29 January 1834, Trumbull Family Papers, AAS.

2. Betts and Bear, eds., *Family Letters of Thomas Jefferson*, pp. 29, 214. "Virtuous, Sensible": Charles Carroll of Annapolis to Charles Carroll of Carrollton, 1 September 1762, quoted in Ann C. Van Devanter, *"Anywhere So Long As There Be Freedom": Charles Carroll of Carrollton, His Family and His Maryland* (Baltimore, 1975), p. 23. Frank Hail Brown, ed., "A Colonial Merchant to His Son; from the unpublished letters of John Brown to his son James (1782–3)," *Rhode Island Historical Society Collections*, vol. 34 (April 1941), p. 49. Timothy Dwight, *Travels in New England and New York*, ed. Barbara Miller Solomon (Cambridge, Mass., 1969), vol. 4, p. 334.

3. Thomas Jefferson to Maria Jefferson Eppes, 7 January 1798, quoted in Sarah N. Randolph, *The Domestic Life of Thomas Jefferson*, 3d ed. (Charlottesville, Va., 1947), p. 207. Thomas E. Buckley, "The Duties of a Wife: Bishop James Madison to His Daughter, 1811," *Virginia Magazine of History and Biography*, vol. 91, no. 1 (January 1983), p. 101. Benjamin Rush, *My Dearest Julia: The Love Letters of Dr. Benjamin Rush to Julia Stockton* (New York, 1979), pp. 16–18.

4. *School of Good Manners*, p. 7. Abigail Adams, *New Letters of Abigail Adams 1788–1801*, ed. Stewart Mitchell (Boston, 1947), pp. 47–48. Maria Silliman Church to Harriet Silliman, 6 October 1839, MSCP.

5. [Anne Grant], *Memoirs of an American Lady* (London, 1808), vol. 1, pp. 295–96. Margaret Cary, quoted in C[aroline] G[ilman] C[urtis], ed., *The Cary Letters* (Cambridge, Mass., 1891), pp. 232–33. Abraham Ridgely to Ann Moore Ridgely, 11 February 1786, RFP.

6. Nancy Shippen, *Nancy Shippen, Her Journal Book*, ed. Ethel Armes (Philadelphia, 1967), p. 41. Sarah Anna Emery, *Reminiscences of a Nonagenarian* (1879; Bowie, Md., and Hampton, N.H., 1978), p. 28. Harriet Beecher Stowe, *The Minister's Wooing* (1859; reprinted in *Stowe: Three Novels*, ed. Kathryn Kish Sklar, New York, 1982), chapter 1, p. 528. That worthy Mrs. Schuyler: [Grant], *Memoirs*, vol. 1, pp. 294–96. On the importance of unruffled ease in manner and person, see Francis D. Nichols, *A Guide to Politeness; or, A System of Directions for the Acquirement of Ease, Propriety and Elegance of Manners* (Boston, 1810), p. 8; and Robert Roberts, *The House Servant's Directory* (1827; Waltham, Mass., 1977), p. 56.

7. Sidney George Fisher, *A Philadelphia Perspective: The Diary of Sidney George Fisher Covering the Years 1834–1871*, ed. Nicholas B. Wainwright (Philadelphia, 1967), p. 111. Ellen H. Rollins [E. H. Arr, pseud.], *New England Bygones* (Philadelphia, 1880), p. 39. Harriet Beecher Stowe, *Uncle Tom's Cabin* (1852; reprinted in *Stowe: Three Novels*, ed. Kathryn Kish Sklar, New York, 1982), chapter 15, p. 187.

8. Catharine E. Beecher, *A Treatise on Domestic Economy* (1841; New York, 1977), pp. 16–17. Maria Silliman Church to Harriet Silliman, 8 February 1842, 26 September 1839, MSCP.

9. Elizabeth Drinker, *Extracts from the Journal of Elizabeth Drinker, from 1759 to 1807 A.D.*, ed. Henry D. Biddle (Philadelphia, 1889), p. 70. On nuclear and extended American families, see Barbara Laslett, "The Significance of Family Membership," in Virginia Tufte and Barbara Myerhoff, eds., *Changing Images of the American Family* (New Haven, 1979). William Wirt, *Memoirs of the Life of William Wirt, Attorney-General of the United States*, ed. John P. Kennedy (Philadelphia, 1854), vol. 1, pp. 36–37. Catherine Robbins, quoted in Susan I. Lesley, *Recollections of My Mother, Mrs. Anne Jean Lyman of Northampton* (1886; Boston, 1899), pp. 39–40.

10. Alexander Anderson, "Diarium Commentarium Vitae Alex. Anderson," typewritten transcript of a journal, 1793–99, NYHS-MC (original manuscript: Rare Book and Manuscript Library, Columbia University). Mary A. White diary, 17, 18 October 1858, OSV. Sarah Connell Ayer, *Diary* (Portland, Maine, 1910), p. 253. Beecher and Stowe, *American Woman's Home*, pp. 303–6.

11. Betsy [Elizabeth] Foote Washington [Mrs. Lund Washington], memorandum book, [c. 1779], 1784, Washington Family Collection, LC-MD. Mary Guion diary, 1805, NYHS-MC. Frances Bowen Moore to Lydia Bowen Clark, 9 March 1790, JICP.

12. [Martha Sellers], *M.S.: The Story of a Life*, ed. Frances Sellers Garrett (Philadelphia, 1901), p. 44.

13. Mary Lee, quoted in Frances Rollins Morse, ed., *Henry and Mary Lee: Letters and Journals* (Boston, 1926), p. 267. Esther Edwards Burr, *Journal . . . 1754–1757*, ed. Carol F. Karlsen and Laurie Crumpacker (New Haven, 1984), p. 213. Anne Eliza Clark Kane to Lydia Bowen Clark, 5 October 1813, JICP. Harriet Manigault, *Diary . . . 1813–1816*, ed. Virginia and James S. Armentrout, Jr. (Rockland, Maine, 1976), p. 79. Burr, ibid., p. 95. Kane to Clark, 15 November 1811.

14. Lucy Larcom, *A New England Girlhood Outlined from Memory* (1889; Williamstown, Mass., 1977), p. 259. Samuella Curd, *Sam Curd's Diary: The Diary of a True Woman*, ed. Susan S. Arpad (Athens, Ohio, 1984), p. 46. Harriet Silliman to Faith Wadsworth, 27 February 1827, WFP.

15. Modified house plans: A[lexander]

J[ackson] Downing, *The Architecture of Country Houses* (1850; New York, 1969), p. 257. Beecher and Stowe, *American Woman's Home*, p. 318. Simon Gratz, "Some Material for a Biography of Mrs. Elizabeth Fergusson, nee Graeme," *Pennsylvania Magazine of History and Biography*, vol. 39, no. 4 (1915), p. 387. [John Bill], "Extracts from the Journal of Philo-Jocundus 1827 [and 1828]," typewritten transcript, NYHS-MC. Faith Silliman Hubbard and Henrietta Silliman to the Benjamin Silliman family, 12 October 1837, FSHP. "There is none good": Maria Silliman Church to Harriet Silliman, 12 July 1836, MSCP. Alexander Mackraby, quoted in *Pennsylvania Magazine of History and Biography*, vol. 11, no. 4 (1887), p. 492. Church to Hubbard, 4 March 1842, MSCP. Elizabeth Drinker's new maid: Cecil K. Drinker, *Not So Long Ago; a Chronicle of Medicine and Doctors in Colonial Philadelphia* (New York, 1937), p. 36. Peter Neilson, *Recollections of a Six Years' Residence in the United States of America* (Glasgow, 1830), p. 193. Lucy Breckinridge, *Lucy Breckinridge of Grove Hill: The Journal of a Virginia Girl, 1862–1864*, ed. Mary D. Robertson (Kent, Ohio, 1979), p. 133. Harriet Beecher Stowe, *Poganuc People* (1878; Hartford, 1977), p. 122. Hubbard to Harriet Silliman, 19 February 1838, FSHP.

16. Martha Blodget, quoted in Marion Tinling, "Cawson's Virginia in 1795–1796," *The William and Mary Quarterly*, 3d ser., vol. 3, no. 2 (April 1946), p. 288. Caroline A. Dustan diary, 7 April 1859, NYPL. Martha Jefferson Randolph, quoted in Betts and Bear, eds., *Family Letters of Thomas Jefferson*, p. 243. Creole's reaction: Eliza Ripley, *Social Life in Old New Orleans* (New York, 1912), p. 32. Josiah Claypoole, quoted in Alfred Coxe Prime, *The Arts and Crafts in Philadelphia, Maryland and South Carolina 1721–1785* (1929; New York, 1969), p. 163. Charles Carroll of Carrollton letterbook, 26 October 1771 (to West and Hobson, London), Arents Collections, New York Public Library; Astor, Lenox and Tilden Foundations; see also Van Devanter, *Anywhere So Long*, pp. 278, 280.

17. Catherine Robbins, quoted in Lesley, *Recollections*, p. 39. Sarah Clarke Whitings to Sophia Griswold, June 1831, BFP-LC.

18. Mrs. Abigail Swett to Eliza Wainwright, 12 September [1822], WP. Burr, *Journal*, p. 192. Annie Crowninshield Warren, *Reminiscences of My Life* (Cambridge, Mass., 1910), p. 55. Fanny Appleton Longfellow, *Mrs. Longfellow: Selected Letters and Journals . . . (1817–1861)*, ed. Edward Wagenknecht (New York, 1956), p. 194. Anne Jean Lyman, quoted in Lesley, *Recollections of My Mother*, p. 166.

19. Sarah Logan Fisher diary, August 1785, HSP. Abigail Adams, quoted in L. H. Butterfield, Marc Friedlaender, and Mary-Jo Kline, eds., *The Book of Abigail and John: Selected Letters of the Adams Family 1762–1784* (Cambridge, Mass., 1975), p. 171. Roger Schofield, "Did the Mothers Really Die? Three Centuries of Maternal Mortality in 'The World We Have Lost,'" in Lloyd Bonfield, Richard M. Smith, and Keith Wrightson, eds., *The World We Have Gained: Histories of Population and Social Structure* (Oxford, 1986), pp. 231–60. Louisa Park to John Park, 5 January 1800, Park Family Papers, AAS. Maria Silliman Church to Faith Silliman Hubbard, [25] November 1843, MSCP. Sidney George Fisher, *A Philadelphia Perspective*, p. 288. Thomas Jefferson, quoted in Randolph, *Domestic Life of Thomas Jefferson*, p. 252.

20. Burr, *Journal*, p. 252. Longfellow, *Mrs. Longfellow*, p. 99. Burr, ibid., p. 142.

21. Longfellow, *Mrs. Longfellow*, p. 196. Maria Silliman Church to Faith Silliman, 18 March 1834, MSCP. Burr, *Journal*, p. 197. Mary Lee, quoted in Morse, ed., *Henry and Mary Lee*, p. 252. Elizabeth Dorsey to Ann Moore Ridgely, 11 March 1787, RFP.

22. Harriet Silliman to Faith Wadsworth, 7 November 1823, SFP. Maria Silliman Church to Silliman, 27 May 1834, MSCP. Lucy Clark Allen, quoted in Allen children, *Memorial of Joseph and Lucy Clark Allen* (Boston, 1891), pp. 64–65.

23. Maria Silliman Church to Harriet Silliman, 16 January 1840, MSCP.

24. Thomas Jefferson to Nathaniel Burwell, 14 March 1818, quoted in *Thomas Jefferson Writings*, ed. Merrill Peterson (New York, 1984), p. 1141. Mary Guion diary [1806?], NYHS-MC. Mary Palmer Tyler, *Grandmother Tyler's Book*, ed. Frederick Tupper and Helen Tyler Brown (New York, 1925), p. 57. Sarah Livingston Jay to Maria Jay, 16 December 1794, SLJ. Harriet Silliman to Faith Wadsworth, 13 August [1827 or 1828?], SFP.

25. Maria Silliman Church to Faith Silliman Hubbard, 2 September 1839, MSCP. Harriet Beecher Stowe, quoted in Annegret S. Ogden, *The Great American Housewife from Helpmate to Wage Earner, 1776–1986* (Westport, Conn., 1986), p. 69. L. H. Cleveland to Charlotte Lambert, 7 October 1818, WP. Sidney George Fisher, quoted in *A Philadelphia Perspective*, p. 288. Stowe, *The Minister's Wooing*, chapter 1, p. 528. The New York farm wife is the creation of Marietta Holley, *My Opinion and Betsy Bobbet's*, quoted in W. Elliot Brownlee and Mary M. Brownlee, *Women in the American Economy: A Documentary History, 1675 to 1929* (New Haven, 1976), pp. 113–14. Mary Beth Norton, *Liberty's Daughters: The Revolutionary Experience of American Women, 1750–1800* (Boston, 1980).

26. "The pleasure of writing a letter": Maria Silliman Church to Henrietta Silliman, [26] October 1837, MSCP. Harriet Beecher Stowe, quoted in Ogden, *Great American Housewife*, p. 69. Elizabeth Wirt to William Wirt, 6 April 1819, WWP. Martha Jefferson Randolph, quoted in Betts and Bear, eds., *Family Letters of Thomas Jefferson*, p. 253. Church to Faith Silliman Hubbard, 21 February 1838, MSCP. Mary Cooper, *Diary . . . 1768–1773*, ed. Field Horne (Oyster Bay, N.Y., 1981), p. 2. Ellen Birdseye Wheaton, *Diary*, ed. Donald Gordon (Boston, 1923), p. 26. "I find the evening": Church to Faith Silliman, 26 November 1833, MSCP. "The evening is a blessed time": Church to Harriet Silliman, [31] October 1837, MSCP. "I am so happy": Wheaton, ibid., p. 224.

27. Edward Shippen, quoted in *Pennsylvania Magazine of History and Biography*, vol. 30, no. 1 (1906), p. 89. The details of Gold Selleck Silliman's collapse are given in Joy Day Buel and Richard Buel, Jr., *The Way of Duty: A Woman and Her Family in Revolutionary America* (New York, 1984), p. 202. Charles Carroll of Carrollton letterbook, 1 March 1773. Burr, *Journal*, p. 142. Mary Guion diary, 16 July 1801. Larcom, *New England Girlhood*, p. 86. Louisa May Alcott, *Louisa May Alcott: Her Life, Letters, and Journals*, ed. Ednah D. Cheney (Boston, 1889), p. 48. Mary Guion diary, 4 February 1805. Abigail Adams, quoted in Butterfield, Friedlaender, and Kline, eds., *Book of Abigail and John*, p. 159. Rush, *My Dearest Julia*, p. 39.

28. Mary Guion diary, 29 November 1802.

29. Raymond C. Werner, ed., "Diary of Grace Growdon Galloway Kept at Philadelphia from June 17, 1778, to July 1, 1779," *Pennsylvania Magazine of History and Biography*, vol. 55, no. 1 (1931), p. 59. J. Hall Pleasants, ed., "Letters of Molly and Hetty Tilghman, Eighteenth-Century Gossip of Two Maryland Girls," *Maryland Historical Magazine*, vol. 21, no. 1 (March 1926), p. 33. Anderson, "Diarium." David B. Warden, *A Chorographical and Statistical Description of the District of Columbia* (Paris, 1816), p. 137. "Gentle mother," "I often think": Sarah Clarke Whitings to Sophia Griswold, 28 August 1832, BFP-LC. Laura Wirt to William Wirt, 6 May 1817, WWP. Louisa Jane Trumbull diary, 7 February 1835, Trumbull Family Papers, AAS. "Safety valves": Maria Silliman Church to Harriet Silliman, 31 March 1841, MSCP.

30. Ralph Waldo Emerson, *Emerson in His Journals*, ed. Joel Porte (Cambridge, Mass., 1982), p. 276. Betts and Bear, eds., *Family Letters of Thomas Jefferson*, p. 36.

31. [Eliza Ware Farrar], *The Young Lady's Friend* (Boston, 1837), p. 57. "A good watcher": Larcom, *New England Girlhood*, p. 191. Beecher, *Treatise*, p. 236. Landon Carter, *The Diary of Colonel Landon Carter of Sabine Hall, 1752–1778*, ed. Jack P. Greene (Charlottesville, Va., 1965), vol. 1, p. 410. George M. Anderson, "An Early Commuter: The Letters of James and

Mary Anderson," *Maryland Historical Magazine*, vol. 75, no. 3 (September 1980), p. 226. Laura Wirt to Mrs. Catharine Gamble, 24 May 1818, WWP. Elizabeth Wirt to William Wirt, 15 April 1819, WWP.

32. Lucy Clark Allen, quoted in Allen children, *Memorial*, p. 108. Burr, *Journal*, p. 114. Sarah Livingston Jay to John Jay, [November 1790], SLJ. Elizabeth Wirt to William Wirt, 15 April 1819, WWP.

33. Sarah Livingston Jay to John Jay, 12 February 1779, SLJ. Martha Jefferson Randolph, quoted in Betts and Bear, eds., *Family Letters of Thomas Jefferson*, pp. 101, 246–47. Faith Silliman Hubbard to Harriet Silliman, 2 October 1839, FSHP. Abigail Adams, *New Letters*, p. 105. Sarah Logan Fisher diary, 18 December 1777, 2 February 1794. Hubbard to Silliman, 27 November 1845, FSHP. Burr, *Journal*, pp. 228–29. Louisa Park diary, 1 May 1801, Park Family Papers, AAS. Mary Fish Noyes and Reverend Joseph Fish, quoted in Buel and Buel, *Way of Duty*, pp. 31–32. Sarah Logan Fisher diary, 10 September 1780.

34. George P. Fisher, *Life of Benjamin Silliman* (New York, 1866), vol. 1, p. 277. Emerson, *Emerson in His Journals*, p. 276.

35. Mary Perkins's sampler was illustrated in *The Magazine Antiques*, September 1982, p. 402. Ayer, *Diary*, p. 209. Carl Van Doren, ed., *The Letters of Benjamin Franklin and Jane Mecom* (Princeton, N.J., 1950), pp. 98–99. Wirt, *Memoirs*, vol. 2, p. 165.

36. "This world is no home": Faith Silliman Hubbard to Harriet Silliman, 20 January 1840, FSHP. Adams, *New Letters*, p. 168. Rachel L. Campbell to Ann Moore Ridgely, 6 July 1799, RFP. Manasseh Cutler, *The Life, Journals and Correspondence*, ed. William Parker Cutler and Julia Perkins Cutler (Cincinnati, 1888), vol. 2, p. 136. Williamina Ridgely to Ann Moore Ridgely, 26 January 1803, RFP. Susan Dabney Smedes, *A Southern Planter* (London, 1889), pp. 134, 140.

37. "Each fold of the bed curtains": [Mrs. A. M. Richards], *Memories of a Grandmother* (Boston, 1854), p. 119. "Letters of Richard Adams to Thomas Adams," *Virginia Magazine of History and Biography*, vol. 22, no. 4 (October 1914), p. 386.

38. "Henry would have been 23": Mrs. Holbrook Curtis to William Curtis, 28 December 1847, quoted in Elizabeth Curtis, ed., *Letters and Journals: Judge William Edmond . . . Judge Holbrook Curtis . . . Judge William Edmond Curtis . . . William Edmond Curtis and Dr. Holbrook Curtis* (New York, 1926), p. 186. "This day is eleven years": Mary Cooper, *Diary*, p. 39. "Resignation," in *Favorite Poems of Henry Wadsworth Longfellow* (Garden City, N.Y., 1947), p. 371.

39. Margaret Cary, quoted in C[aroline] G[ilman] C[urtis], ed., *The Cary Letters* (Cambridge, Mass., 1891), p. 63. Sarah Logan Fisher diary, December 1778, New Year's Day 1786. Maria Silliman Church to Harriet Silliman, 9 January 1838, MSCP. Faith Silliman Hubbard to Silliman, 20 January 1840, FSHP.

40. Sarah Logan Fisher diary, 12 January 1779, [undated] January 1782. Maria Silliman Church to Harriet Silliman, 5 March 1834, MSCP. Faith Silliman Hubbard to Silliman, 3 September 1838, FSHP.

41. Mary Fish Noyes, quoted in Buel and Buel, *Way of Duty*, pp. 33–34. Minerva Rodgers to Commodore John Rodgers, 17 February 1809, RFC. Longfellow, *Mrs. Longfellow*, p. 143. Margaret Morris, quoted in John Jay Smith, ed., *Letters of Doctor Richard Hill and His Children* (Philadelphia, 1854), p. 345. Curd, *Sam Curd's Diary*, p. 119. Maria Silliman Church to Harriet Silliman, 6 April 1834, 9 January 1838, MSCP. Burr, *Journal*, p. 84. Silliman to Eliza Sebor, 8 November [1820], SFP. William Wirt to Elizabeth Wirt, 28 April 1805, WWP.

42. Randolph, *Domestic Life of Thomas Jefferson*, p. 76.

43. Longfellow, *Mrs. Longfellow*, p. 151.

CHAPTER TEN

1. Benjamin Franklin [Anthony Afterwit, pseud.], letter printed in *Pennsylvania Gazette* (10 July 1732), quoted in *The Papers of Benjamin Franklin*, ed. Leonard W. Labaree, vol. 1 (New Haven, 1959), pp. 237–40.

2. Harriet Beecher Stowe [Christopher Crowfield, pseud.], *House and Home Papers* (Boston, 1865), chapter 1, pp. 1–22.

3. "Diary of a French Officer, 1781," *Magazine of American History*, vol. 4, no. 3 (March 1880), p. 209. Henry Wadsworth Longfellow, quoted in John A. Kouwenhoven, *The Arts in Modern American Civilization* (1948; New York, 1967), p. 7. John Bernard, *Retrospections of America 1797–1811*, ed. Mrs. Bayle Bernard (New York, 1887), p. 29. Sarah Anna Emery, *Three Generations* (Boston, 1872), p. 119.

4. Advertisement in the *Charleston City Gazette*, quoted in Alfred Coxe Prime, *The Arts and Crafts in Philadelphia, Maryland and South Carolina 1786–1800* (1932; New York, 1969), p. 198.

5. Mrs. William Thornton, "Diary of Mrs. William Thornton, 1800–1863," *Records of the Columbia Historical Society*, vol. 10, no. 1 (1907), p. 99. Margaret Izard Manigault, quoted in Betty-Bright P. Low, "Of Muslins and Merveilleuses: Excerpts from the Letters of Josephine du Pont and Margaret Manigault," in *Winterthur Portfolio 9*, ed. Ian M. G. Quimby (Charlottesville, Va., 1974), p. 55.

6. Mrs. Manigault, quoted in Low, "Of Muslins," p. 55. Esther Edwards Burr, *Journal . . . 1754–1757*, ed. Carol F. Karlsen and Laurie Crumpacker (New Haven, 1984), p. 170. Eliza Wainwright to Mr. and Mrs. Peter Wainwright, May 1831, WP.

7. Anne Eliza Clark Kane to Harriet Clark, 24 November 1809, JICP. Maria Silliman Church to Faith Silliman, 22 November 1831, MSCP.

8. Mary Boardman Crowninshield, quoted in Margaret Pardee Bates, ed., "Some Letters of Mary Boardman Crowninshield," *Essex Institute Historical Collections*, vol. 83 (April 1947), p. 121.

9. Franklin [Afterwit, pseud.], letter in *Pennsylvania Gazette*. John Smibert, quoted in Jonathan L. Fairbanks et al., *Paul Revere's Boston: 1735–1818*, catalogue of an exhibition at Museum of Fine Arts, Boston (1975), p. 53. Elizabeth DeHart Bleecker McDonald diary, 5 September 1800, NYPL Elizabeth Duché's tea tongs: *Pennsylvania Magazine of History and Biography*, vol. 54, no. 1 (1930), p. 44. Claude Robin, *New Travels through North-America in a Series of Letters* (Boston, 1784), p. 23. John Newton, quoted in Helen Sprackling, *Customs on the Table Top* (Sturbridge, Mass., 1958), p. 10. Thomas Robson Hay, ed., "Letters of Mrs. Ann Biddle Wilkinson from Kentucky, 1788–1789," *Pennsylvania Magazine of History and Biography*, vol. 56, no. 1 (1932), p. 43. [Mrs. Anne Royall], *Sketches of History, Life and Manners, in the United States by a Traveller* (New Haven, 1826), p. 57.

10. Marquis de Chastellux, quoted in Charles H. Sherrill, *French Memories of Eighteenth-Century America* (New York, 1915), p. 55. Philadelphia dinner guest, quoted in *Pennsylvania Magazine of History and Biography*, vol. 16, no. 4 (1892), p. 466.

11. Thomas Cooper, *Some Information Respecting America* (London, 1795), p. 49. François Alexandre Frédéric, duc de La Rochefoucauld-Liancourt, *Travels through the United States of North America in the Years 1795, 1796, and 1797* (London, 1799), vol. 4, p. 100. Sarah Logan Fisher diary, May 1785, HSP. "Travels in the United States of America in the Years 1821, 1822, 1823 to 1824 . . . by a Scotsman," NYHS-MC. Lady Emmeline Stuart Wortley, *Travels in the United States, etc., during 1849 and 1850* (New York, 1851), pp. 41, 139.

12. Sarah Anna Emery, *Reminiscences of a Nonagenarian* (1879; Bowie, Md., and Hampton, N.H., 1978), p. 232. Elizabeth Drinker, *Extracts from the Journal of Elizabeth Drinker, from 1759 to 1807 A.D.*, ed. Henry D. Biddle (Philadelphia, 1889), p. 401.

13. On the development of shop-front windows, see Neil McKendrick, John Brewer, and J. H. Plumb, *The Birth of a Consumer Society: The Commercialization of Eighteenth-Century England* (Bloomington, Ind., 1982). Joshua

Brookes journal 1798–1803, typewritten transcript, NYHS-MC. [Royall], *Sketches*, p. 209.

14. Visitor with a flair for alliteration: [John Bill], "Extracts from the Journal of Philo-Jocundus 1827 [and 1828]," typewritten transcript, NYHS-MC. Julian Ursyn Niemcewicz, *Under Their Vine and Fig Tree: Travels through America in 1797–1799, 1805*, trans. and ed. Metchie J. E. Budka (Elizabeth, N.J., 1965), p. 169. Alicia McBlair Lloyd to Edward Lloyd, 24 November 1836, Lloyd Papers, ms. 2001, Maryland Historical Society Library. Maria Silliman Church to Faith Silliman, 29 September 1835; and Church to Faith Silliman Hubbard, 28 September 1849, MSCP.

15. Anne Hulton, *Letters of a Loyalist Lady: Being the Letters of Anne Hulton, Sister of Henry Hulton, Commissioner of Customs at Boston, 1767–1776* (Cambridge, Mass., 1927), p. 45.

16. On readying the house for George Washington's reception, see *Pennsylvania Magazine of History and Biography*, vol. 13, no. 1 (1889), p. 115. Robert Carter family purchases: Philip Vickers Fithian, *Journal and Letters . . . 1773–1774*, ed. Hunter Dickinson Farish (Williamsburg, Va., 1945), p. 248.

17. Charles Carroll of Annapolis, quoted in Ann C. Van Devanter, *"Anywhere So Long As There Be Freedom": Charles Carroll of Carrollton, His Family and His Maryland* (Baltimore, 1975), p. 27. Franklin [Afterwit, pseud.], letter in *Pennsylvania Gazette*. William Byrd, *The Secret Diary of William Byrd of Westover 1704–1712*, ed. Louis B. Wright and Marion Tinling (Richmond, Va., 1941), pp. 48, 53.

18. Eliza Wainwright to Mr. and Mrs. Peter Wainwright, May 1831, WP. Margaret Izard Manigault to Alice Izard, 22 December 1811, RIFP. Sarah Waring's exchange: Mabel L. Webber, ed., "The Thomas Elfe Account Book, 1768–1775," *The South Carolina Historical and Genealogical Magazine*, vol. 39, no. 3 (July 1938), p. 140. Deborah Franklin, quoted in Rodris Roth, "Floor Coverings in 18th-Century America," in *United States National Museum Bulletin 250* (Washington, D.C., 1967), p. 7.

Anne Eliza Clark Kane to Harriet Clark, 24 November 1809, JICP. John Doggett Letterbook, 22 November 1828, WL-JD. "A pattern which sells": *London Furniture Weekly*, 19 May 1877.

19. The Philadelphian is quoted in Whitfield J. Bell, "Addenda to Watson's Annals of Philadelphia: Notes by Jacob Mordecai, 1836," *Pennsylvania Magazine of History and Biography*, vol. 98, no. 2 (April 1974), p. 138. "If I were a *fairy*": Maria Silliman Church to Faith Silliman Hubbard, 2 September 1839, MSCP. Bates, ed., "Some Letters of Mary Boardman Crowninshield," p. 132.

20. Anna Rawle to Rebecca Rawle Shoemaker, 10 July 1783, "Letters and Diaries of a Loyalist Family of Philadelphia. Written between the years 1780 and 1786," typewritten transcript, HSP. Joseph Lownes to Miss Bailey, undated receipt, WL-JD.

21. Martha Ogle Forman, *Plantation Life at Rose Hill*, ed. W. Emerson Wilson (Wilmington, Del., 1976), pp. 70, 415. A New England girl: Mary Knowlton T[russell], quoted in Thomas Dublin, ed., *Farm to Factory: Women's Letters, 1830–1860* (New York, 1981), p. 159.

22. Rebecca Shoemaker to Samuel Shoemaker, 5 September 1785, "Letters and Diaries of a Loyalist Family." Thornton, "Diary," pp. 138, 143. Martha Jacquelin, quoted in Frances Norton, ed., *John Norton & Sons, Merchants of London and Virginia* (Richmond, Va., 1937), p. 144. Rebecca Rawle Shoemaker letters, quoted in *Pennsylvania Magazine of History and Biography*, vol. 17, no. 2 (1893), p. 232.

23. John Barker Church to Maria Silliman, 29 March 1831, MSCP. Elizabeth Wirt to William Wirt, 6 December 1812, 7 or 8 January 1816, WWP.

24. Sir William Pepperrell, "Pepperrell Manuscripts," *The New England Historical and Genealogical Register*, April 1865, p. 147. Charles Henry Hart, ed., "Letters from William Franklin to William Strahan," *Pennsylvania Magazine of History and Biography*, vol. 35, no. 4 (1911), p. 432. Deborah Franklin on curtains, quoted in Roth, "Floor Coverings," p.

7. Robert Bartlett Haas, ed., "The Forgotten Courtship of David and Marcy Spear, 1785–1787," *Old-Time New England*, vol. 52, no. 3 (January–March 1962), p. 71.

25. Deborah and Benjamin Franklin on a Turkey Carpet, quoted in Roth, "Floor Coverings," p. 7. George Washington, *Letters and Recollections of George Washington* (Garden City, N.Y., 1932), pp. 117–18. On Charles Carroll's order, see Roth, ibid., p. 12.

26. David Spear, quoted in Haas, ed., "The Forgotten Courtship," p. 74. On the Thomas and Caldcleugh advertisement, see Rodris Roth, "Interior Decoration of City Houses in Baltimore: The Federal Period," in *Winterthur Portfolio 5*, ed. Richard K. Doud (Charlottesville, Va., 1969), p. 69. John Barker Church to Maria Silliman Church, 7 August 1831, MSCP. John Gale, quoted in Lois W. Martin, ed., "A Vermont Country Wedding in 1858," *Old-Time New England*, vol. 61, no. 2 (October–December 1970), p. 55.

27. Elizabeth DeHart Bleecker McDonald diary, 2 July (chairs), 16 July (carpeting), 22 July (paper), 21 August (picture) 1800. Thomas Eliot Andrews, ed., "The Diary of Elizabeth (Porter) Phelps," *The New England Historical and Genealogical Register*, January 1967, p. 59. Mary Guion diary, March 1807, NYHS-MC. Phebe Crowell to John Fanning Watson, 23 March 1812; and Watson to Crowell, 27 March 1812, John Fanning Watson Papers, WL-JD. On the Colburns' wedding furniture, see Clifford Stetson Parker, "New Hampshire Courtship in 1826," *Historical New Hampshire*, February 1948, p. 12.

28. John Doggett Letterbook, 22 June 1827. The S. and J. Rawson, Jr., label is illustrated in *The Magazine Antiques*, July 1980, p. 243. Alexis de Tocqueville, *Democracy in America*, ed. Phillips Bradley (1835; New York, 1980), vol. 2, p. 51. Sarah Belknap, quoted in Parker, "New Hampshire Courtship," pp. 13, 18.

29. Benjamin Rush, *My Dearest Julia: The Love Letters of Dr. Benjamin Rush to Julia Stockton* (New York, 1979), p. 17.

Adams, Abigail. *New Letters of Abigail Adams 1788–1801.* Edited by Stewart Mitchell. Boston: Houghton Mifflin, 1947.

Alcott, Louisa May. *Louisa May Alcott: Her Life, Letters, and Journals.* Edited by Ednah D. Cheney. Boston: Roberts Brothers, 1889.

Allen children. *Memorial of Joseph and Lucy Clark Allen (Northborough, Mass.).* Boston: George H. Ellis, 1891.

The American Housewife. New York: Dayton & Saxton, 1841.

Anburey, Thomas. *Travels through the Interior Parts of America.* 2 vols. 1789. Reprint. New York: New York Times and Arno Press, 1969.

Ariès, Philippe. *Centuries of Childhood; a Social History of Family Life.* Translated by Robert Baldick. New York: Alfred A. Knopf, 1962.

————. *Western Attitudes toward Death from the Middle Ages to the Present.* Translated by Patricia M. Ranum. Baltimore: Johns Hopkins University Press, 1974.

Ashe, Thomas. *Travels in America, Performed in the Year 1806, for the Purpose of Exploring the Rivers* . . . London and Newburyport, Mass.: William Sawyer & Co., 1808.

Ayer, Sarah Connell. *Diary of Sarah Connell Ayer, Andover and Newburyport, Massachusetts, Concord and Bow, New Hampshire, Portland and Eastport, Maine.* Portland, Maine: Lefavor-Tower, 1910.

Bacon, Louisa Crowninshield. *Reminiscences.* [Salem, Mass.: Newcomb and Gauss], 1922.

Bailey, Robert. *The Life and Adventures of Robert Bailey from His Infancy Up to December, 1821.* 1822. Reprint, with an introduction by Frederick T. Newbraugh. Marceline, Mo.: Walsworth Publishing, 1978.

Baker, Gary E. "He That Would Thrive Must Ask His Wife: Franklin's Anthony Afterwit Letter." *Pennsylvania Magazine of History and Biography,* vol. 109, no. 1 (January 1985), pp. 27–41.

Barbé-Marbois, François, marquis de. *Our Revolutionary Forefathers; the Letters of François, Marquis de Barbé-Marbois, during His Residence in the United States* . . . *1779–1785.* Translated and edited by Eugene Parker Chase. New York: Duffield & Co., 1929.

Barnes, Emily R. *Narratives, Traditions, and Personal Reminiscences.* Boston: G. H. Ellis, 1888.

Bassett, T. D. Seymour, comp. and ed. *Outsiders inside Vermont: Three Centuries of Visitors' Viewpoints on the Green Mountain State.* Canaan, N.H.: Phoenix Publishing, 1967.

Bayard, Ferdinand M. *Travels of a Frenchman in Maryland and Virginia, with a Description of Philadelphia and Baltimore in 1791; or, Travels in the Interior of the United States, to Bath, Winchester, in the Valley of the Shenandoah, etc., etc., during the Summer of 1791.* 2d ed. 1798. Reprint, translated and edited by Ben C. McCary. Williamsburg, Va.: Colonial Williamsburg, 1950.

Beach, David Nelson. *Beach Family Reminiscences and Annals.* Meriden, Conn.: Journal Press, 1931.

Beaujour, Louis Auguste Félix, baron de. *Sketch of the United States of North America, at the Commencement of the Nineteenth Century, from 1800 to 1810* . . . Translated by William Walton. London: J. Booth, 1814.

Beecher, Catharine E. *Letters to Persons Who Are Engaged in Domestic Service.* New York: Leavitt & Trow, 1842.

————. *A Treatise on Domestic Economy: For the Use of Young Ladies at Home and at School.* 1841. Reprint. New York: Schocken Books, 1977.

Beecher, Catharine E., and Harriet Beecher Stowe. *The American Woman's Home; or, Principles of Domestic Science; Being a Guide to the Formation and Maintenance of Economical, Healthful, Beautiful and Christian Homes.* 1869. Reprint. Hartford: Stowe-Day Foundation, 1975.

Beecher, Lyman. *Autobiography, Correspondence, etc., of Lyman Beecher, D.D.* Edited by Charles Beecher. 2 vols. New York: Harper & Brothers, 1865.

Beeton, Isabella. *Mrs. Beeton's Book of Household Management.* 1861. Reprint. London: Chancellor Press, 1982.

Belden, Louise Conway. *The Festive Tradition: Table Decorations and Desserts in America, 1650–1900.* New York: W. W. Norton, 1983.

Berkin, Carol Ruth, and Mary Beth Norton. *Women of America: A History.* Boston: Houghton Mifflin, 1979.

Bernard, John. *Retrospections of America, 1797–1811.* Edited by Mrs. Bayle Bernard. New York: Harper & Brothers, 1887.

Betts, Edwin Morris, and James Adam Bear, Jr., eds. *The Family Letters of Thomas Jefferson.* Charlottesville: University Press of Virginia, 1986.

Bingham, Millicent Todd. *Emily Dickinson's Home.* New York: Harper, 1955.

Blanchard, Claude. *The Journal of Claude Blanchard, 1780–1783.* Edited by Thomas Balch. Albany: J. Munsell, 1876.

Bowne, Eliza Southgate. *A Girl's Life Eighty Years Ago: Selections from the Letters of Eliza Southgate Bowne.* Introduction by Clarence Cook. New York: Charles Scribner's Sons, 1887.

Boyer, Nathalie Robinson. *A Virginia Gentleman and His Family.* Philadelphia: privately printed, 1939.

Brant, Sandra, and Elissa Cullman. *Small Folk: A Celebration of Childhood in America.* New York: E. P. Dutton, 1980.

Breck, Samuel. *Recollections of Samuel Breck, with Passages from His Notebooks (1771–1862).* Edited by H. E. Scudder. Philadelphia: Porter & Coates, 1877.

Breckenridge, Mrs. Francis A. ("Faith"). *Recollections of a New England Town.* Meriden, Conn.: Journal Publishing, 1899.

Breckinridge, Lucy. *Lucy Breckinridge of Grove Hill: The Journal of a Virginia Girl, 1862–1864.* Edited by Mary D. Robertson. Kent, Ohio: Kent State University Press, 1979.

Brissot de Warville, Jean Pierre. *New Travels in the United States of America, 1788.* Edited by Durand Echeverria. Cambridge, Mass.: Belknap Press of Harvard University Press, 1964.

Brown, Harriet Connor. *Grandmother Brown's Hundred Years, 1827–1927.* Boston: Little, Brown, 1929.

Buckingham, J[ames] S. *America: Historical, Statistic, and Descriptive.* 3 vols. London: Fisher, Son & Co., 1841.

Buel, Joy Day, and Richard Buel, Jr. *The Way of Duty: A Woman and Her Family in Revolutionary America.* New York: W. W. Norton, 1984.

Burke, Emily. *Pleasure and Pain: Reminiscences of Georgia in the 1840's.* Savannah: Beehive Press, 1978.

Burr, Aaron. *Correspondence of Aaron Burr and His Daughter Theodosia.* Edited by Mark Van Doren. New York: Covici, Freide, 1929.

Burr, Esther Edwards. *The Journal of Esther Edwards Burr, 1754–1757.* Edited by Carol F. Karlsen and Laurie Crumpacker. New Haven: Yale University Press, 1984.

Burwell, Letitia M. *A Girl's Life in Virginia before the War.* New York: Frederick A. Stokes, 1895.

Bushman, Richard L. and Claudia L. "The Early History of Cleanliness in America." *The Journal of American History,* vol. 74, no. 4 (March 1988), pp. 1213–38.

Calvert, Karin. "Children in American Family Portraiture, 1670 to 1810." *The William and Mary Quarterly.* 3d ser., vol. 39, no. 1 (January 1982), pp. 87–113.

Carlo, Joyce. *Trammels, Trenchers, and Tartlets: A Definitive Tour of the Colonial Kitchen.* Old Saybrook, Conn.: Peregrine Press, 1982.

Carson, Jane. *Colonial Virginia Cookery Procedures, Equipment, and Ingredients in Colonial Cooking.* 2d ed. Williamsburg, Va.: Colonial Williamsburg Foundation, 1985.

Carter, Landon. *The Diary of Colonel Landon Carter of Sabine Hall, 1752–1778.* Edited by Jack P. Greene. 2 vols. Charlottesville: University Press of Virginia, 1965.

Cary, Wilson Miles. *Sally Cary, a Long Hidden Romance of Washington's Life.* New York: The DeVinne Press, 1916.

Censer, Jane Turner. *North Carolina Planters and Their Children, 1800–1860.* Baton Rouge: Louisiana State University Press, 1984.

Chace, Mrs. Elizabeth [Buffum], and Lucy Buffum Lovell. *Two Quaker Sisters: From the Original Diaries of Elizabeth Buffum Chace and Lucy Buffum Lovell.* Edited by Malcolm Lovell. New York: Liveright, 1937.

Channing, George G. *Early Recollections of Newport, R.I., from the Year 1793 to 1811.* Newport, R.I.: A. J. Ward, C. E. Hammett, Jr.; Boston: Nichols and Noyes, 1868.

Channing, Katharine Minot. *Minot Family Letters, 1773–1871.* Sherborn, Mass.: privately printed, 1957.

Chastellux, François Jean, marquis de. *Travels in North America, in the Years 1780, 1781, and 1782.* Edited by Howard C. Rice, Jr. 2 vols. Chapel Hill: University of North Carolina Press, 1963.

Child, Mrs. L[ydia] Maria. *The American Frugal Housewife. Dedicated to Those Who Are Not Ashamed of Economy.* 12th ed. 1832. Reprint. [Worthington, Ohio: Worthington Historical Society], 1980.

———. *Letters from New York.* New York: C. S. Francis, 1845.

Clark, Clifford Edward, Jr. *The American Family Home 1800–1960.* Chapel Hill: University of North Carolina Press, 1986.

———. "Domestic Architecture as an Index to Social History: The Romantic Revival and the Cult of Domesticity in America, 1840–1870." *Journal of Interdisciplinary History,* vol. 7 (1976), pp. 33–56.

Clark, Thomas D., ed. *South Carolina: The Grand Tour, 1780–1865.* Columbia: University of South Carolina Press, 1973.

———. *Travels in the Old South, a Bibliography.* 3 vols. Norman: University of Oklahoma Press, 1956.

Clinton, Catherine. *The Plantation Mistress: Woman's World in the Old South.* New York: Pantheon Books, 1982.

Closen, Ludwig, baron von. *The Revolutionary Journal of Baron Ludwig von Closen, 1780–1783.* Translated and edited by Evelyn M. Acomb. Chapel Hill: University of North Carolina Press, 1958.

Coke, Edward Thomas. *A Subaltern's Furlough; Descriptive of Scenes in Various Parts of the United States . . . during the Summer and Autumn of 1832.* 2 vols. New York: J. & J. Harper, 1833.

Combe, George. *Notes on the United States of North America during a Phrenological Visit in 1838–9–40.* 2 vols. Philadelphia: Carey & Hart, 1841.

Cooke, Edward S., Jr. "Domestic Space in the Federal-Period Inventories of Salem Merchants." *Essex Institute Historical Collections,* vol. 116 (April 1980), pp. 248–64.

Cooke, Edward S., Jr., et al. *Upholstery in America and Europe from the Seventeenth Century to World War I.* New York: W. W. Norton, 1987.

Cooper, James Fenimore. *Correspondence of James Fenimore-Cooper.* Edited by James Fenimore Cooper. 2 vols. New Haven: Yale University Press, 1922.

———. *Notions of the Americans Picked Up by a Travelling Bachelor.* 2 vols. 1828. Reprint, with an introduction by Robert E. Spiller. New York: Frederick Ungar, 1963.

Cooper, Mary. *The Diary of Mary Cooper: Life on a Long Island Farm 1768–1773.* Edited by Field Horne. Oyster Bay, N.Y.: Oyster Bay Historical Society, 1981.

Cott, Nancy F. *The Bonds of Womanhood: "Woman's Sphere" in New England, 1780–1835.* New Haven: Yale University Press, 1977.

Crowninshield, Mary Boardman. *Letters of Mary Boardman Crowninshield, 1815–1816.* Edited by Francis Boardman Crowninshield. Cambridge, Mass.: Riverside Press, 1905.

Cummings, Abbott Lowell. *Bed Hangings; a Treatise on Fab-*

rics and Styles in the Curtaining of Beds, 1650–1850. Boston: Society for the Preservation of New England Antiquities, 1961.

———. Rural Household Inventories Establishing the Names, Uses and Furnishings of Rooms in the Colonial New England Home, 1675–1775. Boston: Society for the Preservation of New England Antiquities, 1964.

Cummings, George J. "A Leaf from the Life of a Farmer's Boy Ninety Years Ago." Old-Time New England, vol. 19, no. 3 (January 1929), pp. 99–112.

Cummings, Richard Osborn. The American and His Food. Chicago: University of Chicago Press, 1941.

Curd, Samuella. Sam Curd's Diary: The Diary of a True Woman. Edited by Susan S. Arpad. Athens: Ohio University Press, 1984.

Currier, Festus C. Reminiscences and Observations of the Nineteenth Century, More Particularly Relating to the First Half. Fitchburg, Mass.: Sentinel Printing Co., 1902.

C[urtis], C[aroline] G[ilman], ed. The Cary Letters. Cambridge, Mass.: Riverside Press, 1891.

Cutler, Manasseh. The Life, Journals and Correspondence of Rev. Manasseh Cutler. Edited by William Parker Cutler and Julia Perkins Cutler. 2 vols. Cincinnati: Robert Clarke, 1888.

Davidson, Caroline. A Woman's Work Is Never Done: A History of Housework in the British Isles, 1650–1950. London: Chatto & Windus, 1982.

Davidson, Marshall B. Life in America. 2d ed. 2 vols. Boston: Houghton Mifflin, 1974.

Davis, William T. Plymouth Memories of an Octogenarian. Plymouth, Mass.: Memorial Press, 1906.

Dayton, Abram C. Last Days of Knickerbocker Life in New York. New York: George W. Harlan, 1882.

Degler, Carl N. At Odds: Woman and the Family in America from the Revolution to the Present. New York: Oxford University Press, 1980.

Demos, John. "The American Family in Past Time." The American Scholar, vol. 43 (1974), pp. 422–46.

———. "Families in Colonial Bristol, Rhode Island: An Exercise in Historical Demography." The William and Mary Quarterly, 3d ser., vol. 25, no. 4 (October 1968), pp. 40–57.

De Pauw, Linda Grant, and Conover Hunt. Remember the Ladies: Women in America, 1750–1815. New York: Viking Press, 1976.

Derounian, Kathryn Zabelle. " 'A Dear Dear Friend': Six Letters from Deborah Norris to Sarah Wister, 1778–1779." Pennsylvania Magazine of History and Biography, vol. 108, no. 4 (October 1984), pp. 487–516.

Dickinson, Emily. Letters of Emily Dickinson. Edited by Mabel Loomis Todd. 2 vols. Boston: Roberts Brothers, 1894.

The Domestic's Companion, Comprising the Most Perfect, Easy, and Expeditious Methods of Getting through Their Work . . . New York: G. F. Bunce, 1834.

Dow, George Francis. The Arts and Crafts in New England, 1704–1775. Topsfield, Mass.: Wayside Press, 1927.

Dow, George Francis, ed. The Holyoke Diaries, 1709–1856. Salem, Mass.: Essex Institute, 1911.

Downing, A[lexander] J[ackson]. The Architecture of Country Houses. 1850. Reprint. New York: Dover Publications, 1969.

Drayton, John. Letters Written during a Tour through the Northern and Eastern States of America. Charleston, S.C.: Harrison & Bowen, 1794.

Drinker, Cecil K. Not So Long Ago; a Chronicle of Medicine and Doctors in Colonial Philadelphia. New York: Oxford University Press, 1937.

Drinker, Elizabeth. Extracts from the Journal of Elizabeth Drinker, from 1759 to 1807 A.D. Edited by Henry D. Biddle. Philadelphia: J. B. Lippincott, 1889.

Dublin, Thomas. Women at Work: The Transformation of Work and Community in Lowell, Massachusetts, 1826–1860. New York: Columbia University Press, 1974.

Dublin, Thomas, ed. Farm to Factory: Women's Letters, 1830–1860. New York: Columbia University Press, 1981.

Dudden, Faye E. Serving Women: Household Service in Nineteenth-Century America. Middletown, Conn.: Wesleyan University Press, 1983.

Duffy, John. "An Account of the Epidemic Fevers That Prevailed in the City of New York 1791 to 1822." New-York Historical Society Quarterly, vol. 50 (1966), pp. 333–64.

———. Epidemics in Colonial America. Baton Rouge: Louisiana State University Press, 1953.

Duncan, John M. Travels through Part of the United States and Canada in 1818 and 1819. 2 vols. New York: W. B. Gilley, 1823.

Dwight, Timothy. Travels in New England and New York. 1821. Reprint, edited by Barbara Miller Solomon. 4 vols. Cambridge, Mass.: Belknap Press of Harvard University Press, 1969.

Edwards, Lee M. Domestic Bliss: Family Life in American Painting, 1840–1910. Yonkers, N.Y.: Hudson River Museum, 1986.

Ellet, Mrs. [Elizabeth Fries Lummis]. The Practical Housekeeper. New York: Stringer & Townsend, 1857.

Ellet, Mrs. [Elizabeth Fries Lummis], ed. The New Cyclopaedia of Domestic Economy and Practical Housekeeper. Norwich, Conn.: Henry Bill, 1873.

Ellis, Mrs. [Sarah Stickney]. Mrs. Ellis's Housekeeping Made Easy . . . Revised and Adapted to the Wants of the Ladies of the United States. New York: Burgess & Stringer, 1843.

Emerson, Ralph Waldo. Emerson in His Journals. Edited by Joel Porte. Cambridge, Mass.: Belknap Press of Harvard University Press, 1982.

Emery, Sarah Anna. Reminiscences of a Nonagenarian. 1879. Reprint. Bowie, Md., and Hampton, N.H.: Heritage Books, 1978.

———. Three Generations. Boston: Lee and Shepard, 1872.

Evans, Elizabeth. Weathering the Storm; Women of the American Revolution. New York: Charles Scribner's Sons, 1975.

Eve, Sarah. "Extracts from the Journal of Miss Sarah Eve; Written While Living near the City of Philadelphia in 1772–1773." Pennsylvania Magazine of History and Biography, vol. 5, nos. 1 and 2 (1881), pp. 19–36, 191–205.

Fairbanks, Jonathan L., et al. Paul Revere's Boston: 1735–1818.

Boston: Museum of Fine Arts, 1975.

[Farrar, Eliza Ware]. *The Young Lady's Friend*. Boston: John B. Russell, 1837.

Ferguson, Eugene S. "An Historical Sketch of Colonial Heating: 1800–1860." In *Building Early America*, edited by Charles E. Peterson, pp. 165–85. Radnor, Pa.: Chilton Book Company, 1976.

Fisher, Sidney George. *Mount Harmon Diaries of Sidney George Fisher, 1837–1850*. Edited by W. Emerson Wilson. Wilmington: Historical Society of Delaware, 1976.

———. *A Philadelphia Perspective: The Diary of Sidney George Fisher Covering the Years 1834–1871*. Edited by Nicholas B. Wainwright. Philadelphia: Historical Society of Pennsylvania, 1967.

Fithian, Philip Vickers. *Journal and Letters of Philip Vickers Fithian, 1773–1774; a Plantation Tutor of the Old Dominion*. Edited with an introduction by Hunter Dickinson Farish. Williamsburg, Va.: Colonial Williamsburg, 1945.

Flaherty, David H. *Privacy in Colonial New England*. Charlottesville: University Press of Virginia, 1972.

Fletcher, Elijah. *The Letters of Elijah Fletcher*. Edited by Martha von Briesen. Charlottesville: University Press of Virginia, 1965.

Forman, Martha Ogle. *Plantation Life at Rose Hill: The Diaries of Martha Ogle Forman, 1814–1845*. Edited by W. Emerson Wilson. Wilmington: Historical Society of Delaware, 1976.

[Foster, Austin T.]. *A Grandfather's Reminiscences, 1822–1900*. Hartford: N.p., [1922].

Fowler, John, and John Cornforth. *English Decoration in the Eighteenth Century*. Princeton, N.J.: Pyne Press, 1974.

Galateo; or, A Treatise on Politeness and Delicacy of Manners: Also, the Honors of the Table with the Whole Art of Carving. Baltimore: George Hill, 1811.

Galloway, Grace Growden. "Diary of Grace Growden Galloway Kept at Philadelphia from June 17, 1778, to July 1, 1779," edited by Raymond C. Werner. *Pennsylvania Magazine of History and Biography*, vol. 15, no 1 (1931), pp. 32–94.

Gara, Larry, ed. "A New Englander's View of Plantation Life: Letters of Edwin Hall to Cyrus Woodman, 1837." *Journal of Southern History*, vol. 18 (1952), pp. 343–54.

Garrett, Elisabeth Donaghy. "The American Home." Part I: " 'Centre and Circumference,' the American Domestic Scene in the Age of Enlightenment"; Part II: "Lighting Devices and Practices"; Part III: "The Bedchamber"; Part IV: "The Dining Room"; Part V: "Venetian Shutters and Blinds"; Part VI: "The Quest for Comfort: Housekeeping Practices and Living Arrangements the Year Round." *The Magazine Antiques*: January–March 1983, October 1984, August, December 1985; pp. 214–25, 408–17, 612–25, 910–22, 259–65, 1210–23.

———. *The Arts of Independence*. Washington, D.C.: NSDAR, 1984.

Garrett, Wendell D. "The Furnishings of Newport Houses, 1780–1800." *Rhode Island History*, vol. 18, no. 1 (January 1959), pp. 1–19.

Girouard, Mark. *Life in the English Country House, a Social and Architectural History*. New Haven: Yale University Press, 1978.

Goodrich, S[amuel] G[riswold]. *Recollections of a Lifetime; or, Men and Things I Have Seen*. Auburn, N.Y.: Miller, Orton & Mulligan, 1856.

Gordon, Jean, and Jan McArthur. "Living Patterns in Antebellum Rural America as Depicted by Nineteenth-Century Women Writers." In *Winterthur Portfolio 19*, edited by Ian M. G. Quimby, pp. 177–92. Charlottesville: University Press of Virginia, 1984.

Gordon, Michael, ed. *The American Family in Social-Historical Perspective*. New York: St. Martin's Press, 1973.

Gottesman, Rita Susswein. *The Arts and Crafts in New York, 1726–1776*. New York: New-York Historical Society, 1938.

———. *The Arts and Crafts in New York, 1777–1799*. New York: New-York Historical Society, 1954.

———. *The Arts and Crafts in New York, 1800–1804*. New York: New-York Historical Society, 1965.

[Grant, Anne]. *Memoirs of an American Lady; with Sketches of Manners and Scenery in America, as They Existed Previous to the Revolution*. 2 vols. London: Longman, Hurst, Rees & Orme, 1808.

Grattan, Thomas Colley. *Civilized America*. 2d ed. 2 vols. London: Bradbury and Evans, 1859.

Green, Harvey. *The Light of the Home: An Intimate View of the Lives of Women in Victorian America*. New York: Pantheon Books, 1983.

Greven, Philip. *The Protestant Temperament; Patterns of Child-Rearing, Religious Experience, and the Self in Early America*. New York: Alfred A. Knopf, 1977.

Grover, Kathryn, ed. *Dining in America 1850–1900*. Amherst, Mass., and Rochester, N.Y.: University of Massachusetts Press and Margaret Woodbury Strong Museum, 1987.

Grund, Francis J. *The Americans in Their Moral, Social, and Political Relations*. 2 vols. 1837. Reprint (2 vols. in 1). New York: Augustus M. Kelley, 1971.

Haas, Robert Bartlett, ed. "The Forgotten Courtship of David and Marcy Spear, 1785–1787." *Old-Time New England*, vol. 52, no. 3 (January–March 1962), pp. 61–72.

Hale, Edward Everett. *Memories of a Hundred Years*. 2 vols. New York: Macmillan, 1902.

———. *A New England Boyhood*. 1893. Reprint. New York: Grosset & Dunlap, 1927.

Hall, Captain Basil. *Travels in North America, in the Years 1827 and 1828*. 3 vols. Edinburgh: Cadell & Co., 1829.

Hall, Mrs. Basil. *The Aristocratic Journey: Being the Outspoken Letters of Mrs. Basil Hall, Written during a Fourteen Months' Sojourn in America, 1827–1828*. Edited by Una Pope-Hennessy. New York: G. P. Putnam's Sons, 1931.

[Hamilton, Captain Thomas]. *Men and Manners in America*. 2 vols. Edinburgh: William Blackwood, 1833.

Handlin, David P. *The American Home: Architecture and Society, 1815–1915*. Boston: Little, Brown, 1979.

Handlin, Oscar. *This Was America; True Accounts of People and Places, Manners and Customs, as Recorded by European Travelers to the Western Shore in the Eighteenth, Nine-

teenth, and Twentieth Centuries. Cambridge, Mass.: Harvard University Press, 1949.

Harris, Eileen. *Going to Bed.* London: Victoria and Albert Museum, 1981.

———. *Keeping Warm.* London: Victoria and Albert Museum, 1982.

Hart, Albert Bushnell. *How Our Grandfathers Lived.* 1921. Reprint. Ann Arbor, Mich.: Gryphon Books, 1971.

Haswell, [Charles] H. *Reminiscences of New York by an Octogenarian (1816–1860).* New York: Harper & Brothers, 1896.

Havens, Catherine Elizabeth. *Diary of a Little Girl in Old New York.* New York: Henry Collins Brown, 1919.

Haydon, Roger, ed. *Upstate Travels; British Views of Nineteenth-Century New York.* Syracuse, N.Y.: Syracuse University Press, 1982.

Heininger, Mary Lynn Stevens, et al. *A Century of Childhood, 1820–1920.* Rochester, N.Y.: Margaret Woodbury Strong Museum, 1984.

Hellerstein, Erna Olafson, Leslie Parker Hume, and Karen M. Offen, eds. *Victorian Women: A Documentary Account of Women's Lives in Nineteenth-Century England, France, and the United States.* Stanford, Calif.: Stanford University Press, 1981.

Hewitt, Benjamin A., Patricia A. Kane, and Gerald W. R. Ward. *The Work of Many Hands: Card Tables in Federal America, 1790–1820.* New Haven: Yale University Art Gallery, 1982.

Hiltzheimer, Jacob. *Extracts from the Diary of Jacob Hiltzheimer of Philadelphia, 1765–1798.* Edited by Jacob Cox Parsons. Philadelphia: Wm. F. Fell, 1893.

Hiner, N. Ray, and Joseph M. Hawes, eds. *Growing Up in America: Children in Historical Perspective.* Urbana and Chicago: University of Illinois Press, 1985.

Hitchcock, Enos. *The Farmer's Friend; or, The History of Mr. Charles Worthy.* Boston: I. Thomas & E. T. Andrews, 1793.

Hodgson, Adam. *Letters from North America, Written During a Tour in the United States and Canada.* 2 vols. London: Hurst, Robinson & Co., 1824.

Hopkinson, Francis. *The Miscellaneous Essays and Occasional Writings of Francis Hopkinson, Esq.* 3 vols. Philadelphia: T. Dobson, 1792.

Howe, Julia Ward. *Reminiscences, 1819–1899.* Boston: Houghton Mifflin, 1900.

Howe, M. A. DeWolfe, ed. *The Articulate Sisters; Passages from Journals and Letters of the Daughters of President Josiah Quincy of Harvard University.* Cambridge, Mass.: Harvard University Press, 1946.

Howland, Mrs. E[sther] A[llen]. *The New England Economical Housekeeper and Family Receipt Book.* Worcester: S. A. Howland, 1845.

Hoyt, William D., ed. "The Calvert-Stier Correspondence, Letters from America to the Low Countries, 1797–1828." *Maryland Historical Magazine,* vol. 38, no. 2 (June 1943), pp. 123–40.

Hunter, Ethel Ambler. "We Were Not Poor." *Old-Time New England,* vol. 35, no. 3 (January 1945), pp. 48–51.

[Ingraham, Joseph Holt]. *The South-West.* 2 vols. New York: Harper & Brothers, 1835.

Janney, John Jay. *John Jay Janney's Virginia, an American Farm Lad's Life in the Early 19th Century.* Edited by Werner L. Janney and Asa Moore Janney. McLean, Va.: EPM Publications, 1978.

Jensen, Joan M. *Loosening the Bonds: Mid-Atlantic Farm Women, 1750–1850.* New Haven: Yale University Press, 1986.

Jones, Alice Hanson. *American Colonial Wealth: Documents and Methods.* 3 vols. New York: Arno Press, 1977.

Jones, Mary Cadwalader. *Lantern Slides.* Boston: privately printed, 1937.

Kalm, Peter. *The America of 1750; Peter Kalm's Travels in North America. The English Version of 1770.* Reprint, edited by Adolph B. Benson. 2 vols. New York: Dover Publications, 1966.

Kelly, Samuel. *Samuel Kelly, an Eighteenth Century Seaman.* Edited by Crosbie Garstin. New York: Frederick A. Stokes, 1925.

Kendall, Edward Augustus. *Travels through the Northern Parts of the United States in the Years 1807 and 1808.* 3 vols. New York: I. Riley, 1809.

Kerber, Linda K. *Women of the Republic: Intellect and Ideology in Revolutionary America.* Chapel Hill: University of North Carolina Press, 1980.

Kerr, Robert. *The Gentleman's House; or, How to Plan English Residences, from the Parsonage to the Palace . . .* 2d ed. London: John Murray, 1865.

King, Caroline Howard. *When I Lived in Salem, 1822–1866.* Brattleboro, Vt.: Stephen Daye Press, 1937.

Lambert, John. *Travels through Canada, and the United States of North America, in the Years 1806, 1807, and 1808.* 2d ed. 2 vols. London: C. Cradock & W. Joy, 1814.

Landreau, Anthony N. *America Underfoot; a History of Floor Coverings from Colonial Times to the Present.* Washington, D.C.: Smithsonian Institution Press, 1976.

Larcom, Lucy. *Lucy Larcom: Life, Letters, and Diary.* Edited by Daniel D. Addison. Boston: Houghton Mifflin, 1844.

———. *A New England Girlhood Outlined from Memory.* 1889. Reprint. Williamstown, Mass.: Corner House Publishers, 1977.

La Rochefoucauld-Liancourt, François Alexandre Frédéric, duc de. *Travels through the United States of North America in the Years 1795, 1796, and 1797.* 4 vols. London: R. Phillips, 1799.

Lasdun, Susan. *Victorians at Home.* New York: Viking Press, 1981.

Laslett, Barbara. "The Significance of Family Membership." In *Changing Images of the Family,* edited by Virginia Tufte and Barbara Myerhoff, pp. 231–50. New Haven: Yale University Press, 1979.

Laslett, Peter. *The World We Have Lost: England before the Industrial Age.* 2d ed. New York: Charles Scribner's Sons, 1973.

Latrobe, Benjamin Henry. *The Journals of Benjamin Henry Latrobe 1799–1820; from Philadelphia to New Orleans.*

Edited by Edward C. Carter II, John C. Van Horne, and Lee W. Formwalt. 3 vols. New Haven: Yale University Press, 1980.

———. *The Virginia Journals of Benjamin Henry Latrobe, 1795–1798.* Edited by Edward C. Carter II. 2 vols. New Haven: Yale University Press, 1977.

Lea, Elizabeth E[llicott]. *Domestic Cookery.* 1845. Facsimile of the 1853 edition (as *A Quaker Woman's Cookbook*), edited by William Woys Weaver. Philadelphia: University of Pennsylvania Press, 1982.

Leavitt, Judith Walzer. *Brought to Bed: Childbearing in America 1750–1950.* New York: Oxford University Press, 1986.

Lebsock, Suzanne. *The Free Women of Petersburg: Status and Culture in a Southern Town, 1784–1860.* New York: W. W. Norton, 1984.

Lesley, Susan I. *Recollections of My Mother, Mrs. Anne Jean Lyman of Northampton.* Boston: G. H. Ellis, 1886.

Leslie, Miss [Eliza]. *Atlantic Tales; or, Pictures of Youth.* 2d ed. Boston: Munroe & Francis, 1855.

———. *The Behaviour Book: A Manual for Ladies.* 3d ed. Philadelphia: Willis P. Hazard, 1853.

———. *The House Book; or, A Manual of Domestic Economy.* Philadelphia: Carey & Hart, 1840.

———. *Pencil Sketches; or, Outlines of Character and Manners.* Philadelphia: Willis P. Hazard, 1854.

Lewis, Jan. *The Pursuit of Happiness: Family and Values in Jefferson's Virginia.* Cambridge: Cambridge University Press, 1983.

Lewis, Nelly [Eleanor] Custis. *Nelly Custis Lewis's Housekeeping Book.* Edited by Patricia Brady Schmit. New Orleans: Historic New Orleans Collection, 1982.

Little, Nina Fletcher. "An Approach to Furnishing." *The Magazine Antiques*, July 1956, pp. 44–46.

———. *Floor Coverings in New England before 1850.* Sturbridge, Mass.: Old Sturbridge Village, 1967.

———. "Joseph Shoemaker Russell and His Water Color Views." *The Magazine Antiques*, January 1951, pp. 52–53.

———. "Lighting in Colonial Records." *Old-Time New England*, vol. 42 (1952), pp. 96–101.

Lockwood, Charles. *Bricks and Brownstone: The New York Row House, 1783–1929, Architectural and Social History.* New York: McGraw-Hill, 1972.

Longfellow, Fanny Appleton. *Mrs. Longfellow: Selected Letters and Journals of Fanny Appleton Longfellow (1817–1861).* Edited by Edward Wagenknecht. New York: Longmans, Green & Co., 1956.

Loudon, J[ohn] C[laudius]. *An Encyclopaedia of Cottage, Farm, and Villa Architecture and Furniture.* 1833. Reprint. London: Longman, Brown, Green, and Longmans, 1853.

Low, Betty-Bright P. "Of Muslins and Merveilleuses: Excerpts from the Letters of Josephine du Pont and Margaret Manigault." In *Winterthur Portfolio 9*, edited by Ian M. G. Quimby, pp. 29–75. Charlottesville: University Press of Virginia, 1974.

———. "The Youth of 1812: More Excerpts from the Letters of Josephine du Pont and Margaret Manigault." In *Winterthur Portfolio 11*, edited by Ian M. G. Quimby, pp. 172–212. Charlottesville: University Press of Virginia, 1976.

Low, Betty-Bright P., ed. *Sophie du Pont, a Young Lady in America: Sketches, Diaries, and Letters, 1823–1833.* New York: Harry N. Abrams, 1987.

Lyell, Sir Charles. *A Second Visit to the United States of North America.* 2 vols. New York: Harper & Brothers, 1849.

Lynes, Russell. *The Domesticated Americans.* New York: Harper & Row, 1957.

[McDougall, Frances Harriet Whipple]. *The Housekeeper's Book . . .* Philadelphia: William Marshall & Co., 1837.

Mackay, Alexander. *The Western World; or, Travels in the United States in 1846–47.* 3 vols. London: R. Bentley, 1849.

McKearin, Helen. "Sweetmeats in Splendor: Eighteenth-Century Desserts and Their Dressing Out." *The Magazine Antiques*, March 1955, pp. 216–25.

McKendrick, Neil, John Brewer, and J. H. Plumb. *The Birth of a Consumer Society: The Commercialization of Eighteenth-Century England.* Bloomington: Indiana University Press, 1982.

Manigault, Harriet. *The Diary of Harriet Manigault, 1813–1816.* Edited by Virginia and James S. Armentrout, Jr. [Rockland, Maine]: Colonial Dames of America (Chapter II), 1976.

Martineau, Harriet. *Retrospect of Western Travel.* 2 vols. 1838. Reprint (2 vols. in 1), edited by Joseph J. Kwiat. New York: Johnson Reprint Corp., 1968.

———. *Society in America.* 3 vols. 1837. Reprint (3 vols. in 1). New York: AMS Press, 1966.

Mason, Frances Norton. *My Dearest Polly: Letters of Chief Justice John Marshall to His Wife, with Their Background, Political and Domestic, 1779–1831.* Richmond, Va.: Garrett & Massie, 1961.

Matthaei, Julie, A. *An Economic History of Women in America: Women's Work, the Sexual Division of Labor, and the Development of Capitalism.* New York: Schocken Books, 1982.

Maury, Sarah Mytton. *An Englishwoman in America.* London: T. Richardson and Son, 1848.

Mayhew, Edgar deN., and Minor Myers, Jr. *A Documentary History of American Interiors from the Colonial Era to 1915.* New York: Charles Scribner's Sons, 1980.

Michie, Audrey H. "Charleston Upholstery in All Its Branches, 1725–1820." *Journal of Early Southern Decorative Arts*, vol. 11, no. 2 (1985), pp. 20–84.

———. "The Fashion for Carpets in South Carolina, 1736–1820." *Journal of Early Southern Decorative Arts*, vol. 8, no. 1 (1982), pp. 24–48.

Mingay, Gordon. *Mrs. Hurst Dancing, and Other Scenes from Regency Life, 1812–1823.* London: Victor Gollancz, 1981.

Minot family. *Minot Family Letters, 1773–1871.* Compiled by Katharine Minot Channing. Sherborn, Mass.: privately printed, 1957.

Montgomery, Florence M. *Printed Textiles; English and Ameri-*

can Cottons and Linens 1700–1850. New York: Viking Press, 1970.

———. "Room Furnishings as Seen in British Prints from the Lewis Walpole Library." Part I: "Bed Hangings"; Part II: "Window Curtains, Upholstery, and Slip Covers." *The Magazine Antiques*, December 1973, March 1974, pp. 1068–75, 522–31.

———. *Textiles in America, 1650–1870: A Dictionary.* New York: W. W. Norton, 1984.

Moreau de Saint-Méry, M.L.E. *Moreau de St. Méry's American Journey, 1793–1798.* Translated and edited by Kenneth Roberts and Anna M. Roberts. Garden City, N.Y.: Doubleday & Co., 1947.

Morison, Samuel Eliot. "Charles Bagot's Notes on Housekeeping and Entertaining at Washington, 1819." In *Publications of the Colonial Society of Massachusetts. Transactions 1924–1926*, pp. 438–46. Boston, 1927.

Morse, Frances Rollins, ed. *Henry and Mary Lee. Letters and Journals.* Boston: T. Todd Co., 1926.

Mussey, Barrows, ed. *We Were New England: Yankee Life by Those Who Lived It.* New York: Stackpole Sons, 1937.

Neilson, Peter. *Recollections of a Six Years' Residence in the United States of America, Interspersed with Original Anecdotes, Illustrating the Manners of the Inhabitants of the Great Western Republic.* Glasgow: David Robertson, 1830.

Nelson, Christina H. *Directly from China: Export Goods for the American Market, 1784–1930.* Salem, Mass.: Peabody Museum of Salem, 1984.

Nevins, Allan, ed. *America through British Eyes.* New York: Oxford University Press, 1948.

"A Newburyport Wedding One Hundred and Thirty Years Ago; the Bride, Elizabeth Margaret Carter." *Essex Institute Historical Collections*, vol. 87 (October 1951), pp. 309–32.

Nichols, Thomas Low. *Forty Years of American Life, 1821–1861.* 1864. Reprint. New York: Stackpole Sons, 1937.

Niemcewicz, Julian Ursyn. *Under Their Vine and Fig Tree: Travels through America in 1797–1799, 1805, with Some Further Account of Life in New Jersey.* Translated and edited by Metchie J. E. Budka. (*Collections of the New Jersey Historical Society*, vol. 14.) Elizabeth, N.J.: Grassmann Publishing, 1965.

Norton, Mary Beth. *Liberty's Daughters: The Revolutionary Experience of American Women, 1750–1800.* Boston: Little, Brown, 1980.

Nylander, Jane C. "Henry Sargent's *Dinner Party* and *Tea Party.*" *The Magazine Antiques*, May 1982, pp. 1172–83.

———. "Keeping Warm: Coping with Winter in Early 19th-Century New England." *Early American Life*, vol. 11, no. 5 (1980), pp. 46–49.

———. "Summer Housekeeping in Early 19th-Century New England." *Early American Life*, vol. 11, no. 2 (1980), pp. 32–35, 56–57.

Nylander, Richard C., Elizabeth Redmond, and Penny J. Sander, eds. *Wallpaper in New England.* Boston: Society for the Preservation of New England Antiquities, 1986.

Oakley, Ann. *Woman's Work: The Housewife, Past and Present.* New York: Pantheon Books, 1975.

O'Dea, William. *Social History of Lighting.* London: Routledge and Kegan Paul, 1958.

Ogden, Annegret S. *The Great American Housewife from Helpmate to Wage Earner, 1776–1986.* Westport, Conn.: Greenwood Press, 1986.

Olmsted, Frederick Law. *The Cotton Kingdom; A Traveller's Observations on Cotton and Slavery in the American Slave States.* Edited by Arthur M. Schlesinger. New York: Alfred A. Knopf, 1953.

Orr, Lucinda Lee. *Journal of a Young Lady of Virginia, 1782.* Baltimore: J. Murphy and Company, 1871.

Ott, Joseph K. "John Innes Clark and His Family—Beautiful People in Providence." *Rhode Island History*, vol. 32, no. 4 (November 1973), pp. 123–32.

Parker, Clifford Stetson. "New Hampshire Courtship in 1826." *Historical New Hampshire*, February 1948, pp. 3–18.

Parkes, Mrs. William. *Domestic Duties; or, Instructions to Young Married Ladies . . .* 3d American ed. (based on 3d London ed.). New York: J. & J. Harper, 1829.

Parkman, Ebenezer. *The Diary of Ebenezer Parkman 1703–1782. First Part, Three Volumes in One, 1719–1755.* Edited by Francis G. Walett. Worcester: American Antiquarian Society, 1974.

Perry, Hext McCall, ed. *Letters of My Father to My Mother, Beginning with Those Written During Their Engagement, with Extracts from His Journal . . .* Philadelphia: privately printed, 1889.

Peterson, Harold L. *American Interiors from Colonial Times to the Late Victorians.* New York: Charles Scribner's Sons, 1971.

Pike, Martha V., and Janice Gray Armstrong. *A Time to Mourn: Expressions of Grief in Nineteenth Century America.* Stony Brook, N.Y.: Museums at Stony Brook, 1980.

Pollock, Linda. *Forgotten Children: Parent-Child Relations from 1500 to 1900.* Cambridge: Cambridge University Press, 1983.

———. *A Lasting Relationship: Parents and Children over Three Centuries.* Hanover, N.H., and London: University Press of New England, 1987.

Power, Tyrone. *Impressions of America, during the Years 1833, 1834, and 1835.* 2 vols. 1836. Reprint (2 vols. in 1). New York: Benjamin Blom, 1971.

Praz, Mario. *An Illustrated History of Furnishing, from the Renaissance to the 20th Century.* New York: George Braziller, 1964.

Prime, Alfred Coxe. *The Arts and Crafts in Philadelphia, Maryland and South Carolina 1721–1785.* 1929. Reprint. New York: Da Capo, 1969.

———. *The Arts and Crafts in Philadelphia, Maryland and South Carolina 1786–1800.* 1932. Reprint. New York: Da Capo, 1969.

Pynchon, William. *The Diary of William Pynchon of Salem. A Picture of Salem Life, Social and Political, a Century Ago.* Edited by Fitch Edward Oliver. Boston and New

York: Houghton, Mifflin, 1890.

Quincy, Eliza S. M. *Memoir of the Life of Eliza S. M. Quincy.* Boston: John Wilson & Son, 1861.

Randolph, Sarah N. *The Domestic Life of Thomas Jefferson: Compiled from Family Letters and Reminiscences by His Great Granddaughter.* 3d ed. Charlottesville, Va.: Thomas Jefferson Memorial Foundation, 1947.

Rappaport, Samuel, and Patricia Schartle, eds. *America Remembers; Our Best-Loved Customs and Traditions.* Garden City, N.Y.: Hanover House, 1956.

Rhys, Isaac. *The Transformation of Virginia, 1740–1790.* Chapel Hill: University of North Carolina Press, 1982.

Rice, Howard C., Jr., and Anne S. K. Brown, trans. and eds. *The American Campaigns of Rochambeau's Army, 1780, 1781, 1782, 1783.* 2 vols. Princeton, N.J.: Princeton University Press. 1972.

Richards, Caroline Cowles. *Village Life in America, 1852–1872, including the Period of the American Civil War as Told in the Diary of a School-Girl.* Edited by Margaret E. Sangster. 1908. Reprint. Williamstown, Mass.: Corner House Publishers, 1972.

[Richards, Mrs. A. M.]. *Memories of a Grandmother, by a Lady of Massachusetts.* Boston: Gould and Lincoln, 1854.

Ridgely, Mabel Lloyd, ed. *The Ridgelys of Delaware and Their Circle, What Them Befell in Colonial and Federal Times: Letters 1751–1890.* Portland, Maine: Anthoensen Press, 1949.

Ripley, Eliza. *Social Life in Old New Orleans: Being Recollections of My Girlhood.* New York: D. Appleton & Co., 1912.

Roberts, Robert. *The House Servant's Directory.* 1827. Reprint, with a foreword by Charles A. Hammond. Waltham, Mass.: Gore Place Society, 1977.

Robin, Abbé Claude C. *New Travels through North-America in a Series of Letters* ... Boston: E. E. Powars and N. Willis, 1784.

Rollins, Ellen H. [E. H. Arr, pseud.]. *New England Bygones.* Philadelphia: J. B. Lippincott, 1880.

———. *Old-Time Child Life.* Philadelphia: J. B. Lippincott, 1881.

Roth, Rodris. "Floor Coverings in 18th-Century America." In *United States National Museum Bulletin 250. Contributions from the Museum of History and Technology,* Paper 59, pp. 1–64. Washington, D.C.: Smithsonian Institution Press, 1967.

———. "Tea Drinking in 18th-Century America: Its Etiquette and Equipage." In *United States National Museum Bulletin 225. Contributions from the Museum of History and Technology,* Paper 14, pp. 61–91. Washington, D.C.: Smithsonian Institution Press, 1961.

Rothman, David J. "A Note on the Study of the Colonial Family." *The William and Mary Quarterly.* 3d ser., vol. 23, no. 4 (October 1966), pp. 627–34.

Royall, Anne Newport. *Letters from Alabama, 1817–1822.* 1830. Reprint, with an introduction and notes by Lucille Griffith. University: University of Alabama Press, 1969.

Royall, Mrs. Anne. *The Black Book; or, A Continuation of Travels, in the United States.* 3 vols. Washington, D.C.:

privately printed, 1828–29.

[Royall, Mrs. Anne]. *Sketches of History, Life and Manners, in the United States by a Traveller.* New Haven: privately printed, 1826.

Rumford, Beatrix T. "How Pictures Were Used in New England Houses, 1825–1850." *The Magazine Antiques,* November 1974, pp. 827–35.

Rush, Benjamin. *My Dearest Julia: The Love Letters of Dr. Benjamin Rush to Julia Stockton.* New York: Neale Watson Academic Publications, 1979.

Rutman, Darrett B. and Anita H. "Of Agues and Fevers: Malaria in the Early Chesapeake." *The William and Mary Quarterly,* 3d ser., vol. 33, no. 1 (January 1976), pp. 31–60.

Saxe-Weimar Eisenach, Bernhard Karl, duke of. *Travels through North America, during the years 1825 and 1826.* 2 vols. Philadelphia: Carey, Lea & Carey, 1828.

[Schaw, Janet]. *Journal of a Lady of Quality; Being the Narrative of a Journey from Scotland to the West Indies, North Carolina, and Portugal in the Years 1774 to 1776.* Edited by Evangeline Walker Andrews. New Haven: Yale University Press, 1921.

Schoelwer, Susan Prendergast. "Form, Function, and Meaning in the Use of Fabric Furnishings: A Philadelphia Case Study, 1700–1775." In *Winterthur Portfolio 14,* edited by Ian M. G. Quimby, pp. 25–40. Charlottesville: University Press of Virginia, 1979.

Scholten, Catherine M. *Childbearing in American Society, 1650–1850.* Edited by Lynne Withey. New York: New York University Press, 1985.

Schwaab, Eugene L. and Jacqueline Bull, eds. *Travels in the Old South, Selected from Periodicals of the Times.* 2 vols. Lexington: University Press of Kentucky, 1973.

Scott, Donald M. and Bernard Wishy, eds. *America's Families: A Documentary History.* New York: Harper & Row, 1982.

Scott, Mrs. M. L. *The Practical Housekeeper and Young Woman's Friend* ... Toledo, Ohio: Black Steam Printing Establishment, 1855.

Seale, William. *Recreating the Historic House Interior.* Nashville, Tenn.: American Association for State and Local History, 1979.

[Sellers, Martha]. *M. S.: The Story of a Life.* Edited by Frances Sellers Garrett. Philadelphia: Alfred J. Harris, 1901.

Semmes, Raphael. *Baltimore as Seen by Visitors, 1783–1860.* Baltimore: Maryland Historical Society, 1953.

Sessions, Ruth Huntington. *Sixty-Odd: A Personal History.* Brattleboro, Vt.: Stephen Daye Press, 1936.

Sherrill, Charles H. *French Memories of Eighteenth-Century America.* New York: Charles Scribner's Sons, 1915.

Sherrill, Sarah B. "Oriental Carpets in Seventeenth- and Eighteenth-Century America." *The Magazine Antiques,* January 1976, pp. 142–67.

Shippen, Nancy. *Nancy Shippen, Her Journal Book: The International Romance of a Young Lady of Fashion of Colonial Philadelphia, with Letters to Her and about Her.* Compiled and edited by Ethel Armes. Philadelphia: J. B. Lippincott, 1935.

Shorter, Edward. *The Making of the Modern Family*. New York: Basic Books, 1975.

Sigourney, Lydia Howard [Huntley]. *Sketch of Connecticut, Forty Years Since*. Hartford: Oliver D. Cooke & Sons, 1824.

Sigourney, Mrs. Lydia. *Letters to Young Ladies*. New York: Harper & Brothers, 1838.

Silsbee, M[arianne], C. D. *A Half Century in Salem*. Boston and New York: Houghton, Mifflin, 1887.

Sklar, Kathryn Kish. *Catharine Beecher: A Study in American Domesticity*. New Haven: Yale University Press, 1973.

Slater, George A. *The Hills of Home: American Life Pictured in New England in the Last Half of the Nineteenth Century*. New York: William Edwin Rudge, 1931.

Smedes, Susan Dabney. *Memorials of a Southern Planter*. Edited by Fletcher M. Green. New York: Alfred A. Knopf, 1965.

[Smith, Margaret Bayard]. *A Winter in Washington; or, Memoirs of the Seymour Family*. 2 vols. New York: E. Bliss & E. White, 1824.

Smith, Mrs. Samuel Harrison. *The First Forty Years of Washington Society, Portrayed by the Family Letters of Mrs. Samuel Harrison Smith (Margaret Bayard) from the Collection of Her Grandson, J. Henley Smith*. Edited by Gaillard Hunt. New York: Charles Scribner's Sons, 1906.

Smith, Page. "Anxiety and Despair in American History." *The William and Mary Quarterly*. 3d ser., vol. 26, no. 3 (July 1969), pp. 416–24.

Smyth, J.F.D. *A Tour in the United States of America*. 2 vols. London: G. Robinson, 1784.

Sneller, Anne Gertrude. *A Vanished World*. Syracuse, N.Y.: Syracuse University Press, 1964.

Somerville, James K. "The Salem (Mass.) Woman in the Home, 1660–1770." *Eighteenth-Century Life*, vol. 1 (1974), pp. 11–14.

Sprackling, Helen. *Customs on the Table Top; How New England Housewives Set Out Their Tables*. Sturbridge, Mass.: Old Sturbridge Village, 1958.

Sprigg, June. *Domestick Beings*. New York: Alfred A. Knopf, 1984.

Spruill, Julia Cherry. *Women's Life and Work in the Southern Colonies*. 1938. Reprint. New York: W. W. Norton, 1972.

Stannard, David E. *The Puritan Way of Death: A Study in Religion, Culture, and Social Change*. New York: Oxford University Press, 1977.

Stone, Lawrence. *The Family, Sex and Marriage in England, 1500–1800*. New York: Harper & Row, 1977.

Stowe, Harriet Beecher. *Oldtown Folks*. 1869. Reprint, edited by Henry F. May. Cambridge, Mass.: Belknap Press of Harvard University Press, 1966.

———. *Poganuc People: Their Loves and Lives*. 1878. Reprint, with an introduction by Joseph S. Van Why. Hartford: Stowe-Day Foundation, 1977.

Stowe, Harriet Beecher [Christopher Crowfield, pseud.]. *House and Home Papers*. Boston: Ticknor and Fields, 1865.

Strasser, Susan. *Never Done: A History of American Housework*. New York: Pantheon Books, 1982.

Stuart, James. *Three Years in North America*. 2d ed. 2 vols. Edinburgh: Robert Cadell, 1833.

Sutcliff, Robert. *Travels in Some Parts of North America in the Years 1804, 1805, and 1806*. Philadelphia: B. & T. Kite, 1812.

Swan, Susan Burrows. *Plain and Fancy: American Women and Their Needlework, 1700–1850*. New York: Holt, Rinehart & Winston, 1977.

Taylor, George Rogers. " 'Philadelphia in Slices,' by George G. Foster." *Pennsylvania Magazine of History and Biography*, vol. 93, no 1 (January 1969), pp. 23–72.

Thornton, Peter. *Authentic Decor: The Domestic Interior, 1620–1920*. New York: Viking Press, 1984.

———. "Room Arrangements in the Mid-Eighteenth Century." *The Magazine Antiques*, April 1971, pp. 556–61.

Thornton, Mrs. William. "Diary of Mrs. William Thornton, 1800–1863." *Records of the Columbia Historical Society*, vol. 10, no. 1 (1907), pp. 88–226.

Tocqueville, Alexis de. *Democracy in America*. 1835. Reprint, edited by Phillips Bradley. 2 vols. New York: Alfred A. Knopf, 1980.

Trollope, Frances M. *Domestic Manners of the Americans*. 1832. Reprint, edited by Donald Smalley. New York: Alfred A. Knopf, 1949.

Trotter, Isabella. *First Impressions of the New World on Two Travellers from the Old in the Autumn of 1858*. London: Longman, Brown, Green, Longmans & Roberts, 1859.

Trumbull, Harriet and Maria. *A Season in New York, 1801; Letters of Harriet and Maria Trumbull*. Edited and with an introduction by Helen M. Morgan. Pittsburgh: University of Pittsburgh Press, 1969.

Tudor, Henry. *Narrative of a Tour in North America . . . in a Series of Letters Written in the Years 1831–1832*. 2 vols. London: James Duncan, 1834.

Twining, Thomas. *Travels in America One Hundred Years Ago*. New York: Harper & Brothers, 1894.

Tyler, Mary Palmer. *Grandmother Tyler's Book: The Recollections of Mary Palmer Tyler (Mrs. Royall Tyler), 1775–1866*. Edited by Frederick Tupper and Helen Tyler Brown. New York: G. P. Putnam's Sons, 1925.

Van Devanter, Ann C. *"Anywhere So Long As There Be Freedom": Charles Carroll of Carrollton, His Family and His Maryland*. Baltimore: Baltimore Museum of Art, 1975.

Van Valkenburgh, Franklin Butler. *Grandpapa's Letter to His Children from Franklin Butler Van Valkenburgh*. Additional material compiled and edited by Charles H. Vilas. 1899. N.p.: privately reprinted, 1978.

Vinovskis, Maris A. "Angels' Heads and Weeping Willows: Death in Early America." In *Proceedings of the American Antiquarian Society*, vol. 86, part 2 (Worcester, 1976), pp. 273–302.

Wakefield, Priscilla. *Excursions in North America, Described in Letters from a Gentleman and His Young Companion, to Their Friends in England*. London: Darton & Harvey, 1806.

Walsh, Lorena S. "Urban Amenities and Rural Sufficiency: Living Standards and Consumer Behavior in the Colonial Chesapeake, 1643–1777." *Journal of Economic*

History, vol. 43 (1983), pp. 109–17.

Warren, Annie Crowninshield. *Reminiscences of My Life, for My Children.* Cambridge, Mass.: privately printed, 1910.

Webber, Mabel L., ed. "The Thomas Elfe Account Book, 1768–1775." *The South Carolina Historical and Genealogical Magazine,* vol. 35, no. 1 (January 1934)–vol. 42, no. 1 (January 1941).

Webster, Thomas. *An Encyclopaedia of Domestic Economy . . .* New York: Harper & Brothers, 1845.

Webster, T[homas], and Mrs. [William] Parkes. *The American Family Encyclopedia of Useful Knowledge . . .* Edited by D. M. Reese. New York: Derby and Jackson, 1858.

Weld, Isaac, Jr. *Travels through the States of North America, and the Provinces of Upper and Lower Canada during the Years 1795, 1796, and 1797.* 4th ed. 2 vols. London: John Stockdale, 1807.

Wells, Robert V., "Family History and the Demographic Transition." *Journal of Social History,* vol. 9 (1975), pp. 1–19.

———. *Revolutions in Americans' Lives: A Demographic Perspective on the History of Americans, Their Families, and Their Society.* Westport, Conn.: Greenwood Press, 1982.

Welter, Barbara. "The Cult of True Womanhood 1820–1860." *American Quarterly,* vol. 18 (1966), pp. 151–74.

Wertz, Richard W., and Dorothy C. Wertz. *Lying-in: A History of Childbirth in America.* New York: Free Press, 1977.

Whatman, Susanna. *The Housekeeping Book of Susanna Whatman, 1776–1800.* Edited by Thomas Balston. London: G. Bles, 1956.

Wheaton, Ellen Birdseye. *The Diary of Ellen Birdseye Wheaton.* Edited by Donald Gordon. Boston: privately printed, 1923.

Wheeler, Gervase. *Rural Homes; or, Sketches of Houses Suited to American Country Life . . .* New York: Charles Scribner, 1851.

Willich, A[nthony] F. M. *The Domestic Encyclopedia; or, A Dictionary of Facts, and Useful Knowledge. Chiefly Applicable to Rural and Domestic Economy.* 2d American ed. 3 vols. Philadelphia: Abraham Small, 1821.

Winkler, Gail Caskey, and Roger W. Moss. *Victorian Interior Decoration, American Interiors 1830–1900.* New York: Henry Holt, 1986.

Winslow, Anna Green. *Diary of Anna Green Winslow, a Boston School Girl of 1771.* Edited by Alice Morse Earle. 1894. Reprint. Williamstown, Mass.: Corner House Publishers, 1974.

Wolf, Stephanie Grauman. *Urban Village Population, Community, and Family Structure in Germantown, Pennsylvania, 1683–1800.* Princeton, N.J.: Princeton University Press, 1980.

The Workwoman's Guide. London: Simpkin, Marshall, & Co., 1838. Reprint. Guilford, Conn.: Old Sturbridge Village and Opus Publications, Inc., 1986.

Wortley, Lady Emmeline Stuart. *Travels in the United States, etc., during 1849 and 1850 . . .* New York: Harper & Brothers, 1851.

Yarmolinsky, Avrahm. *Picturesque United States of America, 1811, 1812, 1813; Being a Memoir on Paul Svinin . . .* Introduction by R.T.H. Halsey. New York: William Edwin Rudge, 1930.

PHOTOGRAPH CREDITS

The author and publisher wish to thank the museums, galleries, and private collectors named in the illustration captions for supplying the necessary photographs. Other photograph credits are listed below.

A. Baptiste: 53 below, 79; Courtesy William L. Beiswanger: 26 above; David Bohl: 63; Geoffrey Clements: 172; George Fistrovich: 233; © 1987 Hagley Museum and Library and The Nemours Foundation: 118, 134–35; Helga Photo Studio: 18, 19 below, 37, 51, 60, 71, 86 above, 87, 101 above, 113, 116, 130, 143, 157, 184, 232, 261, 265; Courtesy Kennedy Galleries, New York City: 28; Henry E. Peach: 150, 212 left, 221; Joseph Szasfai: 159; © Winterthur Museum: 26 below, 154, 180, 206, 266.